This is an essential and exciting volume. ? men and Christian groups from Catholic: global vision of the early modern church. Brazil and China, as well as much more. *Sixteenth-Century Mission* overturns many false assumptions and valuably fills in many gaps: I wish I had read it when I first started teaching church history decades ago.

Timothy Larsen, McManis Professor of Christian Thought, Wheaton College

Drawing on a broad range of expertise and geographical representation (Australia, Brazil, England, Wales), this collection deliberately challenges the anachronisms built into traditional periodizations of mission history and relocates Protestant missional thinking in the common inheritance of late medieval piety and growing European world consciousness. It points to the problems of Eurocentrism, uncritical dependence on past polemical texts to answer present questions, and the effect on Christian thought of an inadequate grasp of historiographical method in deducing the relationships between thought and action, ideas and causality. In doing so it teaches us much about the importance of communities of faith, of migration movements, and of paying attention not just to exalted successes but to efforts which "end in a melancholic manner." This is a welcome contribution to an understanding not just of the rise of world Christianity, but of global histories in general.

Mark P. Hutchinson, professor of history, Alphacrucis College, Sydney, Australia

Robert Gallagher, Edward Smither, and their team of writers have provided a unique collection of well-researched and informative papers on the little-known area of sixteenth-century Christian mission. The result is a fascinating body of knowledge that opens up many prospects for further research and study on this vital subject. I can imagine more than a few mission strategies being reconsidered and revamped as a result. This is a timely volume for today's world.

Dr. Barry Chant, founding president, Tabor College, Australia

For far too long Reformation historiography has either neglected the Reformers' concerns for missions or mistakenly stressed the absence of any missional efforts during the era. *Sixteenth-Century Mission* is an important, long-overdue corrective to both of these shortcomings. This edited volume offers a refreshing perspective on the global efforts of Protestants and Roman Catholics alike, as the Reformers sought to take the light of Jesus' gospel to the darkest reaches of their known worlds in the early modern period.

Stephen Brett Eccher, associate professor of church history and Reformation studies, Southeastern Baptist Theological Seminary

I commend Robert Gallagher and Edward Smither for editing and Lexham Press for publishing this book. New books on the history of missions are sadly too few. The editors have properly balanced the book between Protestant and Catholic missions. I especially appreciated Ray Van Neste's essay on the Reformers' teaching on and engagement in missions. Van Neste's nuanced essay corrects the common misperception that the Reformers did little about missions. Allen Yeh's essay evaluates the commendable ministry of Bartolomé de las Casas among the indigenous peoples of the Caribbean. De las Casas's advocacy counters the calumny that missionaries always allied themselves with the colonizers. This book should become required reading for courses on the history of missions and the history of the Reformation. I enthusiastically recommend it.

John Mark Terry, emeritus professor of missions, Mid-America Baptist Theological Seminary

Situating the history of the Reformation in the context of global Christianity is exactly what the field needs right now to expand the scope of its focus and to better recognize the intricate ways in which the events of the Reformation in Europe also shaped worldwide Christianity. By tracking both Protestant and Roman Catholic missions in this period, Gallagher and Smither's multi-contributor volume succeeds in offering a welcome addition to the discipline that will be useful for students and scholars alike.

Jennifer Powell McNutt, Franklin S. Dyrness Associate Professor of Biblical and Theological Studies, Wheaton College

Sixteenth-Century Mission is the most exhilarating collection of essays I have ever reviewed. The authors convey the concept of Christian mission from the perspective of the Reformation era's diverse protagonists rather than mimicking the misjudgments of modern antagonists. Their essays will simultaneously scintillate the historical theologian and inspire the practicing missionary. Robert Gallagher and Edward Smither are to be highly commended for editing this book, the authors for composing their contributions, and Lexham Press for publishing what should prove a groundbreaking text in the fields of missiology and the Reformation.

Malcolm B. Yarnell III, research professor of theology, Southwestern Baptist Theological Seminary, and author of *Royal Priesthood in the English Reformation* and *The Formation of Christian Doctrine*

SIXTEENTH-CENTURY MISSION

Explorations in Protestant and Roman Catholic Theology and Practice

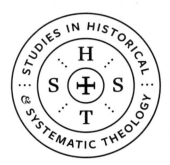

STUDIES IN HISTORICAL
& SYSTEMATIC THEOLOGY

H
S ✠ S
T

SIXTEENTH-CENTURY MISSION

Explorations in Protestant and Roman Catholic Theology and Practice

Edited by **ROBERT L. GALLAGHER** *and* **EDWARD L. SMITHER**

STUDIES IN HISTORICAL AND SYSTEMATIC THEOLOGY

LEXHAM PRESS

Sixteenth-Century Mission: Explorations in Protestant and Roman Catholic Theology and Practice
Studies in Historical and Systematic Theology

Copyright 2021 Robert L. Gallagher and Edward L. Smither

Lexham Press, 1313 Commercial St., Bellingham, WA 98225
LexhamPress.com

Print ISBN 9781683594659
Digital ISBN 9781683594666
Library of Congress Control Number 2021930747

Lexham Editorial: Todd Hains, Jennifer Edwards, Jim Weaver, Danielle Thevenaz
Cover Design: Brittany Schrock
Typesetting: Abigail Stocker

To my Fuller Theological Seminary mentors,
J. Robert Clinton and Paul E. Pierson,
who taught me a great deal about Christian
leadership in the history of missions
through their writings, example, and influence.

Robert L. Gallagher

To Andrew Walls,
who has modeled how to be a historian of mission
and world Christianity and has inspired a new generation of
scholars in this wonderful field of study.

Edward L. Smither

CONTENTS

Contributors xi

Foreword xv
    Dana L. Robert

Acknowledgments... xix

Introduction.. 1
    Edward L. Smither

Part One: Lutheran, Reformed, and Anabaptist Mission

1. Correcting the Record 7
   The Reformers on Evangelism and Missions
    Ray Van Neste

2. Trinity in a Woman's Soul 37
   Recovering a Women's Spirituality for Mission in Jan Hus's
   Dcerka [*The Daughter*]
    Michèle Miller Sigg

3. The Wittenberg Connection in Scandinavia 60
   The Catalyst of the Reformation within Historical Complexity
    Robert L. Gallagher

4. French Reformed Mission before Calvin 1515–1535 91
    Garry Austin

5. Calvin's Geneva 114
   Missions as a Light to the World
    Karin Spiecker Stetina

6. French Reformed Mission in Colonial Brazil 138
    Franklin Ferreira

7. "That There Would Be One Flock Under One Shepherd" 168
   Theodor Bibliander and the Role of Language for Missionary Work
    Gregory J. Miller

8. Characteristics of Anabaptist Mission in
the Sixteenth Century 188
James R. Krabill

9. The Augsburg "Missions Convention" of August 1527
and Early Anabaptist Outreach 208
Charles E. Self

Part Two: Roman Catholic Mission

10. The *Spiritual Exercises* 225
Ignatian Spirituality in Sixteenth-Century Mission in China
Luisa J. Gallagher Stevens

11. Accommodating Christianity to Confucian Culture 244
Matteo Ricci and the Early Jesuit Mission to China (1582–1610)
Alice T. Ott

12. The Jesuit Mission to the Kingdom of Kongo (1548–1555) 264
John Thornton

13. Teresa of Avila and Mary Ward 285
Spirituality and Re-imagining Mission
Amanda J. Kaminski

14. Bartolomé de las Casas 304
Defender of the Indians, Defender of the Word
Allen L. Yeh

15. Sacrificial Labors of Colonization 322
Sixteenth-Century Franciscan Missions in Central Mexico
and in La Florida
Viviana Díaz Balsera

16. The Institutional Inner Logic of Sixteenth-Century
Discalced Franciscan Missions 347
Rady Roldán-Figueroa

Subject Index 369

CONTRIBUTORS

—

GARRY AUSTIN is trained in missiology and served as a campus missionary in Hong Kong. Since 1996, he has been a TESOL language teacher and teacher trainer at the University of Queensland in Brisbane, Australia.

VIVIANA DÍAZ BALSERA (PhD, Yale University) is a professor of Spanish at the University of Miami. She has authored many articles and a number of books on intercultural relations between Spain and the Americas such as *La Florida: Five Hundred Years of Hispanic Presence* (University Press of Florida, 2014).

FRANKLIN FERREIRA (ThM, Seminário Teológico Batista do Sul do Brasil) is currently a pastor of the Trinity Church (*Igreja da Trindade*) and professor of systematic theology and church history at Martin Bucer Seminary (Brazil), where he also serves as director. He is the author of several books in Portuguese, including *A History of the Christian Church, Spiritual Revival in Church, Against Idolatry of the State, The Apostles' Creed,* and a systematic theology (co-authored with Alan Myatt).

RADY ROLDÁN-FIGUEROA (ThD, Boston University) is an associate professor of the History of Christianity at Boston University School of Theology. He is coeditor of *Bartolomé de las Casas, O.P.: History, Philosophy, and Theology in the Age of European Expansion* (Brill, 2018).

ROBERT L. GALLAGHER (PhD, Fuller Theological Seminary) is professor emeritus of intercultural studies at Wheaton College Graduate School. Among Gallagher's recent publications are co-editing *Contemporary Mission Theology: Engaging the Nations* (Orbis Books, 2017), and co-authoring *Encountering the History of Missions: From the Early Church to Today* (Baker Academic, 2017), and *Breaking through the Boundaries: Biblical Perspectives on Mission from the Outside In* (Orbis Books, 2019).

AMANDA J. KAMINSKI (PhD, Graduate Theological Union) is an assistant professor of theology at Texas Lutheran University in Seguin, Texas.

JAMES R. KRABILL (PhD, University of Birmingham, England) is a core adjunct professor at Anabaptist Mennonite Biblical Seminary. Among his many publications, Krabill was general editor of *Mission and Worship for the Global Church: An Ethnodoxology Handbook* and *Creating Local Arts Together: A Manual to Help Communities Reach Their Kingdom Goals* (William Carey Publishers, 2013).

GREGORY J. MILLER (PhD, Boston University) is provost and professor of history at Malone University. His most recent publications include *The Turks and Islam in Reformation Germany* (Routledge Press, 2018).

ALICE T. OTT (PhD, Trinity Evangelical Divinity School) is an affiliate professor of the History of Mission and World Christianity at Trinity Evangelical Divinity School. Her recent publications include *The Sunwoman in the Wilderness* (Asbury Theological Seminary, 2014).

DANA L. ROBERT (PhD, Yale University) is the Truman Collins Professor of World Mission and History of Christianity, and Director of the Center for Global Christianity and Mission, at the Boston University School of Theology. Among her books are *Christian Mission: How Christianity Became a World Religion* (2009); and *African Christian Biography: Stories, Lives, and Challenges* (editor, 2018).

CHARLES E. SELF (PhD, University of California, Santa Cruz) is a professor of Church History at the Assemblies of God Theological Seminary where he teaches apologetics, church history, mission history, leadership development, and discipleship. His published works include *Flourishing Churches and Communities: A Pentecostal Primer on Faith, Work, and Economics for Spirit-Empowered Discipleship* (Christian's Library Press, 2012).

MICHÈLE MILLER SIGG (PhD, Boston University) is the executive director of the *Dictionary of African Christian Biography* at the Center for Global Christianity and Mission at Boston University. She has published articles and book chapters, including "Carrying Living Water for the Healing of God's People: Women Leaders in the *Fifohazana* Revival and the Reformed Church in Madagascar" in *Studies in World Christianity* (2014) and "The *Dictionary of African Christian Biography* and the Story of Ethiopian Christianity," *International Bulletin of Missionary Research* (2015).

EDWARD L. SMITHER (PhD, University of Wales–Trinity St. David; PhD, University of Pretoria) serves as a professor of Intercultural Studies and History of Global Christianity and dean of the College of Intercultural Studies at Columbia International University. His most recent books include *Christian Mission: A Concise Global History* (Lexham Press, 2019) and *Mission in the Early Church: Themes and Reflections* (Cascade Books, 2014).

KARIN SPIECKER STETINA (PhD, Marquette University) is an associate professor of Theology at Talbot School of Theology. Her recent work is *How to Read Theology for All Its Worth* (Zondervan Academic, 2020).

LUISA J. GALLAGHER STEVENS (PhD, Gonzaga University) teaches leadership, spiritual formation, and biblical studies at George Fox University and Portland Seminary. She is the author of *Unscripted Spirituality: Making Meaning of Leadership and Faith in College* (Wipf & Stock, 2021).

JOHN THORNTON (PhD, University California–Los Angeles) is professor of History and African American Studies at Boston University. He is the author of six books and over seventy-five articles in journals. He is the author of *A General History of West Central Africa to 1852* (Cambridge University Press, 2020).

RAY VAN NESTE (PhD, University of Aberdeen) is the dean of the School of Theology and Missions at Union University. His published works include *REF500: How the Greatest Revival since Pentecost Continues to Shape the World Today* (B&H Academic, 2017) and *Forgotten Songs: Reclaiming the Psalms for Christian Worship* (B&H Academic, 2012).

ALLEN L. YEH (DPhil, Oxford University) is an associate professor of intercultural studies and missiology at Biola University. He is the author of *Polycentric Missiology: 21st-Century Mission from Everyone to Everywhere* (IVP Academic, 2016), and co-editor of *Majority World Theologies: Theologizing from Africa, Asia, Latin America, and the Ends of the Earth* (William Carey, 2018).

FOREWORD

The sixteenth century is widely recognized as the beginning of the "golden age" of Roman Catholic missions. The founding of the Jesuits, the global spread of the Mendicant orders, and the activation of women's missionary piety all characterized the century of European expansionism and conquest. While apostolicity and catholicity marked the identity of sixteenth-century Roman Catholics, Protestants remained occupied with the founding of national churches and with navigating the religious strife that accompanied vernacular religious movements. From the vantage point of modern nineteenth-century missions, the Protestant Reformation lacked missionary societies, mission agents, and mission theologies. Earlier generations of scholars thus criticized the sixteenth-century Reformers for the perceived lack of a fully developed missionary dynamic. It took the Pietist movements of later centuries—in conjunction with Scandinavian, Dutch, and British expansionism—to spark the missionary imagination of Protestants.

This volume challenges traditional interpretations by focusing on the thought and practices of both Roman Catholic and Protestant mission in the sixteenth century. By bringing them together, it argues for a more generalized mission consciousness that extended across the Protestant Reform movements and the cross-cultural outreach of Roman Catholic renewal movements. By its structure and content, this book implies that Protestant and Roman Catholic Reformations shared a common missional spirituality grounded in late medieval piety, sharpened by growing engagement with non-Christian lands. Not only did Jan Hus, Guillaume Farel, Martin Luther, John Calvin, Menno Simons, Theodor Bibliander, and other Protestants articulate mission spiritualities and theologies, but Roman Catholic missionaries, such as the Franciscan Twelve Apostles of New Spain, Reformer Bartolomé de las Casas, humanist Matteo Ricci, and the ill-fated Mary Ward, exhibited missionary pieties also associated with later evangelical Protestantism.

To be sure, the organizational superiority of the Roman Catholic religious orders took sixteenth-century missionary activism to new heights, while Protestants bogged down in struggles for survival. But the lack of explicit mission agencies and agents does not mean that the missionary consciousness of Protestantism was deficient. Simply put, the different contexts and capacities for Catholicism and Protestantism led to different priorities as far as cross-cultural missions were concerned. The exceptions prove the rule. For example, the sixteenth-century Protestant overseas mission considered in this volume, that of Huguenots to Brazil, failed because it was crushed by Roman Catholic opposition. And not all Roman Catholic missions were successful, as the failure of the first Jesuit mission to the already-Catholic Kongo kingdom demonstrates.

The central argument of this volume assumes several recent developments in scholarship. First is the rise of World Christianity as a perspective through which to re-evaluate the early modern period. Attention to local and global intersections, and how they shaped each other, allows Roman Catholic and Protestant histories to be brought into dialogue. Recent scholarship has shown the sixteenth century to be one of the most exciting periods for the study of World Christianity. Rather than competition between Protestant nation building and Roman Catholic expansion narratives, World Christianity foregrounds both narratives as matrices of the local and the global. Early modern Europe, therefore, becomes a vibrant site for mission history. When preachers migrated to Scotland and the Low Countries from Calvin's Geneva, and Luther's Wittenberg-based followers spread to Scandinavia, this, too, is relevant to the study of Christianity as a worldwide movement. Though not considered in this volume, research on Hugo Grotius, Gisbertus Voetius, Joan Aventroot, and other European Protestant mission advocates illustrates that sixteenth-century developments fermented missionary apologetics among Protestants prior to their founding viable colonies abroad. And, of course, the work of Jesuits to reconvert European Protestants to Catholicism was a key factor in defining the word "mission" itself. In short, seen through the lens of World Christianity, the sixteenth century was foundational both for Protestant and Roman Catholic mission.

Another assumption undergirding this volume is the redefinition of mission to include the re-evangelization of peoples from ostensibly Christian populations. By defining "mission" narrowly as the effort to convert non-Christians, the breadth of sixteenth century missional consciousness has been obscured. Through its focus on theologies and mission spiritualities, this volume challenges the absolute distinction between missions directed at non-Christians and spiritual revitalization movements directed at other Christians. So, for example, the internal spiritual reorganization of Discalced Franciscans becomes directly relevant to their expansion in Asia; and the vernacularization principle of Lutheran Bible translation becomes key to Protestant missions as well as to the formation of national churches.

A third assumption anchoring this volume is the embrace of interdisciplinary approaches. Although individual articles presuppose particular ecclesial traditions, the cumulative effect highlights the necessity of interdisciplinary and inter-ecclesial perspectives for the sixteenth century to speak to present-day scholars and mission practitioners. Some of the authors use contemporary missiological insights to analyze historical materials. Others combine appreciation for social history research, such as the importance of hymn-singing, ascetic practices, and "lived religion," with intellectual and theological foundations for mission. The public realm of politics is connected to the spiritual dynamics of conversion. Therefore, historical research is essential to mission studies. This point is important for missiology, as historical research often finds itself taking a backseat to mission theology and intercultural studies. Solid historical research proves its foundational importance for understanding mission practices. Conversely, appreciation for mission theory and practice illuminate the meaning of history. At multiple levels, therefore, this volume seeks to make connections across traditional scholarly divisions. Such interdisciplinarity is a necessity for glimpsing the full importance of sixteenth-century studies for both Roman Catholic and Protestant mission history. It is also a reason to pay attention to this work.

Dana L. Robert

Truman Collins Professor of World Christianity and History of Mission
Boston University

ACKNOWLEDGMENTS

—

In editing this book, we were grateful for the opportunity to conduct a workshop on the topic of the history of mission in the sixteenth century at the annual conference of the Evangelical Missiological Society at Dallas International University in Dallas, Texas (October 12–14, 2018). The academic papers presented at the workshop became the foundation of this current volume of unique historical essays.

In addition, we also want to acknowledge and express our appreciation to Dr. Todd Hains, academic editor of Lexham Press, for his enthusiastic encouragement and support throughout the scholastic journey.

Robert L. Gallagher
Edward L. Smither

INTRODUCTION
—

Edward L. Smither

How DID the sixteenth-century global church understand and practice Christian mission?

This question proves more fruitful than the usual questions missiologists and historians often ask of the Reformation: Did the Reformers have a practice and theology of mission? Why did it take so long for Protestants to engage in mission? Was the admonition to make disciples of all nations no longer applicable to the church in every generation?

While making many mistakes, the sixteenth-century church demonstrated faithfulness in Christian mission. The players included a diverse lot—monks, mystics, itinerant preachers, colonialists, women, and men. Our narrative takes us to the ends of the then-known world—to Europe, the Americas, Africa, and Asia. Though cross-cultural outreach had been part of the church's DNA since the first century, it was the sixteenth-century church (the Society of Jesus, in fact) that gave a name to proclaiming Jesus in all of the world—*missions.*

IN THE essays that follow, three themes stand out: the meaning of mission, mission in forgotten places, and the strategy of mission.

The Meaning of Mission. In this project we have resisted offering a definition of Christian mission that might be too located in the twenty-first century. Rather, we have allowed Luther, Calvin, Ignatius of Loyola, Teresa of Avila, and others to define mission on their terms and through their practice. Nevertheless, we are able to sketch out how certain sixteenth-century individuals and movements understood mission.

For the Magisterial Reformers, particularly in the first generation of the Reformation, their focus in mission was evangelizing the existing church in Europe. That said, we will show that disciples of Luther and Calvin also would make disciples in Scandinavia, France, and even in Brazil.

Anabaptist believers largely associated mission with itinerant preaching. Striving to reform the church and preach the gospel while dissenting from a conflation of church and state, Anabaptist missionaries tended to suffer for their faith and ministry more than their Reformed, Lutheran, or Roman Catholic counterparts. In fact, they were routinely persecuted by Reformed, Lutheran, and Catholic Christians.

Sixteenth-century Roman Catholics understood mission as preaching the gospel and establishing the church in all the world. They were the most deliberately global about their focus. Sixteenth-century Roman Catholic mission paralleled Europe's migration to the world, particularly the empires of Spain and Portugal. With missionaries disembarking from the same boats as conquistadores and colonists, it's not surprising that the Jesuits would adopt a military term (*missions*) to describe their work.

Mission in Forgotten Places. Deepening our grasp of global church history, our authors have also shed light on lesser-known mission fields. For example, one author thoroughly surveys Jesuit mission efforts in the kingdom of Kongo—the first wave of sixteenth-century Roman Catholic mission work to the African nation. *Strategy in Mission.* The essays in this book also stimulate discussion on historic mission practice. For example, some of our authors, particularly those surveying Catholic mission, show the correlation between spirituality, ascetic living, and sacrificial mission service. Others, focusing on mission to China, discuss the complexities of what we, today, call contextualization. How does the unchanging gospel find a home in Chinese soil that is cultivated by Confucian thought? Finally, one of our authors reveals the troubling and painful history of mission amid colonial expansion in the Americas, while showing how one sixteenth-century missionary opposed those in power and advocated for justice for indigenous American peoples. Each of these historic themes remain relevant to mission practice today.

WE'VE DIVIDED the book into two main sections. In part one, we engage the narrative of Lutheran, Reformed, and Anabaptist mission history. In the second, we track with the Roman Catholic mission story, focusing largely on the Jesuits, Dominicans, and Franciscans. In both sections, chapters are grouped by affinity (e.g., Reformed, Jesuit) and are largely organized chronologically.

Without further ado, we invite you into the story of sixteenth-century global Christian mission.

Part One

—

LUTHERAN, REFORMED, *and* ANABAPTIST MISSION

1
—

CORRECTING THE RECORD

The Reformers on Evangelism and Missions

Ray Van Neste

Over the past century, many of the books dealing with the history of Christian missions have declared, with varying degrees of certainty, that the Protestant Reformers were derelict in their duty to spread the gospel throughout the entire world.[1] Writers have accused the Reformers of both inactivity and indifference. This unverified opinion has become a virtual certainty among the popular audience. However, is this a fair assessment of what the Reformers did and taught? In this chapter, I will trace the history of this deleterious account of the Reformers in regard to missions and evangelism, critique the methodology of this view, and then present the writings and actions of three Reformers—Martin Luther, Martin Bucer, and John Calvin—in order to show the missional ventures of the Reformers.[2]

A NEGATIVE INTERPRETATION

The Reformation has long been considered by Protestants as a great spiritual revival and doctrinal renewal of the church. However, some writers have argued that the Reformers failed to grasp the missionary imperative

---

1. In this essay, I am addressing missions (the church's part in God's mission) rather than the "mission of God" more broadly conceived.

2. Portions of this material have previously appeared in "The Mangled Narrative of Evangelism and Missions in the Reformation," *Southeastern Theological Review* 8:2 (Fall 2017): 3–27; and in "The Mangled Narrative of Evangelism and Missions in the Reformation," in *Celebrating the Legacy of the Reformation*, ed. Kevin L. King, Edward Hindson, and Benjamin K. Forrest (Nashville: B&H Academic, 2019). This essay is a more complete version of these previous essays.

of the church and have even accused the Reformers of leading the church astray. This view appears to originate with German missiologist Gustav Warneck (1834–1910), a pastor and missions enthusiast whom many regard as the father of Protestant missiology.[3] In his influential survey, Warneck stated that although the conclusion was "painful," nevertheless it is clear that Luther and Calvin's "view of the missionary task of the church was essentially defective."[4] Warneck concedes that Luther preached the gospel earnestly himself, but "nowhere does Luther indicate the heathen as the objects of evangelistic work."[5] Furthermore, Luther "never gives an intimation from which it can be inferred that he held direct mission work among the heathen to be commanded."[6] Warneck concludes "the mission to the heathen world had no interest for [Luther] or his fellow-labourers."[7]

What evidence does Warneck produce to ground such a conclusion? He acknowledges the many obstacles confronting any worldwide effort from Protestants in the sixteenth century, including persecution, lack of contact with "heathen" nations, lack of infrastructure, and the inability to travel to newly discovered lands since Catholic countries (e.g., Spain and Portugal) held sway over the oceans. Still, Warneck faults the Reformers for not lamenting such limitations, suggesting that if they really wanted to reach such far-away areas, there would be indications in their writings of strong yearnings to break through these obstacles to mission.[8] Instead, according to Warneck, we find among the Reformers no idea or activity of missions "in the sense we understand them today."[9]

---

3. For a recent assessment of Warneck's significant place in the development of missiology, see the full chapter on Warneck in Henning Wrogemann, *Theologies of Mission* (Downers Grove, IL: IVP Academic, 2018), 35–46.

4. Gustav Warneck, *Outline of the History of Protestant Missions from the Reformation to the Present Time* (Edinburgh: J. Gemmell, 1884), 17. Three of Warneck's ten German editions were translated into English in 1884, 1901, and 1906.

5. Ibid., 12.

6. Ibid., 16.

7. Ibid., 18.

8. Gustav Warneck, *Outline of the History of Protestant Missions from the Reformation to the Present Time* (Chicago: Revell, 1901), 8–9. The various editions of this book remain consistent in the critique of the Reformers. I drew the first several quotes from an earlier edition because Warneck's points were made more succinctly there.

9. Ibid., 9.

According to Warneck, faulty theology caused the Reformers' defective perception of the imperative of missions. He specified three problematic ideas. First, Warneck says Luther believed the apostles had fulfilled the Great Commission so it no longer applied to the church of his time. However, Warneck acknowledges that Bucer and Calvin did not believe this. Second, Warneck says the Reformers' doctrine of election kept them from sensing any missionary duty. Even though Bucer and Calvin did not think the Great Commission was fulfilled, their belief that the work of salvation was God's work meant there was no human responsibility for the work of missions. Third, the eschatological views of the Reformers inhibited missionary thinking. "Luther and his contemporaries were persuaded that the end of the world was at hand ... so that no time remained for the further development and extension of the kingdom of God on earth."[10]

Warneck's negative representation has been echoed by others through the years. Kenneth Scott Latourette says the Reformers were indifferent to the task of world missions due to their faulty theology, though he does not mention election specifically.[11] Herbert Kane marvels that "spiritual forces released" in the Reformation failed to produce *any* missionary activity, and he blames the same three points of theology that Warneck lists.[12] Stephen Neill finds "exceedingly little" interest in missions from the Reformers.[13] Neill says little about the reasons for this deficiency, but does comment that the Reformation churches did not feel that missions was an obligation on the church. William Hogg says the Reformers "disavowed any obligation for Christians to carry the gospel."[14] Michael Nazir-Ali charges the Reformers with abandoning the responsibility of world missions and blames this on their understanding of election and the idea

---

10. Ibid., 16.

11. Kenneth Scott Latourette, *A History of the Expansion of Christianity: The First Five Centuries* (New York: Harper & Brothers, 1937), 27. Latourette focuses on Luther but does not quote Luther on any of these points. He simply cites Warneck as proof.

12. J. Herbert Kane, *A Concise History of the Christian World Mission: A Panoramic View of Missions from Pentecost to the Present* (Grand Rapids: Baker, 1978), 73.

13. Stephen Neill and Owen Chadwick, *A History of Christian Missions*, 2nd ed (London: Penguin Books, 1986), 189.

14. William Richey Hogg, *Ecumenical Foundations: A History of the International Missionary Council and Its Nineteenth Century Background* (New York: Harper, 1952), 1–2. Hogg cites Warneck as his support.

that the Great Commission no longer applied.[15] According to Ruth Tucker, during the Reformation "the urgency to reach out to others was not seen as a top priority," and she suggests the Reformers did not acknowledge the responsibility to evangelize those without the gospel.[16] She also roots this problem in faulty theology. Johannes Verkuyl blames the Reformers' lack of missions activity on their belief that the Great Commission no longer applied, but he does not reference election or eschatology.[17] Justice Anderson, in a standard missions textbook, attributes the Reformers' lack of missionary zeal to a misunderstanding of the Great Commission and eschatology.[18] The recent *Encountering the History of Missions* by John Mark Terry and Robert Gallagher stands out wonderfully by engaging substantively with the actual writings of the Reformers and appreciating their evangelistic and missional impulse.[19]

This negative interpretation of the Reformers appears commonly in more recent theological writings as well. For example, Ed Stetzer writes, "The church that 'reformed' lost touch with the God who sends, and the mission of the church suffered."[20] Missions professor Alton James says, "the Reformers' theology had little or no room for missions activity" and "a faulty theology served as a hindrance to the early Protestant church being involved in missions."[21] David Allen refers to the "general consen-

15. Michael Nazir-Ali, *From Everywhere to Everywhere: A World View of Christian Witness* (London: Flame, 1990), 42–43.

16. Ruth Tucker, *From Jerusalem to Irian Jaya: A Biographical History of Christian Missions*, 2nd ed (Grand Rapids: Zondervan, 2004), 20. According to Tucker, only in the eighteenth century did Protestants begin "acknowledging their responsibility to evangelize those without the gospel" (98).

17. Johannes Verkuyl, *Contemporary Missiology: An Introduction,* trans. Dale Cooper (Grand Rapids: Eerdmans, 1987), 18–19.

18. Justice Anderson, "Medieval and Renaissance Missions (500–1792)," in *Missiology: An Introduction to the Foundations, History, and Strategies of World Missions*, revised 2d edition, ed. John Mark Terry (Nashville: B&H, 2015), 167–69. Anderson, like several other Free Church authors, says the connection between state and church in the Magisterial Reformers hindered missions since a state church's mission is confined to national interests. However, this fails to account for the missionaries sent out from Geneva to various countries throughout Europe.

19. John Mark Terry and Robert Gallagher, *Encountering the History of Missions* (Grand Rapids: Baker Academic, 2018).

20. Ed Stetzer, *Planting New Churches in a Postmodern Age* (Nashville: Broadman & Holman, 2003), 23.

21. R. Alton James, "Post-Reformation Missions Pioneers," in *Discovering the Mission of God: Best Missional Practices for the 21st Century*, ed. Mike Barnett and Robin Martin (Downers Grove, IL: IVP, 2012), 251, 252.

sus" that the Reformers had almost no missionary vision.[22] Paige Patterson, in a column posted at the website of the Southern Baptist Convention's International Mission Board, charged the Reformers with being ineffectual in missions and cited their doctrine of election as the reason.[23] Ralph Winter says Christians of the Reformation era sent no missionaries, "did not even talk of mission outreach," and did "not even try to reach out."[24]

Clearly, Warneck's argument took root. Few of these works present their own primary source research on the topic. They simply cite or allude to Warneck or to someone who has followed him. Rarely is there evidence of Warneck being read critically. Typically, Warneck's view of the Reformers is simply asserted or assumed as one of the proven facts of historical scholarship. However, this raises the question of whether Warneck was correct or even if he has been properly understood. Thus, we now turn to critical interaction with Warneck, particularly how he defined missions and his appraisal of the Reformers' theology.

WARNECK'S DEFINITION OF MISSIONS

Following the literature just reviewed, popular theological literature and conversation often carry the assumption that the Reformers had no concern for the salvation of souls or the preaching of the gospel. However, this is not what Warneck argued at all. In fact, he concedes that the Reformers were effective in Christianizing Europe and, in this sense, the Reformation "may be said to have carried on a mission work at home on an extensive scale."[25] Warneck also concedes that Luther encouraged any who were taken captive by the Turks (a real threat in the sixteenth century) to be prepared to be a gospel witness to their captors. Luther urges such Christians to faithful living and witness that they might "convert many." This would appear to be significant mission-mindedness but Warneck dismisses it as

---

22. David Allen, "Preaching for a Great Commission Resurgence," in *Great Commission Resurgence: Fulfilling God's Mandate in Our Time*, ed. Chuck Lawless and Adam Greenway (Nashville: B&H Academic, 2010), 286.

23. Paige Patterson, "The Anabaptists, Evangelism, and Missions," May 29, 2017, https://www.imb.org/2017/05/29/anabaptists/.

24. Ralph D. Winter, "The Kingdom Strikes Back: Ten Epochs of Redemptive History," in Ralph D. Winter, Steven C. Hawthorne, ed. *Perspectives on the World Christian Movement: A Reader* (Pasadena: William Carey Library, 2009), 224.

25. Warneck, *History of Protestant Missions*, 8.

simply "the spirit of Christian testimony" rather than proper "missionary work" since this comes from the scattering of persecution rather than the systematic sending out of missionaries.[26] Elsewhere Warneck quotes a long excerpt from an Ascension Sunday sermon of Luther's where he describes how the gospel will go out to the whole world "sped ever farther by preachers hunted and persecuted hither and thither into the world." This, however, cannot be understood as an interest in world missions, Warneck says, because there is "no reference to any systematic missionary enterprise."[27] These are just two examples of many that show that Warneck is operating with a very narrow, even anachronistic, view of missions. To be reckoned as missions, Warneck believes it must be a systematic work, preferably by an institution outside the church that consistently sends missionaries to previously unevangelized areas.[28] As a result, Warneck completely discounts numerous mission-minded statements made by various Reformers because they do not call for the establishment of a missions agency. For example, Martin Bucer's rebuke of Christians for their attitude towards Jews and Turks is diminished because "there is little trace of earnestness as to how one may win their souls to Christ our Lord." Bucer prays for church leaders who will help the church labor for the salvation of Jews, Turks, "and all unbelievers to whom they may ever have any access." Warneck concedes that this sounds like "a direct summons to missions," but it only appears so since Bucer neglects to say anything about "instituting missions."[29] What Warneck means by this is clarified later when he faults Bucer for failing to see the need to devise an "institution for the dissemination of Christianity."[30]

Warneck fails to find any evidence of mission activity or thinking in the Reformers essentially because he has defined missions in accordance with what he and others were doing in the nineteenth century.[31] His argu-

---

26. Ibid., 15. Yet, the original spread of the gospel in Acts resulted from an outbreak of persecution.

27. Ibid., 14.

28. See also Klaus Detlev Schulz, *Mission from the Cross: The Lutheran Theology of Mission* (St. Louis: Concordia, 2009), 45–46.

29. Warneck, *History of Protestant Missions*, 18.

30. Ibid., 19.

31. Jean-François Zorn has shown that the word "mission" was first used in regard to global gospel outreach in the sixteenth century by Roman Catholics. This is why this specific

ments merely prove that the Reformers were not participants in a nine-teenth-century missions agency. But they do not prove that the Reformers had little or no concern about the worldwide spread of the gospel or the salvation of people from all over the world.[32]

This begs the question of a proper definition of missions. Yet such a definition is a topic of debate among contemporary missiologists. David Bosch warns against defining missions "too sharply and too self-confi-dently." He states, "Ultimately, mission remains undefinable; it should never be incarcerated in the narrow confines of our own predilections."[33] Instead of defining missions, he expounds the various elements of mis-sions. He clearly believes that missions involves taking the gospel to a world in need, preaching, planting churches, discipling, and meeting needs in Jesus' name.[34] Bosch argues there is no theological basis for distinguishing "foreign" and "domestic" missions. He refers to the myth "that travelling to foreign lands is the *sine qua non* for *any* kind of missionary endeavor and the final test and criterion of what is truly missionary," and says this idea has been demolished.[35] Bosch's survey suggests that modern missiology has turned away from the narrow definition that governed Warneck's analysis. At the core, missions is the church joining in the mission of God to bring people into fellowship with himself by gospel proclamation, church plant-ing, discipleship, and living out the ethical implications of the gospel.[36]

---

term is not used by the Reformers—it was a new term coined by those in opposition to them ("Did Calvin Foster or Hinder the Missions?" *Exchange* 40 [2011]: 179–81).

32.   The charge that Warneck has anachronistically formulated his analysis is also made by Robert Kolb, "Late Reformation Lutherans on Mission and Confession," *Lutheran Quarterly* 20 (2006): 26. For a thorough critique of Warneck's conception of "mission" see Elias Medeiros, "The Reformers' Commitment to the Propagation of the Gospel to All Nations from 1555 to 1654," PhD diss., Reformed Theological Seminary, Jackson, MS, 2009, especially pages 15–111.

33.   David J. Bosch, *Transforming Mission: Paradigm Shifts in Theology of Mission* (Maryknoll, NY: Orbis Books, 1991), 9.

34.   See his table of contents, as well as his closing comments on page 519.

35.   Bosch, 10. Wrogemann, *Theologies of Mission*, 37, also discusses the geographical lim-itation of "missions" in Warneck's thought.

36.   See further John Mark Terry, Ebbie C. Smith, and Justice Anderson, ed., *Missiology: An Introduction to the Foundations, History, and Strategies of World Missions* (Nashville: Broadman & Holman, 1998, 2). See also Bruce Ashford, ed., *Theology and Practice of Mission: God, the Church, and the Nations* (Nashville: B&H Academic, 2011).

WARNECK'S ASSESSMENT OF
THE REFORMERS' THEOLOGY

Even if Warneck's definition of missions is too restrictive, is there truth to the claim that the Reformers' theology kept them from seeing and embracing the missional mandate of Scripture? We will take up each of the three points of theology Warneck and others have listed as problematic.

First, did the Reformers teach that world missions was no longer an obligation for the church? Calvin explicitly rejects this idea in his commentary on Matthew 28:20: "It ought likewise to be remarked, that this was not spoken to the apostles alone; for the Lord promises his assistance not for a single age only, but *even to the end of the world*."[37] Furthermore, lecturing on Micah 4:3, Calvin stated, "the kingdom of Christ was only begun in the world, when God commanded the Gospel to be everywhere proclaimed, and ... at this day its course is not as yet completed."[38] Whatever one thinks of Calvin's theology or mission involvement, he certainly did not teach that the Great Commission had been fulfilled in the apostolic era.[39]

Neither is it true that Luther taught that the day of missionary obligation had passed.[40] Writing on Matthew 22:9, Luther stated, "This [time for missions] is not yet completed. This era continues so that the servants go out into the highways. The apostles began this work and we continue inviting all. The table will be full at the advent of the last day and when the Gospel has been made known in the whole world."[41] He also stated, "It is necessary always to proceed to those to whom no preaching has been done, in order that the number [of Christians] may become greater."[42] In

---

37. John Calvin, "Commentary on a Harmony of the Evangelists," in *Calvin's Commentaries*, 22 vols., trans. W. Pringle (Grand Rapids: Baker, 1984), 17:391. Emphasis original.

38. John Calvin, "Commentary on Micah," in *Calvin's Commentaries*, 22 vols., trans. W. Pringle (Grand Rapids: Baker, 1984), 14:265.

39. Part of the problem with this misrepresentation of the Reformers is that later readers expect the Reformers to speak of missions from the same texts modern readers do (e.g., Matt 28:19-20).

40. See further Montgomery, "Luther and Missions," *Evangelical Missions Quarterly* 3:4 (1967): 193-202.

41. WA (*Weimer Ausgabe*) 17/1:442.36-37, 1:443.1-2, cited in Ingemar Öberg, *Luther and World Mission: A Historical and Systematic Study with Special Reference to Luther's Bible Exposition* (St. Louis: Concordia, 2007), 134. Werner Elert, *The Structure of Lutheranism*, trans. Walter A. Hansen (St. Louis: Concordia, 1962), 386, has a helpful discussion of how Luther's comments have been misunderstood as suggesting the era of world mission closed with the apostles.

42. Cited in Elert, *Structure of Lutheranism*, 389.

contrast to Warneck's accusation that Luther thought there was no need to take the gospel further because it had already reached the whole world via the apostles, Luther says:

> Their preaching went out to the whole world even though it has not yet reached the whole world. This outcome has begun and its goal is set though it is not yet completed and accomplished; instead, it shall be extended through preaching even farther until the Day of Judgment. When this preaching reaches all corners of the world and is heard and pronounced, then it is complete and in every respect finished and the Last Day will also arrive.[43]

Luther anticipates that people "will be sent by God among the nations as preachers and thus draw many people to themselves and through themselves to Christ."[44] Luther specifically called for the gospel to be taken to the Bohemians, the Russians, and the Muslim Turks.[45] Within a short time after his death, Luther's disciples had set out on mission work to all of these groups.[46] And these men, like those sent to other parts of Europe, went out knowing they were likely to be executed.

Secondly, did the Reformers' doctrine of election prevent them from doing mission work? Warneck says that since Luther saw salvation as a work completely of God's grace, he did not think a "human missionary agency" was part of God's plan.[47] He asserts the same of Bucer and Calvin. For proof he simply cites one statement by Calvin without context: "We are taught that the kingdom of Christ is neither to be advanced nor maintained by the industry of men, but this is the work of God alone; for believers are

---

43. Ascension Sermon, May 29, 1522. WA 10/3:139.17–140.16. Cited in Volker Stolle, *The Church Comes from All Nations: Luther Texts on Mission* (St. Louis: Concordia, 2003), 24. See also Luther's Sermon on Titus 2:11–15, Christmas Postil, 1522. WA 10/1.1:21.3–23.14 (cited in Stolle, *Church Comes from All Nations*, 98–99) where he clearly says the work of taking the gospel to the whole earth is not yet completed.

44. *The Prophet Zechariah Expounded*, LW 20:305–6. Cited in Stolle, *Church Comes from All Nations*, 97.

45. See further Warneck, *History of Protestant Missions*, 13.

46. Öberg, *Luther and World Mission*, 498–99.

47. Warneck, *History of Protestant Missions*, 16. Once again Warneck sees missions only in terms of a sending "agency."

taught to rest solely on His blessing."[48] Later writers often make this same assertion, citing the same quote without context or any mention of where it is found.[49] It is a strong statement, but anyone familiar with Calvin's writings will recognize his affirmation that salvation and the advance of God's kingdom ultimately depends on God alone. However, even a cursory reading of Calvin will show that he also strongly emphasizes human responsibility as well as recognizing that God works through means.[50] For example, Calvin states that the "gospel does not fall like rain from the clouds, but is brought by the hands of men," and God "makes use of our exertions, and employs us as his instruments, for cultivating his field."[51] Warneck does not demonstrate how Calvin's understanding of election hindered missions. Neither do later writers. It is assumed that the doctrine of election "made missions appear extraneous if God had already chosen those he would save,"[52] or "if God wills the conversion of the heathen, they will be saved without human instrumentality."[53] Yet, we have already seen various statements from Luther and Calvin that called upon believers to proclaim the gospel so that people might be saved. Furthermore, if this doctrine made foreign missions moot, why did it not stifle mission work within Europe? Even Warneck concedes that this work in Europe was significant. Why would a belief in God's sovereignty prevent the Reformers from trying to evangelize overseas but not preclude them taking the gospel to France (or other areas of Europe) at the risk of their lives?

Lastly, Warneck asserts that the Reformers did not believe there was much time for mission engagement since the world would end soon. Latourette, Kane, and Tucker all repeat this claim without any citations from Luther or any demonstration of how the idea shaped actions other

---

48. Ibid., 20. I have not been able to find the source of this quote. In the books I have found, authors quote it without citation or simply cite Warneck.

49. See further Kane, *A Concise History*, 74. Olson, C. Gordon, *What in the World Is God Doing? The Essentials of Global Missions* (Global Gospel Publishers, 2011), 103.

50. Jean-François Zorn, "Did Calvin Foster or Hinder the Missions?", 178, 184, is especially helpful on Calvin's emphasis on the necessity of means. See also David Calhoun, "John Calvin: Missionary Hero or Missionary Failure?" *Presbyterion* 5:1 (Spring 1979): 18–20.

51. John Calvin, "Commentaries on the Epistle of Paul to the Romans," in *Calvin's Commentaries*, 22 vols., trans. W. Pringle (Grand Rapids: Baker, 1984), 19:399; "Commentary on a Harmony of the Evangelists," 16:121.

52. Tucker, *From Jerusalem to Irian Jaya*, 97.

53. Kane, *A Concise History*, 74.

than saying the Reformers (particularly Luther) did not think there was time for mission work. However, Warneck conceded that Luther nowhere says the imminent end of the age was a reason for not doing missions. Thus, this connection is merely a guess. However, Warneck says the reason why Luther never makes the connection is that even apart from his eschatology Luther knew nothing of a duty for world mission.[54] So, Luther's eschatology kept him from missions, and we know this because even though we cannot link his views on eschatology and missions, Luther was ignorant of a missions duty anyway. This is a convoluted argument, and yet people have repeated it for over a century.[55]

Thus, all three areas of doctrinal critique fail. Whether or not one agrees with the specific doctrines in view, the arguments fail to prove that these doctrines either were held by the Reformers or that they hindered mission thinking or work.[56]

EVALUATION OF THE REFORMERS THEMSELVES

Now we must turn to the deeds and writings of three Reformers to see what evidence we find of missions involvement and evangelistic impulse. Since we have critiqued Warneck's narrow definition of missions, in the Reformers' words and deeds, we will now turn to the Reformers' active calling of people to faith in Christ and a concern for the gospel to reach the nations.

MISSION WITHIN CHRISTENDOM

One key problem in Warneck and those who follow him is their failure to recognize the missionary setting for Protestants in Europe in the sixteenth century. The gospel was largely unknown by the vast majority of people in Europe, and the Reformers labored to get this gospel message to as many people as possible. Calvin's preface to his *Institutes of the Christian*

---

54. Warneck, *History of Protestant Missions*, 16.

55. See Schulz, *Mission from the Cross*, 51–52, for further refutation of the idea that Luther was certain of the imminent end of the world and that this hindered missions.

56. It will not do to argue as Gordon Olson does that at least we know some people have used the doctrine of election to stifle mission endeavors. Practically every positive doctrine has been abused by someone over the years (*What in the World Is God Doing?*, 104). The question in view is whether the doctrine hindered mission work in the Reformers themselves.

Religion declares that his writing was intended to aid his fellow country-men in France "very many of whom I knew to be hungering and thirst-ing for Christ; but I saw very few who had been duly imbued with even a slight knowledge of him."[57] Calvin expounded the Scriptures to help people know Christ. This is why one biographer says, "Calvin in Strasbourg or Geneva was also a missionary, an envoy."[58] Luther also said that many of the people who attended the church services "do not believe and are not yet Christians." Thus, he said, "the gospel must be publicly preached to move them to believe and become Christians."[59]

Scott Hendrix's *Recultivating the Vineyard: The Reformation Agendas of Christianization* has been particularly helpful in demonstrating the mission element involved in the Reformers' work in Europe.[60] His basic premise is that the "Reformers saw themselves in a missionary situation in which the faith had to be taught to a populace they judged to be inadequately informed."[61] The entire program of the Reformers was to re-evangelize their native lands. Calvin, for example, saw himself as a missionary, labor-ing "to turn nominal believers into real Christians."[62] Of course, Hendrix grants, it took some time before full-fledged international mission work began in Reformation churches, but this developing outward reach was an organic result of Reformation ideas. "The Reformation's own sources state plainly how reformers saw their enterprise as a missionary campaign to renew and replant Christianity in European culture."[63] Nineteenth-century scholars working in a largely Christianized Europe could miss the fact that

---

57. John Calvin, *Institutes of the Christian Religion*, trans. Ford Lewis Battles, *The Library of Christian Classics*, vol. 20 (Philadelphia: Westminster Press, 1960), 9.

58. Bernard Cottret, *Calvin: A Biography* (Grand Rapids: Eerdmans, 2000), 138.

59. Luther, "German Mass," LW 53:62–64. Cited in Stolle, *The Church Comes from All Nations*, 44.

60. Scott Hendrix, *Recultivating the Vineyard: The Reformation Agendas of Christianization* (Louisville: Westminster John Knox, 2004).

61. Ibid., 172.

62. Ibid., 95. Hendrix also cites the revised preface of the 1559 edition of the *Institutes* where Calvin says, "God has filled my mind with zeal to spread his kingdom and to further the public good" (88).

63. Ibid., 163–64. Theodor Bibliander (1509–1564), a biblical scholar from Zurich, who, according to Hendrix, was probably the best informed among the Reformers about Islam.

in the mind of the Reformers the majority of Europe in their day was in need of evangelization.[64]

The training and sending out of pastors which occurred in Geneva and Wittenberg should be understood as an essential element of the Reformers' missionary campaign. The missionary zeal of these pastors is underscored by the fact that many or most of the areas to which they went were hostile to these pastors so they went out at the risk of their lives. Under Calvin's leadership, Geneva became "the hub of a vast missionary enterprise"[65] and "a dynamic center or nucleus from which the vital missionary energy it generated radiated out into the world beyond."[66] Protestant refugees from all over Europe fled to Geneva; they came not merely for safety but also to learn from Calvin the doctrines of the Reformation so they could return home to spread the true gospel. The Register of the Company of Pastors in Geneva records numerous people sent out from Geneva during Calvin's time to "evangelize foreign parts."[67] The records are incomplete, and eventually, due to persecution, it became too dangerous to record the names of those sent out, although it numbered more than one hundred in one year alone. Bruce Gordon refers to the sending of such a large number of missionaries into France the "most audacious missionary effort" undertaken by the Genevan church.[68] By 1557 it was a normal part of business for the Genevan pastors to send missionaries into France. Robert M. Kingdon called it a "concentrated missionary effort."[69] Philip Hughes notes that Geneva became a "school of missions" that had as one of its purposes "to send out witnesses" who would take the gospel "far and wide." Hughes

---

64. Today we can also easily miss that in the sixteenth century various distinct cultures and people groups existed within what is now the boundary of a single country.

65. Raymond K. Anderson, "Calvin and Missions," *Christian History*, 5 no. 4 (Fall 1986): 23.

66. Philip E. Hughes, "John Calvin: Director of Missions," in *The Heritage of John Calvin*, ed. J. H. Bratt (Grand Rapids: Eerdmans, 1973), 45. Portions of this section of the essay are taken from Ray Van Neste, "John Calvin on Missions and Evangelism," *Founders Journal* 33 (1998): 15–21.

67. Alister McGrath, *A Life of John Calvin, A Study in the Shaping of Western Culture* (Oxford: Basil Blackwell, 1990), 182. Cf. Philip Hughes, ed. and trans., *The Register of the Company of Pastors of Geneva in the Time of Calvin* (Grand Rapids: Eerdmans, 1966), 308.

68. Bruce Gordon, *Calvin* (New Haven: Yale University Press, 2009), 312.

69. Robert M. Kingdon, "Calvinist Religious Aggression," in *The French Wars of Religion, How Important Were Religious Factors?*, ed. J. H. M. Salmon (Lexington, MA: D. C. Heath and Company, 1967), 6.

describes Geneva as "a dynamic centre of missionary concern and activity, an axis from which the light of the Good News radiated forth through the testimony of those who, after thorough preparation in this school, were sent forth in the service of Jesus Christ."[70] Zorn suggests that Calvin developed a "missionary theology for Europe."[71] For good reason Hendrix concludes, "The Reformation was a missionary campaign that envisioned a renewed Christian society in Europe."[72]

So, there is no need to discount the words and deeds of the Reformers in regard to the evangelization of their neighbors and neighboring lands, as Warneck did. In fact, given the persecution they faced and the difficulty of travel, we should commend their work. Critics also seem to miss the fact that Germany, for example, did not become a unified nation until later in the nineteenth century, so Protestant preachers were quite often crossing national lines, engaging with other countries according to the thinking of the time. Let us then turn our attention to a sampling from the writings of Luther, Bucer, and Calvin, as representative Reformers, to see the attention given to concern for the salvation of others.

LUTHER (1483–1546)

Although it does not seem to have been picked up in most evangelical missions textbooks, substantial attention has already been given to Luther's comments on evangelism and world mission. Volker Stolle's *The Church Comes from All Nations: Luther Texts on Mission* gleaned significant sections from Luther where he advocates for the task of taking the gospel to all people.[73] Robert Kolb hailed Stolle's work as "more historically sensitive" than Warneck, and it "demonstrates Luther's interest in the spread of the Christian faith."[74] Werner Elert has also drawn from the rich resources of Luther's mission-oriented comments to demonstrate Luther's concern

---

70. Hughes, *Register*, 25. See also Michael A. G. Haykin, "John Calvin's Missionary Influence in France," *Reformation and Revival* 10.4 (Fall 2001): 35–44.

71. Zorn, "Did Calvin Foster or Hinder the Missions," 178.

72. Hendrix, *Recultivating the Vineyard*, 174.

73. Stolle, *The Church Comes from All Nations*.

74. Kolb, "Late Reformation Lutherans on Mission and Confession," 40.

for mission, noting how his conception of mission differed from (and was healthier than) Warneck's view.[75]

Also, Ingemar Öberg, in his *Luther and World Mission: A Historical and Systematic Study with Special Reference to Luther's Bible Exposition*, demonstrated thoroughly Luther's drive to get the gospel to all people.[76] Robert Kolb commended Öberg's work stating that he had mined a "wide variety of sources within Luther's writings with great care and acumen."[77] As a result, Kolb said, Öberg showed the wealth of insights to be found in Luther's writings "for sound mission thinking."[78]

There is no need or space for restating all that Stolle, Öberg, and Elert have gleaned from Luther, but in what follows I will draw some examples from their work and my own observations to demonstrate Luther's evangelistic and missionary concern.[79] Luther's correspondence, alone, was a missionary endeavor as he wrote to people all over Europe urging gospel truths and counseling leaders and others in how to advance the cause of Christ.[80] Furthermore, Luther taught his people to pray for the conversion of unbelievers and for the gospel to be preached over the whole world. In his brief work written to teach his people how to pray, he instructs them to meditate on each petition of the Lord's Prayer turning that into specific prayers. Luther provides an example of how one might pray from each petition, and in the first three petitions, he explicitly prays for the conversion of unbelievers.[81]

This evangelistic concern can also be seen in Luther's exposition of the Lord's Prayer in his Large Catechism. Discussing the second petition, "Your kingdom come," Luther explains that this teaches us, among other things,

---

75. Elert, *Structure of Lutheranism*, 385–402.

76. Öberg, *Luther and World Mission*.

77. Robert Kolb, "Foreword," Öberg, *Luther and World Mission*, viii.

78. Ibid. See also, John Warwick Montgomery, "Luther and Missions," 193–202.

79. Schulz, *Mission from the Cross*, 46–47, note 3, lists more works which highlight the mission emphasis in Luther's writings.

80. For a fascinating graphic display of the geographic distribution of Luther's correspondence, see Ernest G. Schwiebert, *Luther and His Times: The Reformation from a New Perspective* (St. Louis: Concordia, 1950), 4. Plass calls Luther's correspondence "a missionary influence, as was the University of Wittenberg" (Ewald M. Plass, *What Luther Says: An Anthology* [St. Louis: Concordia, 1959], 958).

81. Martin Luther, *A Simple Way to Pray*, trans. Matthew C. Harrison (St. Louis: Concordia, 2012).

to pray that the kingdom "may gain recognition and followers among other people and advance with power throughout the world." Later in the same question he says this petition teaches us to pray both that believers might grow in the kingdom and that "it may come to those who are not yet in it." Concluding, he writes, "All this is to simply say: 'Dear Father, we pray Thee, give us thy Word, that the gospel may be sincerely preached throughout the world and that it may be received by faith and work and live in us."[82] People who pray regularly for the conversion of people around the world are a mission-minded people. Pastors who teach their people to pray this way are mission-minded pastors. Thus, Luther and his churches were mission-minded people.

As noted previously, Warneck conceded that Luther "with all earnestness" urged "the preaching of the gospel, and longs for a free course for it" but said "nowhere does Luther indicate the heathen as the objects of evangelistic work."[83] However, preaching on Matthew 23:15, Luther says, "The very best of all works is that the heathen have been led from idolatry to God."[84] Furthermore, the conversion of the heathen was a significant theme in a number of Luther's hymns, including this one based on Psalm 67:

> Would that the Lord would grant us grace,
> With blessings rich provide us,
> And with clear shining let his face,
> To life eternal light us;
> That we his gracious work may know,
> And what is his good pleasure,
> And also to the heathen show,
> Christ's riches without measure
> And unto God convert them.[85]

Another hymn of Luther's based on Mark 16:15–16 and Luke 24:46–53, says,

---

82. Luther, *Larger Catechism*, 2.51–54; in Theodore G. Tappert, *The Book of Concord: The Confessions of the Evangelical Lutheran Church* (Philadelphia: Fortress Press, 1959), 426–27.

83. Warneck, *History of Protestant Missions*, 1901, 12.

84. Cited in Plass, *What Luther Says: An Anthology*, 957. Also in Elert, *Structure of Lutheranism*, 390.

85. LW 53:234, cited in Öberg, *Luther and World Mission*, 496. Öberg provides other examples as well.

Christ to all his followers says: Go forth
Give to all men acquaintance
That lost in sin lies the whole earth,
And must turn to repentance.
Who trusts and who is baptized, each one
Is thereby blest forever;
Is from that hour a new-born man,
And thenceforth dying never,
The kingdom shall inherit.[86]

In yet another hymn based on Simeon's song in Luke 2:28–32, Luther also taught his people to embrace world evangelization.

It was God's love that sent you forth
As man's salvation,
Inviting to yourself the earth,
Ev'ry nation,
By your wholesome healing Word
Resounding round our planet
You are the health and saving light of lands in darkness;
You feed and lighten those in night
With your kindness.
All God's people find in you
Their treasure, joy and glory.[87]

Luther's hymns were central to the piety of Christians who embraced his teachings. These hymns were sung in families and at work, thus significantly shaping the thinking and living of the people.[88] The inclusion of such explicit mission themes in these hymns is significant.

---

86. Cited in Öberg, *Luther and World Mission*, 496.

87. "In Peace and Joy I Now Depart" (Lutheran Worship 185.3–4), "Lobgesang des Simeon" (Hymn of Simeon), 1524 Evangelisch-Lutherisches Kirchengesangbuch 310.3–4, WA 35:439.8–20. Cited in Stolle, *Church Comes from All Nations*, 49–50.

88. See, for example, Robin Leaver, *The Whole Church Sings: Congregational Singing in Luther's Wittenberg* (Grand Rapids: Eerdmans, 2017); and Christopher Boyd Brown, *Singing the Gospel: Lutheran Hymns and the Success of the Reformation* (Cambridge, MA: Harvard University Press, 2005).

Luther is abundantly clear about the duty of believers, not just magistrates or official clergy, to share the gospel with others. He says "one must always preach the Gospel so that one may bring some more to become Christians."[89] Furthermore, "It would be insufferable for someone to associate with people and not reveal what is useful for the salvation of their souls."[90] Indeed, Luther says, "If the need were to arise, all of us should be ready to die in order to bring a soul to God."[91] Luther recounts his own conversations with Jews where he sought to demonstrate Jesus is the Messiah and to call them to faith.[92] Luther states, "It is certain that a Christian not only has the right and power to teach God's word but has the duty to do so on pain of losing his soul and of God's disfavor." Luther then answers the objection that someone might raise that all are not ordained to the gospel ministry. He says that if you find yourself in a place where there are no other Christians, then one "needs no other call than to be a Christian. ... It is his duty to preach and to teach the gospel to erring heathen or non-Christians, because of the duty of brotherly love."[93]

Here are a few extended sections which demonstrate Luther's concern for personal evangelism and his desire to stir up others to this task. "For this reason, however, he lets us live that we may bring other people also to faith as he has done for us. ... Your preaching should be done so that one brother proclaims to the other the mighty deed of God: how through him you have been redeemed from sin, hell, death, and from all misery, and have been called to eternal life. You should also instruct people how they

---

89. Sermon on the Good Shepherd, 1523. WA 12:540.3-15. Cited in Stolle, *Church Comes from All Nations*, 26.

90. Sermons on the First Books of Moses, WA 24:261.26–262.11. Cited in Stolle, *Church Comes from All Nations*, 16.

91. Plass, *What Luther Says*, 2836.

92. Sermon on Jeremiah 23:6-8, November 25, 1526. WA 20:569.25-570.12. Cited in Stolle, *Church Comes from All Nations*, 61. Luther's interaction with the Jews is too large a subject to delve into here. He urges gentleness toward them for the sake of evangelism in his early work. His later, harsh work is theologically, not racially motivated, where in frustration he calls for punishments with the aim of drawing them to Christ. This is misguided evangelistic zeal with terrible consequences.

93. *The Right and Power of a Christian Congregation*, 1523. LW 39:309-10. Cited by Stolle, *Church Comes from All Nations*, 21.

should come to that light. ... Make it your highest priority to proclaim this publicly and call everyone to the light to which you are called."[94]

"For once a Christian begins to know Christ as his Lord and Savior, ... he is eager to help everyone acquire the same benefits. For his greatest delight is in this treasure, the knowledge of Christ. Therefore, he steps forth boldly, teaches and admonishes others, praises and confesses his treasure before everybody, prays and yearns that they, too, may obtain such mercy."[95]

Far from being concerned only about his own locale, Luther provides a model for missional engagement today. He warns people about getting too caught up with their own setting or language so that they are unable to reach others.[96] As Herbert Blöchle said, "Luther did not speak just on occasions and periodically to the questions about mission to the heathens. His entire theology is rather permeated by a 'missionary dimension'."[97]

MARTIN BUCER (1491–1551)

As noted earlier, Warneck conceded that Bucer had some missionary interest, even though Warneck did not discuss Bucer's book, *Concerning the True Care of Souls,* which is filled with evangelistic pathos and exhortation. In this book Bucer even rebukes the church for failing to mount a more serious missionary endeavor to the Jews and Turks and says that the current threat from the Turks is God's judgment for their failure.[98]

Bucer calls for earnest, zealous, evangelistic labor. To pastors he says, "true carers of souls and faithful ministers of Christ are not to miss anyone anywhere out with the word of salvation, but diligently to endeavor to seek out all those to whom they may have access in order to lead them to Christ

---

94. Sermons on 1 Peter, first edition, 152, WA 12:318.25–319.6. Cited by Stolle, *Church Comes from All Nations,* 20. Luther goes on to say, "Where you see people that do not know this, you should instruct them and also teach them how you learned, that is, how one through the good work and might of God is saved and comes from darkness into light."

95. *Exposition of the Fourteenth and Fifteenth Chapters of the Gospel of St. John,* LW 24:87–88. Cited in Stolle, *Church Comes from All Nations,* 23. Luther goes on to say, "He constantly strives and struggles with all his might, as one who has no other object in life than to disseminate God's honor and glory among the people, that others may also receive such a spirit of grace."

96. See further Luther, *German Mass,* LW 53:62–64. Cited in Stolle, *Church Comes from All Nations,* 43.

97. Quoted in Schulz, *Mission from the Cross,* 48.

98. Martin Bucer, *Concerning the True Care of Souls,* trans. Peter Beale (Carlisle, PA: Banner of Truth, 2009), 87.

our Lord."[99] Bucer calls for perseverance in sharing the gospel with people who do not readily accept it: "faithful members of Christ are not to give up lightly on anyone."[100] In fact, Bucer says, "one should be so persistent with people [in calling them to faith] that to the evil flesh it seems to be a compulsion and urgent pressing."[101] For Bucer, zealous missionary work is rooted in God's desires and stirred by the example of Paul:

> He [God] desires that they should be sought wherever they are scattered, and sought with such seriousness and diligence that one should be ready to be all things to all men, as dear Paul was [1 Cor. 9:22], and even to hazard one's own life, as the Lord himself did, so that the lost lambs might be found and won.[102]

Bucer affirmed God's sovereign election of souls to salvation, but did not see this as conflicting with energetic missionary enterprise:

> But it is not the Lord's will to reveal to us the secrets of his election; rather he commands us to go out into all the world and preach his gospel to every creature. ... The fact that all people have been made by God and are God's creatures should therefore be reason enough for us to go to them, seeking with the utmost faithfulness to bring them to eternal life.[103]

Combining the pastoral care noted previously and evangelistic zeal, Bucer prayed, "May the Lord Jesus, our chief Shepherd and Bishop, grant us such elders and carers of souls as will seek his lambs which are still lost."[104]

---

99. Ibid. 76.
100. Ibid., 78.
101. Ibid.
102. Ibid.
103. Ibid., 77.
104. Ibid., 193.

JOHN CALVIN (1509–1564)

Contrary to the impression or assumption of many, Calvin exhibited deep evangelistic concern.[105] Refugees came to Geneva, fleeing persecution, with many coming to be trained in order to return to their countries as gospel preachers. Pete Wilcox states, "Even if not all of those who attended Calvin's lectures were missionaries in training, the majority were caught up with him in an evangelistic enterprise."[106]

In 1556, Calvin and his fellow ministers helped to support the first mission endeavor to target the New World, with a group sent to Brazil.[107] Warneck discounted this as a mission endeavor because he questioned Calvin's involvement or sympathy and doubted whether the aim was really to evangelize indigenous people or just to provide religious services for the European settlers. However, we have a good account of the Genevan church's actions in the personal journal of Jean de Léry, a member of the church in Geneva. A man seeking to establish a French colony in Brazil sent a letter to Calvin and the Genevan church asking for ministers of the gospel to accompany the settlers. According to de Léry, the letter specifically asked for preachers and other people "well instructed in the Christian religion" so that they might teach the other Europeans and "bring savages to the knowledge of their salvation."[108] The firsthand account we have of the event makes the missionary element of the endeavor crystal clear. Furthermore, the response of the church to this request is striking. De Léry records, "Upon receiving these letters and hearing this news, the church of Geneva at once gave thanks to God for the extension of the reign of Jesus Christ in a country so distant and likewise so foreign and among a nation entirely without knowledge of the true God."[109] This is not the response of a church that has no heart for missions, a church concerned only with stabilizing itself. Rather, this is the result of teaching and preaching which

---

105. See further J. D. Benoit, "Pastoral Care of the Prophet," in *John Calvin: Contemporary Prophet*, ed., Jacob Hoogstra (Grand Rapids: Baker, 1959), 51.

106. Pete Wilcox, "Evangelisation in the Thought and Practice of John Calvin," *Anvil* 12:3 (1995): 212.

107. See further R. Pierce Beaver, "The Genevan Mission to Brazil," in *The Heritage of John Calvin*, ed. John H. Bratt (Grand Rapids: Eerdmans, 1973), 55–73; Kenneth J. Stewart, "Calvinism and Missions: The Contested Relationship Revisited," *Themelios* 34 (2009): 63–78.

108. Beaver, "The Genevan Mission to Brazil," 61.

109. Ibid.

held up the responsibility to proclaim the gospel to all people.[110] Here we see the longing for opportunity to engage in world missions which Warneck says is missing.

Warneck also says the Brazil mission does not qualify as a mission endeavor because it did not last long enough. It is true that because of treachery the effort came to an end. However, obedience and not success has always been the call. While the Brazil mission was still ongoing, a letter was sent to Calvin from one of the missionaries. He described the difficulties of their evangelistic efforts but said, "Since the Most High has given us this task, we expect this Edom to become a future possession of Christ."[111] Not only was this clearly a mission endeavor, the missionaries themselves persevered in a most difficult task buoyed by confidence in a sovereign God.

What kind of preaching led to a church which had such missionaries as these and which responded so jubilantly to mission possibilities despite the difficulties? Calvin's sermons have been too much neglected by scholars, but in his sermons we find the type of exhortation and prayer which would propel evangelistic activity as he regularly and earnestly urged his people to seek the salvation of the nations.[112] For example, preaching on Deuteronomy, Calvin said, "If we have any kindness in us, seeing that we see men go to destruction until God has got them under his obedience: ought we not to be moved with pity to draw the silly souls out of hell and to bring them into the way of salvation?"[113] In his sermons on 1 Timothy, preached in the year leading up to the Brazilian mission, Calvin regularly concludes with a prayer for the salvation of the nations.[114] He tells pastors that God has made them ministers for the purpose of saving souls and thus they must labor "mightily, and with greater zeal and earnestness" for the

---

110. Beaver (61) says Calvin was not in Geneva when the church decided to send these ministers. However, Wilcox (216) corrects this point showing that Calvin was in Geneva and, thus, included among the celebrants.

111. Beaver, "The Genevan Mission to Brazil," 64.

112. T. H. L. Parker's *Calvin's Preaching* (Louisville: Westminster John Knox, 1992) provides a moving description of Calvin's preaching and its power.

113. John Calvin, *Sermons on Deuteronomy*, trans. Arthur Golding (London, 1583; facsimile repr., Edinburgh: Banner of Truth Trust, 1987), 1219. [from a sermon on Dt 33]

114. John Calvin, *John Calvin's Sermons on 1 Timothy*, ed. Ray Van Neste and Brian Denker, vols. 1 and 2 (Jackson, TN: CreateSpace, 2016). For more on Calvin's evangelistic prayers, see Elsie McKee, "Calvin and Praying for 'All People Who Dwell on Earth'," *Interpretation* 63:2 (April 2009): 130–40.

salvation of souls.[115] Even when people reject the salvation offered to them, Calvin tells pastors that they must continue to "devote" themselves to this evangelistic work and "take pains" in calling people to faith so that they might "call as many to God as they can." Calvin urges, "We must take pains to draw all the world to salvation."[116]

Calvin expounds Paul's call to pray "for all men" (1 Tim 2) with application to the church's missionary responsibility to the world: "call upon God and ask him to work toward the salvation of the whole world, and that we give ourselves to this work both night and day."[117] Throughout this sermon Calvin calls for fervent prayer and persistent action for the salvation of souls, urging his people to "have pity and compassion on the poor unbelievers."[118] He tells his people, "The greatest pleasure we can do to men is to pray to God for them, and call upon him for their salvation."[119] It is no surprise, then, that at various places in these sermons Calvin speaks of the salvation of our neighbors as being "dear to us."

This evangelistic compassion is rooted in the character and action of God, as Calvin states in his sermon on 1 Timothy 2:3–5:

> Let us mark first of all when the Gospel is preached to us that it is just as if God reached out his hand (as he says by the prophet Isaiah, Isa. 65:2) and said to us, "Come to me." It is a matter which ought to touch us to the quick, when we see that God comes to seek us, and does not wait until we come to him, but shows that he is ready to be made at one with us, although we were his daily enemies. He seeks nothing but to wipe out all our faults and make us partakers of the salvation that was purchased for us by our Lord Jesus Christ. And thus we see how worthily we have to esteem the Gospel, and what a treasure it is.[120]

Some have said that the ministry of the Reformers was concerned only with teaching further the Christians who were in their midst. These sermons

---

115. Ibid., 2:133.

116. Ibid., 2:141.

117. Ibid., 1:156.

118. Ibid.

119. Ibid., 1:159.

120. Ibid., 1:193.

demonstrate how wrong this is about Calvin. He stated, "It is not enough for us to teach other men faithfully, unless we have a zeal to edify and care for the salvation of all men."[121] He tells his congregation that believers "must draw their neighbors to God in such a way that they must go with them."[122] Specifically speaking to pastors, Calvin encourages them to ask, "Why has God placed me here? To the end that church should increase more and more, and the salvation of men be always sought for."[123]

Some have argued that Calvin's view of predestination prevented any evangelistic impulse. But notice that Calvin is not inhibited from calling all who hear him to Christ. "So often as we preach the doctrine of salvation, we show that God is ready to receive all who come to him, that the gate is open to those who call upon him, and to be assured that their inheritance is prepared for them there above, and they can never be deceived of it."[124] Commenting on James 5:20, Calvin also states:

> To give food to the hungry, and drink to the thirsty, we see how much Christ values such acts; but the salvation of the soul is esteemed by him much more precious than the life of the body. We must therefore take heed lest souls perish through our sloth, whose salvation God puts in a manner in our hands. Not that we can bestow salvation on them; but that God by our ministry delivers and saves those who seem otherwise to be nigh destruction.[125]

In fact, Calvin strongly rebukes those who lack evangelistic concern.

> So then let us mark first of all that all who care not whether they bring their neighbors to the way of salvation or not, and those who do not care to bring the poor unbelievers also, instead being willing to let them go to destruction, show plainly that they make no account of God's honor. ... And thus we see how cold we are and

---

121. Ibid., 1:130.

122. Ibid., 2:130.

123. Ibid., 2:127–28.

124. Ibid., 2:388.

125. John Calvin, "Commentaries on the Catholic Epistles," in *Calvin's Commentaries*, 22 vols., trans. W. Pringle (Grand Rapids: Baker, 1999), 22:361.

negligent to pray for those who have need and are this day in the way to death and damnation.[126]

Rather than someone who was merely concerned with organizing the new Protestant church or for deeper teaching, we find in Calvin a true shepherd who cares for his people and yearns for the salvation of souls.[127] As he stated, "We cannot bestow our lives and our deaths better than by bringing poor souls who were lost, and on their way to everlasting death, to salvation."[128]

CONCLUSION

In his work on missions history, Stephen Neill says, "When everything favorable has been said that can be said [about the Reformers' commitment to mission], and when all possible evidences from the writings have been collected, it amounts to exceedingly little."[129] This brief article has shown this to be untrue. I have shown this without including the large number of quotes others have cited in the writings of the Reformers on this topic. It is time for the narrative to change. The evidence is ample; the conclusion is clear. The charge of apathy regarding missions among the Reformers is common but unfair. If we reject an anachronistic, narrow, unscriptural definition of missions, it is obvious that the Reformers were significantly mission-minded and present to us a largely untapped resource for mission strategy, especially as the West is once again increasingly devoid of the gospel. Of course, they did not launch full-blown, overseas mission projects as later Christians would, but that is due to the limitations of their time and not due to a lack of concern for missions.[130] Indeed, their work laid the foundation for the later expansion of world mission endeavor. Rather than denigrating these forebearers, we need to examine their work afresh to see what lessons they may have for us in this hour of great need for gospel advance.[131]

---

126. Calvin, *Sermons on 1 Timothy*, 1:201.

127. See also Michael A. G. Haykin and C. Jeffrey Robinson, *To the Ends of the Earth: Calvin's Missional Vision and Legacy* (Wheaton, IL: Crossway, 2014).

128. Ibid., 1:297.

129. Neill and Chadwick, *History of Christian Missions*, 189.

130. See further Paulus Scharpff, *History of Evangelism: Three Hundred Years of Evangelism in Germany, Great Britain, and the United States of America* (Grand Rapids: Eerdmans, 1966), 12.

131. See further Schulz, *Mission from the Cross*, 67.

BIBLIOGRAPHY

Allen, David. "Preaching for a Great Commission Resurgence." In *Great Commission Resurgence: Fulfilling God's Mandate in our Time*, edited by Chuck Lawless and Adam Greenway, 281–98. Nashville: B&H Academic, 2010.

Anderson, Justice. "An Overview of Missiology." In *Missiology: An Introduction to the Foundations, History, and Strategies of World Missions*, edited by John Mark Terry, Ebbie Smith, and Justice Anderson, 1–17. Nashville: B&H, 1998.

———. "Medieval and Renaissance Missions (500–1792)." In *Missiology: An Introduction to the Foundations, History, and Strategies of World Missions*, edited by John Mark Terry, Ebbie Smith, and Justice Anderson, 183–98. Nashville: B&H, 1998.

Anderson, Raymond K. "Calvin and Missions." *Christian History*, 5, no. 4 (Fall 1986): 23.

Ashford, Bruce, ed. *Theology and Practice of Mission: God, the Church, and the Nations*. Nashville: B&H Academic, 2011.

Beaver, R. Pierce. "The Genevan Mission to Brazil." In *The Heritage of John Calvin*, edited by John H. Bratt, 55–73. Grand Rapids: Eerdmans, 1973.

Benoit, Jean-Daniel. "Pastoral Care of the Prophet." In *John Calvin, Contemporary Prophet*, edited by Jacob Hoogstra, 51–67. Grand Rapids: Baker, 1959.

Bosch, David J. *Transforming Mission: Paradigm Shifts in Theology of Mission* (Maryknoll, NY: Orbis Books, 1991).

Brown, Christopher Boyd. *Singing the Gospel: Lutheran Hymns and the Success of the Reformation*. Cambridge, MA: Harvard University Press, 2005.

Bucer, Martin. *Concerning the True Care of Souls*. Translated by Peter Beale. Carlisle, PA: Banner of Truth, 2009.

Calhoun, David. "John Calvin: Missionary Hero or Missionary Failure?" *Presbyterion* 5, no.1 (Spring 1979): 16–33.

Calvin, John. *Calvin's Commentaries*. Translated by W. Pringle. 22 vols. Grand Rapids: Baker, 1984.

————. *Institutes of the Christian Religion*. Translated by Ford Lewis Battles. Edited by John T. McNeill. 2 vols. Philadelphia: Westminster Press, 1960.

————. *Sermons on Deuteronomy*. Translated by Arthur Golding. Reprint, Edinburgh: Banner of Truth Trust, 1987.

————. *Sermons on 1 Timothy*, edited by Ray Van Neste and Brian Denker. 2 vols. Jackson, TN: CreateSpace, 2016.

Cottret, Bernard. *Calvin: A Biography*. Grand Rapids: Eerdmans, 2000.

Elert, Werner. *The Structure of Lutheranism*. Translated by Walter A. Hansen. St. Louis: Concordia, 1962.

Gordon, Bruce. *Calvin*. New Haven: Yale University Press, 2009.

Haykin, Michael A. G. "John Calvin's Missionary Influence in France." *Reformation and Revival* 10, no. 4 (Fall 2001): 35–44.

————, and C. Jeffrey Robinson. *To the Ends of the Earth: Calvin's Missional Vision and Legacy*. Wheaton, IL: Crossway, 2014.

Hendrix, Scott. *Recultivating the Vineyard: The Reformation Agendas of Christianization*. Louisville: Westminster John Knox, 2004.

Hogg, William Richey. *Ecumenical Foundations: A History of the International Missionary Council and Its Nineteenth Century Background*. New York: Harper, 1952.

Hughes, Philip E. "John Calvin: Director of Missions." In *The Heritage of John Calvin*, edited by John H. Bratt, 40–54. Grand Rapids: Eerdmans, 1973.

————, ed., trans. *The Register of the Company of Pastors of Geneva in the Time of Calvin*. Grand Rapids: Eerdmans, 1966.

James, R. Alton. "Post-Reformation Missions Pioneers." In *Discovering the Mission of God: Best Missional Practices for the 21st Century*, edited by Mike Barnett and Robin Martin, 250–66. Downers Grove, IL: IVP, 2012.

Kane, J. Herbert. *A Concise History of the Christian World Mission: A Panoramic View of Missions from Pentecost to the Present*. Grand Rapids: Baker, 1978.

Kingdon, Robert M. "Calvinist Religious Aggression." In *The French Wars of Religion: How Important Were Religious Factors?* edited by J. H. M. Salmon, 6–11. Lexington, MA: D. C. Heath and Company, 1967.

Kolb, Robert. "Late Reformation Lutherans on Mission and Confession." *Lutheran Quarterly* 20, no. 1 (2006): 26–43.

Latourette, Kenneth Scott. *A History of the Expansion of Christianity: The First Five Centuries*. New York: Harper & Brothers, 1937.

Leaver, Robin. *The Whole Church Sings: Congregational Singing in Luther's Wittenberg*. Grand Rapids: Eerdmans, 2017.

Luther, Martin. *A Simple Way to Pray*. Translated by Matthew C. Harrison. St. Louis: Concordia, 2012.

McGrath, Alister. *A Life of John Calvin: A Study in the Shaping of Western Culture*. Oxford; Basil Blackwell, 1990.

McKee, Elsie. "Calvin and Praying for 'All People Who Dwell on Earth'." *Interpretation* 63, no. 2 (April 2009): 130–40.

Medeiros, Elias. "The Reformers' Commitment to the Propagation of the Gospel to All Nations from 1555 to 1654." PhD diss., Reformed Theological Seminary, Jackson, MS, 2009.

Montgomery, John Warwick. "Luther and Missions." *Evangelical Missions Quarterly* 3, no. 4 (1967): 193–202.

Nazir-Ali, Michael. *From Everywhere to Everywhere: A World View of Christian Witness*. London: Flame, 1990.

Neill, Stephen, and Owen Chadwick. *A History of Christian Missions*. 2nd ed. New York: Penguin Books, 1986.

Öberg, Ingemar. *Luther and World Mission: A Historical and Systematic Study with Special Reference to Luther's Bible Exposition*. St. Louis: Concordia, 2007.

Olson, C. Gordon, and Don Fanning, *What in the World Is God Doing?: Essentials of Global Missions: An Introductory Guide*. Lynchburg, VA: Global Gospel Publishers, 2013.

Parker, T. H. L. *Calvin's Preaching*. Louisville: Westminster John Knox, 1992.

Patterson, Paige. "The Anabaptists, Evangelism, and Missions." May 29, 2017. https://www.imb.org/2017/05/29/anabaptists/.

Plass, Ewald M. *What Luther Says: An Anthology*. St. Louis: Concordia, 1959.

Scharpff, Paulus. *History of Evangelism: Three Hundred Years of Evangelism in Germany, Great Britain, and the United States of America*. Grand Rapids: Eerdmans, 1966.

Schulz, Klaus Detlev. *Mission from the Cross: The Lutheran Theology of Mission*. St. Louis: Concordia, 2009.

Schwiebert, Ernest G. *Luther and His Times: The Reformation from a New Perspective*. St. Louis: Concordia, 1950.

Stetzer, Ed. *Planting New Churches in a Postmodern Age*. Nashville: B&H, 2003.

Stewart, Kenneth J. "Calvinism and Missions: The Contested Relationship Revisited." *Themelios* 34, no. 1 (2009): 63–78.

Stolle, Volker. *The Church Comes from All Nations: Luther Texts on Mission*. St. Louis: Concordia, 2003.

Tappert, Theodore G. *The Book of Concord: The Confessions of the Evangelical Lutheran Church*. Philadelphia: Fortress Press, 1959.

Terry, John Mark, and Robert Gallagher. *Encountering the History of Missions* (Grand Rapids: Baker Academic, 2018).

Tucker, Ruth. *From Jerusalem to Irian Jaya: A Biographical History of Christian Missions*. 2nd ed. Grand Rapids: Zondervan, 2004.

Van Neste, Ray. "John Calvin on Missions and Evangelism." *Founders Journal* 33 (1998): 15–21.

———. "The Mangled Narrative of Evangelism and Missions in the Reformation." In *Celebrating the Legacy of the Reformation,* edited by Kevin L. King, Edward Hindson, and Benjamin K. Forrest, 235–60. Nashville: B&H Academic, 2019.

———. "The Mangled Narrative of Evangelism and Missions in the Reformation." *Southeastern Theological Review* 8:2 (Fall 2017): 3–27.

Verkuyl, Johannes. *Contemporary Missiology: An Introduction.* Translated by Dale Cooper. Grand Rapids: Eerdmans, 1987.

Warneck, Gustav. *Outline of the History of Protestant Missions from the Reformation to the Present Time*. Edinburgh: J. Gemmell, 1884.

———. *Outline of the History of Protestant Missions from the Reformation to the Present Time*. Authorized translation from the seventh German edition by George Robson. New York: Revell, 1901.

Wilcox, Pete. "Evangelisation in the Thought and Practice of John Calvin." *Anvil* 12, no. 3 (1995): 201–17.

Winter, Ralph D. "The Kingdom Strikes Back: Ten Epochs of Redemptive History." In *Perspectives on the World Christian Movement: A Reader,* 4th ed., edited by Ralph D. Winter and Steven C. Hawthorne, 209–27. Pasadena, CA: William Carey Library, 2009.

Wrogemann, Henning. *Theologies of Mission*. Downers Grove, IL: IVP Academic, 2018.

Zorn, Jean-François. "Did Calvin Foster or Hinder the Missions?" *Exchange* 40, no. 2 (2011): 170–91.

2

—

TRINITY IN A WOMAN'S SOUL

Recovering a Women's Spirituality for Mission in Jan Hus's Dcerka [The Daughter]

Michèle Miller Sigg

More than a century before the beginning of the sixteenth-century Reformation, Czech theologian Jan Hus was embroiled in another, lesser-known Reform movement in the kingdom of Bohemia. In the midst of this struggle, a few years before his execution in 1415, Hus wrote a devotional text addressed to a female audience entitled "Regarding the Knowledge of the True Way of Salvation."[1] Known in popular tradition as *Dcerka* [*The Daughter*], this text remains unnoticed in contemporary scholarship.[2] This short text is exceptional for its welcoming tone and its positive treatment of women.

In this study, my purpose is to introduce readers to this exceptional, little-known text of female spirituality, and to bring it to the attention of the scholarly community. This is but the first step in recovering Hus's text for an Anglophone audience because the only extant translation from the Czech original is a version in French made by Paul de Vooght

---

1. The only translation of *Dcerka* from the Czech is that of Josepha Pilny and Paul de Vooght in, "Un Classique de La Littérature Spirituelle: La Dcerka de Jean Huss," *Revue d'histoire de la Spiritualité*, no. 48 (1972): 275–314. I translated de Vooght's French text into English with partial help from Dan Török. Further work is needed to produce an authoritative English translation.

2. See Thomas A. Fudge, *Jan Hus: Religious Reform and Social Revolution in Bohemia* (London: I. B. Tauris, 2010), 86. Another translation of the title "Dcerka – O poznání cesty pravé k spasení" is "Daughter – How to Find the Correct Way to Salvation," according to ed. Danhelka, in František Ryšánek, Anežka Vidmanová-Schmidtová, Amedeo Molnár, and František Graus, *Magistri Iohannis Hus opera omnia*, vol. 4 (Prague: Acad., Scientiarum Bohemoslovaca, 1988), 163–86. Work abbreviated as "MIHO."

and published in 1972.[3] I argue that its recovery would fill a gap in the corpus of texts related to female spirituality and mission, given that the uniqueness of *The Daughter* first lies in the fact that Jan Hus, a leading male Reformer, was writing exclusively to a female audience to educate them.[4] Furthermore, the text does not instruct women along the lines of their traditional gender roles in family or church, but instead functions as a spiritual instructional manual to equip them for an active public role, alongside their male counterparts. These elements make *The Daughter* a remarkable text in the late-medieval and early-modern literary corpus, and worthy of more scholarly attention. Lastly, I argue that *The Daughter* belongs in the larger corpus of missiological texts because it presents a holistic mission spirituality for women.[5]

The Daughter was an important text for women in fifteenth century Bohemia since Hus's positive and encouraging message to women was revolutionary at the time. According to Thomas A. Fudge, Hus may have written to these pious women "because of his conviction that women were sometimes more ardent proponents of religious truth than the theologians of Prague in the early fifteenth century."[6] Hus believed that God had endowed women with exceptional religious insight, making them devoted followers, just like the women in Jesus' ministry.[7]

Furthermore, *The Daughter* rejected the negative views of women in contemporary theology. The medieval theology of creation considered females to be socially subordinate and inherently inferior to men.[8] It was common for preachers and theology instructors to teach that God had not created the female body in his image, and that the woman was responsible

---

3. de Vooght, "Un Classique de La Littérature Spirituelle: La Dcerka de Jean Huss," 275–314. De Vooght's article begins with a commentary, and then includes the full translation of *Dcerka* into French. I have made a full translation of de Vooght's text into English for the purposes of this article.

4. Pavlína Rychterová, "The Vernacular Theology of Jan Hus," in *A Companion to Jan Hus*, ed. František Šmahel (Leiden: Brill, 2015), 207, note 120.

5. "Holistic mission spirituality" means "prophetic spirituality," which is a term coined by Fudge that I will explore later in the study.

6. Thomas A. Fudge, *Jan Hus Between Time and Eternity: Reconsidering a Medieval Heretic* (Lanham, MD: Lexington Books, 2015), 6.

7. Ibid.

8. John M. Klassen, *Warring Maidens, Captive Wives and Hussite Queens: Women and Men at War and at Peace in Fifteenth Century Bohemia* (New York: Columbia University Press, 1999), 162.

for bringing sin into the world using her sexuality.[9] Another teaching was that God had only created man in his own image and therefore only man had the power to govern.[10] Hus departed from tradition in rejecting these views, particularly the belief that God had not made woman in his own image.[11] Instead, he taught that men and women were equal, and that, as worthy members of God's economy, women were fully competent to contribute to the life of society or to any religious community.[12]

The first half of this study describes the social, religious, and literary context in which Hus composed *The Daughter,* looking at the vernacular theology movement and the role of Bethlehem Chapel, the institution in Prague where Hus preached for ten years. The second half of the chapter concentrates on the text itself where I present the context of its composition and literary genre, then give an overview of the text and a detailed outline with excerpts from the English translation. I conclude with a presentation of "prophetic spirituality" as a framework for understanding this text in the context of missions.

VERNACULAR THEOLOGY AND SOCIAL CHANGE IN FOURTEENTH AND FIFTEENTH CENTURY BOHEMIA

In the high Middle Ages, Bohemia was a highly charged context in which grassroots religious movements like the Béguines were flourishing.[13] Popular preachers urged the local people to practice a rigorous piety that included asceticism, the sharing of belongings, sexual restraint, listening

---

9. Ibid.

10. R. Howard Bloch, *Medieval Misogyny and the Invention of Western Romantic Love*, ACLS Humanities E-Book (Chicago: University of Chicago Press, 1991), 27.

11. Klassen, *Warring Maidens*, 162, 165. On the issue of equality, for example, in the prologue to *The Daughter*, Hus affirms both male and female virginity by referring to "Jesus Christ, true God and true man, who raised virginity above other states, when he decided to be born of a pure virgin and to remain a virgin, in order to confirm for us both female and male virginity, to uplift it and to exalt it above other states."

12. Klassen, *Warring Maidens*, 163. In spite of what seems to be an egalitarian outlook, Hus's views of marriage were more traditional for the time—he allowed men to physically abuse their wives. On the other hand, he discouraged women from marrying to avoid these issues in a marital relationship.

13. Originating in the twelfth century, Béguines represented a lay movement of women who grew up in urban contexts primarily in northern Europe in the later Middle Ages. They did not take formal religious vows, and there was no original rule of life. Yet they embraced the values of the *vita evangelica*, imitating the practices of the early church by living a life

to sermons, Bible study, prayer, meditation, and frequent Eucharist.[14] Béguines lived in wooden houses and followed their own spiritual rule of life, subsisting on private donations or the proceeds from their handicrafts. They offered education for young girls and cared for the sick and the elderly.[15] As they, along with local preachers, nuns, and the educated laity, felt the desire to read Scripture, portions of the Bible were translated into the vernacular in the last decades of the fourteenth century. Eventually the demand was so great that the whole Bible was translated into Czech around 1414. This gave the common people access to the written text of their faith from which they could develop a spirituality and religious practices similar to those of the regular and secular clergy.[16]

The Daughter was one of several texts that Hus wrote in the vernacular after his exile from Prague and it followed another important treatise in Czech, the Exposition of the Faith.[17] Both texts belonged to a growing corpus of vernacular theology that is likely to have contributed to the origins of the Czech Reformation.[18] By contrast with Luther, Hus and his followers linked theology to an intentional effort to transform societal structures and relations.[19] Their point of departure differed with that of the Lutheran Reformation that began with Luther's internal conflict regarding the question of salvation. For him, the primary struggle took place within one's heart and conscience, putting everything else in second place.[20] On the other hand, in the context of the Czech Reformation,

---

of simplicity and chastity in the service of the poor. See Philip Sheldrake, A Brief History of Spirituality (Hoboken, NJ: John Wiley & Sons, 2013), 90–91.

14. Klassen, Warring Maidens, 160.

15. Ibid., 161. The first house of Béguines in Prague was founded in 1279, and by 1415 there were at least eighteen such groups.

16. Ibid., 162. The regular clergy belong to religious orders, and the secular clergy are parish priests or deacons.

17. Ota Pavlíček, "The Chronology of the Life and Work of Jan Hus," in A Companion to Jan Hus (Leiden: Brill, 2015), 58.

18. Marcela Kličova Perett in Preachers, Partisans, and Rebellious Religion: Vernacular Writing and the Hussite Movement (Philadelphia: University of Pennsylvania Press, 2018), 17 ,shows that the vernacularization of theological education increased religious factions and radicalism, and Hus deliberately sought to have the laity follow his teaching instead of the church's in his later years.

19. Rudolf Říčan, C. Daniel Crews, and Amedeo Molnár, The History of the Unity of Brethren: A Protestant Hussite Church in Bohemia and Moravia (Bethlehem, PA: Moravian Church in America, 2008), 7.

20. Ibid., 110.

Hus, the Hussites, and after them the Brethren, were led by the question of what was the will of God; what kind of church did Christ wish to have; what should a faithful Christian be like; how should a true priest live; what sort of order was to be valid in the congregation of Christ's church; what then must be done that the holy will of God be fulfilled in the congregation, in the family, in private, and in public life?[21]

Therefore, Hus's guiding purpose for reform embraced all of life—from individual piety and family life in the private sphere, to social responsibility in the public arena. Through the medium of vernacular theology, his message gained influence among the laity who wanted access to theological education in Czech. The common people sought to surpass nominal observance and to live out an intentional commitment to the Christian faith.[22] To feed this hunger for learning, a body of writing emerged—texts that had formerly addressed monastics, but now targeted the laity. These treatises simplified scholastic theology in an effort to make it understandable to the laity and to encourage virtuous Christian behavior, feeding into a "theology of piety."[23] Hus's text, *The Daughter*, is a salient example of vernacular theology, a literary tradition that was influenced by women.[24]

DEVOTIO MODERNA

At this time throughout Europe, groups such as the *Devotio Moderna*, or the Brothers and Sisters of the Common Life, sought to establish a new spiritual ideal with religious practices that were accessible to lay people.[25] *The Imitation of Christ* by Thomas à Kempis, a member of the Brothers of the Common Life, was a bestselling text in this tradition.[26] However, the Czech *Devotio Moderna* and Hus's writings not only taught practices relevant to individual faith and to the church, but also advocated religious action that directly engaged with the socio-political realm. Joseph Macek

---

21. Ibid.
22. Perett, *Preachers, Partisans, and Rebellious Religion*, 7.
23. Ibid., 8–9.
24. Ibid., 10.
25. Ibid., 11. See also Sheldrake, *A Brief History of Spirituality*, 107.
26. Perett, *Preachers, Partisans, and Rebellious Religion*, 11.

notes, "The reforming and revolutionary tendencies co-mingle in the work of Hus and in the reform movement. ... It would be completely false to want to limit the concept of the 'reforms' only to the religious and ecclesiastical domain."[27] According to Vilém Herold, "The figure of Jan Hus has become not only the symbol of an era in Czech and European history that is named after him, but has also come to represent a philosophical and ethical movement aimed at improving or reforming the existing social order. This was linked, above all, with an ongoing effort to improve the condition of the contemporary church through reform."[28] The authors of the *Devotio Moderna* movement focused their teaching on everyday piety, reminding the laity of what was most important in a life of faith.[29] According to Philip Sheldrake, "The evangelical piety and lay emphasis of the movement had a significant influence on both Protestant and Catholic Reformations."[30] In Bohemia, Hus's influence was significant because he focused a large proportion of his reform efforts on his vernacular texts.[31]

THE ROLE OF BETHLEHEM CHAPEL

Bethlehem Chapel was the ideal location to disseminate an important message to a large public. One of the largest buildings in Prague used for public meetings at almost 800 square meters, it could accommodate 3,000 souls.[32] Founded in 1392 in Prague as a secular (nonparochial) establishment, its primary purpose was to serve as a venue for vernacular preaching only.[33] In 1402, at age 32, Hus agreed to take over the pulpit at Bethlehem Chapel. Between 1402 and October 1412, when he went into exile, he gave 3,500 sermons there, which is approximately one sermon a day for ten years.[34]

Hus was a charismatic preacher with a university education and his sermons drew such crowds that they filled the chapel capacity on any given

---

27. Joseph Macek, *Jean Hus et Les Traditions Hussites (Xve–XIXe Siècles)*, Series Civilisations et Mentalités (Paris: Plon, 1973), 208. Translation from the French by Sigg.

28. Vilém Herold, "The Spiritual Background of the Czech Reformation: Precursors of Jan Hus," in *A Companion to Jan Hus* (Leiden: Brill, 2015), 70.

29. Perett, *Preachers, Partisans, and Rebellious Religion*, 10.

30. Sheldrake, *A Brief History of Spirituality*, 108.

31. Rychterová, "The Vernacular Theology of Jan Hus," 170.

32. Perett, *Preachers, Partisans, and Rebellious Religion*, 25.

33. Ibid., 20.

34. Ibid., 28–29.

day.[35] He influenced liturgical reform by introducing the practice of congregational singing, and his teaching strengthened popular religion and
lay piety.[36] The walls of Bethlehem Chapel also served didactic purposes,
being inscribed with biblical passages and other instructive texts, as well
as paintings, some of which were copies of biblical scenes by Nicholas of
Dresden and his followers. Influenced by Waldensian ideals, Nicholas of
Dresden painted Jesus in all his humility, thus shining a damning light,
by stark comparison, on the rich lifestyle of the Roman clergy.[37] It was in
this context that Hus frequently voiced his critiques of clerical authorities,
and starting in 1410, established himself as an alternate authority for the
common people to follow.[38]

Bethlehem Chapel was the ideal place for Hus's subversive preaching and an answer to the growing demand for preaching in Bohemia. The
founders wanted Bethlehem Chapel to be more than a place of ongoing
reform but a community where change had already occurred, and therefore embodied renewed parish life.[39] Rules prescribed where the priest
could reside, how to deal with compensation for services, and included
precautions on how to deal with greed.[40] In accepting this post, Hus was
eager to follow the tradition set by his immediate predecessors and ardent
reformers, Prague University Masters John Protiva and Stephen of Kolín.[41]

---

35. Fudge, *Jan Hus: Religious Reform and Social Revolution in Bohemia*, 58–59.

36. Craig D. Atwood, *The Theology of the Czech Brethren from Hus to Comenius* (University
Park, PA: Penn State Press, 2009), 52, quoting Fudge.

37. Ibid., 52–54.

38. Perett, *Preachers, Partisans, and Rebellious Religion*, 35, 39. The texts included his reform
program written in Latin and Czech, entitled *De sex erroribus* ("On the Six Errors"), meant to
educate the laity about the abuses of the clergy. In 1949, reconstruction work in Bethlehem
Chapel uncovered the text "On the Six Errors" (of the church). See Atwood, *The Theology of
the Czech Brethren*, 52.

39. Perett, *Preachers, Partisans, and Rebellious Religion*, 24–26. The founders were two
Prague burghers, Hanuš of Mühlheim and John Kříž, who endowed Bethlehem Chapel and
defined its mission. See Rychterová, "The Vernacular Theology of Jan Hus," 175.

40. Perett, *Preachers, Partisans, and Rebellious Religion*, 26.

41. Rychterová, "The Vernacular Theology of Jan Hus," 175.

INTRODUCING *THE DAUGHTER*

Hus wrote *The Daughter*—a text that Hussitologists consider his most charming text in Czech—in early 1413, during his period of exile from Prague.[42] The text specifically addresses pious women, possibly nuns or Béguines, living in the vicinity of Bethlehem Chapel.[43] According to John Klassen, *The Daughter* may have served as a theological model since Hus treated the sexes equally and gave gender-neutral examples of sin in the text: "Hus's daughter was likely a construct used to make a theological point and a tool with which Hus mediated the values of his culture. She may have been an alternative male identity whom Hus presented to his readers in order to lead men to greater fullness and totality."[44] Paul De Vooght calls *The Daughter* "a profession of faith, not a theological and abstract one, but one that is existential, warm, and communicative, from a man who is transmitting to his chosen audience his deep conviction regarding the meaning of life."[45] Fudge compares *The Daughter* to *The Imitation of Christ* by Thomas à Kempis and describes it as "a classic within the later medieval literature of Christian spirituality."[46] He sees *The Daughter* as a "profound witness to the vibrancy of medieval spirituality," and wonders whether there are "connections between Hus, his work on spirituality, and the religious practices of his followers including the radical, revolutionary movement centered at Tábor."[47]

There is no question about the authenticity of the text's authorship, and the primary textual source of the Bible. Chapter 4, on temptation, draws heavily—as was often the practice in the Middle Ages—on his mentor John Wycliffe's writings, and other parts from Pseudo-Bernard.[48] Overall, the spiritual doctrine of *The Daughter* was not radical, and did not pose a problem for the Inquisition or the Council of Constance.[49]

---

42. Ibid., 196.

43. Ibid., 207. One of the women was the daughter of Tomáš of Štítný. See Ota Pavlíček, 58.

44. Klassen, *Warring Maidens*, 165–66.

45. de Vooght, "Un Classique de La Littérature Spirituelle: La Dcerka de Jean Huss," 278.

46. Fudge, *Jan Hus between Time and Eternity*, 6–7.

47. Ibid., 6. This is a truncated exposé of the comparison between the Czech Reformation and the sixteenth-century Reformation.

48. Fudge, *Jan Hus: Religious Reform*, 86. See Wycliffe's sermon on Easter, according to Rychterová, "The Vernacular Theology of Jan Hus," 197.

49. de Vooght, "Un Classique de La Littérature Spirituelle: La Dcerka de Jean Huss," 282–83.

OVERVIEW OF THE TEXT

The title of *The Daughter* is borrowed from the refrain that introduces each of the ten chapters—"Hear, daughter, look and incline your ear"—a partial paraphrase of Psalm 44:11 in the Vulgate.[50] The use of the tender, fatherly term "daughter" underlines Hus's pastoral role in the text and establishes a family rapport with his audience. The refrain's source is a psalm written in the style of a love song with strong echoes of Song of Solomon describing a royal wedding in which the poets ("the sons of Korah") divide their praises between the king and the queen. This literary device both amplifies the role of the woman-queen and underlines the symbiotic male-female relationship of the royal couple. Hus's choice to use as a refrain an excerpt from a love song addressed to a queen can be interpreted as an expression of his deep and respectful affection for his female audience.

The text contains ten short chapters, each "devoted to an aspect of spiritual understanding aimed at facilitating a life of piety and devotion."[51] The style suggests that Hus may have intended the text to be an oral performance.[52] At times Hus's style is rather dramatic, and not without comical elements, as if it were a performance.

In the prologue, Hus outlines the themes of the book:

> Hear, O daughter, and listen carefully, for I want you to learn about yourself, to know in whose image you have been created. Second, so that you can learn about your conscience. Third, so that you can learn about the misery of this life. Fourth, so that you can learn about the temptations of this world. Fifth, so that you can learn about the three enemies. Sixth, so that you can do penance properly. Seventh, so that you can respect the dignity of the soul. Eighth, so that you can realize that there will be a day of judgement. Ninth,

---

50. František Šmahel, "Instead of Conclusion: Jan Hus as Writer and Author," in *A Companion to Jan Hus* (Leiden: Brill, 2015), 402, note 125. The reference is Psalm 45:10 (44:10 Vg). The verse is part of a psalm described as "an ode to a royal wedding." Traditionally, the expression "Hear, O daughter" was a mariological reference or addressed the church. Applying it to ordinary laywomen was a radical move for Hus. Throughout the rest of the chapter, for the sake of consistency, I use this translation of the refrain, "Hear, daughter, look and incline your ear," from Dan Török's translation.

51. Fudge, *Jan Hus: Religious Reform*, 87.

52. Ibid.

so that you can respect eternal life. Tenth, so that you can love the Lord God more than anything. [53]

According to this outline, Hus was offering in *The Daughter* the foundations of a well-rounded theological worldview that included a healthy understanding of the self in relation to God (chapters 1–2), an exposé of the contemporary spiritual and social contexts (chapters 3–5), the practices needed to combat evil in order to lead a righteous life (chapters 6–7), and an eschatological outlook (chapter 9).[54] The final lesson (chapter 10) was the "greatest commandment"—to love the Lord with all one's heart—the guiding principle of the gospel.

A CLOSER LOOK AT THE TEXT

Lesson One

For medieval women, the most powerful of Hus's teachings in *Dcerka* was the first lesson because it emphasized that God had created them, like men, in his own image:

> Hear, daughter, look and incline your ear to what I have said, that you must know yourself above all, knowing in whose likeness you were created. … The soul possesses three faculties through which it remembers God, knows him and prays to him: the first faculty is memory, the second reason, and the third will. Memory remembers God, reason looks towards God, and will possesses him and understands him. … And when these three things are united in the soul, then they hold in it the image and likeness of the Holy Trinity who has created you in its own likeness with power, wisdom and complete freedom.

Hus plays on parallel triads to make his point in this chapter. He transposes the image of the three persons of the Trinity onto another trinity of memory, reason, and will in the woman's soul. This powerful equivalence

---

53. *Dcerka*, MIHO, vol. 4, 163, translated from the French, in Fudge, *Jan Hus between Time and Eternity*, 7. All other passages are translated by Sigg.

54. Klassen, *Warring Maidens*, 165.

communicates that woman is an autonomous being—that is, not deriva-
tive of man—and that she is independent of man in her salvific relationship to God.

Lesson one may also be the most lyrical of Hus's chapters, since he
so explicitly expresses his care for these women whom he holds in high
regard for their exceptional spirituality: "When you think of God, you will
not have far to go; you will find him inside yourself and you will find your
delight in him."[55] He closes the chapter with an exhortation and a lesson
that again communicates his warm affection. One could call this Hus's
existential creed for women:

> Do not be ignorant of what a glorious creature you are, in the like-
> ness of God, and who is very dear to him. ... Remember what you
> are, where you come from, and where you are going. What are you?
> You are a creature of God, reasonable, glorious, and beautiful in her
> soul. Where do you come from? You find your origin in God. And
> where are you going? Towards God into eternal joy, if you do not, in
> the end, soil his image through sin. Remember that God made you
> eternal and that he wants to live eternally in your soul.[56]

Lesson Two

In this lesson, Hus presents the conscience as a tool for self-knowledge
and a means to achieve righteous living through the practice of discernment: "Hear, daughter, look and incline your ear. Listen also and see that
the conscience is the knowledge of self, in other words, that by which man
knows himself, whether he is guilty of sin or not, and that he can determine
whether he has sinned or not."[57] He explains that the conscience plays a
cautionary role in relation to salvation:

---

55. Sigg, "*Dcerka* Translation into English from the French," chapter 1, paragraph 3.

56. Sigg, "*Dcerka* Translation," chapter 1, paragraph 3.

57. Because my translation is based on the French, it is not clear whether in the original,
Hus's generalizations about humanity used the masculine (e.g. "Man sins ... he falls into
temptation") or were gender neutral ("One sins ... one falls into temptation"). Therefore, I
have chosen to follow de Vooght's lead and have adopted the French use of the masculine for
generalizations about humanity, with a few exceptions where appropriate.

Hear, daughter, look and incline your ear, because it is good that you know your conscience. … [Know that] whichever way you turn, what you deposited in your soul and in your conscience, whether it is good or evil, your conscience will keep it as long as you are alive and will give it back to you after your death.

The conscience is also a tool that one must hone ("it is possible that the conscience can make a mistake") and learn to use effectively:

He [man] must guard himself from too broad a conscience as much as from too scrupulous a conscience, because a conscience that is too broad often mistakes evil for good, sin for innocence. … Man must also guard himself from an overly scrupulous conscience because it can lead him to despair. It can tell him that he is too evil.

Hus expounds on the various sins that can cloud the judgment of the conscience such as ignorance, negligence, pride, unresolved questions and error, and excessive fear. To combat these sins and train the conscience, he recommends the use of the Holy Scripture because it "shed[s] light on his conscience, even concerning his previous actions, as well as those he commits and those he will commit later." Humility is key in the process of discernment. "Know also that the conscience of a servant of God must be humble and afflicted, in order for humility to exclude pride and affliction to exclude lust or vain rejoicing."[58]

Lesson Three

This lesson teaches about what Hus calls "the misery of life:"

Hear, daughter, look and incline your ear because it is necessary for you to recognize the misery of life. Know that misery consists in the insufficiency of good, and that it exists in the soul and in the body. Misery is found in the soul that does not have divine grace and that, as a result, doesn't truly know God.

Along with lesson four, this lesson is one of the longest chapters in the treatise. In both of these chapters, Hus seeks to impart knowledge of the

---

58. Sigg, "*Dcerka* Translation," chapter 2, paragraphs 4–6.

evils in the world and the temptations that humankind will have to confront. In lesson three, Hus enumerates the miseries of the body (including "work, thirst, hunger, extreme heat, cold, or frost, nakedness, drunkenness, and other suffering to which man is chained until he dies") and of the soul (including anger, evil thoughts, obstinacy, avarice, small mindedness, complaining, slander, greed, and pride).

This lesson gives a sense of both the dramatic and comical quality of Hus's text that he would have gained from live presentations:

> And who could enumerate, let alone describe all the miseries that man can know in this world! ... If he reaches old age, his heart becomes sad, his head wobbles, his soul becomes somber and his breath rank, his face becomes wrinkled, his height shrinks, his eyes blink and weep. His nose runs, his mouth drools, his teeth fall out, his lips rot. His hair falls out, his ears no longer hear, his voice becomes hoarse, his heart weakens. Wheezing rips through his lungs, raspiness clenches his throat, and so many other miseries![59]

Lesson Four[60]

The objective of this lesson, the longest of all ten lessons, is to "learn to recognize the temptations of this world." Hus painstakingly picks apart what he has defined as the devil's six principal attacks against the faithful. Among these are the concept of *carpe diem*—"You are young, take advantage of the world;" and that of "cheap grace"—"What are you worried about? ... You will certainly be saved, live here below as you wish." This is a particularly performative passage in which Hus refutes the devil's arguments, speaking as if he were Jesus during his temptation:

> Fifth, when you say, demon: "What are you worried about, since God by suffering for you gave sufficient satisfaction to justice," demon, I know that the merciful Lord, by suffering for me, has given full satisfaction. This is exactly why I strive not to render vain his holy

---

59. Sigg, "*Dcerka* Translation," chapter 3, paragraphs 6–8.

60. This lesson draws heavily on Wycliffe's Sermon on Easter, according to Rychterová, "The Vernacular Theology of Jan Hus," 197. This is what accounts for the stylistic difference and the theatrical approach in addressing the devil directly.

death for my salvation, as when you lost the kingdom of heaven prepared for you and which I am concerned about. When you also say: "You are a child of God elected to be saved," demon, I hope to God that I am among the elect, and so as not to irritate our merciful Father, I do not want to listen to your perverse speech. When you tell me: "Live down here as you wish, joyfully, among carnal pleasures and sensuality, you will be saved no matter what," demon, you lie! For I know that the rich man, who lived as you advise me to, is dead and was buried in hell thanks to you.[61]

To the devil's attacks, Hus offers a strategic defense particularly adapted to the needs of his female audience. He underlines the importance of knowing one's own temperament to respond to the devil because a person "with an unstable temperament is easily fooled by the devil." The first defense is that "man avoid the darkness, solitude and its drawbacks, especially from anxiety, because in this case, the devil easily leads men to despair." Then, turning his attention to a particular challenge for women, he teaches a way to confront what could be understood as postpartum depression:

This is why young women suffer great terrors and temptations during the pains of childbirth and after the birth of the child, because they are greatly unsettled in their natural dispositions and their weakness has become greater. That is why it is good for these suffering and fearful women not to remain alone and to avoid darkness.

The second defense is to seek "to be enlightened by faith, hope and love because, to defeat the devil, it is very useful for him to be, by the grace of God, enlightened by Scripture." Hus points out that this was Christ's defense during his temptation by the devil. The third defense is to be active in the service of God, "on the one hand by praying, on the other, if we know how to write, by writing, or by praising him through song or by conversing with joy with other reasonable people who love God and

---

61. Sigg, "*Dcerka* Translation," chapter 4, paragraphs 8–10.

especially by not remaining alone too long in the things that are not necessary for salvation."[62]

Lesson Five

In this lesson, the goal is to learn how to "recognize three enemies of every man in this world. They try to defeat his soul. They are: the body, the world, and the devil." Hus describes the need to cry out to God for help because "my body formed from mud suggests to me slimy, impure, and voluptuous thoughts, the world suggests to me vain and futile ones, and the devil's thoughts full of lies and evil. Behold these three enemies, the body, the world, and the devil have surrounded my soul."[63]

Lesson Six

Here Hus teaches the meaning of true penitence: "Listen and know that you must do penance and see what you must do penance for." True penitence is what ultimately leads to a righteous life:

> Lend your spiritual ear and also listen with your physical ear so that you understand that it is right to do penance, to repent from your past sins and to have the will not to commit any others. For the true penitent is he who repents to such an extent of committed sins that he will not commit any more voluntarily, in such a way that he doesn't attach any sin to himself, even though he cannot live without venial sins in this miserable life.[64]

Lesson Seven

The theme of this chapter—learning to appreciate the dignity of one's soul—both mirrors and complements the lesson taught in chapter 1. It represents another expressive passage that employs architectural imagery to further develop the biblical metaphor of the soul as the temple of God:

> God lives there by his grace and is pleased there more than in all the temples and monasteries and chapels made of any kind of materials

---

62. Ibid.
63. Ibid., chapter 5, paragraphs 10–11.
64. Ibid., chapter 6, paragraph 11.

and however beautiful they may be, because temples exist and must not exist for any other reason until the day of Judgment except to preserve the soul as an eternal dwelling place for the Lord God.[65]

The latter part of the chapter includes a reflection on the wounds of Christ and an exhortation to emulate his obedience—obedience that ultimately led to his sacrifice on the cross. The implication is that the truly obedient Christian woman has to be ready to suffer and die for her faith, just as Christ did.

Lesson Eight

This chapter and the following introduce the reader to a well-informed eschatological outlook. The devout Christian must meditate on the last judgment and to be prepared for the time of its arrival: "The date of this Judgment is hidden to us so that we will always be alert and will remain in the expectation of the Lord. This Judgment is terrible because before the supreme Judge, he will destroy all his enemies by fire."[66]

Lesson Nine

In chapter 9, Hus presents the hope of heaven for those who have been faithful in their early life. He encourages his listeners to engage in a happy contemplation: "Listen therefore, my daughter, to the eternal Sovereign and, with a pious spirit, lend an ear to the thought of your happiness and contemplate through your reason how consoling is the Kingdom of heaven. Listen and look so as to reach a true reckoning of eternal life."[67]

Lesson Ten

The final chapter sums up the teaching from all the previous lessons, in a reiteration of the Great Commandment: "Hear, daughter, look and incline your ear in order to understand that in tenth place I have said: You must love the Lord, your God, above all things, for if you observe this precept, you will easily keep all the other directives already given. Hear and incline

---

65. Ibid., chapter 7, paragraphs 11–12.
66. Ibid., chapter 8, paragraph 12.
67. Ibid., chapter 6, paragraphs 12–13.

you ear in order to know that to love God is truly to want the glory of God."[68] Hus then ends his treatise with a warning and with a Trinitarian closing benediction in the style of Paul the Apostle:

> Listen to this, my daughter, look and lend an ear; hear me well, use your reason, apply yourself, so that you understand, that you remember and that you follow through. For what is the use of what is written and that you read it, understand it and do not follow it? This is why apply yourself, in order to read, understand, love, and know God, in order to combat, to defeat the work, the body, and the devil, and so that your work will achieve rest, that your cries will be transformed into joy, and so that after the darkness of this world, you may see the Sun of justice, Jesus Christ, along with his Mother and all the saints, and so that, being glorified, you may rejoice with them. In this may the powerful God the Father, the Son of God full of wisdom, the Holy Spirit who is love, that is one all-powerful God, blessed throughout all centuries, help you! Amen.[69]

PROPHETIC SPIRITUALITY AS FRAMEWORK AND APPLICATION FOR MISSION

Fudge describes the religious discipline that Hus teaches in *The Daughter* as "prophetic spirituality," a spirituality that Hus considered to be "essential to the reform and religious life of later medieval Christianity."[70] According to Fudge, "Prophetic spirituality cultivates active participation in an accepted and intentional *Heilsgeschichte* wherein creation is restored, redemption is achieved, and history is overcome by the reign of God."[71]

Fudge identifies five characteristics of prophetic spirituality: (1) faith as a heart relationship to Christ rather than literal doctrinal compliance; (2) discipline and action; (3) an outward orientation that emphasizes orthopraxy (right action) over orthodoxy (right belief); (4) "eschatological disobedience" defined as conditional obedience to civil and church authorities;

---

68. Ibid., chapter 10, paragraph 13.

69. Ibid., chapter 10, paragraph 14.

70. Fudge, *Jan Hus between Time and Eternity*, 5.

71. Ibid., 23. *Heilsgeschichte* is defined as an interpretation of history emphasizing God's saving acts and viewing Jesus Christ as central in redemption.

and (5) readiness to suffer for Christ. These elements point to the framework and application of mission: heart conversion, the practice of piety and mercy, the quest for justice, and the potential for suffering. I will briefly show how these characteristics of prophetic spirituality are expressed in Hus's teaching in the text.

FAITH AS A HEART RELATIONSHIP WITH CHRIST

This principle is found in many places throughout the text—particularly lessons one and seven—where Hus uses the language of passionate love and beauty, almost as if he is describing the bond between lovers. In lesson seven, Hus develops the idea of the soul as the temple of God—a place of worship and of love. This passage is similar in tone and content to lesson one:

> Hear, daughter, look and incline your ear, and appreciate the dignity of your soul, because your soul, which is spirit, is a reasonable creature, resembling the Holy Trinity and who surpasses all the other creatures without reason. ... In this way, your soul is more precious to God than heaven and earth. ... It is this holy soul that is the temple of the Lord.[72]

Hus then gives a series of reasons to explain why the soul is beloved of God: (1) it is a place of prayer; (2) it is where we offer "a pleasing sacrifice to God, that is, humble thoughts and a contrite spirit"; (3) "because it [the soul] includes an altar on which Christ offers himself. This altar is living faith and the flame that must never go out in the soul is the love of the Lord God"[73]; (4) "the resemblance to the Holy Trinity and to Christ's Passion are inscribed therein"; (5) because God is more pleased to live there than in religious buildings made by humankind. The poignant image of the dwelling place refers back to the first lesson about the soul and pairs it with the idea of the soul as the temple of the Lord: "When you think of God, you will not have far to go; you will find him inside yourself and you will find your delight in him."[74] These images of living faith, the undying flame of

---

72. Sigg, "*Dcerka* Translation," chapter 7.
73. Ibid.
74. Ibid., chapter 1.

love, and architectural beauty evoke the language of love and devotion in the Psalms or Song of Solomon.

DISCIPLINED AND ACTIVE SPIRITUALITY
THAT EMPHASIZES ORTHOPRAXY

According to Fudge, prophetic spirituality "is not withdrawal from the world or human affairs. Spirituality gives politics its moral structure and purpose."[75] Prophetic spirituality functions as a theological and moral compass intimately connected to realities in everyday life. Hus offers tools to teach his audience how to lead an exemplary life while confronting the realities of sin and evil. Lesson two teaches how to use one's conscience to live a righteous life. Lesson three instructs the audience about the misery of life and the spiritual challenges present in the world. Lesson four teaches how to recognize temptations and offers a list of strategies for resisting the devil's attacks. In lesson five, Hus shows his audience how to identify the enemies of all those who wish to lead a righteous life: the body, the world, and the devil. Much like a general instructing his troops before a battle, he seeks to impart an understanding of the sources of sin, evil, and the temptations that flow from them so that devout Christians are well equipped for the spiritual struggle.

ESCHATOLOGICAL DISOBEDIENCE AND SUFFERING FOR CHRIST

Prophetic spirituality necessarily implied "eschatological disobedience" that Fudge describes in this way:

> Jan Hus' *The Daughter* teaches the duty of eschatological disobedience. … Eschatology implies that human society is condemned and that history itself is doomed and cannot survive the kingdom of God. Eschatology places demands on history and on spirituality. Hus understood this. Disobedience was not defiance but an integral part of spirituality. Hus (and the Taborites after him) refused to be complicit; therefore, they became disobedient both to church and civil authority.[76]

---

75. Fudge, *Jan Hus between Time and Eternity*, 8.

76. Ibid., 7. A Taborite was a member of the radical and militant branch of Hus's followers. In 1420, they gave their fortified settlement south of Prague the biblical name of "Tabor." They

For Hus and the Hussites after him, obedience to civil and ecclesiastical authorities was conditional, based on a critical examination of their underlying motives and whether the outcome would be just. Herein lies the basis for Hus's radical social reform, and the civil and religious disobedience that accompanied it. For Hus, spirituality brought together both life in the world and the possibility of reforming the church.[77]

Consequently, those who embraced prophetic spirituality had to be ready to suffer the consequences of their choice to be agents of change in society. The experience of suffering was connected to the relationship with Christ, whose suffering the devout Christian shared out of love for the truth. True followers of Christ had to die to self and sin, and then give themselves totally to his service. Hus expounded on this in lesson seven:[78]

> See how cruel were his [Christ's] wounds. ... Not only did [the Son of God] want to receive wounds, but he wanted to die, and not an easy death, but the most atrocious and cruel death. ... Lend an ear, my daughter ... walk in his footsteps. Observe ... how many thousands of martyrs have already followed [this road before you], virgins and pure youth, and you would still be afraid?" He who leads you is the way, the truth, and the life: a path where one cannot lose oneself, a truth that cannot deceive, and a life that will never end ... my daughter ... do not fear suffering. See, the Lord cried over you; you too, cry over yourself. He sweat drops of blood because of you and he shed his blood and you, [being] grateful, remember with tenderness. He died for you and you, die to sin for the Lord and for yourself. [79]

Therefore, the faithful Christian had no other choice but to walk the *via dolorosa*, the way of the cross, as an act of love.

---

were strict biblicists and received the Eucharist in both kinds (bread and wine), like their more moderate coreligionists, the Utraquists. However, they denied transubstantiation and the Real Presence and only accepted baptism and the Eucharist as sacraments They formed an independent church that used Czech in the liturgy. They took up arms and destroyed many churches until their decisive defeat in 1452.

77. Fudge, *Jan Hus between Time and Eternity*, 8.

78. Ibid., 23. This included a concept of spiritual struggle that appeared in the theology and writings of the early Hussite movement.

79. Sigg, "*Dcerka* Translation," chapter 7.

CONCLUSION

The Daughter was written just a year or two before Hus's execution in 1415. His death unleashed an open rebellion in the kingdom of Bohemia. Rican argues that Hus's teaching linked theology to "an attempt to change social structures and relations" in contrast with Luther and Calvin, who failed to emphasize living faith to produce a new life.[80] This is why, contrary to the Lutheran Reformation, "the Czech Reformation was also a political revolution."[81] This holistic understanding of reform was present in the teachings of the Unity of the Brethren, the descendants of the Hussite church and forebears of the Moravians, who believed that "the Reformation, from the times of Hus, meant a call to place the whole of life under the Word of God, in which the Gospel resounds as a call to a new and devoted obedience."[82]

This holistic integration of private faith and public life that Hus taught in *The Daughter* is still an effective basis for a missionary outlook today. Prophetic spirituality was for Hus, and is still today, a call to action that should inspire obedience to God's will in the world.[83] Hus taught this spirituality in a work addressed to a community of women because he believed their active participation in the life of the church was central to the renewal of church and society—in other words, mission. By delivering a positive message to women about themselves and encouraging their active roles in the church, Hus's text empowered them to be agents of change in Bohemian church life and society. *The Daughter* can therefore be considered to be an early, foundational text for a gender-inclusive holistic mission spirituality.

The Daughter teaches the key elements of prophetic spirituality—faith as a heart relationship with Christ, disciplined and active social engagement, the emphasis on responding compassionately to the needs of society, conditional obedience in relation to political and church authorities, and suffering for Christ in the work of mission. These characteristics still represent, today, the guiding principles of holistic mission practice. The true test of robust mission teaching can be found in Hus's summary of this spirituality in the final lesson of *The Daughter*. There he reminds his female

---

80. Říčan, *The History of the Unity of Brethren*, 7.

81. Ibid.

82. Ibid., 110.

83. Fudge, *Jan Hus between Time and Eternity*, 23.

audience of Jesus' teaching in the Great Commandment: "Hear, daughter, look and incline your ear, in order to understand that … you must love the Lord, your God, above all things, for if you observe this precept, you will easily keep all the other directives already given."[84]

BIBLIOGRAPHY

Atwood, Craig D. *The Theology of the Czech Brethren from Hus to Comenius.* University Park, PA: Penn State Press, 2009.

Bloch, R. Howard. *Medieval Misogyny and the Invention of Western Romantic Love.* ACLS Humanities E-Book. Chicago: University of Chicago Press, 1991.

De Vooght, Paul, and Josepha Pilny. "Un Classique de La Littérature Spirituelle: La Dcerka de Jean Huss." *Revue d'histoire de la Spiritualité* no. 48 (1972): 275–314.

Fudge, Thomas A. *Jan Hus between Time and Eternity: Reconsidering a Medieval Heretic.* Lanham, MD: Lexington Books, 2015.

———. *Jan Hus: Religious Reform and Social Revolution in Bohemia.* London, New York: I. B. Tauris, 2010.

Herold, Vilém. "The Spiritual Background of the Czech Reformation: Precursors of Jan Hus." In *A Companion to Jan Hus*, edited by František Šmahel, 69–95. Leiden: Brill, 2015.

Klassen, John M. *Warring Maidens, Captive Wives and Hussite Queens: Women and Men at War and at Peace in Fifteenth Century Bohemia.* New York: Columbia University Press, 1999.

Macek, Joseph. *Jean Hus et Les Traditions Hussites (XVe–XIXe Siècles).* Civilisations et Mentalités. Paris: Plon, 1973.

Pavlíček, Ota. "The Chronology of the Life and Work of Jan Hus." In *A Companion to Jan Hus*, edited by František Šmahel, 9–68. Leiden: Brill, 2015.

Perett, Marcela Kličova. *Preachers, Partisans, and Rebellious Religion: Vernacular Writing and the Hussite Movement.* Philadelphia: University of Pennsylvania Press, 2018.

---

84. Sigg, "*Dcerka* Translation," chapter 10, paragraph 13.

Říčan, Rudolf, C. Daniel Crews, and Amedeo Molnár. *The History of the Unity of Brethren: A Protestant Hussite Church in Bohemia and Moravia*. Bethlehem, PA: Moravian Church in America, 2008.

Rychterová, Pavlína. "The Vernacular Theology of Jan Hus." In *A Companion to Jan Hus*, edited by František Šmahel, 170–213. Leiden: Brill, 2015.

Ryšánek, František, Anežka Vidmanová-Schmidtová, Amedeo Molnár, and František Graus. *Magistri Iohannis Hus opera omnia*. Prague: Acad., Scientiarum Bohemoslovaca, 1988.

Sheldrake, Philip. *A Brief History of Spirituality*. Hoboken, NJ: John Wiley & Sons, 2013.

Sigg, Michèle Miller. *Dcerka:* Translation into English from the French text by Paul de Vooght and Joseph Pilny. Unpublished manuscript, 2019.

Šmahel, František. "Instead of Conclusion: Jan Hus as Writer and Author." In *A Companion to Jan Hus*, edited by František Šmahel, 370–409. Leiden: Brill, 2015.

3

—

THE WITTENBERG CONNECTION IN SCANDINAVIA

The Catalyst of the Reformation within Historical Complexity

Robert L. Gallagher

The development of Reformation Scandinavia was an interlocking of Wittenberg's theology and practice within a complex array of historical events. Some of the significant meshing instances are the support of monarchs, nobility, and populace in the midst of rising nationalism to eliminate the political and financial burden of the Catholic papacy; established cultural, financial, and geographical connections between the Germanic and northern states; and information propagation through the new invention of the printing press. In northern Europe, the Reformation was a political revolution with religious outcomes, and not so much a religious revolution with political outcomes. Yet, the key catalyst of the Reformation in the midst of the complex set of historical proceedings was the graduates of Wittenberg University in Saxony. Wittenberg became a revolutionary center of missions whereby its students preached and published Martin Luther's radical ideas throughout Scandinavia, notably in Denmark, Sweden, and Finland.

REFORMATION WITTENBERG:
A CENTER OF MISSIONS TRAINING

Between 1520 and 1560, approximately 5,000 of the 16,000 students at Wittenberg's university were from nations other than Germany, making the institution an important center of missions training.[1] Through his teaching at the university, Luther promoted a renewed interest in the gospel, and many of his students returned to their home countries across Europe spreading the Reformation, which resulted in societal conversion.[2] This was especially true of Scandinavia, which, similar to Germany, wanted to discard papal dominance.[3] As Paul E. Pierson puts it,

---

1. If historians use the terms "mission" and "missionary" for Protestant cross-cultural workers sent to preach Christ's gospel to Catholic and Orthodox people in regions of Africa, Asia, Europe, and Latin America, then the same designations may also be used for Wittenberg's Protestant students sent by Martin Luther to proclaim the Reformation gospel message in Catholic Scandinavia. Furthermore, discovering the writings of Augustine enabled Luther to break from Aristotle, Thomas Aquinas, and the structure of Scholasticism that gradually led him to a series of theological breakthroughs, including the foundational reinterpretation of Romans 1:16–17, which David J. Bosch calls "the 'missionary text' of the Protestant theological paradigm." See *Transforming Mission: Paradigm Shifts in Theology of Mission* (Maryknoll, NY: Orbis Books, 1991), 239–40.

2. See further Thomas Coates, "Were the Reformers Mission-Minded?" *Concordia Theological Monthly* 40 (October 1969): 603; and Eugene W. Bunkowske, "Was Luther a Missionary?" *Concordia Theological Quarterly* 49 (April–June 1985): 170. A number of historians maintain that Luther believed that missionary involvement was no longer a charge of the church because of the impending second coming, and that the early apostles had fulfilled the Great Commission. See J. Herbert Kane, *A Concise History of the Christian World Missions: A Panoramic View of Missions from Pentecost to the Present*, rev. ed. (Grand Rapids: Baker, 1982), 73–75; Stephen Neill and Owen Chadwick, *A History of Christian Missions*, 2nd ed. (New York: Viking Penguin, 1986), 187–89; Norman E. Thomas, ed., *Classic Texts in Mission and World Christianity* (Maryknoll, NY: Orbis Books, 1995), 32–35; Kenneth B. Mulholland, "From Luther to Carey: Pietism and the Modern Missionary Movement," *Bibliotheca Sacra* 156 (January–March 1999): 86; Ruth A. Tucker, *From Jerusalem to Irian Jaya: A Biographical History of Christian Missions*, 2nd ed. (Grand Rapids: Zondervan, 2004), 97; and Carlos F. Cardoza-Orlandi and Justo L. González, *To All Nations from All Nations: A History of the Christian Missionary Movement* (Nashville: Abingdon Press, 2013), 138–39, 182–83. Gustav Warneck claimed that during the early sixteenth century, the politically and socially turbulent times caused the Reformers to neglect missions, and since the German reformer rejected Catholic monasticism, Lutheranism was devoid of a medium for missions. See Werner Elert, *The Structure of Lutheranism*, trans. W. A. Hansen (St. Louis: Concordia, 1962), 385; Bosch, *Transforming Mission*, 243; Stanley H. Skreslet, *Comprehending Mission: The Questions, Methods, Themes, Problems, and Prospects of Missiology* (Maryknoll, NY: Orbis Books, 2012), 38; and Justice Anderson, "An Overview of Missiology," in *Missiology: An Introduction to the Foundations, History, and Strategies of World Missions*, ed., John Mark Terry (Nashville: B&H Publishing, 2015), 14.

3. See Ernest G. Schwiebert, *Luther and His Times* (St. Louis: Concordia, 1950), 293.

Some scholars have accused Luther and Calvin of having no missionary vision, and have affirmed the missionary activity of the Anabaptists. That view is incorrect. Lutheran missionaries to the Scandinavian countries followed the older medieval Christendom pattern of mission. They won the rulers to the new faith, and the church was reformed following the Lutheran model. ... Most Lutheran missionaries were Luther's former students. They took the movement to Denmark, Sweden, and Finland.[4]

THE WITTENBERG CONNECTION IN DENMARK

In the early sixteenth century, Denmark was undergoing economic and social change with the expansion of the urban merchant classes in tension with the nobility who were seeking to secure and strengthen their aristocratic power. Interest in Luther's ideas came to Denmark early, and the people showed strong interest since German economic and political influences were flourishing in the kingdom. In addition, the towns were geographically close to the ferment of the German Reformation, and the majority of the population clustered in large urban centers, which allowed for ready information distribution. Reformers who had studied at Wittenberg promptly carried the ideas of Luther into Denmark with the support of the Oldenburg monarchy beginning with King Christian II.

KING CHRISTIAN II: PROGRESSIVE DESPOT

By 1518, Luther's authority had reached the courts of Christian II of Denmark where Wolfgang von Utenhof (ca. 1495–1542), a Wittenberg graduate in canon law, and General Johann Rantzau (1492–1565) tutored the future king in Wittenberg belief (Christian III [1503–1559; r. 1533–1559]). Moved by his tutors' witness to Reformation ideas, the young prince as a member of the delegation of his uncle, Duke Joachim of Brandenburg (1499–1535), attended the Diet of Worms, and heard Luther's defense before Charles V,

---

4. Paul E. Pierson, *The Dynamics of Christian Mission: History through a Missiological Perspective* (Pasadena, CA: William Carey International University Press, 2009), 141. For a consideration of the Reformers' missional impetus, see Robert L. Gallagher, "Encountering Reformation Missions," in *Encountering the History of Missions: From the Early Church to Today*, Robert L. Gallagher and John Mark Terry, Encountering Missions Series (Grand Rapids: Baker Academic, 2017), 130–49. Also, see David J. Valleskey, "Luther's Impact on Mission Work," *Wisconsin Lutheran Quarterly* 92 (April 1995): 100.

the Holy Roman Emperor (1500–1558; r. 1519–1556). Luther's bold argument intrigued the crown prince.

King Christian II, the cousin of Prince Christian, contacted the University of Wittenberg in 1520 requesting Saxon clergy to help establish a humanistic curriculum at the University of Copenhagen. To answer the royal call, Luther sent the Christian humanists Mathias Gabler and Martin Reinhart from Wittenberg. Gabler imparted Greek for a number of years at the university, and Reinhart taught Wittenberg doctrine for a year. Further, Christian II allowed Reinhart to preach in German at the church of Saint Nicholas in Copenhagen—the first minister to teach Lutheranism in Denmark with royal permission.[5]

On his return from the Stockholm Massacre in 1521,[6] the king sent Reinhart back to Wittenberg to entice the university's chancellor, Andreas Bodenstein von Karlstadt (1486–1541)—a close associate of Martin Luther— or Luther himself, to come to Denmark and assist him in the expected reforms.[7] Pope Leo X (1475–1521; p. 1513–1521) had already excommunicated Luther from the Catholic Church, and soon thereafter, the Reformer disappeared to Wartburg Castle under the protection of Frederick III, Elector of Saxony (1463–1525).[8] Thus, Karlstadt accepted the royal invitation.[9] He

---

5. For an explanation of Reinhart's accomplishments as an active reformer, see R. Nisbet Bain, *Scandinavia: A Political History of Denmark, Norway, and Sweden, from 1513 to 1900* (Cambridge: Cambridge University Press, 1905), 90, and Amy Nelson Burnett, "Communion Preparation in the Early Years of the Reformation," in *From Wittenberg to the World*, ed. Charles P. Arand, Erik H. Herrmann, and Daniel L. Mattson (Göttingen: Vandenhoeck and Ruprecht, 2018), 61.

6. As a consequence of the coronation of Christian II of Denmark as the new king of Sweden, conflict arose between Swedish pro-unionists (in favor of the Kalmar Union, then dominated by Denmark), and anti-unionists (supporters of Swedish independence, and opposed to King Christian II). The Stockholm Massacre was a trial of those opposed to Christian II that led to the beheading of nearly 100 nobles in Stockholm (1520).

7. For further understanding of Andreas Bodenstein von Karlstadt, see Alejandro Zorzin, "Andreas Bodenstein von Karlstadt (1486–1541)," in *The Reformation Theologians: An Introduction to Theology in the Early Modern Period*, ed. Carter Lindberg (Oxford: Blackwell, 2002), 327– 37, and Ronald J. Sider, *Karlstadt's Battle with Luther: Documents in a Liberal-Radical Debate* (Philadelphia: Augsburg Fortress Press, 1978), 38–48.

8. During this period (May 1521 to March 1522), Luther translated the New Testament from Greek into German in ten weeks so that all people might have the opportunity to read the Bible. See Lamin Sanneh, *Translating the Message: The Missionary Impact on Culture* (Maryknoll, NY: Orbis Books, 2009), 89.

9. Ole Peter Grell, "Scandinavia," in *The Early Reformation in Europe*, ed. Andrew Pettegree (Cambridge: Cambridge University Press, 1992), 96. For an awareness of how Karlstadt played a key role in the development of Lutheran theology, see Sider, *Andreas Bodenstein von Karlstadt:*

arrived in Copenhagen the next year only to stay for less than a month before returning to Germany since the Wittenberg chancellor was suspicious that the king had little intention of separating from Rome, and furthermore, he was worried about his safety.

Led by the nobles of Jutland, the Danish aristocracy overthrew and exiled Christian II in 1523 at the Danish Council (*Rigsrådet*) because of the king's attempts to lessen their political influence by recklessly appointing and dismissing bishops. The Council elected his uncle, Duke Frederik of Holstein and Schleswig, who had supported the rebellion, as monarch (Frederik I [1471–1533; r. 1523–1533]). The overthrown king and his wife Isabella, rather than confront the unrest, retreated to the Netherlands under the protection of his brother-in-law, Emperor Charles V, converting to Lutheranism while in exile at the city of Lier. Beginning in 1524, the royal couple visited Wittenberg on a number of occasions where they stayed at the home of Barbara and Lucas Cranach the Elder (1472–1553)—a close friend of Luther, and a portrait painter of the leaders of the Protestant Reformation—and sat under the preaching of Martin Luther.

Christian II financially supported the translation of Lutheran hymns and sermons, and the Bible into the Danish vernacular. In Wittenberg, for example, he directed the first two Danish publications of Luther's German New Testament in 1524, and again five years later; and had some of the copies smuggled into Denmark.[10] The deposed king primarily viewed the new Reformation ideas as a tool of political reform to break the meshing dominance of the nobility and the Catholic Church.

Characteristically, the exiled monarch hoped to harmonize his new Lutheran beliefs with his political ambitions to recover the throne of Denmark believing that the new translations would keep the Danish commoner in the faith of the banished king. He supposed that the Danish publications would stir the peasants to demand his return supported by the parish priests who suffered a socio-economic gulf with the higher clerics. When Christian II visited Wittenberg in 1526, Luther supported this notion, and wrote that the Danes were committing blasphemy by rejecting their

---

The Development of His Thought, 1517–1525, ed. Heiko A. Oberman, Studies in Medieval and Reformation Thought, vol. 11 (Leiden: E. J. Brill, 1974), 7.

10. The first Danish translation of the entire Scripture was Christian III's Bible of 1550.

God-anointed king, and would suffer the consequences of the Lord's judgment. Ten years after the Reformation in Denmark, Luther still supported
Christian II, and wrote to King Christian III asking for his royal colleague's
pardon.[11]

KING FREDERIK I: RISING REFORMATION RUMBLINGS

Frederik I began his reign in 1523. Reformation rumblings were already on
the rise in Schleswig-Holstein and Jutland since the year before Lutheran
preachers from Germany had invaded these duchies.[12] In 1522 in the town
of Husum, Schleswig-Holstein, the Wittenberg-trained Catholic priest
Hermann Tast (1490–1551) preached Reformation teaching in Low German
with such an enthusiastic response from the populace that he had to move
from the private home of Mathias Knutzen, a merchant and town-coun-
selor, to the market square.[13] In 1525, Franz Hamer (1496–1553), a former
Catholic colleague who also had studied at Wittenberg, joined Tast in
preaching in the southwestern part of Schleswig-Holstein. Ole Peter Grell
verifies, "The Wittenberg connection was to characterize the Reformation
in Schleswig-Holstein from the outset."[14]

---

11. See further Martin Schwarz Lausten, "Luther and the Reformation in Denmark," in
Luther After 1530: Theology, Church, and Politics, ed. Helmar Junghans (Göttingen: Vandenhoeck
& Ruprecht, 2005), 118–19. King Christian II's marriage to the Habsburgs complicated his
position. In 1530, he returned to the Catholic faith when both his opponents, Frederick I and
Gustav Vasa, joined the Reformation. Subsequently, with this change of allegiance, Christian
II reconciled with his brother-in-law, Charles V, the Holy Roman Emperor.

12. For an appreciation of German Lutheran preachers following Luther's teachings, see
WA 10 I, 1. 540, 12 ff., Luther cited in Elert, 1962, 387; WA 12:540.3-15, Luther cited in Volker
Stolle, *The Church Comes from All Nations*, trans. K. Schulz (St. Louis: Concordia Academic
Press, 2003), 26; and Alfred Koschade, "Luther on Missionary Motivation," *Lutheran Quarterly*
17 (August 1965): 235.

13. See further Grell, "Scandinavia," in *The Reformation World*, ed. Andrew Pettegree
(London: Routledge, 2000), 260. In 1511, Hermann Tast studied theology at the University
of Wittenberg.

14. Grell, "Scandinavia," in *The Reformation in National Context*, ed. Bob Scribner, Roy
Porter, and Mikuláš Teich (Cambridge: Cambridge University Press, 1994), 114. At the Diet
of Copenhagen in 1527, Frederik I promised to uphold the privileges of the church, yet did
not support the legal authority of the bishops. See N. K. Andersen, "The Reformation in
Scandinavia and the Baltic," in *The Reformation (1520-1559)*, ed. Geoffrey Rudolph Elton, The
New Cambridge Modern History, 2nd ed., vol. 2 (Cambridge: Cambridge University Press,
2008), 147. Inspired by Lutheran teaching, Frederik I declined to interfere with the "preaching
of God's word," and allowed any doctrine that was in agreement with the Bible, even though at
his coronation he had promised the conservative Danish hierarchy that he would deal with the
heretics. On that occasion the new king declared, "[We will] not allow any heretics, disciples of

The city of Viborg in Jutland became the center of the Danish Lutheran Reformation under the direction of Hans Tausen (1494-1561)[15]—a former Johannite monk who had studied at Wittenberg where he became a Luther enthusiast and a disciple of Melanchthon—and Jørgen Jensen Sadolin (ca. 1490-1559) who also was Wittenberg-educated. They became parish priests in the two mendicant monasteries at Viborg after town citizens had destroyed twelve redundant churches and monasteries in the region. In 1526, Tausen and Sadolin formed a school to train Protestant preachers, and published pamphlets from the press of the German printer Hans Vingaard who had settled in Viborg. The Reformation movement spread rapidly from Viborg among the larger market towns such as Malmø, starting in 1527 through the preaching of the priest Klaus Mortensøn Tondebinder and monk Hans Olufsen Spandemager, together with monk Tausen in Copenhagen—all the while relying heavily on popular and local magisterial support.[16]

The practical and economic aspects of Protestantism helped foster the new teaching. Without the toleration of the state, though, the Reformation would have seen little progress in Denmark, as already witnessed by the involvement of Christian II and Frederick I. The expansion was based on the movement's creed of the priesthood of all believers (no distinction between clergy and laity), and the desire for gospel-focused services in the vernacular in common with widespread social dissatisfaction with the Roman hierarchy and clergy.[17] The solidarity among the lay nobility against

---

Luther or others to preach or to teach, secretly or openly against the heavenly God, the belief of the holiest church, the holiest father the Pope, or the Roman church, but where they are found in this kingdom, we promise to punish them on life and property"(Grell, "Scandinavia," 104). In spite of this coronation charter, it was during the reign of Frederik that the Lutheran movement began to advance in Denmark fueled by the feudal crisis within Danish society.

15. See further Martin Schwarz Lausten, "Hans Tausen," in *The Oxford Encyclopedia of the Reformation*, ed. Hans J. Hillerbrand, vol. 4 (New York: Oxford University Press, 1996), 1451; and Lausten, "The Early Reformation in Denmark and Norway, 1520-1559," in *The Scandinavian Reformation: From Evangelical Movement to Institutionalisation of Reform*, ed. Ole Peter Grell (Cambridge: Cambridge University Press, 1995), 14.

16. Malmø was an important Danish trading center whereby the northern German towns connected through shipping not only bringing imported goods, but also German Lutheran preachers and publications to Denmark.

17. The movement based its theology on the teachings of Wittenberg. See James Atkinson, *Martin Luther: Prophet to the Church Catholic* (Grand Rapids: Eerdmans, 1983), 10; Jerry K. Robbins, ed., *The Essential Luther: A Reader on Scripture, Redemption, and Society* (Grand

Luther's teaching began to break down as they increasingly wanted the privileged clergy to carry a greater responsibility for the increased royal tax-burden, and objected to the dominance of uneducated clergy in the parish churches.[18] These events represented a direct interference by the Danish laity with Catholic governance. Further, the peasants demanded social reorganization in the areas of education, social welfare for the poor, and health care, misinterpreting the Wittenberg message as a rejection of the existing social and political order.

To evade growing pressure from the Catholic bishops who had suspended Tausen in 1526, Frederik appointed the Wittenberg graduate as his personal court chaplain to give him immunity from heresy charges; and ordered both Lutherans and Catholics to share the same churches, as well as issuing royal letters protecting Reformation preachers.[19] One year later, at the Council of Nobles (*Herredag*) in Odense, Denmark, officially severed relations with the papacy. The council of the aristocracy agreed that future appointed bishops no longer needed the approval of the pope, and candidates would pay the Danish king for the privilege of the office, instead of Rome. The church in Denmark had now separated into two sections: the official Catholic Church, governed by bishops; and the Lutherans with their own parishes, pastors, and services. "Ten years of conflict and spiritual war between the defenders of the Roman church and the eager aggressive Lutheran preachers followed."[20]

Rapids: Baker Books, 1991), 50; and Bernhard Lohse, *Martin Luther's Theology: Its Historical and Systematic Development* (Minneapolis: Fortress Press, 1999), 202.

18.   The increased taxation was to pay for the raising of an army against the military threat from the deposed king, Christian II, who was endeavoring to solicit military help from his reluctant brother-in-law, the Emperor Charles V, who had just been victorious against the French. See Grell, "Scandinavia," 114.

19.   See Bain, *Scandinavia*, 90, and Lausten, "The Early Reformation," 14.

20.   Lausten, "Luther and the Reformation," 122. Under the rule of Frederik, religion became a matter of personal conscience with Lutherans permitted to preach "the word of God." Yet, the year 1527 saw the king close Franciscan houses and monasteries in twenty-eight Danish towns, and sporadically offer small stipends to retiring monks. Tausen's preaching at the church of Saint Nicholas in Copenhagen introduced reform to the city, and the printing press of Vingaard established at Viborg in 1528, aided the dissemination of Protestant views throughout Denmark, despite the intrepid opposition of Bishop Rønne of Copenhagen. In the meantime, due to skillful propaganda, King Frederik weakened the power of the Catholic Church, and averted a religious war. "Doctrinally he preferred toleration; structurally he preferred a church subservient to state interests" (Christopher Ocker, *Luther, Conflict, and Christendom: Reformation Europe and Christianity in the West* [Cambridge: Cambridge University Press, 2018], 89).

KING CHRISTIAN III: COMPLETION OF LUTHERAN REFORMATION

In 1526, Frederik permitted Christian, his eldest son, to establish over sixty Lutheran parishes around Haderslev and Tønning (Duchy of Schleswig), a wedding gift for his son's marriage to the Lutheran Dorothea of Saxony-Lauenburg (1511–1571). Duke Christian managed to entice two German Wittenberg theologians to Haderslev: Eberhard Weidensee (ca. 1486–1547) held a doctorate in canon law from the University of Leipzig also having spent time in Wittenberg, and Johann Wenth (ca. 1490–1541), a recent Wittenberg graduate. Both played a significant role in reforming Haderslev-Tønning. Weidensee held the role of superintendent or bishop, and Wenth authored the Danish Protestant Church Ordinance (1537–1539) and the Schleswig-Holstein Church Ordinance (1542). Both served under the guidance of Johannes Bugenhagen of the Duchy of Pomerania (1485–1558), a theology faculty member at Wittenberg University. "By the end of 1527 most of the parish churches in the towns of Schleswig-Holstein had received Protestant ministers, in many cases Wittenberg-educated Germans who had been introduced personally by either King Frederik I or Duke Christian."[21]

The German leaders of the Danish Protestant movement initiated the Reformation by creating the first Lutheran church diocese in Scandinavia, modeled after Wittenberg. Under the auspices of Duke Christian, the Wittenberg Reformers turned the collegiate-chapter school into an academy for retraining the local Catholic priests in Haderslev to become Lutheran ministers, while expelling the mendicant orders such as the Dominicans and Franciscans. Practically, the majority of the Catholic clergy remained in office after the retraining. Within a few years, the Haderslev academy became a model for other seminaries in Denmark such as at Malmø in 1529 with the teachers Peder Laurentsen and Carmelite Frans Vormordsen—a learned humanist.

At the Diet of Kiel in 1526, a synod of clergy, the duke presented the first draft of the Haderslev Articles, written by Weidensee and Wenth. This document instructed the Reformation pastors to persecute the Anabaptists who were gaining influence in the duchies, along with how to preach, practice, and live the Lutheran faith, including the compulsory decree that all

---

21. Grell, "Scandinavia," 115.

ministers should marry. Thereafter, the ministers pledged allegiance to Christian, the Duke of Holstein and Schleswig.[22] "It is the first evangelical Church Order to emerge in Scandinavia, and its dependence on Luther and Wittenberg is obvious. Thus, Duke Christian as early as 1526 established a princely Lutheran territorial church in his tiny duchy in Schleswig, which was identical to similar much larger territorial churches in Germany."[23]

By 1530, the Reform movement had established itself in the majority of towns and cities throughout Denmark. At the Diet of Copenhagen that same year, the Lutheran pastors presented "Forty-three Articles," which outlined their Protestant beliefs. These Articles became popular with the people, and when Frederik died in 1533, most of Denmark was Lutheran.[24] The full realization of a Lutheran national church, however, occurred in 1537 after Christian III won the civil war against the Catholic nobles (1534-1536). He then removed the Catholic bishops from their office, and nationalized the monasteries, nunneries, and priories, resulting in many Catholic priests marrying and continuing their ministry as Lutherans.

In the confiscation of Catholic property after the religious reform, the royal land expanded from 15 to 60 percent of the national acreage. As the supreme head of the church, Christian III appointed Bugenhagen—Luther's pastor at Saint Mary's church in Wittenberg—to lead the ecclesiastical reorganization (1537-1539). This task included modeling the University of Copenhagen after Wittenberg,[25] and placing national education in the hands of the church, supervised by Hans Tausen (the king's chaplain), and the Lutheran bishops.[26] Tausen drafted the first Lutheran

---

22. See Andersen, "The Reformation in Scandinavia," 144; and E. Dunkley, *The Reformation in Denmark* (London: SPCK, 1948), 45.

23. Lausten, "Luther and the Reformation," 121.

24. See further, Trygve R. Skarsten, *The Scandinavian Reformation: A Bibliographical Guide* (St. Louis: Center for Reformation Research, 1985), 31-32.

25. Christian III had little respect for Danish theologians, and repeatedly sent invitations to Luther to supply his Copenhagen school with Wittenberg theologians. See Leif Grane, "Teaching the People: The Education of the Clergy and the Instruction of the People in the Danish Reformation Church," in *The Danish Reformation against Its International Background*, ed. Herausgegeben von Leif Grane and Kai Hørby (Göttingen: Vandenhoeck & Ruprecht, 1990), 167; and C. E. Flöystrup, "The Church in Denmark," *Church Quarterly Review* 64 (April–July 1907): 87.

26. See Paul Douglas Lockhart, *Denmark, 1513-1660: The Rise and Decline of a Renaissance Monarchy* (Oxford: Oxford University Press, 2007), 64.

Church Ordinance in 1537,[27] and adopted Philipp Melanchthon's Augsburg Confession as the normative for Danish Lutheran theology.[28]

N. K. Andersen explains:

> The type of Christianity contained in the ordinance is Lutheranism, as formulated by Melanchthon. Once the Reformation was established, the direct influence from Wittenberg also became much more powerful. The preachers' simple belief in the Bible gradually gave way to a Christianity dictated by Luther's catechism. The evangelical awakening of the years of strife before 1536 lost heart; the congregation became passive, and growing emphasis was laid on the church as an institution, and on the dignity of the clergy.[29]

DANISH LUTHERAN THEOLOGY ALIGNS WITH WITTENBERG

As Christian III continued corresponding with Luther and other Wittenberg Reformers such as Peder Palladius (1503–1560)—a Danish Wittenberg graduate who became the first Lutheran bishop of Zealand at thirty-four years of age—Danish Lutheran theology aligned itself with Wittenberg.[30] Palladius had studied for six years at the University of Wittenberg where he became a doctor of theology in 1537. He had not taken part in the Reformation struggle, yet recommended by Luther and Melanchthon, and approved by King Christian, Bugenhagen consecrated him with six other priests as new bishops at Copenhagen in 1537. Since Bugenhagen was only a parish priest, he did this without the mantle of apostolic succession.

---

27. For the Lutheran Church Ordinance and Bugenhagen's involvement, see Andersen, "Reformation in Scandinavia," 150.

28. See further Eric W. Gritsch, *A History of Lutheranism* (Minneapolis: Augsburg Fortress, 2002), 50–52; and Robert Kolb, *Luther's Wittenberg World: The Reformer's Family, Friends, Followers, and Foes* (Minneapolis: Fortress Press, 2018), 200.

29. Andersen, "The Reformation in Scandinavia," 151. For the influence of the Catechism, see Martin Luther, *Luther's Works: Liturgy and Hymns*, vol. 53 (Philadelphia: Fortress Press, 1965), 64.

30. Wittenberg teaching promoted that although the apostles began missions, the church was to continue and include the whole world in its responsibility. God is unfolding his missions' purposes, and the Christian should spread the gospel among non-Christian people. See further, Koschade, 1965, 227, 231, 233, 235; Bunkowske, 162; and Luther cited in C. R. Lindquist, *Remonking the Church*, PhD diss., Fuller Theological Seminary, 1990, 57.

Palladius was involved in the restructuring of the Danish Protestant church through advising the king on church affairs (in Denmark as well as in Norway and Iceland). His influence extended to presiding over the meetings of the Lutheran bishops; teaching theology at the University of Copenhagen; pastorally administrating 390 parishes within his bishopric; being a popular and productive speaker; advocating for the removal of Catholic images and rituals, which he believed were idolatrous; and writing Reformation theological materials that he designed for the common people to understand.

The most celebrated of Palladius's writing projects was the translation of the Latin Bible into Danish in 1550, which Christian III approved, and encouraged every Lutheran church to obtain a copy. Other important writings were his *Book of Visitations* (1556) on the application of Lutheran teaching for various life situations, *Introduction to the Prophetic and Apostolic Books* (1557)—that ran sixteen Latin editions as well as Danish, English, German, and Polish translations—and *On Repentance and Justification* (1558), all of which enjoyed a wide readership throughout Scandinavia and Germany.

Niels Palladius (ca. 1510–1560), Peder's brother, studied for a decade at Wittenberg from 1534 before returning to teach at a convent in southern Denmark.[31] On revisiting Wittenberg for a short time, he then came back to his homeland, and accepted a pastorate in Copenhagen (1550) before becoming the Lutheran bishop of Lund a year later. He wrote over twenty books teaching the lessons of Wittenberg in Danish, Icelandic, and Latin, including a guide for Danish pastors, *Useful and Necessary Rules for Conducting Sermons* (1556), and in the same year, *Oration on the True and Catholic Church*, which helped direct the organization and practice of the Lutheran churches.[32]

---

31. Between 1534 and 1537, Peder and Niels Palladius were studying at the same time in Wittenberg.

32. A Danish contemporary of the Palladius brothers was Niels Hemmingsen (1513–1560), whom after studying in Wittenberg (1537–1542) and shaped by Melanchthon's method of biblical interpretation, taught at the University of Copenhagen in Greek and dialectics, and became the chair of theology in 1553. His writings modelled the ethics of the Christian life and practice for the fledgling Protestant church of Denmark such as his *Handbook of Theology* (1555), *Pastor* (1562), as well as commentaries on the Psalms and a number of New Testament books. See Kolb, *Luther's Wittenberg World*, 202.

THE WITTENBERG CONNECTION IN SWEDEN

The Swedish war of independence began after the 1521 "Stockholm Massacre" of Christian II, and the subsequent election of Gustav Vasa as the independent Swedish king in 1523. Vasa desired political freedom from Denmark, and religious independence from Rome. It was amid this economic and nationalistic malaise that the sparks of the Swedish Reformation originated and spread, fanned by Luther's Wittenberg students.

As was the case in Denmark, there were strong cultural and economic ties between Sweden and Germany in the early sixteenth century, which contributed to the German flow of Protestant ideas.[33] There were sizeable German populations in Malmø, Copenhagen, and Stockholm, for example, who were attracted to the new Wittenberg beliefs. German merchants first introduced Lutheranism to the large German colony in Stockholm with the German Lutheran, Nicholaus Stecker of Eisleben (b. 1483), a Wittenberg graduate, becoming their first Lutheran minister in 1524.[34] Other Wittenberg-influenced theologians followed into the courts of King Vasa, namely, Laurentius Andreae (ca. 1470–1552) and the brothers Olaus (1493–1552) and Laurentius (1499–1573) Petri. All three men had reached their Protestant belief through biblical humanism. The impact of these three men infected the nation of Sweden with the Wittenberg message.

SPREADING WITTENBERG THEOLOGY

Olaus Petri and his younger brother Laurentius were educated in the Carmelite monastery at Örebro, as well as the universities of Uppsala and Leipzig. In 1516, Olaus went to Wittenberg for two years to study for his masters in theology. There he witnessed the events that unfolded after Luther presented his *Theses*; and when Laurentius joined the university community around 1524, both brothers then experienced the German practical reforms of Melanchthon and Luther that influenced their theology.[35]

---

33. See Andersen, "Reformation in Scandinavia," 158.

34. See further Frank C. Senn, *Christian Liturgy: Catholic and Evangelical* (Minneapolis: Augsburg Fortress, 1997), 401–2; and Anderson, "Reformation in Scandinavia," 157.

35. For an illustration of Luther's preaching of the need for missions that influenced the Petri brothers and Laurentius Andreae, see Ewald M. Plass, *What Luther Says: An Anthology*, vol. 2 (St. Louis: Concordia, 1959), 958–60.

In 1519, Olaus returned to Strängnäs, in the Swedish part of the Danish realm, to teach at the cathedral school and became secretary to Bishop Matthias Gregersson (b. 1501-1520). There he taught Wittenberg theology to Laurentius Andreae (ca. 1470-1552), and together they preached the Reformation message.[36] Yet, their proclamation was not without opposition from the defenders of the old faith such as Bishop Hans Brask of Linköping (1464-1538) who vowed to crush the rising "Lutheran heresy." Andreae became archdeacon of the bishopric of Strängnäs after Christian II executed his superior in 1521, Bishop Matthias.

In protecting the "Lutheran heretics," Vasa invited Olaus Petri to be the secretary of Stockholm, and preach at *Storkyrkan* (Cathedral of Saint Nicholas) in 1524, and in the same year, Laurentius Andreae—who studied canon law in Rome—as the king's principal advisor. Vasa appointed Laurentius Petri as his counselor when Olaus's brother returned from Wittenberg in 1527. Andreae became the political engineer of the king's ideas of Reformation, Laurentius Petri the conductor of ecclesiastical transformation—aligning the Swedish church with Lutheran Reformation practices—and Olaus Petri the communicator of the Protestant message.[37] Andreae "formulated a programme for a national church. He argued that, since the church was the community of the faithful, the Christian people, its property belonged to the people whose king administered it. The Bible and not the pope's decree was the supreme authority, and Luther's writings must therefore be read and tested in the light of God's word."[38]

Stirred by the polemical writings of Olaus Petri against the doctrines of the Catholic Church, a *Riksdag* (parliament of nobles) gathered at Västerås in 1527 and agreed with King Vasa—after he cried and threatened to resign—to establish a Swedish Lutheran church modeled after the Wittenberg reform. In turn, the king pressured Peder Månsson, the Catholic bishop of Västerås (1462-1534; b. 1524-1534), to appoint three other bishops without papal consent. He also installed Laurentius Petri as a professor of theology at the University of Uppsala in 1527, and four years later

---

36. See Andersen, "Reformation in Scandinavia," 157.

37. Altman K. Swihart contends that Olaus Petri was "the intellectual leader of the Reformation in Sweden," *Luther and the Lutheran Church (1483-1960)* (London: Peter Owen, 1960), 224-38.

38. Andersen, "Reformation in Scandinavia," 156.

appointed him as the archbishop of Uppsala (the first Lutheran archbishop of Sweden).

DISTRIBUTION OF REFORMATION LITERATURE

The work of Andreae and the Petri brothers continued to affect the nation with the Protestant message well into the mid-sixteenth century. Together they published a Swedish New Testament in 1526 following Luther's German version. In the same year, Olaus published a devotional book, *Useful Instructions*, based on Luther's *Personal Prayer Book* (1522). Five years later, he published a number of polemical writings opposing the Catholic tradition. In 1531, Olaus printed a liturgical manual for a simplified Swedish mass and catechism followed by a Swedish translation of the Old Testament in 1536. "His production dominated the entire book market. In the next few years, his numerous writings assisted in a gradual transformation of the Swedish liturgy, and the acceptance of services in the vernacular."[39]

Olaus Petri explained the new faith mainly through publishing.[40] Additionally, he translated Luther's works into Swedish such as his *Book of Sermons* (1531); implemented another of Luther's ideas by having the mass sung in Swedish for the first time; and edited vernacular hymnals because he believed that they were edifying, instructive, and "expressed the prayer of the heart."[41] Altogether, Olaus published sixteen books in the decade 1530 to 1540 bringing Wittenberg theology to the Swedish people, and thereby tripling the number of books printed in the Swedish language. In 1541, Olaus in collaboration with his brother Laurentius, and Andreae, translated the entire Bible into Swedish (Gustav Vasa Bible), and its use in every Lutheran parish influenced religious education well into the next

---

39. Andersen, "Reformation in Scandinavia and the Baltic," 160.

40. See Grell, "Scandinavia," 113.

41. C. Bergendoff, *Olavus and the Ecclesiastical Transformation in Sweden (1521-1552): A Study in the Swedish Reformation* (New York: The Macmillan Company, 1928), 160. Not only were Wittenberg's publications expanding the effect of the Reformation faith, but also Luther's production of music. For Luther, music expressed biblical truths in service to theology, but was secondary to Scripture. See Luther, *The Table Talk of Martin Luther* (London: George Bell & Sons, 1884), 296; Luther, *Luther's Works*, 323–24; Paul Peters, "Luther's Practical Mission-Mindedness," *Wisconsin Lutheran Quarterly* 66 (April 1969): 119; Carl F. Schalk, "Martin Luther's Hymns Today," *Hymns* 34 (July 1983): 133; H. Guicharrousse, *Les Musiques de Luther* (Geneva: Labor et Fides, 1995), 20–27, 67–68; and Gracia Grindel, "The Rhetoric of Martin Luther's Hymns: Hymnody Then and Now," *Word & World* 26 (Spring 2006): 179.

century. In addition, thirty years after the Vasa Bible, Laurentius Petri authored an exposition of the creeds and the Christian life that served as a Lutheran catechism.[42]

ROYAL POLITICAL INTRIGUES

Throughout these Swedish Reforms, the popular cause of Protestantism was strongest in the capital of Stockholm. Vasa had contended with repeated agrarian uprisings before 1540, as the people, sponsored by the Catholic priests, objected to excessive royal taxes—to pay for the ongoing war of liberation from Denmark—and supported traditional Catholicism. Plagued by constant financial troubles, Vasa appropriated Franciscan and Dominican monasteries for secular use at places such as Viborg, to buttress the national treasury to pay for defense expenses; and in doing so, he inadvertently facilitated the Reform movement.[43] Grell summarizes:

> From 1524 to 1542, a succession of peasant rebellions and one major civil war had dominated events in Denmark and Sweden in particular. These revolts were all primary social and economic in origin, but more often than not, they were conditioned by the growing conflict between new and old in the religious domain.[44]

During this period of social disorder, Luther sent Georg Norman (d. 1553) in 1539—a graduate of the University of Wittenberg, and a Pomeranian noble who was a disciple of Melanchthon—to tutor the Swedish Princes Erik and Johan.[45] Gustav appointed Norman as *ordinator* and *superattendant*" with royal authority over "bishops, prelates, and all divines" of the Swedish church, and to appoint and discharge "all divines and preachers."[46] During the parliament of Örebro in 1539, Norman with the German

---

42. See further R. Woodward, *Piæ Cantiones: A Collection of Church and School Song* (London: Chiswick Press, 1910), 205–66; and James A. Scherer, "Luther and Mission: A Rich but Untested Potential," *Missio Apostolica: Journal of the Lutheran Society for Missiology* 2 (May 1994): 18.

43. See further Wayne te Brake, *Shaping History: Ordinary People in European Politics, 1500–1700* (Berkeley, CA: University of California Press, 1998), 54–55.

44. Grell, "Scandinavia," 112.

45. Ocker, *Luther, Conflict, and Christendom*, 87. Erik XIV (1533–1577; r. 1560-1568), and Johan III (1537–1592; r. 1568–1592).

46. Nils Forsander, *Olavus Petri: The Church Reformer of Sweden* (Rock Island, IL: Augustana Book Concern, 1918), 79.

councilor Conrad von Pyhy (d. 1553), encouraged Vasa to take full control of the Swedish church because of continuing peasant protests—caused by economic hardships and dissatisfaction with church governance—and the Reformers' unwillingness to submit to secular authority. With this political maneuver, the king slowly worked towards the completion of Lutheran Reform in the Swedish church. Norman implemented the Swedish Reformation according to the German pattern in both theology and practice.[47] The next year saw a new church organization because of the royal Reformation that remained until the king's death in 1560.[48] Between 1539 and 1544, German Lutheran views held sway in Sweden because of Georg Norman's influence.[49]

After King Vasa died, subsequent royal political intrigues hindered the formation of Protestantism for the next decade. A Protestant Church Order finally occurred in 1571, whereby, Laurentius Petri defined the practice of the church, followed by a complete embrace of Lutheran theology in 1593.[50] Furthermore, Andreae steered the church through the reigns of the king's two older sons in keeping the country aligned to Luther's theology: Erik XIV promoted Calvinist teaching throughout his realm, and when he died in 1568, Johann III tried to return Sweden to Catholic allegiance, which met resistance from the nobility and people.

THE WITTENBERG CONNECTION IN FINLAND

Finland shared an economic, social, and religious history with Sweden for almost 700 years from around 1150 until the Finnish War of 1809. Consequently, sixteenth-century Swedish politics swayed Finland to change from Catholicism to Lutheranism without any peasant rebellions. The Swedish authorities dissolved Catholic churches, and promoted Swedish language services to help congregations understand the sermons. As the academic language moved from Latin to Swedish, Finnish

---

47. See Andersen, "Reformation in Scandinavia," 162.

48. Ocker, *Luther, Conflict, and Christendom*, 87.

49. In 1559, Gustav Vasa sent a missionary, named Michael, to Lapland. See William Brown, *The History of Mission: Or, of the Propagation of Christianity Among the Heathen, Since the Reformation*, vol. 1 (Philadelphia: McCarty & Davis, 1820), 20.

50. See further Gritsch, *A History of Lutheranism*, 52–53.

was by-passed. This led to a disruption in education that detrimentally affected the training of local clergy.[51]

ENCOUNTERS WITH LUTHER'S REFORMATION

Luther's teaching began penetrating the Finnish sections of Gustav Vasa's territory through nobleman Petrus Särkilahti (d. 1529), who as a disciple of Erasmus of Rotterdam (1469-1536) began reading Luther's works at the University of Leuven around 1520.[52] In 1522 he returned to Turku—the center of Finnish territory in the Swedish realm—and while rector of the cathedral school became the first priest in the Swedish realm to marry. Särkilahti also distributed the publications of Olaus Petri and Martin Luther among the priests in the region preaching against the Catholic worship of saints and images, as well as celibacy and monastic life.

Among Särkilahti's followers was Mikael Agricola (1510-1557). Father Bartholomeus, Agricola's parish priest in Pernå sent him to Viipuri for priestly training. There he first encountered Luther's Reformation teaching and Erasmus's humanism, together with Lutheran services under the auspices of the German Count Johann, who served the king of Sweden. On returning to Turku in 1528, Agricola became a scribe for the Dominican Bishop Martinus Johannis Skytte (ca. 1477-1550; b. 1528-1550), and met Petrus Särkilahti who enthusiastically shared Luther's Reformation message.

INFLUENCES OF WITTENBERG'S COMMUNITY

Bishop Skytte of Turku, a biblical humanist and Catholic Reformer, sent Agricola as a priest to Wittenberg in 1536 for three years, where he studied under Luther, and specialized in the Greek New Testament with Melanchthon. This understanding of the first-century language enabled him to start a 718-page translation of the New Testament into Finnish in 1537, which he completed in 1543. While attending Wittenberg University,

---

51. J. Wuorinen, *A History of Finland* (New York: Columbia University Press, 1965), 65.

52. Luther taught that all Christians were to be missionaries as they lived for their neighbor. See Elert, *The Structure of Lutheranism*, 392-93; WA 412, 18, Luther cited in Lindquist, *Remonking the Church*, 48; and LW 39:309-10, Luther cited in Stolle, *The Church Comes from All Nations*, 21-22.

Agricola also translated and printed three liturgical books into Finnish with Luther's theology heavily influencing the contents (1549).

The first book centers on practical Christian ministry in the areas of baptisms, marriages, and funerals, together with words of comfort for the sick, grieving, and dying. Except for the portions on baptism and marriage, which came from Luther, Agricola translated the remainder of the ministerial topics from the writings of Olaus Petri. Again, he based the second booklet primarily on Olaus Petri's writings on how to conduct a church service. The final liturgical book focused on the sufferings of Christ based on the four Gospels. This work also is strongly influenced by Wittenberg scholarship, in particular the teachings of the German Bugenhagen.

Agricola returned to Turku in 1551 as rector of the cathedral school (Finland's clerical seminary). Three years later, Gustav Vasa consecrated him as bishop of Turku: the first Lutheran bishop of Finland. Agricola's Reformation activities extended far beyond his administrative responsibilities in bringing Wittenberg theology and practice to the churches of Finland. His writings not only promoted Luther's ideas, but also the Finnish language, and his treatises focused on the deconstruction of medieval piety by emphasizing the atoning death and resurrection of Christ. Agricola's writings and translations helped guide Lutheran pastoral practice and preaching in Reformation Finland. Andersen claims, "After the synod at Uppsala in 1536, the publication of liturgical books in Finnish became an urgent necessity, but only with Agricola's *Book of Ritual* and *Order of the Mass*, both of which appeared in 1549 based on Olavus Petri's corresponding works, did Finnish religious life take on a definite shape."[53]

Another Finnish Reformer influenced by Wittenberg who was likewise a part of the circle of Martinus Skytte was Paavali Juusten (ca. 1516–1575). He first moved from Viborg to Turku in 1536 for further education. Bishop Skytte ordained Juusten as a priest in 1540, and he became the acting headmaster of the Viborg School (1541–1543) before the bishop sent him to study at Wittenberg between 1543 and 1546.

Juusten returned to Finland and succeeded Agricola as the headmaster of the Turku cathedral school in 1548. In 1554, Gustav Vasa, supported by Bishop Botvid Sunesson of Strängnäs (d. 1562; b. 1536–1555; 1561–1562),

---

53. Andersen, "Reformation in Scandinavia," 166.

appointed Juusten as the inaugural bishop of Viborg, and nine years later, Erik XIV appointed him bishop of Turku. Additionally, King Johann III sent Bishop Juusten as an ambassador to Russia in 1569 to negotiate with Ivan IV (1530–1584; r. 1547–1584; aka. the Terrible) a peace treaty between Sweden and Russia. The first Tsar of Russia, however, imprisoned the Swedish delegation for over two years, finally releasing them in 1572. In the last year of his life, Juusten authored the Finnish-language catechism (1574), the story of his Moscow travels (1574), a mass book (1575), and the Chronicle of Finnish bishops (1575), all designed to help guide the Finnish church in Wittenberg theology.

SUMMARY OF LUTHERAN MISSION ACTIVITY

CULTURAL AND ECONOMIC TIES

Interest in Lutheranism came easily to Scandinavia because of the existing German economic and political influences. The Reformation movement spread quickly from Viborg in Denmark to some of the larger market towns such as Malmø because it was an important trading port connected to the northern German towns. The ships not only brought imported goods, but also German Lutheran preachers and publications to Denmark. Geographically positioned near the centers of the German Reformation, the majority of the Nordic population clustered in large urban centers, which allowed for ready information distribution. In addition, large German colonies in Malmø, Copenhagen, and Stockholm made a willing pathway for the new Wittenberg preachers and beliefs.

There were also robust cultural and economic ties between Sweden and Germany, which contributed to the German flow of Luther's ideas. Duke Albrecht of Prussia, for example, made a treaty with Gustav Vasa, and sent Reformation pamphlets to Sweden along with Prussian counselors to help the king Lutheranize the Swedish church, and separate from the pope.

In turn, Finland shared cultural and economic connections with Sweden, and subsequently, Swedish political powers influenced Finland to change religious affiliation from Rome to Stockholm without stirring the populace waters.

EDUCATIONAL TRAINING CENTERS

Luther was a part of a team of theological colleagues of Reformation at Wittenberg who trained students to spread the message across Europe, including Scandinavia. All were committed to the reform of Lutheranism, although some followed the Wittenberg theology and manner more closely than others did. As Wittenberg-educated preachers penetrated northern duchies with Luther's message, they accordingly trained Lutheran workers using the University of Wittenberg as a template.

Hans Tausen and Jørgen Sadolin formed a training school at Viborg in Jutland to train Protestant preachers, most of whom were Catholic priests who effortlessly changed association. In Haderslev, Denmark under the auspices of Duke Christian, Wittenberg alumni Eberhard Weidensee, and Johann Wenth, turned the Catholic seminary into an academy to train Lutheran pastors (again the majority being former Catholic priests) modelled after Wittenberg University. The Haderslev academy became a Wittenberg educational model for other seminaries to duplicate such as at Malmø and Copenhagen.

In Sweden, Olaus Petri implanted his Wittenberg seminary training into the Strängnäs cathedral school under Bishop Matthias. Similarly, Mikael Agricola and Paavali Juusten, Finnish Wittenberg graduates, supported by Bishop Skytte, followed the Lutheran educational pattern at the clerical seminary in Turku.[54]

CHRISTIAN HUMANISM

Christian humanism was an important prerequisite of the Lutheran movement in northern Europe. Students who returned from European universities such as Wittenberg brought back Christian humanist ideas. King Christian II of Denmark requested Luther to help establish a humanistic academic curriculum at the University of Copenhagen. Subsequently, the Saxon Reformer sent the Christian humanists Mathias Gabler and Martin Reinhart from Wittenberg.

---

54. See further Robert L. Gallagher, "Historic Models of Teaching Christian Mission: Case Studies Informing an Age of World Christianity," in *Teaching Christian Mission in an Age of World Christianity*, ed. Robert A. Danielson and Linda F. Whitmer, Association of Professors of Mission Series (Wilmore, KY: First Fruits Press, 2017), 127–50.

In Sweden, Laurentius Andreae and the Petri brothers, Olaus and Laurentius, had reached their Protestant belief through biblical humanism. The influence of these three men greatly affected Sweden with the Reformation message.

Luther's teaching arrived in Finland through Petrus Särkilahti who, as a disciple of the leading humanist Erasmus of Rotterdam, began reading Luther's works. Särkilahti then influenced Bishop Skytte of Turku, a biblical humanist and Catholic Reformer, who in turn, sponsored Mikael Agricola and Paavali Juusten to study at Wittenberg under Luther and Philipp Melanchthon.

COMMITTED MESSENGERS

The transforming effect of the Wittenberg students in northern Europe was considerable and played a major role in the unfurling of Lutheranism. The Wittenberg influence in Denmark, for instance, came through students and faculty such as Johannes Bugenhagen, Mathias Gabler, Franz Hamer, Niels Hemmingsen, Andreas Karlstadt, brothers Peder and Niels Palladius, Martin Reinhart, Jørgen Sadolin, Hermann Tast, Hans Tausen, Eberhard Weidensee, Johann Wenth, and Wolfgang von Utenhof.

In Sweden, Laurentius Andreae, Georg Norman, brothers Olaus and Laurentius Petri, and Nicholaus Stecker had attended Wittenberg University, and on returning home, proclaimed and secured the Reformation message and praxis. Moreover, in Finland, the Reformers Mikael Agricola and Paavali Juusten, who had studied at Wittenberg, promoted the Finnish Reformation and literature. In spreading the Reformation teaching, contemporaries of Luther had to interpret what it meant to be in the Wittenberg circle in their own ministry contexts. Nonetheless, these highly educated men shared a common commitment to spread Luther's ideas of what it meant to follow Christ in word and deed.

ROYAL SPONSORSHIP AND REJECTION OF CATHOLICISM

The practical and economic aspects of Protestantism helped foster the new Lutheran teaching launched from the biblical humanism of Wittenberg University by skilled graduate preachers. Without the toleration of the state, though, the Reformation would have seen little progress in northern Europe. Government leaders played an important role in declaring

Wittenberg theology by allowing the Reformation canon time and space to develop. However, the Scandinavian states wanted to discard papal dominance, and in the case of Sweden, the power of the Danish Crown. In the process, northern Europe shifted towards Protestantism, and severed all relations with the pope. In doing so, nationalism suppressed the Catholic Church's power and stole its possessions. The result was a theological, social, and physical separation that still rages today in many regions of the world.

Reformers who had studied at Wittenberg promptly carried the ideas of Luther into Scandinavia with the support of the Oldenburg monarchy in Denmark: beginning with the irresolute King Christian II, the progressive despot, followed by the Reformation rumblings during the reign of Frederik I, and finally Christian III, completing the Lutheran Reformation.

Gustav Vasa in Sweden protected and promoted the Wittenberg Lutherans as long as they were willing to submit to his royal authority. In Finland, the conservative Lutheran Reformers cooperated with King Vasa, and the Reformation slowly seeped into the Finnish church and society with the backing of Vasa's Catholic Reform-minded bishops such as Skytte and Sunesson.

PEASANT SUPPORT AND REBELLIOUS UPRISINGS

Wherever the Wittenberg preachers extended Luther's Reformation, they relied heavily on popular support. The movement's creed of egalitarianism between clergy and laity, and the desire for gospel preaching and services in the vernacular, entwined with widespread social dissatisfaction with royal and Roman hierarchy. A succession of peasant rebellions and a major civil war from 1524 to 1542, had dominated events in Denmark and Sweden. Economic hardships and dissatisfaction with church governance were the origin of these uprisings, though the growing tension between the contemporary Reformation and the medieval papacy served as a catalytic agent. The peasants of northern Europe demanded a social reorganization in the areas of education, social welfare for the poor, and health care, misunderstanding the Wittenberg message of the priesthood of all believers as a rejection of the existing social and political order.

During the reign of Frederik I, the Lutheran movement began to advance in Denmark empowered by the feudal crisis within Danish society.

Tast preached Reformation teaching in Husum, Denmark, with such a keen response from the people that he shifted from a merchant's private home to the town's market square. Throughout the Swedish Reforms, the popular cause of Protestantism was strongest in the urban centers. In rural Sweden, Vasa had to contend with continuing and multiple uprisings before 1540, as the populace, sponsored by the Catholic priests, primarily objected to excessive royal taxes.

INFORMATION DISTRIBUTION

The Wittenberg Reformation in Europe used the printed word to promote its message. C. S. Lewis gives perspective to the importance of publications: "The Reformation was a process that occurred on three planes: firstly, in the thought and conscience of the individual, secondly in the intertangled realms of ecclesiastical and political activity, and thirdly on the printed page."[55] The Johannes Gutenberg printing press of 1436 led the way for a wave of printed books in Europe. This ingenious invention also gave rise to the fame of the German priest and professor of theology who started the Protestant Reformation since Gutenberg's invention catapulted his preaching across Europe and Scandinavia. Martin Luther was the first rock star of the age of printing. "The Reformation could not have occurred as it did without print," writes Andrew Pettegree. "Print propelled Martin Luther, a man who had published nothing in the first 30 years of his life, to an instant celebrity. In the process he changed Western religion and European society forever."[56]

The Reformation movement spread rapidly aided by the dissemination of Protestant views throughout Denmark, Sweden, and Finland. The Wittenberg Reformers in northern Europe not only used preaching, but also the printed page to transform society. The printing press was the mechanism that propelled Wittenberg teaching via theological writings, Bible translations, and Church Articles and Orders.

---

55. C. S. Lewis, *English Literature in the Sixteenth Century: Excluding Drama* (Oxford: Clarendon Press, 1954), 157.

56. Andrew Pettegree, *Brand Luther: How an Unheralded Monk Turned His Small Town into a Center of Publishing, Made Himself the Most Famous Man in Europe—and Started the Protestant Reformation* (New York: Penguin Press, 2015), 11–12.

Theological Writings

Tausen and Sadolin in Denmark published adaptations of Luther's pamphlets from the Viborg printing press. Peder Palladius wrote Reformation theological materials designed for the common people to understand about the application of Lutheran teaching for various life situations, which enjoyed wide readership throughout Scandinavia and Germany. Neil Palladius, Peder's brother, wrote over twenty books teaching the lessons of Wittenberg in Danish, Icelandic, and Latin. This included a guide for Danish pastors, which helped direct the organization and practice of the Lutheran churches. Niels Hemmingsen, a Danish contemporary of the Palladius brothers, and a Wittenberg graduate, modelled in his writings the ethics of the Christian life and practice for the fledgling Protestant church of Denmark.

Olaus Petri dominated the Swedish book market. He published sixteen books in the decade between 1530 and 1540 bringing Wittenberg theology to the Swedish people. His numerous writings assisted in the transformation of the Swedish liturgy, and the acceptance of services in the vernacular. He published devotional books, polemical writings opposing the Catholic tradition, and a liturgical manual for a Swedish mass and catechism. Additionally, he translated Luther's works into Swedish and edited vernacular hymnals.

In Reformation Finland, Mikael Agricola brought Wittenberg theology and practice to the churches. His writings and translations not only promoted Luther's ideas, but also the Finnish language, and helped guide Lutheran pastoral practice and preaching. Agricola translated the liturgical works of Olaus Petri, Luther, and Melanchthon that shaped Finnish Lutheran worship. While attending Wittenberg University, he published Finnish liturgical books with Luther's theology, the ministerial topics of Olaus Petri, and the teachings of Johannes Bugenhagen, heavily influencing the contents.

Bible Translations

Luther's missional strategy included his interest in Bible translation—again through the impact of the printing press. Luther's Bible was not the first German translation, but by using the common language of the people, he standardized the vernacular, which fostered nationalism. His translation quickly became the most widely circulated. Luther's German

Bible became the template to follow as other European nations translated the Scriptures into their languages—a translation that formed the basis of the Danish, Finnish, Icelandic, Norwegian, and Swedish versions.

The most celebrated of Peder Palladius's writing projects was his translation of the Latin Bible into Danish, which Christian III encouraged every Lutheran church to obtain a copy. Andreae and the Petri brothers published a Swedish New Testament following Luther's German version. Olaus Petri shadowed with a Swedish translation of the Old Testament. Olaus in collaboration with his brother Laurentius, and Andreae, eventually translated the entire Bible into Swedish, known as the Gustav Vasa Bible.

Agricola produced a translation of the New Testament into Finnish using Luther's German, Erasmus's Latin, and Olaus Petri's Swedish translations. When he began his New Testament translation, there was no standard written form of the Finnish language. Thus, he started developing one. In addition, he initiated an Old Testament translation, including the Psalms of David.

Church Articles and Orders

Another important aspect of the Reformation information distribution was the publication of Church Articles and Orders that guided the Scandinavian churches in Lutheran theology and practice. Christian III of Denmark presented the Haderslev Articles that instructed Reformation pastors how to preach, practice, and live the Lutheran faith. At the Diet of Copenhagen, Lutheran pastors produced the "Forty-three Articles," which outlined their Protestant beliefs, and became popular with the people. Tausen drafted the first Lutheran Church Ordinance, and adopted Philipp Melanchthon's Augsburg Confession as the normative of Danish Lutheran theology. Moreover, the Swede Laurentius Petri authored an exposition of the creeds and the Christian life that served as a Lutheran catechism.

CONCLUSION

The development of Reformation Scandinavia was an interlocking of Wittenberg's theology and practice with a complex array of historical events. The catalytic change agents of the Scandinavian Reformation in the midst of this complexity, however, were the Christian graduates of Wittenberg University who promoted Martin Luther's revolutionary teaching.

BIBLIOGRAPHY

Andersen, N. K. "The Reformation in Scandinavia and the Baltic." In *The Reformation (1520–1559)*, edited by Geoffrey Rudolph Elton, 144–71. The New Cambridge Modern History, vol. 2, 2nd ed. Cambridge: Cambridge University Press, 2008.

Anderson, Justice. "An Overview of Missiology." In *Missiology: An Introduction to the Foundations, History, and Strategies of World Missions*, 2nd ed., edited by John Mark Terry, 3–18. Nashville: B&H Publishing, 2015.

Atkinson, James. *Martin Luther: Prophet to the Church Catholic*. Grand Rapids: Eerdmans, 1983.

Bain, R. Nisbet. *Scandinavia: A Political History of Denmark, Norway, and Sweden, from 1513 to 1900*. Cambridge: Cambridge University Press, 1905.

Bergendoff, C. *Olavus and the Ecclesiastical Transformation in Sweden (1521–1552): A Study in the Swedish Reformation*. New York: The Macmillan Company, 1928.

Bosch, David J. *Transforming Mission: Paradigm Shifts in Theology of Mission*. Maryknoll, NY: Orbis Books, 1991.

Brown, William. *The History of Mission: Or, of the Propagation of Christianity Among the Heathen, Since the Reformation*. Vol. 1. Philadelphia: McCarty & Davis, 1820.

Bunkowske, Eugene W. "Was Luther a Missionary?" *Concordia Theological Quarterly* 49 (April–June 1985): 161–79.

Burnett, Amy Nelson. "Communion Preparation in the Early Years of the Reformation." In *From Wittenberg to the World*, edited by Charles P. Arand, Erik H. Herrmann, and Daniel L. Mattson, 60–67. Göttingen: Vandenhoeck and Ruprecht, 2018.

Cardoza-Orlandi, Carlos F., and Justo L. González. *To All Nations from All Nations: A History of the Christian Missionary Movement*. Nashville: Abingdon Press, 2013.

Coates, Thomas. "Were the Reformers Mission-Minded?" *Concordia Theological Monthly* 40 (October 1969): 600–11.

Dunkley, E. *The Reformation in Denmark*. London: SPCK, 1948.

Elert, Werner. *The Structure of Lutheranism*. Translated by W. A. Hansen. St. Louis: Concordia, 1962.

Flöystrup, C. E. "The Church in Denmark." *Church Quarterly Review* 64 (April–July 1907): 80–104.

Forsander, Nils. *Olavus Petri: The Church Reformer of Sweden.* Rock Island, IL: Augustana Book Concern, 1918.

Gallagher, Robert L. "Encountering Reformation Missions." In *Encountering the History of Missions: From the Early Church to Today,* Robert L. Gallagher and John Mark Terry, 130–49. Encountering Missions Series. Grand Rapids: Baker Academic, 2017.

———. "Historic Models of Teaching Christian Mission: Case Studies Informing an Age of World Christianity." In *Teaching Christian Mission in an Age of World Christianity,* edited by Robert A. Danielson and Linda F. Whitmer, 127–50. Association of Professors of Mission Series. Wilmore, KY: First Fruits Press, 2017.

Grane, Leif. "Teaching the People: The Education of the Clergy and the Instruction of the People in the Danish Reformation Church." In *The Danish Reformation against Its International Background,* edited by Herausgegeben von Leif Grane and Kai Hørby, 164–76. Göttingen: Vandenhoeck & Ruprecht, 1990.

Grell, Ole Peter. "Scandinavia." In *The Reformation World,* edited by Andrew Pettegree, 257–76. London: Routledge, 2000.

———. "Scandinavia." In *The Reformation in National Context,* edited by Bob Scribner, Roy Porter, and Mikuláš Teich, 111–30. Cambridge: Cambridge University Press, 1994.

———. "Scandinavia." In *The Early Reformation in Europe,* edited by Andrew Pettegree, 94–119. Cambridge: Cambridge University Press, 1992.

Grindel, Gracia. "The Rhetoric of Martin Luther's Hymns: Hymnody Then and Now." *Word & World* 26 (Spring 2006): 178–87.

Gritsch, Eric W. *A History of Lutheranism.* Minneapolis: Augsburg Fortress, 2002.

Guicharrousse, H. *Les Musiques de Luther.* Geneva: Labor et Fides, 1995.

Kane, J. Herbert. *A Concise History of the Christian World Missions: A Panoramic View of Missions from Pentecost to the Present.* Rev. ed. Grand Rapids: Baker, 1982.

Kolb, Robert. *Luther's Wittenberg World: The Reformer's Family, Friends, Followers, and Foes.* Minneapolis: Fortress Press, 2018.

Koschade, Alfred. "Luther on Missionary Motivation." *Lutheran Quarterly* 17 (August 1965): 224–39.

Lausten, Martin Schwarz. "Luther and the Reformation in Denmark." In *Luther After 1530: Theology, Church, and Politics*, edited by Helmar Junghans, 115–30. Göttingen: Vandenhoeck & Ruprecht, 2005.

———. "Hans Tausen." In *The Oxford Encyclopedia of the Reformation*, edited by Hans J. Hillerbrand, 1451. Vol. 4. New York: Oxford University Press, 1996.

———. "The Early Reformation in Denmark and Norway, 1520–1559." In *The Scandinavian Reformation: From Evangelical Movement to Institutionalisation of Reform*, edited by Ole Peter Grell, 12–41. Cambridge: Cambridge University Press, 1995.

Lewis, C. S. *English Literature in the Sixteenth Century: Excluding Drama.* Oxford: Clarendon Press, 1954.

Lindquist, C. R. *Remonking the Church.* PhD diss., Fuller Theological Seminary, 1990.

Lockhart, Paul Douglas. *Denmark, 1513–1660: The Rise and Decline of a Renaissance Monarchy.* Oxford: Oxford University Press, 2007.

Lohse, Bernhard. *Martin Luther's Theology: Its Historical and Systematic Development.* Minneapolis: Fortress Press, 1999.

Luther, Martin. *Luther's Works: Liturgy and Hymns.* Vol. 53. Philadelphia: Fortress Press, 1965.

———. *The Table Talk of Martin Luther.* London: George Bell & Sons, 1884.

Mulholland, Kenneth B. "From Luther to Carey: Pietism and the Modern Missionary Movement." *Bibliotheca Sacra* 156 (January–March 1999): 85–95.

Neill, Stephen, and Owen Chadwick. *A History of Christian Missions.* 2nd ed. New York: Viking Penguin, 1986.

Ocker, Christopher. *Luther, Conflict, and Christendom: Reformation Europe and Christianity in the West.* Cambridge: Cambridge University Press, 2018.

Peters, Paul. "Luther's Practical Mission-Mindedness." *Wisconsin Lutheran Quarterly* 66 (April 1969): 116–22.

Pettegree, Andrew. *Brand Luther: How an Unheralded Monk Turned His Small Town into a Center of Publishing, Made Himself the Most Famous Man in Europe—and Started the Protestant Reformation.* New York: Penguin Press, 2015.

Pierson, Paul E. *The Dynamics of Christian Mission: History through a Missiological Perspective.* Pasadena, CA: William Carey International University Press, 2009.

Plass, Ewald M. *What Luther Says: An Anthology.* Vol. 2. St. Louis: Concordia, 1959.

Robbins, Jerry K., ed. *The Essential Luther: A Reader on Scripture, Redemption, and Society.* Grand Rapids: Baker Books, 1991.

Sanneh, Lamin. *Translating the Message: The Missionary Impact on Culture.* 2nd ed. Maryknoll, NY: Orbis Books, 2009.

Schalk, Carl F. "Martin Luther's Hymns Today." *Hymns* 34 (July 1983): 130–33.

Scherer, James A. "Luther and Mission: A Rich but Untested Potential." *Missio Apostolica: Journal of the Lutheran Society for Missiology* 2 (May 1994): 17–24.

Schwiebert, Ernest G. *Luther and His Times.* St. Louis: Concordia, 1950.

Senn, Frank C. *Christian Liturgy: Catholic and Evangelical.* Minneapolis: Augsburg Fortress, 1997.

Sider, Ronald J. *Karlstadt's Battle with Luther: Documents in a Liberal-Radical Debate.* Philadelphia: Augsburg Fortress Press, 1978.

———. *Andreas Bodenstein von Karlstadt: The Development of His Thought, 1517–1525.* Studies in Medieval and Reformation Thought, edited by Heiko A. Oberman. Vol. 11. Leiden: E. J. Brill, 1974.

Skarsten, Trygve R. *The Scandinavian Reformation: A Bibliographical Guide.* St. Louis: Center for Reformation Research, 1985.

Skreslet, Stanley H. *Comprehending Mission: The Questions, Methods, Themes, Problems, and Prospects of Missiology.* Maryknoll, NY: Orbis Books, 2012.

Stolle, Volker. *The Church Comes from All Nations.* Translated by K. Schulz. St. Louis: Concordia Academic Press, 2003.

Swihart, Altman K. *Luther and the Lutheran Church (1483–1960).* London: Peter Owen, 1960.

te Brake, Wayne. *Shaping History: Ordinary People in European Politics, 1500–1700.* Berkeley, CA: University of California Press, 1998.

Thomas, Norman E., ed. *Classic Texts in Mission and World Christianity.* Maryknoll, NY: Orbis Books, 1995.

Tucker, Ruth A. *From Jerusalem to Irian Jaya: A Biographical History of Christian Missions.* 2nd ed. Grand Rapids: Zondervan, 2004.

Valleskey, David J. "Luther's Impact on Mission Work." *Wisconsin Lutheran Quarterly* 92 (April 1995): 96–123.

Woodward, R. *Piæ Cantiones: A Collection of Church and School Song.* London: Chiswick Press, 1910.

Wuorinen, J. *A History of Finland.* New York: Columbia University Press, 1965.

Zorzin, Alejandro. "Andreas Bodenstein von Karlstadt (1486–1541)." In *The Reformation Theologians: An Introduction to Theology in the Early Modern Period*, edited by Carter Lindberg, 327–37. Oxford: Blackwell, 2002.

4
—

FRENCH REFORMED MISSION BEFORE CALVIN 1515–1535

Garry Austin

Although France outlawed Lutheranism in 1521, some French Christians recognized Martin Luther as the "German Hercules" who wrestled with the papacy.[1] These reform-oriented French believers were not strictly Lutherans, or even followers of Luther, although the Roman Catholic authorities quickly labelled them as such. Through the study of Scripture and observations of the state of the established church, these individuals reached similar conclusions to Luther, which were confirmed when they purchased and read his works, as well as those of Zwingli and others. They included members of the royal court, humanist scholars, Catholic monks, merchants, artisans, and laborers, but these evangelical believers were united in their convictions that the Bible was true and trustworthy, that salvation was found in Christ alone through faith, and that the teachings, rituals, and hierarchy of the Catholic Church had moved people away from the truth.[2] While some remained within the Roman Catholic Church, others rejected the papacy completely and actively protested against its excesses.

---

1. In Jonathan A. Reid, *King's Sister, Queen of Dissent: Marguerite of Navarre (1492–1549) and Her Evangelical Network* (Leiden: Brill, 2009), 249. This is taken from a poem by Nicolas Bourbon, first published in 1530.

2. Ibid., 37. Reid, and many French Reformation authors, use the term "evangelical" to refer to this group of French Christians. Reid credits French historian, Pierre Imbert de la Tour (1914) with developing a systematic categorization among religious believers of this era. R. J. Knecht (1982), for example, stated that "evangelical preachers were increasingly active" in 1523 (143). Jean-Henri Merle d'Aubigne used "evangelical" throughout his *History of the Great Reformation in the Sixteenth-Century in Germany, Switzerland, etc.* (1851).

By the start of the Wars of Religion in 1562, up to 10 percent of France had become Protestant, gathering in 2,150 Reformed churches, some with congregations of over 10,000, despite decades of severe persecution.[3] Most histories, if they mention these results at all, attribute them almost exclusively to John Calvin, despite the fact that he arrived late on the scene and escaped from France soon after his conversion. Geoffrey Treasure, for example, attributes the development of the French Protestant church mostly "to Calvin, the haven at Geneva for French refugees, and the missionary enterprise launched from that city."[4] Jason Zuidema laments that "several centuries of history ... have lionized Calvin."[5]

By looking beyond Luther and Calvin, this chapter seeks to introduce other key people and the events and processes which helped to contribute to the growth of French Protestantism. There was a significant French evangelical mission which began in the period from 1515 to 1535. It was truly a mission to promote faith in the gospel according to the Bible, not an internal reform of the Catholic Church from the inside. Many members of the movement came to similar conclusions to their German counterparts that the Catholic Church hierarchy was an antichrist system, a dominant deception.[6] They believed that France had fallen into darkness and that they had the responsibility to be bearers of the gospel light. Reform and translation efforts preceded Luther's rise to fame in Paris around 1520 and led to the formation of the "Circle of Meaux" in the early 1520s. Their activities and ideas spread across France and into neighboring French-speaking Swiss cantons. With the growing harvest came increasing arrests and executions, leading to events which disrupted the evangelical community, and caused many Reform-minded believers, including the newly converted John Calvin, to flee from France.

---

3. Mark Greengrass, *The French Reformation* (Oxford: Blackwell, 1987), 43.

4. Geoffrey Treasure, *The Huguenots* (New Haven: Yale University Press, 2013), 1.

5. Jason Zuidema, "Guillaume Farel in Early French Reform," in *Early French Reform: The Spirituality of Guillaume Farel*, ed. Jason Zuidema and Theodore Van Raalte (Farnham: Routledge, 2011), 3.

6. Ibid, 117–79. An excellent starting point for understanding French evangelical belief and vision is *A Summary and Brief Exposition*, written by William Farel, originally in 1525. See the translation of the 1529/1534 editions by Jason Zuidema in *Early French Reform: The Spirituality of Guillaume Farel*, ed. Jason Zuidema and Theodore Van Raalte (Farnham: Routledge, 2011), 117–79. See pages 135–37 on attitudes to the mass; or pages 145–48, for teaching about the adoration of saints, and about the pope and the Catholic system.

FRENCH EVANGELICAL MISSION
BEFORE LUTHER

Scholars across Paris read Luther's ideas and actions as early as 1518, and students read and discussed them widely by 1520.[7] Without question, though, a recognition of the need for reform in France preceded Luther's influence. At the turn of the century, Jan Standonck was directing a strong Reform agenda at the College de Montaigu in the University of Paris, however his attempts at national church reform failed due to lack of state support.[8] Of greater significance was his student, Erasmus of Rotterdam, who began studying theology in Paris in 1495. His interest in ancient texts turned scholarly attention to the message of biblical and early Christianity.[9] An advocate of reform within the Catholic Church, Erasmus never joined the ranks of the evangelicals, but provided a great service in publishing his annotated Greek New Testament in Basel in 1516.[10]

The thought leader of the French gospel mission was the biblical humanist, Jacques Lefevre d'Etaples, who had been a professor at College de Lemoine at the University of Paris. Lefevre's literary reputation attracted many scholars to the university and from them came many leaders for the evangelical mission. Publishers profited as they disseminated his views widely, and Lefevre communicated personally with many others on the cusp of reform. Two of his published works were of particular importance in launching the Reformation in Germany. His Christ-centered commentary on Psalms (1509) and his commentary on the Epistles of Paul (1512). In the preface of the latter, Lefevre reveals his hope that recent New World conquests "were opening new avenues for preaching the gospel."[11] Luther quoted Lefevre in his Wittenberg lectures on Romans in 1515, one year before the annotated Greek New Testament of Erasmus appeared.[12] These texts guided Luther to his convictions on justification by faith.

---

7. Lucien Febvre and Henri-Jean Martin, *The Coming of the Book: The Impact of Printing 1450–1800*, trans. Henry-Jean Martin (London: Verso Editions, 1984), 296. See also Reid, 20, where it is noted that Lefevre sent greetings to Luther as early as 1519.

8. R. J. Knecht, *Francis I* (New York: Cambridge University Press), 133.

9. Ibid., 135.

10. Anthony Levi, *Renaissance and Reformation: The Intellectual Genesis* (New Haven: Yale University Press, 2002), 251.

11. Reid, *King's Sister*, 116.

12. Vivian H.H. Green, *Luther and the Reformation* (New York: Capricorn Books, 1964), 46.

Beyond writing, however, Lefevre gathered and taught many of the men who became the leaders of French reform. One future Reformer converted at this time was Guillaume Farel, to whom Lefevre reportedly said, "God will renew the world, and you will see it."[13] Farel moved from zealous Catholic devotion to vehement rejection of "diabolical" papal teaching. Through Lefevre's influence, God's Word and purpose became his all-consuming passion.[14] This strong emotion would fuel his reform efforts and guide his own writing.

Another student of Lefevre, Guillaume Briconnet, the bishop of Meaux, was instrumental in making space for a gospel mission within the French Catholic Church. In 1517, he surveyed his diocese and discovered that "the people neither knew nor loved the faith enough to live better lives" due to clergy absenteeism, ignorance, and preference for alms collection over spiritual education.[15] As early as 1519, Paris scholar, Pierre Richard commended Briconnet for his scheme of thirty-two preaching circuits, involving "secular clergymen—the best and the brightest ... of the University of Paris, hasten from town to town and castle to castle, dispersing the gospel throughout your diocese, not seeking their own profit but that of Jesus Christ."[16] At this time, it seemed a model of Catholic Reform. Lefevre and his group may have already been engaged in this work from Paris, but Briconnet would soon call them to work directly in Meaux.

The internal reform efforts of Lefevre and Briconnet were soon provided with a different model. In February 1519, Basel publisher Johann Froben informed Luther that he had printed and sent 600 copies of his works to France and Spain.[17] The flood of subsequent material flowing from Wittenberg stirred great interest among publishers and booksellers in the humanist network, who became significant players in the French Reformation.[18] Letters from Paris to Basel and Wittenberg suggested a very positive French reception of Luther's works. Even the University of Paris

---

13. William Maxwell Blackburn, *William Farel and the Story of the Swiss Reform,* new ed. (Edinburgh: William Oliphant and Co., 1877), 34.

14. Farel quoted in Zuidema, "Guillaume Farel in Early French Reform," 8.

15. Quoted in Reid, *King's Sister,* 160.

16. Paris scholar, Pierre Richard to Briconnet in ibid., 163.

17. Knecht, *Francis I,* 140.

18. Febvre and Martin, *The Coming of the Book,* 296.

Theology Faculty, the Sorbonne, initially welcomed Luther's attacks on the much-hated indulgences.[19] Most importantly, Luther's works were read by Lefevre's circle and this strengthened their resolve to promote gospel teaching. Published books, tracts, placards, and letters all became vital instruments of mission in the coming years.

A FRENCH REFORM MOVEMENT
IGNITES (1520-1525)

The mood changed quickly in Paris. The Sorbonne condemned Luther's doctrines as heretical in April 1521, and the *Parlement* of Paris outlawed his works.[20] They also condemned Lefevre, whose Christian humanist opinions challenged accepted traditions.[21] They banned all new unauthorized theological or scriptural writings, announcing these laws with trumpets, imposing fines and threatening imprisonment. Nonetheless, they struggled to enforce such laws.[22] In this environment, a clandestine network developed which continued to translate, publish, and disseminate works considered "offensive to the Catholic faith" throughout Paris and across France.[23]

These publications bore widespread fruit quickly following the paths of the already flourishing book trade. Far from Paris, Boniface Amerbach, son of the Basel printworks founder, was completing his doctorate in the southern papal enclave of Avignon.[24] Amerbach requested that Froben send him "news and pamphlets of the German and Swiss reformers ... to pass on to his eager friends in Avignon."[25] One Franciscan preacher in that city, Francois Lambert, was reading Luther's works but fled to Wittenberg when his peers reported him. As he traveled, other Reformers accommodated him and helped to consolidate his reformed doctrine, including Huldrych

---

19. Knecht, *Francis I*, 140.

20. Reid, *King's Sister*, 20. The French word *parlement* denotes a supreme court. There were several of these in various parts of France. They had authority to set laws and were sometimes used to advise the king.

21. Jonathan Arnold, *The Great Humanists: An Introduction* (New York: I.B. Tauris, 2011), 219.

22. Febvre and Martin, *The Coming of the Book*, 297.

23. Knecht, *Francis I*, 142.

24. Earle Hilgert, "Johann Froben and the Basel University Scholars, 1513-1523," in *The Library Quarterly* 41, no. 2 (1971): 145.

25. Amerbach to Froben in Greengrass, *The French Reformation*, 1.

Zwingli, who he disputed against in July 1521.[26] In Wittenberg, Lambert and two other French converts, Anemond de Coct and Claude de Tauro, formulated "ambitious plans to promote the evangelical movement in Savoy, France, and Italy."[27] They soon met French refugees in Hamburg with a printing press and access to ships bound for France.[28] At Lambert's request, Luther found him a position in Strasbourg, and also sent de Coct with missional letters to the duke of Savoy and to the French court.[29]

Meanwhile, the reform efforts of Briconnet were taking shape. Meaux, just outside Paris, has been referred to as both the "cradle" and "springboard" of the French Reformation.[30] In fact, it was more like a powder keg with a very short wick. Briconnet asked Lefevre for help to overcome clergy resistance to his reforms. As anti-Lutheran sparks continued to fly in Paris, Lefevre moved his carefully chosen, highly educated mission team to Meaux. Among them were "Michel d'Arande, Gerard Roussel, Guillaume Farel, Pierre Caroli, Martial Mazurier, and Francois Vatable, all of whom were open in varying degrees to the new doctrines and would go on to play leading roles in the religious controversies of the next thirty years."[31]

According to Lefevre, the goals of their program were "to know the gospel, to follow the gospel, and to proclaim the gospel everywhere."[32] Under the leadership of Lefevre and the patronage of Briconnet, they preached in the cathedral and churches, and in the market places of the 32 circuits. They read the works of the German Reformers, wrote new works, translated the New Testament into French, and taught and distributed copies to the laity across the diocese to support the preaching work.[33] Getting the Bible to the people was their priority goal and achievement. In Meaux, they encouraged the people who could to "read the gospel at

---

26. Pietro Delcorno, "Between Pulpit and Reformation: The Confessions of Francois Lambert" in *Franciscan Studies* 71 (2013): 123.

27. Reid, *King's Sister*, 255. See also Blackburn, *William Farel*, 83.

28. Jean Henri Merle d'Aubigne, *History of the Reformation of the Sixteenth Century*, trans. Henry White (New York: Robert Carter & Brothers, 1851), 461.

29. Reid, *King's Sister*, 256.

30. David Nicholls, "France," in *The Early Reformation in Europe*, ed. Andrew Pettegree (Cambridge: Cambridge University Press), 123.

31. Reid, *King's Sister*, 20.

32. Ibid., Quoting from the preface of Jacques Lefevre d'Etaples, 1522 Latin *Introductory Commentary of the Four Gospels*.

33. Reid, *King's Sister*, 20.

home, ponder it, then come and listen to a preacher's exposition giving the correct interpretation."[34] This method reached local garment industry workers, and harvest workers from across France who "went home with the gospel in their hearts" and began Bible groups in rural areas like Landouzy, north of Paris.[35] Across France, these New Testaments soon "penetrated into obscure hamlets to which no missionary of the 'new doctrines' could find access."[36]

ROYAL SUPPORT FOR THE GOSPEL MISSION

In June 1521, just two months after the *parlement* condemned and banned Luther's works, Briconnet gained an important ally, Marguerite d'Angouleme, sister of King Francis I, and the future Queen of Navarre (r. 1527–1549). Although only twenty-seven at the time, she played an active role in introducing evangelical ideas to the royal court and in gaining court support for a national church reform program based on the gospel-focused teaching of Lefevre and the administrative strategies of Briconnet. Marguerite corresponded with Briconnet on a wide range of topics but *le doctrine evangelique* was at the center of their concerns.[37] As part of his spiritual guidance, in a February 1522 letter, he urged Marguerite to "become Captain [of our band] so that others will be inspired to enter into the Promised Land."[38]

Despite royal patronage, complaints about "Lutheran" preaching in Meaux soon reached *parlement*. In April 1523, Briconnet, who had sponsored the distribution of Scripture portions, was forced to impose restrictions on the preachers. In October 1523, he published criticisms of Luther for his rejection of the ecclesiastical hierarchy.[39] His reform influence con-

34. David J. Nicholls, "The Nature of Popular Heresy in France, 1520–1542," in *The Historical Journal* 26, no. 2 (1983): 267.

35. Blackburn, *William Farel*, 68.

36. Henry Martyn Baird, *History of the Rise of the Huguenots: Vol. 1, S. 1* (London: Hodder and Stoughton, 1880), 79.

37. Reid, *King's Sister*, 191. See also page 37, note 3, on the sixteenth-century use of the term *evangelique*.

38. Ibid., 186.

39. Ibid., 203–4.

sequently began to wane, but, as Reid notes, "Marguerite pushed forward," committed "to an ever more assertive reform program."[40]

ARRESTS AND EXECUTIONS AND THE FURTHERANCE OF THE GOSPEL

Historical records of arrests and executions allow us to gauge the widespread influence of evangelicals, and occasionally to glimpse their mission strategies, and the types of people reached. One famous case is of Louis de Berquin, a nobleman serving the king and the humanist cause, who had been collecting and translating the works of Erasmus, Luther, and other Reformers, making these available to the royal court and to the public. He was seized in May 1523 along with his library and his own reform-oriented writings. Among his charges were that he had encouraged the evangelical movement in the northern city of Amiens.[41] Marguerite pleaded with her brother, the king, who ordered him released. Meanwhile, authorities arrested a friend of Lefevre, Jean Guibert, an Augustine hermit of the Livry forests near Meaux. Before his arrest, he had been going door to door in the peasant villages promoting the gospel and "the perfect pardon that it offers to the burdened soul."[42] His freedom came after a four-year trial, which ended with a much-celebrated not-guilty verdict.[43] Another Augustine monk, Jean Valliere, was not so fortunate, dying in a public burning on August 8, 1523, near Notre Dame in Paris. Authorities made an example of him for "conniving with 'the party of the heretic Luther,' and for reading and commenting on Lutheran books"—possibly translations by Berquin.[44] Inevitably, despite royal protection, and a series of arrests and releases, Berquin, who was greatly favored by Marguerite, would eventually give his final testimony in April 1529 "before a crowd of 20,000 onlookers."[45]

---

40. Ibid., 185.
41. Ibid., 79.
42. Merle d'Aubigne, *History of the Reformation*, 488.
43. Reid, *King's Sister*, 354.
44. Ganoczy, *The Young Calvin* (Philadelphia: Westminster Press, 1987), 49.
45. Reid, *King's Sister*, 365.

GUILLAUME FAREL AND THE
NAVARRE NETWORK

Not everyone chose to stay in such an environment. Guillaume Farel, an outspoken member of Lefevre's team in Meaux and a professor of philosophy and rector of the College of Cardinal Lemoine in Paris, had contributed to the reputation of both places as centres "of Lutheran heresy."[46] In April 1523, Farel rejected the restrictions that Briconnet had imposed on the preachers of Meaux. Traveling through the south of France on his way to Switzerland, he preached in his hometown of Gap and brought his brothers, Daniel, Walter, and Claude, into the Reformation.[47] Farel also won the afore-mentioned Anemond de Coct, a knight and brother of the lord of Chartelard; and, a respected Franciscan preacher, Pierre Sebiville in Grenoble.[48] While de Coct proceeded to Wittenberg and met Lambert, Sebiville stayed and preached in Grenoble. When Farel arrived in Basel, Switzerland, in January 1524, he received a letter from Lefevre in Meaux, which said, "You have wisely distanced yourself from those who wish us evil, to take up residence among true Christians."[49] He reports that the common people of Meaux, since receiving the French New Testaments, "had become so avid for the word of God that they would now rather suffer anything than be deprived of it."[50] Farel's arrival in Basel was anything but secretive. In February, he staged a successful public disputation supported by the Basel Reformer, Johannes Oecolampadius.[51]

Strategically, Farel's arrival in Basel connected the evangelical leaders of Meaux, the German-speaking Reformers, and the French refugees, such as Lambert and de Coct, into an enduring international solidarity of about one hundred individuals and their followers, which Reid calls the "Navarre Network."[52] Farel would actively pursue the furtherance of the Reformation in French-speaking Swiss cantons. He would be active in corresponding and publishing. The French refugees in Basel, meanwhile,

---

46. Ibid., 299.
47. Merle d'Aubigne, *History of the Reformation*, 464.
48. Ibid., 422.
49. Reid, *King's Sister*, 260.
50. Ibid., 261.
51. Blackburn, *William Farel*, 92–93.
52. Reid, *King's Sister*, 257.

"formed an evangelical society in Switzerland with the view of rescuing their country from its spiritual darkness" and gathered intelligence from across France.[53] In cities far and wide, they promoted secret church groups, or conventicles.[54]

The work of mission was achieved through the efforts of many. De Coct, for example, helped to connect the French royal court, particularly Antoine Papillon, with Zwingli in Zurich. Lambert was now based in Strasbourg, but in 1526 became the professor of theology at the new University of Marburg. These French Reformers-in-exile began writing and publishing tracts in French and translating the works of others, well supported by their German-speaking hosts.[55] Early printed works included Farel's booklet on *The Lord's Prayer and the Creed*, in August 1524.[56]

Despite facing many opponents, Farel played a leading role in furthering the Reformation among Swiss French speakers. Much of his ministry involved the strategic use of conflict. Even in Basel, Farel conflicted with Erasmus who demanded his expulsion from that city. At that time, Oecolampadius laid his hands on Farel and commissioned him to preach in the nearby French dukedom of Montbeliard.[57] This tough assignment proved to be a training ground for Farel.

Letters to Farel in July 1524 demonstrate how the reports of his missionary efforts encouraged those remaining in France. Lefevre was exultant about what he had heard: "Christ is spread through a good part of Europe by dint of a pure understanding. And I hope that Christ will visit this blessing on our France. Let Christ hear our prayers and victory would favour our works everywhere from the very beginning."[58]

---

53. Merle d'Aubigne, *History of the Reformation*, 474. Included in this group at various times were Farel, de Coct, Lambert, Michel Bentin, Nicolas d'Esch, and Pierre Toussain, both from Metz, Antoine Du Blet, a merchant, and Jean Vaugris, the printer, both from Lyon. Each of these is known to have traveled extensively.

54. Ibid., 308.

55. Reid, *King's Sister*, 255.

56. Greengrass, *The French Reformation*, 13.

57. Reid, *King's Sister*, 281.

58. Henry Heller, "Reform and Reformers at Meaux 1518–1525" (PhD diss., Cornell University, 1969), 308.

Gerard Roussell had been the cathedral preacher in Meaux and was a close confidant of Lefevre and Marguerite. His letter to Farel shows clear understanding of the missionary imperative:

> The simple and ignorant are leaders of the Christian restoration. ... It already renews the time in which the Gospel is carried forward by the downcast seeing as they will be sent throughout the whole world just as the poor apostles were sent out to the world at the beginning of Christianity.[59]

Roussel requested Farel's help in obtaining printing equipment for Meaux to make "greater and more effective use of the printed page to help disseminate evangelical ideas."[60]

LEADERSHIP AND LITERATURE HELP
THE GOSPEL INFLUENCE SPREAD

Meanwhile, Marguerite in France began to coordinate appointments of key network members to spread their influence. She had d'Arande preaching at the royal court, where she also circulated the letters from Briconnet and Lefevre's translations of Paul. She also arranged for evangelical preaching in her territories across France with d'Arande preaching in Alencon and Bourges, with Aime Meigret and Pierre de Sebiville preaching in Rouen, Grenoble, and Lyon, where the royal court was settled in 1524.[61] Antoine Papillon, the king's *Grand Conseil*, corresponded with Zwingli, informing him that "d'Arande and Marguerite were in contact with a whole circle of humanists from Lyon and Grenoble who were evangelizing in the region and establishing familiar relations with the German Reformers."[62] However, Meigret and Sebiville were arrested for heresy in Lyon in May 1524. When released they continued preaching "salvation by faith in Jesus Christ alone."[63] Church authorities later silenced Sebiville "under pain of

---

59. Ibid., 314.
60. Landa, "The Reformed Theology of Gerard Roussel," 36.
61. Reid, *King's Sister*, 21.
62. Ibid., 80–81.
63. Ibid., 263, 265.

death," but believers in Grenoble continued to meet secretly, to discuss the Gospel, and to pray.[64]

For the movement to spread under such conditions, they needed good material and a well-planned strategy. By November 1524, the French refugees in Switzerland had procured and reprinted Lefevre's revised French New Testament helped by Lyon publishers, Jean Vaugris and Conrad Resch.[65] Together they developed a distribution system.

> Farel and his friends consigned the books to certain pedlars or colporteurs, simple and pious men, who, laden with their precious burden, passed from town to town, from village to village, and from house to house, in Franche Comte, Lorraine, Burgundy, and the adjoining provinces, knocking at every door. They procured the books at a low rate "that they might be the more eager to sell them." Thus, as early as 1524 there existed in Basle a Bible society, a tract society, and an association of colporteurs, for the benefit of France.[66]

Published sermons were popular and helped to magnify each preacher's influence and to spread the message beyond where preachers could go.[67] In one printed sermon, preached to thousands in the Lyon cathedral, Meigret preached that "faith in Jesus Christ means to believe that we will never gain paradise except by the virtue of the faith ... that we have in him." He also asks, "To what state of affairs have we come that when someone preaches and declares the gospel to you, you call him a heretic or a Lutheran, but someone who glorifies human tradition and inventions is in your opinion a preacher of the gospel?"[68]

CONTINUED GROWTH AMID PERSECUTION

A number of events beyond France helped to further restrict the evangelical mission. In February 1525, King Francis I was imprisoned by Charles V of Spain after the battle of Pavia. While Marguerite, the evangelical patron

---

64. Merle d'Aubigne, *History of the Reformation*, 472.

65. Febvre and Martin, *The Coming of the Book*, 301–2

66. Merle d'Aubigne, *History of the Reformation*, 475.

67. Zuidema, "Guillaume Farel in Early French Reform," 10.

68. From the sermon by Aime Meigret in Larissa J. Taylor, *Soldiers of Christ* (New York: Oxford University Press, 1992), 103.

and protector, negotiated the release of her brother, the Sorbonne and the *parlement* seized their opportunity to attack the evangelicals. They ordered an investigation into Meaux, the suppression of Scripture translations, and a campaign against the "evil and damnable sect and heresy of Luther," which they claimed included some of the magistrates.[69] Berquin was rearrested in the king's absence.

The suppression of the evangelicals was supported by many in Paris who feared that the spreading Peasants' War in Lorraine was in fact a Lutheran invasion.[70] Certainly, members of the evangelical network were active there. Lambert briefly visited the area in 1524,[71] while Farel, Pierre Toussain, and Nicolas D'Esch helped raise "a substantial circle of commoners and nobles in Metz [but it was] not powerful enough to stand up against the duke of Lorraine."[72] Several preachers in this region died by execution—Chatelain of the Sorbonne in January 1525,[73] and Wolfgang Schuch, seven months later in Nancy, forsaking his life to protect his congregation in St. Hippolyte near Metz.[74]

Trouble soon disrupted Lefevre's gospel plans for Meaux when the focus shifted to direct attacks on Rome and its traditions. First, two leading preachers, Martial Mazurier and Pierre Caroli were censured.[75] Then, in March 1525, authorities arrested two more preachers, Jean Pauvan and Matthias Saulnier, and charged them with "impugning the power of the Pope, the concept of purgatory, the cult of the saints, monastic vows, [and] the efficacy of the sacraments."[76] They executed Pauvan at the stake in Paris in August 1526 and whipped and branded a popular lay preacher, Jean Le Clerc, a wool carder from Meaux, for replacing papal indulgences placards with others attacking the pope.[77] Although he died several months later, having smashed shrine images in Metz in the Lorraine region,

---

69. Greengrass, *The French Reformation*, 9–10.

70. Reid, *King's Sister*, 22.

71. Merle d'Aubigne, *History of the Reformation*, 461–462.

72. Reid, *King's Sister*, 279, footnote 85.

73. Merle d'Aubigne, *History of the Reformation*, 464.

74. Ibid., 480.

75. Reid, *King's Sister*, 297.

76. Heller, "Reform and Reformers at Meaux," 327.

77. Ibid., 325.

His deep biblical learning, which was appreciated by fellow evangelicals at Metz and noted by the crowd at the time of his execution, was exactly what the Meaux group intended to produce: lay people learned in the Scriptures who were capable of perpetuating the faith.[78]

The arrests and execution were meant to discourage those who would not conform to the traditional practices and beliefs. However, the attraction of the gospel message and the evident corruption of the Catholic Church meant secret evangelical groups would continue to form around the country.[79]

> In a barn, at night, by the dim light of the candle—for they must not raise suspicion—or by daylight in the forest glade … the illiterate gathered around him who could read. He was a vicar or a monk, brought over to the new ideas, or sometimes a schoolmaster or a lawyer, barrister, proctor, or notary; he would read, and around him hard-headed peasants, the women that spun, the children with large, wondering eyes, muttered inwardly the strong words of the Bible, or the exhortations of the theologian [and] from that day, in some obscure corner of "the most Christian Kingdom," a Protestant community was born.

Consequently, those charged with investigating charges against the preachers of Meaux discovered "alarming evidence of heresy among the people."[80] Noel Beda, the Sorbonne leader, complained that by rejecting "meritorious works," and resting all the weight of salvation on faith alone … thousands of men, seduced by these doctrines, have learned to say, "Why should I fast and mortify my body?"[81] When opposition ended the public mission to Meaux, "an underground evangelical cell" continued there.[82]

---

78. Reid, *King's Sister*, 307.

79. Henry Hauser, "The French Reformation and the French People in the Sixteenth Century" in *The American Historical Review* 4, no 2 (1899): 219.

80. Nicholls, *France*, 124.

81. Noel Beda in Merle d'Aubigne, *History of the Reformation*, 480.

82. Reid, *King's Sister*, 74.

With Marguerite occupied trying to secure her brother's release, the Paris authorities announced in October 1525 that they would prosecute the members of the Meaux mission. For safety, the aged Jacques Lefevre, with Gerard Roussel, Michel d'Arande, and two Franciscan preachers, fled to Strasbourg. The leaders of the Reformed church there—Martin Bucer, Wolfgang Capito, Matthew Zell, and Marguerite's cousin, Sigismund Hohenlohe—welcomed the new arrivals.[83] Farel was at this time preaching at a French refugee church there.[84]

From Strasbourg, Roussel reported to Briconnet how impressed he was with the doctrines and practice there.[85] Briconnet, however, had advised Marguerite "if preaching the gospel caused scandal, then one ought to desist lest God be dishonored and the people's hearts be hardened against His message."[86] Under pressure, Briconnet turned against the evangelical cause, imprisoning so-called heretics and sending at least one to the stake. These severe measures "forced artisans who were committed to the evangelical cause to flee the diocese." They were reported to be "proselytizing" and "agitating" in Troyes and also at Soissons.[87]

THE MISSION SPREADS TO THE PROVINCES

Paris-based persecution helped move the mission into regional cities and towns, especially due to Marguerite's appointments. In Alencon near Normandy, Marguerite appointed Pierre Caroli in November 1525 to implement a Meaux-style program. He raised up laity, including women, to preach, arguing, "God can illuminate the heart of a woman with the true sense of Scripture if she has a simple goodness in her."[88] To encourage Bible study and publish evangelical literature, Marguerite moved her printer, Simon Du Bois, to Alencon in 1529 since Paris had become too dangerous.[89] Du Bois was strongly supported by the evangelical preacher,

---

83. Ibid., 344.

84. Blackburn, *William Farel*, 122.

85. Paul Landa, "The Reformed Theology of Gerard Roussel, Bishop of Oloron (1536)" (PhD diss., Vanderbilt University, 1976), 41.

86. Reid, *King's Sister*, 241.

87. Ibid., 363.

88. Taylor, *Soldiers of Christ*, 197.

89. Reid, *King's Sister*, 370–71.

Étienne Lecourt, who Marguerite appointed administrator of the hospital for the poor.[90] Lecourt also preached among the Conde-sur Sarthe peasants.[91] In 1530, Bucer reported to Luther that Normandy had become a "little Germany"[92] with evangelical districts around Rouen, Vexin, and Caux, as well as nearby Saintonge where, "about 1534 ... many congregations sprang up, composed of fishermen and vinedressers."[93] John Calvin was also in Saintonge at this time, studying in the library of Louis de Tillet, canon of Angouleme.[94] This growth ran parallel with persecutions. Thirty-seven heresy trials in Rouen from 1528–1533 resulted in five executions and extensive punishments affecting clergy, nobles, and commoners alike.[95] Preachers like Lecourt used their heresy trials to present their gospel propositions, which emphasized "the need of grace for salvation" and that "everyone should have a Bible in French."[96] Lecourt fought an "aggressive battle against his accusers" but they finally executed him in December 1533.[97]

Judicial records also indicate that more than forty cities in France had evangelical groups by 1535.[98] In Bourges, south of Paris, where Marguerite's authority and mission leadership was strong, Michel d'Arande ministered freely to large crowds beginning in 1523. Marguerite appointed respected evangelical scholars to the University of Bourges, including jurist Andrea Alciato and Melchior Wolmar, who taught Greek and law at the University of Orleans before coming to Bourges. John Calvin and his friends may have accepted Lutheran ideas while boarding with Wolmar in Orleans.[99] Meanwhile in Toulouse, an evangelical cell had formed at the university. Authorities interrupted an evangelical gathering of over fifty people and arrested twenty-two attendees, including their leader, university professor,

90.   Ibid., 405.

91.   Hauser, *The French Reformation and the French People*, 225.

92.   Bucer to Luther in Reid, *King's Sister*, 26.

93.   Hauser, "The French Reformation and The French People," 225.

94.   Ganoczy, *The Young Calvin*, 83.

95.   Reid, *King's Sister*, 393.

96.   Larissa J. Taylor, *Preachers and People in the Reformations and Early Modern Period* (Boston: Brill Academic, 2003), 198–99.

97.   Reid, *King's Sister*, 394.

98.   Ibid., 382.

99.   Ganoczy, *The Young Calvin*, 68.

Jean de Caturce. They executed Caturce soon after and publicly punished another professor, Jean de la Boyssone.[100] Nonetheless, based on heresy trial numbers, the protestant community continued to grow exponentially.[101] Persecution did not stifle mission.

PROGRESS IN PARIS

Evangelicals in Paris continued with their mission cautiously. Pierre Toussain, who had already spent time in prison for his convictions, had come to Paris to study. He complained to Farel about the cowardice of the evangelicals there. When Farel wrote to Roussel about this in 1526, Roussel insisted that ministry and "the harvest of souls" must be faced with wisdom, and not only with courage. Their approach had to be "prudent and crafty."[102] To this end, evangelicals conducted various activities without attracting the attention of the authorities.[103] Simon Du Bois had collaborated with Louis de Berquin printing evangelical literature in Paris, until the latter's arrest and execution in 1529.[104] Bookshops such as the *Ecu de Bale* (Books of Basel) continued to sell pro-Reform works despite the bans.[105] Supporters in the royal court and around the city, distributed and discussed Lefevre's New Testament and other Reformist publications. Meanwhile, during this time Marguerite had completed and published her collection of evangelical poems, *Mirrors of the Sinful Soul*. [106]

The early 1530s showed some signs of better days for the evangelicals of Paris. The sons of Francis I had been released from Spanish captivity in early 1529. Francis then began seeking alliances with the Protestant princes of Germany. In March 1530, at Marguerite's insistence, the king appointed royal professorships in biblical languages.[107] The "free and independent courses they provided" attracted large numbers of students. During Lent in 1531, Gerard Roussel preached at the Louvre with Marguerite in attendance.

---

100. Reid, *King's Sister*, 386–87.

101. Greengrass, *The French Reformation*, 37.

102. Reid, *King's Sister*, 311.

103. Ibid., 350.

104. Ibid., 367.

105. Febvre and Martin, *The Coming of the Book*, 302–3.

106. Patricia Francis Cholakian and Rouben Charles Cholakian, *Marguerite de Navarre: Mother of the Renaissance* (New York: Columbia University Press, 2006), 154–55.

107. Ibid., 151.

It was also during this time that Calvin began to make an appearance among the evangelicals, although little evidence of conversion appears until 1533. In June of 1531, John Calvin arrived to study Greek and Hebrew in Paris, reconnecting with his school friend, Nicolas Cop, whose father, Guillaume Cop, was the king's physician, and "the generous evangelical merchant," Etienne de la Forge.[108] De la Forge and the goldsmith, Christopher Herault, were leaders of an evangelical cell in Paris with connections to Marguerite's network and to Farel in Switzerland.[109]

Marguerite's ability to make appointments opened further opportunities for the gospel. Jean Du Bellay, was appointed as bishop of Paris in 1532, with his brother Rene assisting him.[110] In early 1533, permission was gained for Gerard Roussel to preach during Lent in Paris. During the campaign, over 4,000 people attended daily, more than the initial venues were able to contain.[111] Despite the "wild popularity of his sermons,"[112] there were also large street protests. There were soon other reasons for protest. On November 1, 1533, Nicolas Cop, as the new rector of the University of Paris, decided to give a bold evangelical sermon. Quoting Erasmus and Luther, he condemned the practices of the theologians, and stated: "Blessed are the persecuted! Let us not be afraid of confessing the Gospel. Should we strive to please men rather than God? Should we fear those who can kill the body yet are powerless over the soul?"[113]

The Catholic authorities were enraged and arrested many evangelicals, but Cop fled to Basel. It was hard to predict how Francis I would react. He had recently met with Pope Clement VII for the wedding between the king's son, Henry, and the Pope's niece, Catherine de Medici. Francis I assured the conservatives, "We are angry and displeased ... to learn that ... this damned heretical Lutheran sect is flourishing in our good town of Paris." Nonetheless, by February 1534, the king had imprisoned Beda for his

---

108. Ganoczy, *The Young Calvin*, 72, 75.

109. Reid, *King's Sister*, 79.

110. Ibid., 419.

111. Cholakian and Cholakian, *Marguerite de Navarre*, 168.

112. Reid, *King's Sister*, 380.

113. Knecht, *Francis I*, 244–45.

verbal attacks on the royal lecturers.[114] Others in the Sorbonne continued the offensive against the evangelicals.

ADVANCES IN SWITZERLAND AND THE AFFAIR OF THE PLACARDS

Across the eastern border, Guillaume Farel "proved to be a pioneer missionary of the first rank, and most of French-speaking Switzerland entered the Reformed fold through his efforts."[115] As he and his co-workers promoted the Reformation, they used the newly published French Bibles and Farel's *Summaire* (1529) to consolidate the converts.[116] Farel soon had workers and congregations scattered across French-speaking Switzerland. An astute recruiter and trainer of young men, he raised up leaders like Pierre Viret in Orbe (and later Lausanne); Christopher Fabri from Montpellier; Antoine Marcourt as pastor of the church in Neuchatel; Anthony Froment and Pierre Robert Olivetan who helped to win Geneva, where he also famously called John Calvin to serve. But in 1534, Calvin was only twenty-five, newly converted and mostly unknown.

An incident occurred in Paris at this time known as the Affair of the Placards, which many authors credit with turning Francis I against the evangelicals. On the night of October 17–18, 1534, the streets of Paris and other major cities in the region were suddenly and secretly covered in strongly worded placards against the mass. Jonathan Reid argues that it was clearly the work of "a well-coordinated cabal."[117] The clandestine evangelical cell network, according to William Maxwell Blackburn, sought to "arouse the public attention of all, from the king to the cottager."[118] To this end, they sent Feret, a man in the king's service, to seek help and advice from Farel and the ministers in Switzerland.[119]

---

114. Ibid., 245–46.

115. Donald H. MacVicar, "William Farel, Reformer of the Swiss Romand: His Life, His Writings and His Theology" (PhD diss. abstract, Union Theological Seminary, 1954) in *Church History* 24, no. 2 (1955): 175.

116. Zuidema, "Guillaume Farel in Early French Reform," 12.

117. Reid, *King's Sister*, 40.

118. Blackburn, *William Farel*, 285–86.

119. Ibid.

Farel's reputation for using "dramatic action ... to promote Reformed belief" was widespread.[120] Network leaders in France had heard about Farel's successes in bringing Reformation to a large number of towns and cities in Switzerland. They would have known about the use of placards in Neuchatel, and Geneva in 1532 to oppose papal indulgences and to offer in their place a "heavenly pardon."[121] Each time, the placards were followed by opposition and persecutions; but each time, Farel capitalized on the reaction.[122] In 1533, Farel had invited the Lyon printer Pierre de Vingle to base himself in Neuchatel, where he was assisted by Antoine Marcourt.[123] It is very likely, then, that Farel was a key instigator of the placards which descended on Paris in October 1534. Antoine Marcourt later confessed to the authorship of the placards and the pamphlets which followed in January.[124] Nonetheless, given that the 1530 Neuchatel placard was equally provocative, it is likely that Farel delegated that task to Marcourt who was assisting de Vingle, the printer.[125] Farel and those who had requested his help sought a confrontation to move the reform along faster.

Most authors depict the placards affair as only negative. Knecht, for example, says it had a "shattering" effect on Paris and caused a "wave of hysteria."[126] Reid argues that it angered "the magistrates and the king, thus turning the political tide in favour of the traditionalists and dealt the evangelicals a hard blow."[127] Damaging the reputation of Marguerite and her network and resulting in hundreds of arrests and many executions, "the Placards scuttled any chance of an evangelical reformation succeeding."[128] On the "most-wanted list of heretics" were many associated with Marguerite, including Caroli and others from Alencon, Simon Du Bois,

---

120. Frans P. van Stam, "Piety in Tumultuous Times: Farel the Flamboyant Herald of Reformed Belief," in *Between Lay Piety and Academic Theology*, eds. Frans P. van Stam, U. Hascher-Burger, A. Den Hollander, and W. Janse (Leiden: Brill, 2010), 292–93.

121. Blackburn, *William Farel*, 244.

122. Ibid., 177–72.

123. Febvre and Martin, *The Coming of the Book*, 314.

124. C. Louise Salley, "Antoine Marcourt: Reformateur et Pamphletaire du 'Livre des Marchans' aux Placards de 1534, by Gabrielle Bertoud," *Church History* 43, no. 1 (March 1974): 108.

125. Blackburn, *William Farel*, 172.

126. Knecht, *Francis I*, 249.

127. Reid, *King's Sister*, 79.

128. Ibid., 380.

and "several of Marguerite's servants as well as members of an evangelical cell in Paris with whom she and her court were in direct contact."[129] Many key leaders, such as Etienne de la Forge, died following the distribution of Marcourt's follow-up pamphlets in January 1535. It was at this time that Calvin escaped to Switzerland.

CONCLUSION

It would be easy to conclude that all hope for a Lutheran Protestant Reformation in France was lost, given the devastation which faced the evangelicals following the placards affair in October 1534. To some authors it seemed that Farel had failed, that Marguerite's influence was now over. When faced with this situation and the large number of French Protestants in 1562, many have assumed that Calvin alone deserved the credit. This chapter has argued, however, that Lefevre and his team laid the foundations for the gospel mission, made the Scriptures available in French, and distributed them widely. By her patronage and direct involvement, Marguerite protected and placed evangelicals in positions of influence across France. A wide range of others joined the mission, promoting the gospel in various ways. Some boldly preached despite the risk of execution, while others moved cautiously, producing and distributing Reformation literature, and organizing secret prayer and study groups. Still others fled and established Reformation bases beyond the borders of France. Guillaume Farel was the most prominent of these, supported by civil authorities, reformed clergy, and French refugees, who imbibed his passion for mission.

As the number of evangelicals grew, despite persecutions, across regional France and in French-speaking Switzerland, attention turned to Paris in the hope it might be won to the Reformation. Cell leaders in Paris, hoping to mirror the dramatic intervention which brought reform to Neuchatel and Geneva, collaborated with Farel and the Swiss ministers and ran a campaign which, although costly in terms of lives, greatly challenged the French nation. Although the Affair of the Placards of 1534 is often seen as the end of evangelical outreach in France, it could be thought of as a culmination. It was, in fact, part of that process that had been begun and consolidated by Lefevre, influenced by the writings of Luther and the

---

129. Ibid., 434.

German Reformers, trialed by the team at Meaux, supported and extended by Marguerite, taken across borders by Farel and the French refugees, and then fostered by evangelical believers all over France and French-speaking Switzerland.

BIBLIOGRAPHY

Arnold, Jonathan. *The Great Humanists: An Introduction.* New York: I.B. Tauris, 2011.

Baird, Henry Martyn. *History of the Rise of the Huguenots: Vol. 1.* London: Hodder and Stoughton, 1880.

Blackburn, William. M. *William Farel: And the Story of the Swiss Reform.* New ed. Edinburgh: William Oliphant & Co., 1877.

Cholakian, Patricia Francis, and Rouben Charles Cholakian. *Marguerite De Navarre Mother of the Renaissance.* New York: Columbia University Press, 2006.

Delcorno, Pietro. "Between Pulpit and Reformation: The Confessions of François Lambert." *Franciscan Studies* 71 (2013): 113–33.

Febvre, Lucien, and Henri-Jean Martin. *The Coming of the Book: The Impact of Printing, 1450–1800.* London: Verso Editions, 1984.

Ganoczy, Alexandre. *The Young Calvin.* Philadelphia: Westminster Press, 1987.

Green, Vivian Hubert Howard. *Luther and the Reformation.* New York: Capricorn Books, 1964.

Greengrass, Mark. *The French Reformation.* Oxford: Basil Blackwell, 1987.

Hauser, H. "The French Reformation and the French People in the Sixteenth Century." *The American Historical Review* 4, no. 2 (1899): 217–27.

Heller, Henry. "Reform and Reformers at Meaux 1518–1525." PhD diss., Cornell University, 1969.

Hilgert, Earle. "Johann Froben and the Basel University Scholars, 1513–1523." *The Library Quarterly* 41, no. 2 (1971): 141–69.

Knecht, R. J. *Francis I.* New York: Cambridge University Press, 1982.

Landa, Paul. "The Reformed Theology of Gerard Roussel, Bishop of Oloron (1536–1555), Based upon a Critical Edition of his 'Familiere Exposition Du Simbole, de la Loy et Oraison Dominicale en Forme de Colloque' and his 'Forme de Viste de Diocese' (ca. 1548)." PhD diss., Vanderbilt University, 1976.

Levi, Anthony. *Renaissance and Reformation: The Intellectual Genesis*. New Haven: Yale University Press, 2002.

MacVicar, Donald H. "William Farel, Reformer of the Swiss Romand: His Life, His Writings and His Theology." PhD diss. abstract, Union Theological Seminary in *Church History* 24, no. 2 (1955): 175.

Merle D'Aubigné, Jean Henri. *History of the Reformation of the Sixteenth Century, Volumes 1–4*. Translated by Henry White. New York: Robert Carter & Brothers, 1851. Accessed from https://www.hathitrust.org/.

Nicholls, David J. "The Nature of Popular Heresy in France, 1520–1542." *The Historical Journal* 26, no. 2 (1983): 261–75.

Nicholls, David. "France." In *The Early Reformation in Europe*, edited by Andrew Pettegree, 120–41. Cambridge: Cambridge University Press, 1992.

Reid, Jonathan A. *King's Sister, Queen of Dissent: Marguerite of Navarre (1492–1549) and Her Evangelical Network*. Leiden: Brill, 2009. Accessed from https://brill.com/.

Salley, C. Louise. "Antoine Marcourt: Reformateur et Pamphletaire du 'Livre des Marchans' aux Placards de 1534, by Gabrielle Bertoud." *Church History* 43, no. 1 (March 1974): 108.

Taylor, Larissa. *Preachers and People in the Reformations and Early Modern Period*. Boston: Brill Academic, 2003.

———. *Soldiers of Christ: Preaching in Late Medieval and Reformation France*. New York: Oxford University Press, 1992.

Treasure, Geoffrey. *The Huguenots*. New Haven: Yale University Press, 2013.

Van Stam, Frans P. "Piety in Tumultuous Times: Farel the Flamboyant Herald of Reformed Belief." In *Between Lay Piety and Academic Theology*, edited by Van Stam, Frans P., U. Hascher-Burger, A. Den Hollander, and W. Janse, 289–307. Leiden: Brill, 2010.

Zuidema, Jason, and Theodore Van Raalte. *Early French Reform: The Theology and Spirituality of Guillaume Farel*. Farnham: Routledge, 2011.

5

—

CALVIN'S GENEVA

Missions as a Light to the World

Karin Spiecker Stetina

As a young professor, Karl Barth describes his struggle to adequately understand and portray John Calvin and Reformed theology. Having to teach on the Reformed tradition without much first-hand knowledge, Barth determined to immerse himself in Calvin's writings. The brilliant theologian describes how he wrestled with the Reformer day and night and even dismissed his class more than once due to feeling insufficiently prepared to lecture on Calvin. He describes the Reformer as "a cataract, a primeval forest, a demonic power, something directly down from Himalaya, absolutely Chinese, strange, mythological."[1] In a letter penned on June 8, 1922, to his friend, Eduard Thurneysen, the young theologian declares himself as lacking "the means, the suction cups, even to assimilate this phenomenon, not to speak of presenting it adequately"; yet he would "gladly and profitably set myself down and spend all the rest of my life just with Calvin."[2] This oft-quoted account reveals the challenge of properly interpreting and assessing the Reformer and his followers. Barth's words stand as a warning against oversimplifying Calvin and Reformed thought by interpreting them based on uninformed caricatures. Yet this very pitfall often occurs when it comes to determining the Reformed tradition's relationship to missions.

---

1. Karl Barth and Eduard Thurneysen, *Revolutionary Theology in the Making: Barth-Thurneysen Correspondence, 1914–1925* (Louisville: Westminster John Knox, 1964), 101.

2. Ibid.

The perennial question of whether Calvin and Calvinism have fostered or hindered missions has divided scholars since the sixteenth century.[3]

Many scholars contend that the Reformed tradition has had a negative impact on missions. Starting with the sixteenth century and Roman Catholic theologian Robert Bellarmine (1542–1621) critics have often disparaged Calvin and other Reformers for their lack of zeal for the conversion of non-Christian peoples. Bellarmine damningly proclaimed, "In this one century the Catholics have converted many thousands of heathens in the new world" while the Protestants "have among them a very large number of Jews, and in Poland and Hungary have the Turks as their near neighbors," yet "have hardly converted so much as a handful."[4] In the early twentieth century, German Protestant missiologist Gustav Warneck (1834–1910) portrayed Calvin and the Reformed view of missions as "defective" and disinterested in converting the "heathen world."[5] As has been well-documented by other missions scholars, similar sentiments are articulated by Kenneth Scott Latourette,[6] W. R. Hogg,[7] J. Herbert Kane,[8] Stephen Neill,[9] and even Ruth A. Tucker.[10] Scholarship by W. Stanford Reid,[11] David Calhoun,[12]

3. Jean-François Zorn, "Did Calvin Foster or Hinder the Missions?" *Exchange* 40.2 (2011): 170–91.

4. Robert Bellarmine, *Controversaie*, book IV quoted in Stephen Neill, *History of Christian Missions* (Baltimore, MD: Penguin Books, 1964), 221.

5. See Gustav Warneck, *Outline of a History of Protestant Missions from the Reformation to the Present Time* (Chicago: Fleming H. Revell, 1901), 8–9, 18.

6. Kenneth Scott Latourette, *A History of the Expansion of Christianity* (Grand Rapids: Zondervan, 1937), 25–26.

7. William Richey Hogg, "The Rise of Protestant Missionary Concern, 1517–1914," in *The Theology of Christian Mission*, ed. by Gerald H. Anderson (New York: McGraw-Hill, 1961), 101.

8. J. Herbert Kane, *A Concise History of the Christian World Mission: A Panoramic View of Missions from Pentecost to the Present*, rev. ed. (Grand Rapids: Baker, 1982), 73.

9. Stephen Neill, *A History of Christian Missions*, 187.

10. Ruth Tucker, *From Jerusalem to Irian Jaya: a Biographical History of Christian Missions*, 2nd ed. (Grand Rapids: Zondervan, 2004), 97–98.

11. W. Stanford Reid, "Calvin's Geneva: A Missionary Centre," *The Reformed Theological Review* 42, no. 3 (1983): 65–74.

12. David B. Calhoun, "John Calvin: Missionary Hero or Missionary Failure?" *Presbyterion* 5, no. 1 (1979): 16–33.

Kenneth J. Stewart,[13] Michael Haykin,[14] and Frank A. James III[15] has sought to dispel the negative interpretations of the Reformed tradition, and to portray Calvinism as "missiologically challenged." Yet the uncharitable perspectives remain, with Calvinists often portrayed as the cold and callous "frozen chosen" who care little about sharing the good news of the gospel due to their strong emphasis on God's sovereignty and the doctrine of predestination. This work aims to give a more nuanced view of John Calvin and the early Reformed tradition's relationship to missions by focusing on Calvin and Geneva's aim to spread the gospel by being a light in a dark world. The Reformer and the believers in Geneva, in part in response to Roman Catholicism and the widespread persecution of Protestants, sought to be a light to the world by being a Christian refuge and training center for the gospel. By focusing on teaching God's Word and the core gospel truths contained in it, Geneva represents a shift in missions from a narrow focus on converting heathens to the Christian church, to a more holistic approach of promoting the reign of Jesus Christ through the preaching, teaching, and living out of the pure gospel for the glory of God.

WHAT IS MISSIONS?

To evaluate John Calvin and Geneva's relationship to missions, one must first answer the question, *what is missions*? Is missions the fulfilling of the Great Commission to "make disciples of all nations"? (Matt 28:19) If so, what is meant by making *disciples* and *all* nations? Is missions being witnesses "in Jerusalem, and in Judea and Samaria, and the ends of the earth"? (Acts 1:8). If so, what does it mean to be *witnesses* and what is implied by each of these places? What priority should be given to each place? Is missions being a "light for the Gentiles"? (Acts 13:47). If so, who are the *Gentiles* and what does it mean to be a *light* for them? All too often, the Reformed tradition's relationship to missions has been evaluated based on defining missions simply as overseas evangelism ("to the ends of the earth") to convert "heathens" ("Gentiles") to the Christian church. Is this a broad enough

---

13. Kenneth J. Stewart, "Calvinism and Missions: The Contested Relationship Revisited," *Themelios* 34 no. 1 (2009): 63–78.

14. Michael A. G. Haykin, *To the Ends of the Earth: Calvin's Missional Vision and Legacy* (Wheaton, IL: Crossway, 2014), 25–26.

15. Frank A. James III, "Calvin the Evangelist," *Reformed Quarterly* 19, no. 2 (2001): 4.

understanding of the Christian calling to be Christ's witnesses? Geneva's view of missions suggests that it is not.

John Stott's statement on the proper missionary motive helps us consider how to effectively understand and assess Calvin and Geneva's relationship to missions. Drawing on Romans 1:1–6, Stott writes the following:

> If God desires every knee to bow to Jesus and every tongue to confess Him, so should we. ... The highest of all missionary motives is neither obedience to the Great Commission (important as that is), nor love for sinners who are alienated and perishing (strong as that incentive is, especially when we contemplate the wrath of God), but rather zeal—burning and passionate zeal—for the glory of Jesus Christ. ... Only one imperialism is Christian, and that is concern for His Imperial Majesty Jesus Christ, and for the glory of his empire or kingdom. Before this supreme goal of the Christian mission, all unworthy motives wither and die.[16]

Stott, like Calvin and his followers, does not see the conversion of the heathen to the Christian religion as the primary goal of Christian missions. Both Bellarmine and Warneck are correct in pointing out that global missions was not the major emphasis for the Genevan Reformer and his disciples. Calvin's Geneva, instead, expanded its missional focus to the promotion of Christ's reign through the communication and living out of the pure gospel to *all* people, including the local Genevans and the French.

Calvin's writings reveal his heart for the Genevan church to be a beacon of light to *all* people.[17] He implores his parishioners and students to recognize the importance of this calling:

---

16. John Stott, *Romans: God's Good News for the World* (Downers Grove, IL: InterVarsity Press, 1994), 53.

17. "We now have a full revelation in the gospel: let us not, therefore, do this injury to God, to put away the brightness which he hath caused to shine before our eyes; seeing the Son of justice, that is to say, our Lord Jesus Christ, is now made manifest to us" (Selection of sermons, 177). "Seeing the truth of God cannot reign among us, unless the gospel be preached, we ought to esteem it highly, knowing that he otherwise holdeth himself afare off. ... May we attend to what God hath enjoined upon us, that he would be pleased to show his grace, not only to one city or a little handful of people, but that he would reign over all the world; that every one may serve and worship him in spirit and in truth" (Selections, 119, 124).

God has not deposited the *teaching* of His salvation with us not for the purpose of keeping it to ourselves, but of our pointing out the way of salvation to *all* mankind. This, therefore, is the common duty of the children of God,—to promote the salvation of their brethren.[18]

The Reformer and the Genevans do not show a strong interest, like the Roman Catholic Church (and Bellarmine), in expanding the Imperial Church (religion) and its reign by colonizing foreign countries. While Calvin was a magisterial Reformer who worked with the Genevan city council to establish true religion and the city of Geneva sent missionaries to Brazil in the hopes of establishing the reign of Christ, they did not focus their resources on establishing the Reformed church as a political power in foreign nations. Rather, their primary concern appears to be the extension of Christ's kingdom so the glory of God might be recognized, enjoyed, and promoted by all peoples. This conviction is evident in Geneva's short-lived overseas work in Brazil. The Genevan trained minister and Brazilian missionary Jean de Léry's statement about the Genevan church's reaction to the Brazilian voyage speaks to their concern for the expansion of Christ's kingdom. He reports that "upon receiving these letters and hearing this news, the church of Geneva at once gave thanks to God for the extension of the reign of Jesus Christ in a country so distant and likewise so foreign and among a nation entirely without the knowledge of the true God."[19] While the Genevans, like the Catholics, were concerned with communicating the gospel to other nations, they did not limit missions to this endeavor. They recognized that European countries, including Switzerland and France, where they helped plant over 2,000 churches, were also in dire need of true faith, rather than religion.

The Reformation in Geneva centered around the restoration of the pure gospel. Without it, human souls were in peril. The Reformer saw false teaching, particularly that of the Roman Catholic Church, threatening the communication of the pure gospel. To be a good missionary one must

---

18. Writing about Daniel 12:3 (emphasis added), in John Calvin, *Calvin's Complete Commentaries* (Corona, CA: E4 Group, 2013), Kindle locations 315248–50.

19. R. Pierce Beaver, "The Genevan Mission to Brazil," in *The Heritage of John Calvin: Heritage Hall Lectures, 1960–1970*, ed. John H. Bratt (Grand Rapids: Eerdmans, 1973), 61.

first be a good theologian of the gospel.[20] Calvin proclaims the necessity of knowledge of the gospel:

> Without the gospel everything is useless and vain; without the gospel we are not Christians; without the gospel all riches is poverty, all wisdom folly before God; strength is weakness, and all the justice of man is under the condemnation of God. But by the knowledge of the gospel we are made children of God, brothers of Jesus Christ, fellow townsmen with the saints, citizens of the Kingdom of Heaven, heirs of God with Jesus Christ, by whom the poor are made rich, the weak strong, the fools wise, the sinner justified, the desolate comforted, the doubting sure, and slaves free. It is the power of God for the salvation of all those who believe.[21]

The gospel needs to go out to the heathens (pagans or foreigners) as well as to Roman Catholics, Jews, and unconverted Protestants.[22] If, following Philippians 2:10–11, the primary motive of missions is a concern for Christ's reign, missions can and should take on a variety of forms. The Reformer and his city recognized that God's Word is the true source of the gospel. When it is properly proclaimed, both in words and in actions, it has the power to save (Rom 1:16) and does not return void (Isa 55:11). With these principles in mind, the city of Geneva sought to not only send missionaries and pastors to other countries such as Brazil, France, Italy, Hungary, Poland, England, Scotland, and the Netherlands, but also to intentionally focus on being a light and a training center for the promotion of Christ's kingdom in Switzerland.

---

20. Frank A. James, III, "Calvin the Evangelist," 4.

21. John Calvin, from his "preface" to *Pierre Robert Olivétan's French Translation of the New Testament in 1534*, in Joseph Haroutunian, and Louise Pettibone Smith, *Calvin: Commentaries* (Louisville: Westminster John Knox, 2006), 66.

22. In his commentary on Hosea 2:4–5, Calvin writes, "Such apostasy prevails under the Papacy, and has for many ages prevailed, how senseless they are in their boasting, while they would be thought to be the holy Catholic Church, and the elect people of God? For they are all born by wantonness, they are all spurious children. The incorruptible seed is the word of God; but what sort of doctrine have they? It is a spurious seed. Then as to God all the Papists are bastards. In vain then they boast themselves to be the children of God, and that they have the holy Mother Church, for they are born by filthy wantonness." Calvin, *Calvin's Complete Commentaries*, Kindle locations 320689–91.

THE WORD AS THE SOURCE OF TRUTH

With all the attention given to his doctrine of election, Calvin could be mistakenly given the derogatory title, Doctor of Predestination. However, it seems more appropriate to call him a servant of the Word, as a plaque in St. Pierre's Cathedral in Geneva reads, since God's Word was the focal point of his thought, ministry, and missional perspective.[23] Calvin's biblical emphasis appears from the first pages of his foundational work, *Institutes of the Christian Religion*, which he conceived as an instruction manual for reading the Bible and a defense of the true faith. He opens the 1560 edition:

> Although Holy Scripture contains a perfect doctrine, to which one can add nothing, since in it our Lord has meant to display the infinite treasures of his wisdom, yet a person who has not much practice in it has good reason for some guidance and direction, to know what he ought to look for in it, in order not to wander hither and thither, but to hold to a sure path, that he may always be pressing toward the end to which the Holy Spirit calls him. Perhaps the duty of those who have received from God fuller light than others is to help simple folk at this point, and as it were to lend them a hand, in order to guide them and help them to find the sum of what God meant to teach us in his Word. Now, that cannot be better done through the Scriptures than to treat the chief and weightiest matters comprised in the Christian philosophy. It is very necessary to help in this way those who desire to be instructed in the doctrine of salvation. Consequently, I was constrained, according to the ability that the Lord gave me, to undertake this task.[24]

This pedagogical work seeks to teach biblical truth and repudiate false religions that go against the word of God and the gospel of Christ.[25] In his

---

23. Kenneth S. Kantzer, "Calvin and the Holy Scriptures," in *Inspiration and Interpretation* ed. John F. Walvoord; (Grand Rapids: Eerdmans, 1957), 115.

24. John Calvin, *Calvin: Institutes of the Christian Religion*, ed. John T. McNeill, trans. Ford Lewis Battles (Louisville: Westminster John Knox, 2006).

25. In the *Institutes* Calvin refutes many errors, including the "Papal Mass: A Sacrilege by Which Christ's Supper Was Not only Profaned but Annihilated" and "The Five Other Ceremonies, Falsely Terms Sacraments: Although Commonly Considered Sacraments Hitherto, They Are Proved Not to Be Such, and Their Real Nature Is Shown." John Calvin and Ford Lewis Battles, *Calvin: Institutes of the Christian Religion* (Louisville: Westminster John Knox, 2006), IV, XVIII, 1429 and IV, XIX, 1448.

prefatory address to King Francis I, he speaks of this concern, writing that "the fury of certain wicked persons has prevailed so far in your realm that there is no place in it for sound doctrine."[26] Calvin sees the proper understanding of Scripture as the remedy to counteract false teachings, including those propagated by the Roman Catholic Church. The *Institutes*, his commentaries on nearly every book of the Bible, and the numerous sermons (2,000 of which are recorded by stenographer Denis Raguenier from 1549–1564) give us insight into his Word-centered ministry and missionary impulse in Geneva.

The central role that Scripture played in Calvin's life and missional work is evident in his acceptance of the position of Professor of Sacred Letters in the church of Geneva, which he held until his death.[27] After his return to Geneva in 1541, he preached and lectured on God's Word multiple times a week for more than twenty years.[28] Additionally, on Friday mornings he led local area ministers in the study of Scripture. The Reformer also helped reorganize an academy in Geneva in 1559, which became the first official Protestant university, with the explicit purpose of training both youth and ministers to understand and share the good news of Jesus Christ. The draft of Geneva's *Confession of Faith* (1536) that Calvin and Farel established to define the city's public theology reflects Geneva's Word-centeredness. It opens with the declaration that "we affirm and desire to follow Scripture alone as the rule of faith and religion, without mixing with it any other thing which might be devised by the opinion of men apart from the Word of God."[29] The Word was central to Calvin and Geneva's missiology. They recognized that when the Word is rightly preached, heard, and received, it is a catalyst of salvation. Calvin reminds the Genevans about the importance of preaching God's Word when evangelizing; for all hope of salvation

---

26. Prefatory Address to King Francis I of France. Ibid., 9.

27. Paul Traugott Fuhrmann, "Calvin, the Expositor of Scripture," *Interpretation: A Journal of Bible and Theology* 6 (April 1952): 190.

28. T. H. L. Parker, *Calvin's Preaching* (Louisville: Westminster John Knox, 1992), 153–62.

29. There is some debate regarding the authorship of the *Genevan Confession*. Calvin's early biographer and colleague, Theodore Beza, credits Calvin as the author and later suggests that he "drew it up." Most scholars agree that Farel was the primary author. Regardless, it is probable that Calvin was influential in its composition. For more information see John Kelman Sutherland Reid's discussion in *Calvin: Theological Treatises*, trans. with introductions and notes by J. K. S. Reid (London: SCM Press, 1954), 25.

rests in the proclamation of the gospel.[30] Calvin preaches that "the will of God is opened to us, as often as we hear His Word preached, whereby He calleth and exhorteth us all to repentance."[31] That's what Geneva sought to do: reveal the will of God to people through the preaching and teaching of the Word.

GENEVA AS A BIBLE AND MISSIONS TRAINING CENTER

Calvin's colleague and successor, Theodore Beza, describes Geneva as, by God's providence, the "purest light to arise out of the thickest darkness."[32] The academy that Calvin helped establish had two arms: the college for the education of the youth, and the seminary for the training of ministers. The draft of *Ecclesiastical Ordinances* (1541) reveals Calvin's original intention to institute a school in Geneva "for instructing children to prepare them for the ministry as well as for civil government."[33] This training center, which came to fruition after Calvin's return to Geneva, helped open the doors for the Christian education of all youth in Geneva and beyond. No longer was higher learning limited to boys born into families of wealth or position.

The academy was dedicated to glorifying God with the Bible serving as the foundation of all learning.[34] Prior to their banishment, Calvin had taught Old Testament, and William Farel had taught New Testament. Biblical study, rather than logic and canon law (which was the norm in Catholic institutions), continued to be the priority when the academy was revived in 1559. It quickly gained a reputation as the premier Protestant institution in Europe with the seminary rapidly doubling in size and

---

30. Sermon II on 2 Timothy 1:8–9, in John Calvin, *A Selection of the Most Celebrated Sermons of John Calvin* (Philadelphia: Charles Desilver, 1860), 14–37.

31. Sermon VII on 1 Timothy 2:3–5. Ibid., 108

32. Theodore Beza, *The Life of John Calvin* (Philadelphia: Westminster Press, 1909), 84.

33. Jean Calvin and John Kelman Sutherland Reid, *Calvin: Theological Treatises*, trans. with introductions and notes by J .K. S. Reid (London: SCM Press, 1954), 63.

34. Ibid. In 1559 printer Robert Estienne published the statutes of the academy in both French and Latin. Robert Estienne, *L'ordre Dv College De Geneue* (Geneva: L'Olivier de Rob. Estienne, 1859), https://babel.hathitrust.org/cgi/pt?id=njp.32101068146321&view=1up&seq=5. These statutes reveal the biblical emphasis at the academy. In his thorough study of Geneva and the academy's *Ordre du College de Geneve* Ivan Zabilka points out Calvin's important contribution to universal education. Ivan L Zabilka, "Calvin's Contribution to Universal Education," *The Asbury Theological Journal* 44, no. 1 (Spring 1989): 77–96.

attracting students from all over, but particularly France.[35] The curriculum, which was heavily influenced by the humanist principle of *ad fontes* (going back to original sources), trained students to study the Bible in the original languages. The professors included scholars such as Bonaventure Bertram (Hebrew), François Berauld and Isaac Casaubon (Greek), and Theodore Beza and Lambert Daneau (theology). On Saturday afternoons ministry students would rotate giving and critiquing each other's sermons with local pastors also providing feedback.[36] The rigorous academic and spiritual training helped prepare the students for future ministry both in Geneva and beyond. The future professor Lambert Daneau recalls his experience as a student in Geneva:

> In 1560, I came to your Academy, full of enthusiasm, not because it was near the French border, for there were others nearby, but because it offered to me the *purest* source of that heavenly doctrine. … I will say freely that so many leading lights, so many talented and famous men in all branches of knowledge were in that city, that it seemed to me to be one of the richest markets for intellectual commerce in the world.[37]

Geneva became the flagship of the Reformed faith, with pastors describing it as a nursery for future pastors, missionaries, and international Calvinism.[38] In a letter written to persecuted French Protestants who were requesting pastors for their growing congregations, Calvin replies, "Send us wood, and

---

35. It is a bit unclear the exact number of students enrolled in the seminary and in the college. Most scholars agree that 162, as recorded in the rector's book, is the initial number in the seminary. Some suggest that in four short years there were over 300 and others over 1,200. It seems more probable that the larger number includes the combined number of students. Zabilka, 86. James Edward McGoldrick, "John Calvin: Erudite Educator," *Mid-America Journal of Theology* 21 (2010): 121–32.

36. Karin Maag discusses this practice in "Preaching Practice: Reformed Students' Sermons," in *The Formation of Clerical and Confessional Identities in Early Modern Europe*, ed. Wim Janse and Barbara Pitkin (Leiden: Brill, 2006), 135–36.

37. Cited in Scott M. Manetsch's *Calvin's Company of Pastors: Pastoral Care and the Emerging Reformed Church, 1536–1609* (Oxford: Oxford University Press, 2015), 49. Emphasis added.

38. Karin Maag, *Seminary or University? The Genevan Academy and Reformed Higher Education, 1560–1620* (Aldershot: Scolar Press, 1995), 62–63; Manetsch, *Calvin's Company of Pastors,* 59

we will send you arrows."[39] That is just what the Genevan seminary sought to do. Under Calvin and Theodore Beza's direction, scores of students were trained to rightly handle the word of God and to spread the gospel of Christ. Graduates included such notable figures as Belgian Reformer Guido de Bres (author of the Belgic Confession), German Reformer Caspar Olevianus (who penned the Heidelberg Catechism), and Scottish Reformer John Knox (founder of the Presbyterian Church in Scotland). In a letter written from Geneva, Knox proclaims the Protestant city to be "most perfect school of Christ that was ever in the earth since the days of the apostles. In other places I confess Christ to be truly preached, but manners and religion so sincerely reformed I have not yet seen in any other place besides."[40] Many Protestant churches in France express similar sentiments. For example, in a letter written on September 24, 1613, to the Company of Pastors recommending a candidate to the seminary, a French church in Rouen writes the following:

> We would ask that he could have entry to your consistories to learn that good order which was first born among you and then spread the churches of France. We also ask you to use him sometime, as you do others of the same statutes, to preach in the villages of your area, so that by speaking in public he may be able to train his voice and grow in confidence.[41]

Geneva sent at least eighty-eight church planters to Calvin's country of origin, a dangerous undertaking due to France's anti-Protestant stance. The seminary even became known as "Calvin's school of death" due to the large number of graduates who were martyred for their passionate, unwavering, evangelistic faith in Christ.[42]

---

39. Cited in Louis Delmas, *The Huguenots of La Rochelle: A Translation of "The Reformed Church of La Rochelle, an Historical Sketch,"* (New York: Randolph, 1880), 40.

40. Knox wrote this in letter XIII to Mr. Lock on December 9, 1556. John Knox in *Writings of the Rev. John Knox: Minister of God's Word in Scotland* (Philadelphia: Presbyterian Board of Publication, 1842), http://books.google.com/books?id=XvoQAAAAIAAJ, 454.

41. Cited in Maag, "Preaching Practice," 139.

42. Jeremy Walker, "An Outline of the Life of John Calvin," *Banner of Truth* (blog), February 3, 2009, https://banneroftruth.org/us/resources/articles/2009/an-outline-of-the-life-of-john-calvin/.

Philip E. Hughes, who translated and published *The Register of the Company of Pastors of Geneva in the Time of Calvin*, attests to the missional character of the academy and the Protestant city:[43]

> Calvin's Geneva was something very much more than a haven and a school. It was not a theological ivory tower that lived to itself and for itself, oblivious to its responsibility in the gospel to the needs of others. Human vessels were equipped and refitted in this haven ... that they might launch out into the surrounding ocean of the world's need, bravely facing every storm and peril that awaited them in order to bring the *light of Christ's gospel* to those who were in the ignorance and darkness from which they themselves had originally come. They were taught in this school in order that they in turn might teach others the truth that had set them free.[44]

Calvin's comments on Acts 8:4 corroborate the missional emphasis in Geneva. Elaborating on the passage that discusses the scattering of faithful Christians abroad due to the persecution of the New Testament church, the Reformer writes, "Therefore, if we desire to be counted their brethren, let us prick forward ourselves so diligently, that no fear or bitterness of cross discourage us, but that we go forward in showing forth the profession of faith."[45] He implores believers to "never be weary of furthering the doctrine of Christ; for it is an absurd thing that exile and flight, which are the first exercises of martyrdom, should make us dumb and fainthearted."[46] Calvin urges them to see persecution and the scattering of the faithful not as a defeat, but rather as a work of God's divine providence, to "bring light out of darkness and life out of death."[47] Geneva sought to be just such a light, training people to bring Christ to the dark world, even if it meant persecution and death.

---

43. Philip E. Hughes, *The Register of the Company of Pastors of Geneva in the Time of Calvin* (Eugene, OR: Wipf & Stock, 2004).

44. Philip E. Hughes, "John Calvin: Director of Mission," in *The Heritage of John Calvin: Heritage Hall Lectures, 1960–1970*, ed. John H. Bratt (Grand Rapids: Eerdmans, 1973), 44–45. Emphasis added.

45. John Calvin, *Commentary upon the Acts of the Apostles*, edited from the original English translation of Christopher Fetherstone by Henry Beveridge (Edinburgh: T&T Clark, 1859), 328.

46. Ibid.

47. Ibid.

TEACHING AND PREACHING AS MISSION

As a servant of the Word, John Calvin did not just preach *about* the gospel, he preached *the gospel*. As C. H. Spurgeon comments, Calvin "now is often looked upon as a theologian only, but he was really one of the greatest of gospel preachers." When the Reformer "opened the Book and took a text, you might be sure that he was about to preach 'Through grace are ye saved, and that not of yourselves, it is the gift of God.'"[48] Calvin's ultimate goal was the propagation of the gospel of Christ, so that God might be properly worshiped and glorified. The teaching and preaching of God's Word were God's primary means of communicating the pure gospel and realizing the kingdom of God. Elaborating on 2 Timothy 1:8–9, Calvin proclaims that "if the gospel be not *preached*, Jesus Christ is, as it were, buried. Therefore, let us stand as witnesses, and do Him this honor, when we see *all the world* so far out of the way; and remain steadfast in this wholesome doctrine."[49] Calvin is adamant that salvation is based on God's sovereign work alone. God, however, uses preaching and teaching as his instruments to communicate the gospel. In his comments on Matthew 13:37, "The one who sows the good seed is the Son of Man" (ESV), Calvin asserts the following:

> When Christ says, not that the ministers of the word sow, but that he alone sows, this is not without meaning ... yet as he makes use of our exertions, and employs us as his instruments, for cultivating his field, so that He alone acts by us and in us, he justly claims for himself what is, in some respects, common to his ministers. Let us, therefore, remember, that the Gospel is preached, not only by Christ's command, but by his authority, and direction; in short, that we are only his hand, and that He alone is the Author of the work.[50]

For Calvin, God—not the Church or the pope—is our Savior and sovereign Master, and God alone determines what is to be taught. God, however, uses the mouths of preachers and teachers to communicate the gospel. Calvin also addresses this in a sermon on Deuteronomy, in which he answers the

---

48. C. H. Spurgeon, "Good Earnests of Great Success," Sermon No. 802 delivered on January 12, 1868, https://www.ccel.org/ccel/spurgeon/sermons14.xv.html.

49. Sermon II on 2 Timothy 1:8–9 in Calvin, *A Selection of the Most Celebrated Sermons of John Calvin*, 14.

50. Calvin, *Calvin's Complete Commentaries*, Kindle locations 382899–900.

critical questions of *Why do we come to the sermon?* and *Why is there this order in the Church?*

> It is so that God may govern us and that we may have our Lord Jesus Christ as our Sovereign Teacher, so that we may be the flock that he leads. Now, that cannot be unless we all hear his voice, distinguishing it from the voice of strangers; so that we may not be carried here and there like reeds shaken by every wind, but may be stayed on the purity of Holy Scripture and our faith so grounded there that the devil will never shake it.[51]

The spread of the gospel and the reign of Christ are the God-appointed work of the church. They are accomplished not just by overseas missions and the evangelizing of the heathens, but also by rightly communicating God's Word through local preaching and teaching. Without the proper preaching and the teaching of sound, biblical doctrine, salvation is at risk.

Calvin understood the significant role that Geneva played in the communication of the gospel. In a letter to Heinrich Bullinger in 1549, he writes, "When I consider how very important this corner is for the propagation of the kingdom of Christ, I have good reason to be anxious that it should be carefully watched over."[52] The true church is dependent upon the faithful proclamation of the word of God, whereby God teaches his people. Calvin understands this writing, "There is no other way of raising up the church of God than by the light of the word, in which God himself, by his own voice, points out the way of salvation. Until the truth shines, men cannot be united together, so as to form a true church."[53] It does not happen by churches colonizing other countries or individuals adhering to a leader's teachings. While God uses the "outward voice of men," it is not to increase the power of the church in the world. Instead, it is to draw others to God.[54]

---

51. Cited in Parker, *Calvin's Preaching*, 50.

52. Jean Calvin, Jules Bonnet, and Henry Beveridge, *John Calvin: Tracts and Letters* (Edinburgh: Banner of Truth Trust, 2009), 2:227.

53. *Commentary on Micah* 4:1–2, in Calvin, *Calvin's Complete Commentaries*, Kindle locations 344192–93.

54. Commenting on Isaiah 2:3, Calvin writes, "By these words he first declares that the godly will be filled with such an ardent desire to spread the doctrines of religion, that everyone, not satisfied with his own calling and his personal knowledge, will desire to draw others with him. ... This points out to us also the ordinary method of collecting a church, which is,

God appoints ministers of the gospel, depositing the teaching of his salvation with them, to point "the way of salvation to all mankind." This appointment is not limited to the church leaders, but is the "common duty of the children of God."[55]

THE ROLE OF SOUND DOCTRINE

Calvin communicates the vital role that sound doctrine plays in spreading the good news and reconciling humanity to God. Doctrine, for the Genevan professor, is not just an academic discipline, but a lifeline for the unbeliever. While Catholic institutions during that time stressed the significance of studying canon law and logic, priding themselves on being bastions of higher learning, Geneva trained people to be disciples of Scripture. Real knowledge and true religion are not based on human understanding, but on a correct apprehension of God, which is only fully available in his Word. Calvin proclaims this idea in his *Institutes*:

> Now, in order that true religion may shine upon us, we ought to hold that it must take its beginning from heavenly doctrine and that no one can get even the slightest taste of right and sound doctrine unless he be a pupil of Scripture. Hence, there also emerges the beginning of true understanding when we reverently embrace what it pleases God there to witness of himself. But not only faith, perfect and in every way complete, but all right knowledge of God is born of obedience. And surely in this respect God has, by his singular providence, taken thought for mortals through all ages.[56]

The teaching of sound doctrine has a twofold function—to gather sheep, and to ward off wolves. God supplies the teacher with the word of God

---

by the outward voice of men; for though God might bring each person to himself by a secret influence, yet he employs the agency of men." Calvin, *Calvin's Complete Commentaries*, Kindle locations 179383–86.

55. Commenting on Daniel 12:3 he writes, "God has deposited the teaching of his salvation with us, not for the purpose of our privately keeping it to ourselves, but of our pointing out the way of salvation to all mankind. This, therefore, is the common duty of the children of God." Calvin, *Calvin's Complete Commentaries*, Kindle locations 315249–50.

56. Calvin, *Institutes of the Christian Religion*.

and the Holy Spirit to accomplish both.[57] Ignorance and false teaching cor-
rupts sound doctrine and perverts the gospel, putting the flock at risk and
detracting from the glory of Christ.[58] God uses the proper communication
of the Word, however, to spread the kingdom of his Son. There can be no
true religion and godliness, according to Calvin, without the sound doctrine found in the word of God.[59]

Calvin's lengthy section in the *Institutes* entitled "The True Church"
helps establish the ecclesiology and in turn the missiology of Geneva and
the Reformed faith. Calvin holds that there is both a visible (institutional
church) and invisible church (made up of God's elect). The visible church,
the "mother of believers," has a vital role in bringing about the invisible
church by communicating sound doctrine so that the gospel can take root
in the heart.[60] He identifies two primary biblical marks of the true church:

---

57. Commenting on Titus 1:9, he writes, "The pastor ought to have two voices: one, for
gathering the sheep; and another, for warding off and driving away wolves and thieves. The
Scripture supplies him with the means of doing both; for he who is deeply skilled in it will
be able both to govern those who are teachable, and to refute the enemies of the truth. This
twofold use of Scripture Paul describes when he says, That he may be able to exhort and to
convince adversaries." Calvin, *Calvin's Complete Commentaries*, Kindle locations 550562–65.

58. In discussing Acts 20:30, Calvin writes, "For the sincerity of the word of God doth
then flourish when the pastors join hand in hand to bring disciples unto Christ, because this
alone is the sound state of the Church, that he be heard alone; wherefore, both the doctrine of
salvation must needs be perverted, and also the safety of the flock must needs go to nought,
where men be desirous of mastership. And as this place teacheth that almost all corruptions
of doctrine flow from the pride of men, so we learn again out of the same that it cannot otherwise be, but that ambitious men will turn away from right purity, and corrupt the word of
God. For seeing that the pure and sincere handling of the Scripture tendeth to this end, that
Christ alone may have the preeminence, and that men can challenge nothing to themselves,
but they shall take so much from the glory of Christ, it followeth that those are corrupters of
sound doctrine who are addicted to themselves, and study to advance their own glory, which
doth only darken Christ. Which thing the Lord doth confirm in the seventh of John (John 7:18)."
Calvin, *Calvin's Complete Commentaries*, Kindle locations 491937–45.

59. In his commentary on Acts 17:4 he writes, "Nevertheless, let us know that the truth
and the sound doctrine of the word of God is the rule of godliness, so that there can be no
religion without the true light of understanding." Calvin, *Calvin's Complete Commentaries*
Kindle locations 489748–50.
Commenting on Acts 4, he writes, "Howsoever the ministers of sound doctrine be as sheep
in the mouths of wolves, yet doth God spread abroad the kingdom of his Son; he fostereth the
light of the gospel which is lighted; and he is the protector of his children." Calvin, *Calvin's
Complete Commentaries*, Kindle location 479402.

60. He describes this role in the fourth book of *Institutes*, "The External Means or Aids by
Which God Invites Us into the Society of Christ and Holds Us Therein" (*Institutes*, IV). Calvin,
Institutes of the Christian Religion, Kindle locations 24904–5.

The pure ministry of the Word and pure mode of celebrating the Sacraments are, as we say, sufficient pledge and guarantee that we may safely embrace as church any society in which both of these marks exist. The principle extends to the point that we must not reject it so long as it retains them, even if it otherwise swarms with many faults.[61]

Geneva took seriously the biblical call for the church to be marked by "pure ministry of the Word." Not only did the academy train future ministers to do just that, but Calvin's Geneva also established a biblically grounded confession and catechism to help standardize the doctrinal teaching. Ministers of Geneva were required to adhere to this catechism. Calvin's catechism had a tremendous impact on the spread of the Reformed faith, being translated from French into Latin, Greek, Hebrew, Italian, German, and Spanish. It found its way to Scotland, Hungary, Poland, and the Netherlands. The doctrinal work also served as a model for the Heidelberg Catechism. The communication of sound biblical doctrine stands at the heart of Geneva's missiology.

FIGHTING FALSE RELIGION AND PROMOTING TRUE RELIGION

For Calvin's Geneva, a key to the spread of the gospel was not only the establishment of sound biblical doctrine, but also fighting against false teaching. This included responding to threats from other religions (such as Judaism and Islam) as well as heretical beliefs being propagated from within Christianity (such as those promoted by Roman Catholicism and the Anabaptists). While Calvin believes that the promises concerning the gospel were not only for those of the new covenant but also for the Old Testament Jews, he warns the church of the dangers of being influenced by the false beliefs of Jews of their day, who are blind and disobedient to the gospel truth.[62] He maintains a hope that they will turn to Christ and

---

61. *Institutes*, IV:1:12, in Calvin, *Institutes of the Christian Religion*, Kindle locations 25177–80.

62. "Let no one perversely say here that the promises concerning the gospel, sealed in the Law and the Prophets, were intended for the new people." (*Institutes* II.10.3). Calvin, *Institutes of the Christian Religion* (Presbyterian Publishing Corporation), Kindle locations 11445–48.

calls believers to seek to win them over to Christianity, writing "when we have to do with any Jews, which are not acquainted with our customs, and that we go about to win them and draw them to the obedience of the Gospel: we must for a time (in being conversant with them) abstain from the things which they think to be foresended [prohibited]."[63] More threatening than the Jews, however, according to Calvin, were the Papists, who depose Christ and rest their beliefs upon the "fancies of men."[64] Calvin writes this warning to the church:

> Though the Pope have oppressed the Church with his sacrilegious tyranny, yet doth he make boast of the title of the Church; yea, he deceiveth men under the vain title of the Church, that he may put out the clear light of sound doctrine. But if we shall come thoroughly to examine the matter, we may easily refute such a gross mock, because he alone beareth rule, having deposed Christ. He doth in word confess that he is Christ's vicar; but in very deed after that he hath by a beautiful banishment obey Christ, the King of kings, that there may be one sheepfold and one Shepherd (John 10:16).[65]

He likens the Papists to the Pharisees, who corrupt the church and "extinguish the Gospel." They are even willing to align themselves with heretics, according to Calvin, if it furthers their power. Their bad example should cause the church to labor with greater boldness in the defense of true and sound doctrine.[66]

---

63. Sermon on Galatians 2:6–8. The Ninth Sermon, John Calvin, *Sermons on Galatians* (Albany, OR: AGES Software, 1998), http://media.sabda.org/alkitab-7/LIBRARY/CALVIN/CAL_SGAL.PDF, 136.

64. Ibid. He continues, "But contrariwise, if the Papists would bring us to this point, that we should continually forbear the eating of flesh upon Fridays and Saturdays, and in Lent season, and upon other days of their appointing: whichsoever of us should agree to that, he were a traitor to the Gospel, and we should rather die a hundred times. For why? We must keep the liberty that is purchased for us by our Lord Jesus Christ. If it be said, and how so? Ought a man to trouble the whole world, and to be so willful for a little liquorousness [pleasant desire] of eating flesh? The question is not whether a man should eat flesh or no: but whether God ought to be obeyed and the thing used which he permitteth, or whether we should rest upon the fancies of men."

65. Acts 15:16. Calvin, *Calvin's Complete Commentaries*, Kindle locations 488643–49.

66. Ibid., Kindle locations 465862–65. The Reformer writes about John 7:32, "Meanwhile, since the Pharisees had such ardent zeal and such incessant toil for defending their tyranny

The Catholics, however, were not the only ones endangering the gospel and true worship. Calvin sees any Christian who promotes an unbiblical view of Christ as a threat. This includes Servetus and the Anabaptists. Without a proper understanding of Christ as fully human and fully divine, united in one person, salvation is not possible.[67] The principal aim for the true believer is not to confuse and mislead others, but "to teach the ignorant and to show them the way of salvation."[68]

CONCLUSION

The Latin phrase *post tenebras lux* (after the darkness light), has become synonymous with Calvin's Geneva for a good reason. The biblical metaphor of light was a significant theme for the Reformer and the Swiss city. Calvin personally understood what it was like to be enlightened by God and to move from the darkness of ignorance and sin to being a child of God. Calvin's personal conversion changed the trajectory of his life. He saw his calling to be obedient to Christ, regardless of the personal cost. This led him to minister in Geneva, a city that William Farel describes as having "little sympathy for the gospel," when he all he wanted was a quiet life of study in Strasbourg. He even returned to Geneva after being expelled, though "there is no place on earth of which" he was "more afraid."[69] Calvin's conviction that people are to obey God and his Word dominated his life, theology, and missiology. The Reformer understood that the ultimate goal of the Christian is to glorify Christ and to draw others to him. Calvin spurred the citizens of Geneva to also recognize their calling to be "children of light" and to make themselves servants

---

and the corrupt state of the Church, how much more zealous ought we to be in maintaining the kingdom of Christ! The Papists in the present day are not less mad or less eager to extinguish the Gospel; and yet it is monstrously wicked that their example does not, at least, whet our desires, and cause us to labor with greater boldness in the defense of true and sound doctrine."

67. Ibid., Kindle locations 460159–62. Calvin writes, "And in the present day, Servetus and the Anabaptists invent a Christ who is confusedly compounded of two natures, as if he were a Divine man. In words, indeed, he acknowledges that Christ is God; but if you admit his raving imaginations, the Divinity is at one time changed into human nature, and at another time, the nature of man is swallowed up by the Divinity."

68. John Calvin, *Sermons on the Epistle to the Ephesians* (London: Banner of Truth Trust, 1987), 463.

69. E. William Monter, *Calvin's Geneva* (Eugene, OR: Wipf and Stock, 2012), 70

of God's Word. In a sermon on Ephesians 4:29-30, Calvin preaches the following:

> We are all the children of light, after having been enlightened by faith, and are commanded to carry in our hands "burning lamps," (that we may not wander in darkness) and even to point out to others the way of life (Luke 12:35). But, as the preaching of the Gospel was committed to the apostles above others, and is now committed to the pastors of the Church, this designation is given to them, in a peculiar manner, by Christ. "They are placed in this rank on the condition, that they shall shine, as from an elevated situation, on all others."[70]

While pastors have the special role to preach the gospel, Calvin encourages the Genevans to recognize that all children of God are called to win others to Christ. Having received God's gracious mercy, Christians are called to be heralds of Christ.[71] As the book of Hebrews communicates, the church is not simply to gather for its own sake, but is also to seek to restore those who have wandered away and lead others to the truth of the gospel.[72] Having been enlightened by God, believers are to give light to unbelievers "who wander and reel and stumble."[73] Calvin asserts this idea in a sermon on Ephesians 4:6–8:

> Generally, because we have the gospel freely preached here among us, and because we ought everywhere to be like a burning lamp to show the way of salvation [John 5:35]. And particularly, by every man discharging his own duty that we give no cause of offence to our neighbors, but rather endeavor to draw to us those are estranged from God and his truth.[74]

---

70. Calvin, *Calvin's Complete Commentaries*, Kindle locations 375403-7.

71. He writes this in his comments on Psalm 51:16. Ibid., Kindle locations 143926-28.

72. Comments on Hebrews 10:25 in Ibid., Kindle locations 556876-77.

73. Sermons on Ephesians 5:8-11. Calvin, *Sermons on the Epistle to the Ephesians*, 513.

74. Calvin, *Sermons on the Epistle to the Ephesians*, 340. "Having said, 'Not forsaking the assembling together,' he adds, But exhorting one another; by which he intimates that all the godly ought by all means possible to exert themselves in the work of gathering together the Church on every side; for we are called by the Lord on this condition, that everyone should afterwards strive to lead others to the truth, to restore the wandering to the right way, to extend a helping hand to the fallen, to win over those who are without. But if we ought to

Calvin's Genevans understood their calling to glorify God by being a light in a dark world. This awareness shaped how they approached missions. In response to Roman Catholicism and the persecution of Protestants, Reformed Protestants developed a more holistic gospel. Though they sent out missionaries to foreign countries, they did not limit missions to converting heathens to the Imperial Church. Rather, in accordance with Acts 13:47, they situated missions in their ecclesiology. Geneva sought to be a light, so the whole world might have the opportunity to glorify Christ as Lord. The most effective way to be a light was by training pastors to teach and preach God's Word and the core gospel truths contained in it. In doing so, Geneva promoted the communication of the pure gospel, both within the local church and abroad; to fulfill Matthew 5:14: "You are the light of the world. A city set on a hill cannot be hidden" (ESV).

BIBLIOGRAPHY

Barth, Karl, and Eduard Thurneysen. *Revolutionary Theology in the Making: Barth-Thurneysen Correspondence, 1914–1925.* Louisville: Westminster John Knox, 1964.

Beaver, R. Pierce. "The Genevan Mission to Brazil." In *The Heritage of John Calvin: Heritage Hall Lectures, 1960–1970,* edited by John H. Bratt, 55–73. Grand Rapids: Eerdmans, 1973.

Calhoun, David B. "John Calvin: Missionary Hero or Missionary Failure?" *Presbyterion* 5, no. 1 (1979): 16–33.

Calvin, John. *Commentary upon the Acts of the Apostles.* Edited from the original English translation of Christopher Fetherstone by Henry Beveridge. Edinburgh: T&T Clark, 1859.

———. *A Selection of the Most Celebrated Sermons of John Calvin.* Philadelphia: Charles Desilver, 1860.

———. *Calvin: Theological Treatises.* Translated with introductions and notes by J. K. S. Reid. London: SCM Press, 1954.

———. *Sermons on the Epistle to the Ephesians.* London: Banner of Truth Trust, 1987.

---

bestow so much labor on those who are yet aliens to the flock of Christ, how much more diligence is required in exhorting the brethren whom God has already joined to us?"

———. *Calvin: Institutes of the Christian Religion*. Edited by John T. McNeill. Translated by Ford Lewis Battles. Louisville: Westminster John Knox, 2006.

———. and Jules Bonnet, and Henry Beveridge. *John Calvin: Tracts and Letters*. Edinburgh: Banner of Truth Trust, 2009.

———. *Calvin's Complete Commentaries*. Corona, CA: E4 Group, 2013. Kindle.

———. *Sermons on Galatians*. Albany, OR: AGES Software, 1998. http:// media.sabda.org/alkitab-7/LIBRARY/CALVIN/CAL_SGAL.PDF.

Beza, Theodore. *The Life of John Calvin*. Philadelphia: Westminster Press, 1909.

Delmas, Louis. *The Huguenots of La Rochelle: A Translation of "The Reformed Church of La Rochelle, an Historical Sketch."* New York: Randolph, 1880.

Estienne, Robert. *L'ordre Dv College De Geneue*. Geneva: L'Olivier de Rob. Estienne, 1859. https://babel.hathitrust.org/cgi/pt?id=njp.3210106 8146321&view=1up&seq=5.

Fuhrmann, Paul. "Calvin, the Expositor of Scripture." *Interpretation: A Journal of Bible and Theology* 6 (April 1952): 188–209.

Haroutunian, Joseph, and Louise Pettibone Smith. *Calvin: Commentaries*. Louisville: Westminster John Knox, 2006.

Haykin, Michael A. G. *To the Ends of the Earth: Calvin's Missional Vision and Legacy*. Wheaton, IL: Crossway, 2014.

Hogg, William Richey. "The Rise of Protestant Missionary Concern, 1517–1914." In *The Theology of Christian Mission*, edited by Gerald H. Anderson, 95–111. New York: McGraw-Hill, 1961.

Hughes, Philip E. *The Register of the Company of Pastors of Geneva in the Time of Calvin*. Eugene, OR: Wipf & Stock, 2004.

———. "John Calvin: Director of Mission." In *The Heritage of John Calvin: Heritage Hall Lectures, 1960–1970*, edited by John H. Bratt, 40–54. Grand Rapids: Eerdmans, 1973.

James, Frank A. III. "Calvin the Evangelist." *Reformed Quarterly* 19, no. 2/3 (Fall 2001): 3–6.

Kane, J. Herbert. *A Concise History of the Christian World Mission: A Panoramic View of Missions from Pentecost to the Present*. Rev. ed. Grand Rapids: Baker, 1982.

Kantzer, Kenneth S. "Calvin and the Holy Scriptures." In *Inspiration and Interpretation*, edited by John F. Walvoord. Grand Rapids: Eerdmans, 1957.

Knox, John. *Writings of the Rev. John Knox: Minister of God's Word in Scotland*. Philadelphia: Presbyterian Board of Publication, 1842. http://books.google.com/books?id=XvoQAAAAIAAJ.

Latourette, Kenneth Scott. *A History of the Expansion of Christianity*. Grand Rapids: Zondervan, 1937.

Maag, Karin. "Preaching Practice: Reformed Students' Sermons." In *The Formation of Clerical and Confessional Identities in Early Modern Europe*, edited by Wim Janse and Barbara Pitkin, 133–48. Leiden: Brill, 2006.

———. *Seminary or University?: The Genevan Academy and Reformed Higher Education, 1560–1620*. Aldershot: Scolar Press, 1995.

Manetsch, Scott M. *Calvin's Company of Pastors: Pastoral Care and the Emerging Reformed Church, 1536–1609*. Oxford: Oxford University Press, 2015.

McGoldrick, James Edward. "John Calvin: Erudite Educator." *Mid-America Journal of Theology* 21 (2010): 121–32.

Monter, E. William. *Calvin's Geneva*. Eugene, OR: Wipf and Stock, 2012.

Neill, Stephen. *A History of Christian Missions*. Baltimore, MD: Penguin Books, 1964.

———, and Owen Chadwick. *A History of Christian Missions*. 2nd ed. London: Penguin Books, 1986.

Parker, T. H. L. *Calvin's Preaching*. Louisville: Westminster John Knox, 1992.

Reid, W. Stanford. "Calvin's Geneva: A Missionary Centre." *The Reformed Theological Review* 42, no. 3 (1983): 65–74.

Spurgeon, C. H. "Good Earnests of Great Success." Sermon No. 802 delivered on January 12, 1868. https://www.ccel.org/ccel/spurgeon/sermons14.xv.html.

Stewart, Kenneth J. "Calvinism and Missions: The Contested Relationship Revisited." *Themelios* 34, no. 1 (2009): 63–78.

Stott, John. *Romans: God's Good News for the World*. Downers Grove, IL: InterVarsity Press, 1994.

Tucker, Ruth A. *From Jerusalem to Irian Jaya: A Biographical History of Christian Missions.* 2nd ed. Grand Rapids: Zondervan, 2004.

Walker, Jeremy. "An Outline of the Life of John Calvin." *Banner of Truth* (blog). February 3, 2009. https://banneroftruth.org/us/resources/articles/2009/an-outline-of-the-life-of-john-calvin/.

Warneck, Gustav. *Outline of a History of Protestant Missions from the Reformation to the Present Time.* Chicago: Fleming H. Revell Company, 1901.

Zabilka, Ivan L. "Calvin's Contribution to Universal Education." *The Asbury Theological Journal* 44, no. 1 (Spring 1989): 77–96.

Zorn, Jean-François. "Did Calvin Foster or Hinder the Missions?" *Exchange* 40, no. 2 (2011): 170–91.

6

—

FRENCH REFORMED MISSION IN COLONIAL BRAZIL

Franklin Ferreira

This chapter presents the motivations that led a group of French Protestants, under the leadership of Nicolas Durand de Villegagnon, to a small island in Guanabara Bay, in Brazil, which became Fort Coligny. I will describe the voyage from Europe, their arrival in Rio de Janeiro, and the initial problems among the settlers. Originating from Geneva, Switzerland, and Rouen, Honfleur, and Paris, France, the French Protestants headed for that fateful bay, where trouble soon arose. This led them to flee to the mainland where a few managed to escape back to France, while others were captured and martyred. This essay considers the work of these men, such as preaching and evangelizing the French and Indians, celebrating the Lord's Supper and practicing Christian discipline, and concludes with an evaluation of their accomplishments, which blazed a new trail in propagating the Reformed faith.

BRAZIL AS A COLONY

THE EUROPEAN DISCOVERY OF BRAZIL

The sailors saw the first birds on April 22, 1500, and spotted land later that afternoon. Because it was Easter week [*Páscoa* in Portuguese], Pedro Álvares Cabral, the commander-in-chief of a Portuguese fleet, gave the name of *Pascoal* to the first high mountain he saw. It was the Terra of Vera

Cruz [Land of Vera Cruz].[1] His initial destination was India, but after several setbacks, he landed in what he later called the Terra de Santa Cruz [Land of Santa Cruz] (1501), when Amerigo Vespucci found out it was not an island, and finally called it Brazil (1503), due to a tree called Pau Brasil [Brazilwood].[2] Upon arriving in the country, they docked at a large bay, named Porto Seguro [Safe Haven].[3] On Sunday, April 26, the first mass in Brazil was celebrated on the island of Coroa Vermelha by Friar Henrique de Coimbra, the leader of the friars of St. Francis, the first religious representatives of Portugal.

A few days later, the ceremony was repeated on the mainland, this being the grand official mass. They raised a large wooden cross, and the artillery fired a salvo as the commander-in-chief of the fleet took formal possession for the king of Portugal, Manuel I, the Fortunate, and named it Vera Cruz. As the supply ship commanded by Gaspar de Lemos sailed to Portugal to announce the discovery of new lands, the rest of the fleet set sail for India.[4]

RIO DE JANEIRO BEFORE THE FRENCH

The Portuguese discovered Guanabara Bay on January 1, 1502. Due to the custom of calling any river mouth a "river" and due to the date, the sailors referred to it as Rio de Janeiro [January River]. They founded a trading post to exchange spices with the natives, but it was soon destroyed in retaliation for the behavior of one of its foremen.[5] In 1519, Fernão de Magalhães

---

1. S.B. Holanda et al., *História geral da civilização brasileira: A época colonial* (São Paulo: Difel, 1976), 35. Little is known of Pedro Álvares Cabral. He is known to have been born in Belmont in 1467 or 1468. He was in his early thirties when he took over command of the fleet. This was made up of ten warships, a round carrier, and some other merchant vessels incorporated into the expedition.

2. Today it is known that the Portuguese fleet landing here was not the work of chance. "Cabral brought strict recommendations to see if, within the Portuguese jurisdiction under the Treaty of Tordesillas, the land whose existence was more than suspected in Portugal was worth anything." Rocha Pombo, *História do Brasil, vol. 1: O descobrimento e a colonização* (Rio de Janeiro: W. N. Jackson, 1967), 23. The Treaty of Tordesillas, signed at Tordesillas in Spain on June 7, 1494, divided the newly discovered lands outside Europe between the Portuguese Empire and the Spanish Empire (crown of Castile), along a meridian west of the Cape Verde islands, off the west coast of Africa. The lands to the east would belong to Portugal and the lands to the west to Spain.

3. Which is not the current Porto Seguro, but the bay of Santa Cruz, which has the current name of Esbrália Bay.

4. Holanda et al., *História geral da civilização brasileira*, 36.

5. Hélio Viana, *História do Brasil: Período Colonial* (São Paulo: Melhoramentos), 121.

traveling through this land found traces of the old trading post. One of his pilots, João Lopes de Carvalho, lived with the Tupinambás Indians for four years (1510–1514), and took his son with him whose mother was an Indian woman he had met on a previous visit to the region. Neither survived the Spanish expedition that completed the first circumnavigation of the world in 1522.[6] Rio de Janeiro remained abandoned until 1531, when Martin Afonso de Souza landed with his expedition. During the three months he stayed there, he built a stronghold and two brigantines,[7] and then headed for São Vicente. Shortly thereafter, Hereditary Captaincies were created,[8] and São Vicente was granted to Martin Afonso, which included Rio de Janeiro. Despite the excellent position of support to navigators, Martin Afonso did not plan to populate such a locality.[9]

Except for the captaincies of Pernambuco and São Vicente, the project proved to be a complete failure. In 1549, Portugal established the General Government, with Tomé de Souza. Six Jesuits accompanied him, after which four more arrived. Duarte da Costa brought sixteen with him to catechize Indians and settlers, but his effort had little impact. And long before Villegagnon arrived, the French visited the Brazilian coast. In June 1503, Captain Binot Paulmier of Gonneville set sail from Honfleur for an expedition to the West Indies. Six months later, he arrived on the north coast of Santa Catarina, Brazil. In 1521, Huges Roger made two further trips, a feat repeated by Jean Parmentier in 1525. The expedition by Villegagnon was the fourth to reach the beaches of Brazil from France.[10]

---

6. Pedro Calmon, *História do Brasil: As origens: século XVI* (Rio de Janeiro: Livraria José Olympio, 1959), 151.

7. A two-masted sailing vessel.

8. The captaincies of Brazil were administrative divisions and hereditary fiefs of Portugal in the colony of Brazil.

9. It is from this period that the name "carioca" (*caraí*, lord; *oca*, house) was given to any construction made to protect a fort or freshwater deposit, and was given, by extension, to the stream that flowed into the beach. Ibid. 151.

10. Laércio Caldeira da Andrada, *A Igreja dos Fiéis, Coligny, no Feudo de Villegaignon* (Rio de Janeiro: 1947), 32. For a narrative of the astounding and sad conquests of the Spaniards, Portuguese, and French, refer to Justo L. González, *Uma história ilustrada do cristianismo, vol. 7: A era dos conquistadores* (São Paulo: Vida Nova, 1990).

THE PROTESTANT REFORMATION IN FRANCE

THE BEGINNING OF THE REFORMATION IN FRANCE

In 1512, while an obscure Augustinian monk traveled to Rome to settle matters of his order, Jacques Lefèvre d'Etaples, a doctor of theology at the University of Paris, broke away from the ecclesiastical theology that dominated the church and emphasized a return to Scripture.[11] Regarding the Reformation in France, Merle D'Aubigné stated:

> The Reformation had to combat not only infidelity and superstition in France, but also a third antagonist, who had not yet been found, at least with such force, among the people of German origin: immorality. ... The violent enemies that the Reformation encountered simultaneously in France gave it a very special character. Nowhere else did it remain so often in prison, or resembled more the primitive Christianity in faith, in charity, and in the number of martyrs.[12]

Guillaume Briçonnet, bishop of Meaux, rallied around Lefèvre where those with reforming tendencies gathered due to their persecution from the teachers of Sobornne in Paris. Guillaume Farel also joined the Reformation, and later, not being discouraged by hardship and persecution, won over the cities of Montbelliard, Neuchatel, Lausanne, Aigle, and finally Geneva to the Reformed faith. On October 30, 1522, Lefèvre published a French translation of the Gospels. On November 6, he published the remaining books of the New Testament, and on October 12, 1524, he published all of these books. In 1525 he published a version of the Psalms.[13]

In Meaux, a new persecution took place, and the first martyrs shed their blood. Among these were Jean Leclerc (d. 1524), a wool carder, and pastor of the Reformed church in that city. By this time Luther's writings were arriving in France, exerting great influence on the thinking of such men. The writings which captivated the hearts and minds of the French Protestants, however, would come mainly from Strasbourg and Geneva,

---

11. For further information, see Philip Edgcumbe Hughes, *Lefèvre: Pioneer of Ecclesiastical Renewal in France* (Grand Rapids: Eerdmans, 1984).

12. D.H. Merle D'Aubigne, *História da Reforma do Décimo-sexto Século*, vol. 4 (São Paulo: Casa Editora Presbiteriana), 115.

13. D'Aubigne, *História da Reforma*, 115.

the city of John Calvin. Calvin's conversion gave the Reformation a writer who could popularize the new teaching. It was the persecution of French Protestants that led Calvin to publish the first edition of *The Institutes of the Christian Religion* in 1536,[14] as his intention was to defend French Christians as loyalists and to suggest the end of persecution. Calvin, in fact, led both the French and the Geneva Protestants. More than 155 pastors, trained in Geneva, were sent to France between 1555 and 1556.[15]

For those who are unconvinced of the missionary character of Calvin's work in Geneva, it is eye-opening to consult the Record of the Company of Pastors, especially the period from 1555 to 1562.[16] The names mentioned amount to eighty-eight persons sent—the majority under an alias—to almost all fields of Europe. For security reasons, however, many names are not mentioned, and in the year when the greatest number was sent—1561—the number of missionaries reached 142, more than many current missionary forces.[17] The chart below shows the following data on missionaries sent from Geneva from the period between 1555 and 1562:[18]

---

14. The first edition appeared in Basel in the year 1536. It was a book of 516 pages, but small enough in size to fit large pockets, and could circulate covertly through France. The success of such work was immediate and surprising. In nine months, the edition was exhausted, which, being in Latin, was accessible to readers of different nationalities. Calvin continued to prepare successive editions of the *Institutes* that grew as the years went by. They were edited some nine times, the latest editions dating from 1559 and 1560. In the final edition of 1559, it reached 1,500 pages. Refer to Timothy George, *Teologia dos Reformadores* (São Paulo: Nova Vida, 1993), 176–79.

15. Pierre Courthial, "A idade de ouro do calvinismo na França," in *Calvino e sua influência no mundo ocidental*, ed. Stanford W. Reid (São Paulo: CEP, 1990), 88. John Calvin's influence extended to various countries, such as Switzerland, France, the Netherlands, Germany, Hungary, Poland, England, Scotland, and the United States. The main factors that contributed to its influence spreading so widely were: preaching (it was central to Calvin's exposition and communication); his teaching role at the Geneva Academy; it earned the almost fierce loyalty of a wide variety of personality types; voluminous correspondence with men and women from all over Europe; his formal writings: he gave what he wrote a broader and more systematic theological focus. For more information on Calvin's impact on Western culture, see Stanford Reid, "A propagação do calvinismo no século XVI," ed. Stanford W. Reid, 35–59.

16. Philip Hughes, ed., *The Register of the Company of Pastors of Geneva in the Time of Calvin* (Grand Rapids: Eerdmans, 1966).

17. Philip Hughes, "John Calvin: Director of Mission," in *The Heritage of John Calvin*, ed. John H. Bratt (Grand Rapids: Eerdmans, 1973), 46.

18. Carter Lindeberg, *As Reformas na Europa* (São Leopoldo: Sinodal, 2001), 325.

1555	5 (4 to Piedmont, Italy)	1559	32 (all to France)
1556	5 (2 to Piedmont, 2 to Brazil)	1560	13 (1 to London)
1557	16 (4 to Piedmont, 1 to Antwerp, Belgium)	1561	12 (all to France)
1558	23 (1 to Turim, Italy)	1562	12 (all to France)

MISSIONARIES SENT FROM GENEVA (1555-1562)

Many people seek to find compelling mission statements from Calvin, and concerning this, R. Pierce Beaver, who served as a missionary and teacher in China, said:

> While Calvin had not explicitly urged the Reformed churches to carry out missions, he certainly was not hostile to world evangelization. In fact, his theology logically calls for missionary action, although he did not announce this. Isolated passages from Calvin's Commentaries strongly support the idea of missions. For example: Calvin declares that there are no people or social class in the world excluded from salvation, because God wants the gospel to be proclaimed to everyone without exception. Now the preaching of the gospel offers life, and therefore … God invites all equally to share in salvation." (See 1 Timothy 2:4)[19]

THE HEROIC PERIOD

At this time, the French Protestants began to be called Huguenots, a word of obscure origin, which they used as their honorific title. Reformed faith, first sown by the testimony and martyrdom of many, spread among the people, and manifested itself in theology and philosophy, in the sciences and arts, in the city and countryside, in family and professional life, and

---

19. R. Pierce Beaver, "The Genevan Mission to Brazil," in John H. Bratt (ed.), *The Heritage of John Calvin*, ed. John H. Bratt (Grand Rapids: Eerdmans, 1973), 56. For further information regarding the relationship between Calvin and missions, refer also to Antônio Carlos Barro, "A consciência missionária de João Calvino," *Fides Reformata* 3/1 (January–July 1998): 38–49.

even in politics. This same faith was present in all social classes, peasants and nobles, together with bourgeois and artists.

The French Protestants already counted on the support of Marguerite d'Angoulême, sister of King Francis I and wife of Henry, king of Navarre. Although she never made a public profession of faith, she gave shelter in her court to several Reformers who sought refuge, Farel among them. The persecutions became even more severe when, on July 24, 1539, Francis I reinforced them by promulgating an edict, but the king died in 1547. He was succeeded by Henry II, who continued with the persecutions, but conversions only increased. Until 1555, however, there were no organized Reformed churches in France. It was in this year, on July 12, 1555, that the Villegagnon's expedition left Le Havre with six hundred people. The church of Paris was organized in September 1555. This was a period of sowing the gospel, as congregations gathered in clandestine assemblies. In those churches, the new Reformed believers would meet to read the Scriptures, pray, and sing Psalms, listening to any itinerant preacher.

Such a situation was one of the characteristics of the French Reformed church. Although it received support from Geneva, few French clerics converted to the Reformed faith. For this reason, a far greater number of men from practically every occupation exercised "secret ministries" in those days. The Paris congregation, for example, in 1540 chose as its preacher Claude Le Peintre, a traveling goldsmith, who spent about three years in Geneva. Then he was burned at the stake. The congregation of Meaux then chose a carder in 1546.[20] From Geneva came Calvin's *Institutes of Christian Religion*, as well as catechetical, liturgical, and controversial writings. Several colporteurs were burned for spreading the French-language Scriptures, leaflets, and song books. Jean Crespin in his *Martyrology* or *Book of Martyrs*, with additions completed in 1619 by Pastor Simon Goulart, tells the story of 789 martyrdoms and mentions the names of 2,120 other Protestants sentenced to death or murdered.[21]

The first National Synod of the Reformed Churches met secretly in Paris from May 26 to May 28, 1559, according to Theodore Beza to "establish an agreement in doctrine and discipline, in accordance with the Word

---

20. D'Aubigne, *História da Reforma*, 169.

21. Courthial, "Calvinismo na França," 91.

of God."[22] A Parisian pastor, François de Morel, presided over this Synod, which brought together representatives of sixty of the one hundred existing churches in France. Growth in the French church was remarkable, for in 1555 there were only five organized churches: Paris, Meaux, Angers, Poitiers, and Loudon. According to Pierre Courthial, "There is no doubt that if the scourge of religious wars had not hit the country, France would have become predominantly Protestant."[23] This Synod adopted a confession of faith and a norm of discipline, both influenced by Calvin's teachings. The Huguenots reached twenty-five hundred congregations in 1562.

> The Huguenots became so powerful and well organized that they formed a kingdom within a kingdom. The government's understanding of this situation resulted in the change from the government policy of constant, fierce, and bloody persecution adopted between 1538 and 1559 to (from 1562) a policy of religious war that led France back to Rome.[24]

The commander of the Protestants at this time was Admiral Gaspard of Chantillon Coligny. Son of a marshal, he was knighted by King Francis I because of his participation in the Battle of Ceresole in Italy. From the age of twenty-two, Coligny was part of the French court having been a protégé of the Duke of Guise until breaking up with him because of his conversion to the Reformed faith. He was the head of the French Protestant party, and one of the most respectable men of his time. It was he who, at thirty-six years of age, sponsored the sending of the Huguenots to Brazil during the rule of King Henry II.

This is the background to the expedition of Villegagnon to Rio de Janeiro, and an understanding of some of the factors that explain the expansion and influence of the Reformed faith. We can now move to the adventure that involves the sending of two men (with a group of French immigrants sent by Coligny) across the Atlantic to Brazil. The record for 1556 states that on Tuesday, August 25, Pierre Richier and Guillaume Chartier were elected to minister on the islands off the Brazilian coast that had recently

---

22. Courthial, "Calvinismo na França," 93.
23. Courthial, "Calvinismo na França," 89.
24. Earle E. Cairns, *O Cristianismo Através dos Séculos* (São Paulo: Vida Nova, 1988), 257.

been conquered by France, and "were then commissioned into the Lord's care and sent with a letter" from the church of Geneva.[25] This project testifies to the broad vision, shared by Calvin and his colleagues in Geneva, regarding missionary work. And this was the context and motivations that brought the Huguenot missionaries to Brazil.

THE FRENCH IN RIO DE JANEIRO

PREPARATIONS AND LEAVING

The expedition began in the minds of Nicolas Durand de Villegagnon, nephew of the grand master of the Order of St. John of Jerusalem (also known as the Order of Malta, and called the "Scorpions of the Mediterranean" by the Ottomans), Villiers de I'Isle-Adam.[26] At the age of twenty-one, he entered the Order of St. John of Jerusalem, which had recently been expelled from Rhodes by Solomon II, settling in Malta in 1530. After a time of study, in 1541 he took part in an expedition against the Sultan of Algiers and left a written account of this combat in Latin. The following year, he was deployed to Hungary to fight the Turks. In 1548, already famous in military circles, he was commissioned to transport young Mary Stuart, the bride of Francis II, from Scotland to France, circumventing the surveillance of English ships. In 1551 he again fought the Turks, this time on the Island of Malta. That same year, as a reward for his services, he was appointed by Henry II to be Vice Admiral of Brittany, having the port of Brest under his supervision, with full freedom to fulfill his commitments to the Order. Soon afterwards he fought in Tripoli, but by the time he reached this stronghold the fighting was over, for its commandant, Francisco Vallier, had already surrendered.[27]

All these actions, including the protest against the Grand Master of his Order, who wanted to blame Vallier for Tripoli's defeat, earned Villegagnon a reputation in France, to where he retired in disgust after this defeat. In 1552 he was appointed to oversee the defense of the port of Brest. Villegagnon, however, entered into conflict with the captain of

---

25. Hughes, "John Calvin: Director of Mission," 47–48.

26. Calmon, *História do Brasil*, 269.

27. Pombo, *História do Brasil*, vol. 1, 206–7. Refer also to Calmon, *História do Brasil*, 269.

the stronghold, and without the king's support, "began to grow bored in France, accusing France of enormous ingratitude, since in its service he had spent all his youth in the military career."[28]

However, an acquaintance of Villegagnon resided in the town of Brest, and during an informal conversation told him about his travels, especially about the European discovery of Brazil. This was enough to stir the adventurer's mind. And it is precisely in these motivations that he brought this expedition to Brazil. Being a Roman Catholic knight of St. John, he sought support from the Reformed Admiral Gaspard de Coligny. Only this man could finance such a trip. And in this endeavor arose the idea of founding in overseas colonies where Reformed Christians could serve and worship God in freedom. This was commendable at a time when French Protestants were being slaughtered. Villegagnon, feeling the absolute need for Coligny's consent and support, adopted the safest, though not the most honorable, tactic: flattering the admiral. Villegagnon pretended to be inclined to converting in a maneuver to "let him glimpse the prompt accomplishment of one of the Huguenot chief's favorite projects, tampering him with the hope of creating a shelter for his persecuted fellow Europeans across the Atlantic."[29]

ARRANGEMENTS FOR THE TRIP

Villegagnon, according to Jean de Léry, the Reformed historian of the expedition, expressed to several French leaders a desire not only to "retire to a distant country where he could freely serve God according to the Reformed gospel, but also to prepare a refuge for all who wished to flee from persecution."[30] Such persecution was, indeed, already dreadful at that time. Thus he gained the support of the most prominent retired nobles in France, including Admiral Coligny himself, who interceded on behalf of Villegagnon before King Henry II, showing him that the kingdom would profit greatly from such an expedition. "In view of this, the sovereign ordered that he should be given two fully equipped ships, including artillery and ten thousand francs for the expenses of the voyage."[31] He would

---

28. Jean Crespin, *A Tragédia da Guanabara ou: A história dos protomártires do cristianismo no Brasil* (Rio de Janeiro: Typo-Lith, Pimenta de Mello & C., 1917), 15.

29. Pombo, *História do Brasil*, vol. 1, 207.

30. Jean de Léry, *Viagem à terra do Brasil* (São Paulo: Livraria Martins, 1924), 45–46.

31. de Léry, *Viagem à terra do Brasil*, 46.

also bring from Brest more artillery, gunpowder, bullets, guns, wood, and other accessories for building and for the defense of a fort. But he needed people to establish this overseas colony. Thus, he "published everywhere that he needed God-fearing, peaceful, and good people, for he knew that they would be more useful to him than anyone else because of their hope of forming a congregation whose members would be devoted to divine service."[32] Villegagnon's major staff consisted of Catholics and Reformed members.[33] But they lacked people. Villegagnon then asked the king for permission to recruit more settlers, only this time in the prisons of Rouen, Paris, and other cities. This human dross would create problems for the admiral. The number of six hundred settlers was reached. By a singular neglect, which highlights a profound ignorance in colonial matters on the part of Villegagnon and its protectors, "the essential principle of every society in formation had been forgotten: no one had considered the family. The whole expedition was made up of only men, and it is understood that, under such conditions, it was impossible to do a permanent work."[34]

Still evading any clear profession of faith, on July 12, 1555, Villegagnon left the Le Havre port with the two ships and a transport. As soon as they found themselves on the high seas, a storm threw them against the shores of England, and eventually they landed at Dieppe, in France. "Most of those who had yielded to the admiral's eloquence took advantage of that pretext to abandon him, leaving him only about eighty men, the very worst, because they were, besides a few mercenaries, the relapses that had been recruited in prison."[35] The ships having been finally repaired, they set sail on August 14, 1555. After various setbacks such as "docking, lack of drinking water, pestilences, excessive heat, headwinds, storms, bad weather from the torrid zone, and other things that would be tedious to list,"[36] having also been bombed by the Spaniards in Tenerife, they arrived in Rio de Janeiro

---

32. Pombo, *História do Brasil*, vol. 1, 209.

33. Jean Cointac, who later played a crucial role in the controversy with the Protestants, lord of Boules, and a doctor from Sorbonne; La Chapelle, de Boissi, Le Thoret et De Sausacque (who became the commander of the future Fort Coligny), and Nicolas Barré (expedition navigator), the latter, Protestant. Another one was a Franciscan cosmographer, André Thevet, who only stayed three months in Rio de Janeiro.

34. Pombo, *História do Brasil*, vol. 1, 209.

35. Crespin, *A Tragédia da Guanabara ou*, 19.

36. de Léry, *Viagem à terra do Brasil*, 47.

on November 10, 1555, to the sound of cannon fire, and the sailors shouting for joy after such a turbulent voyage.

SETTLEMENT AND THE ARRIVAL OF THE PASTORS OF GENEVA

Before disembarking all passengers to what cartographers would later call *France Antarctique* (Antarctic France), Villegagnon was careful to explore all the sea-stops, entering the immense Guanabara Bay, recognizing all points of the coast, including the smaller and larger islands. While he explored the bay, he fortified Rat Island (now called Fiscal Island), which he called Ratier, where he built some wooden shelters and laid some cannons. This fortification barred all entry to the Bay, but the undertow displaced the artillery pieces, endangering the garrison. Meanwhile, he "eventually settled on a deserted island where, after landing his artillery and other luggage, he began building a fort to secure themselves against both the savages and the Portuguese," on Serigipe Island (today called the Island of Villegagnon). This island offered unquestionable advantages to become the center of resistance of the position; it dominated the entrance of the bay, and was difficult to access since it was surrounded by reefs that stood almost at water level. What is hard to understand is Villegagnon's intent to found a colony on an island. To make matters worse, the admiral, relying on the provisions of the land, did not bring enough food. This greatly annoyed the settlers as their diet consisted of fruits and roots rather than bread, and rationed water instead of wine.

As soon as the French landed, Villegagnon put them to work on the island's fortification. Communications with the mainland were forbidden, and in a semi-slavery regime, within a few months the entire contour of the island was walled. In the words of Jean de Léry:

> At the ends of this island there are two hills on which Villegagnon had two houses built, the one where he resided, was built in the center of the island in a stone from fifty to sixty feet high. On both sides of this rock we flattened and prepared small spaces where not only the room, where we would gather for the lecture and the meal, were built, but also several other shelters that could seat some eighty people, including Villegagnon's entourage. But other than the house built on the rock, and a few masonry-clad artillery ramparts,

the rest were nothing more than rough wood-and-straw huts built in the style of the savages, who, in fact, built them. In a nutshell, this was the fort that Villegagnon called Coligny, thinking this would please Mr. Gaspar de Coligny, Admiral of France, without whose support, as I said at the beginning, he had never had the means to make the trip or build any fort in Brazil.[37]

One of the island's major drawbacks, however, was that it offered no drinking water. To remedy this, when possible, a large cistern was opened, which could contain and hold water for six months. But even seeking isolation, it was inevitable not to have contact with the Indians on the continent, because that was where the French went when they needed food. And the Indians made themselves very helpful for the French.

These Indians were the Tupinambás (the Tamoios of the Portuguese chronicles), who provided meat, fish, manioc flour, and fruits of the land for the French, as well as drinking water. The Indians even helped in the fortification of the island, bringing materials from the continent. But Villegagnon wanted to treat them with the same rigor as he treated the French, inasmuch as the main load of work fell on them, while the French drifted into idleness. On February 4, 1556, the ships that brought the expedition, that until then were docked in the Bay, returned to France.

To make matters worse, the French wanted to rebel. In a letter that Villegagnon wrote to Calvin asking for more pastors, he stated that the revolt stemmed from the fact that he had forbidden indigenous women from entering the Fort unaccompanied by their husbands. A number of mercenaries had begun living with such women.[38] A total of twenty-six mercenaries gathered together to conspire against and kill the admiral. The leader arranged with the others to kill the admiral. They tried to entice five Scottish guards who protected Villegagnon. These guards pretended to be part of the conspiracy, learning about the whole situation, and reported it to their supervisor. Vengeance did not take long. Villegagnon and those on his side, duly warned, armed themselves and arrested four of the leading conspirators, to whom they "inflicted very severe punishment, to the

---

37. de Léry, *Viagem à terra do Brasil*, 95.
38. Crespin, *A Tragédia da Guanabara ou*, 21.

fear of the others, and to retain control of their duties; two of those were put in prison with chains, and were ordered to publicly perform forced labor for a while."[39]

The leader of the plot was killed. This spread terror among the French of the colony and among the Tupinamba Indians. The Indians fled the coast, and even an epidemic was transmitted to them. Some frightened French fled to the mainland and founded the village of La Brigueterie, which provided shelter for the French pirates, who visited the coast all the way from Cabo Frio.

Villegagnon, in this disintegrating environment, tried to get a draft of troops from King Henry II, but the French government "did not want to understand the problem properly or hesitated to openly risk such an adventure."[40] In this context, the admiral requested help from Geneva. It was the only way to save the colony: to use the need of security for the French Reformed church. And he needed better quality reinforcements. The letter was sent on the ships that had returned to Europe.

> His letter was not preserved in any of Calvin's correspondence or in the Canton archives. Jean de Léry ... furnishes its content. The letter asked the Church of Geneva to immediately send to Villegagnon ministers of God's Word and with them many "well-educated people in the Christian religion" to reform him and his people and "bring the savages to the knowledge of their salvation." Given that the issue of missions was already clear before the Church of Geneva, "after receiving these letters and hearing the news" ... the Church of Geneva in one voice gave thanks to God for the expansion of the Kingdom of Jesus Christ in such a distant country, so different and among an entire nation without the knowledge of the true God.[41]

Calvin was in Frankfurt, Germany, at that time, but was informed of all the important matters taking place in Geneva and was always providing advice. There is no doubt that he was consulted about the mission, because the leaders carried letters from him to Villegagnon. Nicholas des Gallars,

---

39. Crespin, *A Tragédia da Guanabara ou*, 23.

40. Pombo, *História do Brasil*, vol. 1, 213.

41. Beaver, "The Genevan Mission to Brazil," 61.

Calvin's trusted man, and later, in 1557, pastor of the Reformed congregation of Rue Saint-Jacques in Paris, wrote a letter dated September 16, informing Calvin that the group had left Geneva "full of ardor" on the eighth of that same month. The church of Geneva had chosen two ministers for the mission: Pierre Richier and Guilhaume Chartier, fifty and thirty years old, respectively.[42] Eleven recruits were sent with them to work, four were carpenters, one worked with leather, one was a blacksmith, and one a tailor. Their names were: Pierre Bourdon, Matthieu Verneuil, Jean de Bourdel, André La Fon, Nicolas Denis, Martin David, Nicolas Raviquet, Nicolas Carmeau, Jacques Rousseau, Jean Gardien (who probably worked on the illustrations of Léry's book) and "I, Jean de Léry, who joined the company, as much for the strong desire God had given me to contribute to His glory, as for the curiosity of seeing this new world."[43] Léry was a shoemaker, having learned this profession while very young, for at eighteen he was in Geneva, studying theology. At the time of his trip to Brazil, he was twenty-three years old.

Admiral Coligny had also received a letter requesting reinforcement, so he then requested by letter that his friend Phillipe de Corguilleray, and Mr. Du Pont, to undertake the trip to Brazil, leading the Huguenot group. Mr. Du Pont lived in Bossy, near Geneva, and even at an advanced age agreed to lead the expedition. "Not even his personal affairs and the love he devoted to his children kept him from accepting the trust the Lord placed upon him."[44]

They left Geneva on September 8, 1556, had a meeting with Admiral Coligny in Chatillon-Sur-Loing, who encouraged them to pursue the endeavor. After a short stay in Paris, they moved to Rouen and then to Honfleur, near Normandy, where they joined a large group of Huguenots, recruited through the efforts of Admiral Coligny. The group was three

---

42. Crespin, *A Tragédia da Guanabara ou*, 25–26. Refer also to Philip Hughes, ed., *The register of the company of pastors of Geneva in the time of Calvin*, 317. Mention was made in reference to the sending of the ministers to Brazil on August 25, 1556. Pierre Richier was a doctor in theology and former Carmelite friar. He converted to Protestantism, and after his studies in Geneva, went to Brazil in 1556, where he returned the following year, was sent to La Rochelle, where he organized a church, and died in 1580. Guilhaume Chartier, a native de Vitré, Brittany, studied in Geneva and eagerly accepted the commissioning for America. After this expedition, little is known of him, except that he became chaplain of Jeane d'Albret.

43. de Léry, *Viagem à terra do Brasil*, 48–49.

44. Crespin, *A Tragédia da Guanabara ou*, 25.

hundred people. The commander of the expedition was the master of Bois
Le Conte, the nephew of Villegagnon, who commissioned three ships with
supplies and other items necessary for the trip to set sail on November 19
at the king's expense. Le Conte, who was elected Vice Admiral, was aboard
the "Petite Roberge" with about eighty people including soldiers and sailors. The other ships were the "Great Roberge," with 120 people aboard; on
the third boat, which was called "Roseé," there were almost ninety people,
including six boys, who were taken to learn the native language, and five
girls with a housekeeper.[45]

These were the first French women sent to Brazil. After many adven-
tures (even contrary to the opinion of the Huguenots, two English merchant ships were boarded and looted, one Irish, one Portuguese, and one
Spanish, the latter being towed to Brazil), on March 10, 1557, the expedition arrived in Rio de Janeiro, where they were welcomed with great joy by
Villegagnon. Léry, always an eyewitness, tells us that everyone gathered
at the beach, thankful to God for having protected them during the trip.
Then came Villegagnon, who greeted them with a large smile, embracing
them all. The pastors presented their credentials and the letters from John
Calvin, and Villegagnon said, "As for me, I have longed and wholeheartedly
desired this and welcome you very much, especially because I aspire for our
church to be the most well reformed of all. I want vices to be repressed, the
luxury of clothing condemned, and that all who might harm God's service
be removed from our midst." Then looking up at the heavens and clasping
his hands together, he said, "Lord God, I thank you that you have sent me
what I have been so intensely praying for so long." And turning again to
the companions, he continued:

> My children (for I want to be your father), just as Jesus Christ had
> nothing of this world for himself and did everything for us, so I
> (hoping that God will preserve my life until we strengthen our-
> selves in this country and you can discharge me) intend to do every-
> thing here for all who come for the same purpose as you came. It is
> my intention to create here a refuge for the persecuted faithful of
> France, Spain or any other country overseas, so that, without fear

---

45. de Léry, *Viagem à terra do Brasil*, 50.

of the king or emperor or any potentates, they may serve God with purity according to His will.[46]

These were the first words spoken by Villegagnon upon the arrival of the expedition on March 10, 1557. Then he gave orders to gather all the people in the fort, and Pierre Richier celebrated the first Protestant service in the Americas. A week later, the Lord's Supper was also celebrated according to the Reformed rite, on March 21. Villegagnon himself was the first to partake of it, after confessing his Reformed faith to the whole congregation.[47]

The Huguenots soon began working on fortification of the island, and Richier encouraged them, calling Villegagnon a new "Paul." To demonstrate his goodwill, Villegagnon created the Council of Notables, just like the one in Geneva, in which he was a moderator. But the apparent peace was broken during Pentecost in 1557. At the celebration of the previous Lord's Supper, Jean Cointac began to cast doubt on whether it was right to mix water to the wine at the consecration ceremony. He had come to Brazil with the promise that he would be ordained a bishop of the church, made by Villegagnon himself, but having been disapproved by the Genevan pastors, he began to spread discord. Quoting St. Cyprian, St. Clement, and the ecumenical councils, he was refuted by Pierre Richier, who used only the Scriptures to contradict such views. This then sparked violent debates about the nature of Christ's presence in the Eucharist. Shortly after, Villegagnon publicly sought to refute Richier during the celebration of a wedding. To avoid further debate, it was decided that Guilhaume Chartier would go to Geneva to be counseled by Calvin, leaving Guanabara on June 4, 1557, on one of the ships that set sail, loaded with redwood and other goods. Villegagnon's letter to Calvin, which Chartier was carrying, was never found. The Vice Admiral himself was willing to accept the Reformer's arbitration, but until the answer came, Richier was prevented from administering the sacraments, or from alluding in his sermons to the issues that caused the controversy. This was before Pentecost. On that date in June, Villegagnon, along with Cointac, gave orders to mix water with wine, and to follow the Catholic rite. When he was reminded of his earlier

---

46. de Léry, *Viagem à terra do Brasil*, 77.
47. de Léry, *Viagem à terra do Brasil*, 80–83.

commitment, he publicly denounced Reformed theology as heretical. Léry informs us that Villegagnon received "letters from Cardinal Lorraine and others advising him to stop sustaining the Calvinist heresy"[48] from a ship that docked at Cabo Frio during those days.

After humiliating Le Thoret, the Calvinist who was the commander of the fortress (who fled swimming to a British ship anchored offshore and headed for France), Lord Du Pont made it clear to the admiral that if he did not follow the Reformed faith, they would be under no obligation to follow him. After several hardships and humiliations, in October the Huguenots left the island to take refuge on land in the village of La Briqueterie, having remained there for about two months. It was an opportunity to evangelize the Indians, who treated them very kindly. Even the lords of La Chapelle and Boissi were expelled for not denying the Reformed faith.

Villegagnon also declared the council void, undertaking sole command of the fortress. He forbade Richier to preach and gather the Huguenots to pray unless the minister ratified a new formula for prayers, because according to him, the old ones were erroneous. In the small village, the French lived without any amenities, without wine even for their ceremonies, eating and drinking with the Indians (their diet consisted of roots, fruits, and fish) who turned out to be kinder than the French of the island, Villegagnon in particular.

In February 1558 a small boat called "Le Jacques" docked at Guanabara. According to Léry, this ship had embarked on the voyage sponsored by several French Reformed leaders, with the purpose of "exploring the land and choosing a place suitable for the location of seven hundred to eight hundred people who were to arrive later that same year in large groups of Flanders to colonize the country."[49] The ship's hull was already half-decayed, and was loaded with redwood, pepper, cotton, monkeys, parrots, and other products of the land. Since the ship did not belong to Villegagnon's company, he could not stop the Huguenots from embarking.[50] The captain agreed to transport them, and on January 4, 1558, he started the Atlantic crossing. The ship was small with only twenty-five sailors and fifteen

---

48. de Léry, *Viagem à terra do Brasil*, 227.

49. de Léry, *Viagem à terra do Brasil*, 227.

50. S. B. Holanda, et. al., *História geral da civilização brasileira*, 157.

passengers.[51] Even though he did not oppose the passengers from embarking, Villegagnon sent secret instructions to be handed over to the first judge
in France, telling him to execute the Huguenots as traitors and heretics.
This message was in a waterproof urn, but at the end of the trip, it fell
into the hands of a Huguenot judge, and was later used against its author.

Due to the excessive load, the vessel was about to sink just as soon as it
left the shore. Once the emergency repairs had been made, they discussed
the convenience of continuing the journey or to have the passengers stay
in Guanabara. Most of the Huguenots decided to continue their journey,
but faced with the ship's master's reply about the insecurity of the voyage,
Léry "and five other companions were already determined to return to the
land of the savage, only nine or ten leagues away, considering the possibility of the shipwreck, and hunger."[52] At the time of departure, one of the
Huguenots extended his arms in friendship to Léry and said, "I beg you to
stay with us, for despite the uncertainty of reaching France; there is more
hope of saving us on the side of Peru or any other island than in the claws of
Villegagnon, which, as you can imagine, will never give you rest."[53] In this
way the expedition historian was saved from suffering a similar fate as his
returning brothers. These were: Pierre Bourdon, Jean du Bourdel, Matthieu
Verneuil, André La Fon, and Jacques le Balleur. The others returned to
France, experiencing major storms. Passengers and crew were reduced to
eating leather (from belts, shoes, etc.) and remains, and reached Nantes,
more dead than alive. On May 24, 1558, they finally sighted Britain. They
docked at Hodierne, where they bought food, and finally, on May 26, they
entered the port of Blavet in Britain. All of them arrived safe and sound.
After saying goodbye to the Breton sailors, the Huguenots went to Nantes,
where they were very kindly treated by qualified doctors.

MARTYRDOM OF THE HUGUENOTS

The martyrdom of the Huguenots must be understood in the context of the
dramatic change that took place in Villegagnon's character. Since the Lord's
Supper controversy in June 1557, he became bitter and violent. The settlers

---

51. de Léry, *Viagem à terra do Brasil*, 227.
52. de Léry, *Viagem à terra do Brasil*, 229.
53. de Léry, *Viagem à terra do Brasil*, 229.

could identify the admiral's mood by the bright colors of his garments.[54] Both Léry and Crespin report his cruelties to the inhabitants of the fortress. Some thirty or forty men and women from another Tupinambá enemy tribe, who sold them to the French, were treated with extreme cruelty. One was tied to a piece of artillery, and the admiral himself spilled molten bacon on the poor Indian's buttocks.[55] Villegagnon's butlers, both reformed, were expelled from the Fort. An artisan starved to death, in spite of begging for food to the mentally unstable admiral. The climax was the expulsion of Jean Cointac from the fortress. When the Huguenots fled to La Briqueterie, Cointac was already there. He had been expelled by Villegagnon, and spent his days cursing the admiral. Then he fled to Bertioga, when the French and Tupinambás were going to attack Sao Vicente. Subsequent events were shared by eyewitnesses with Lord Du Pont in Paris, after their return from the colony.

The five Huguenots set out to sea, and only later did they notice that their longboat had no mast. They improvised one, along with a sail, and set off, heading for the coast. Having faced severe weather, after five days they landed on a beach near the Fort of Coligny. After being treated kindly by the local Indians, they headed for the fortress due to the illness of one of the Huguenots. They stayed on the beach for four days, and then they sailed to the Fort of Coligny.

They headed straight for La Briguiterie, and upon disembarking they were treated well by Admiral Villegagnon, who was there on private business. He at first welcomed them, but soon turned against them. He first took their longboat, and after twelve days began to think that they were spies of the Huguenots who had left with "Le Jacques."

Being the representative of Henry II on the island, it was his duty to prove the faith of the Huguenots, and envisioning this as the opportunity to get rid of them, he formulated a questionnaire with several controversial points, sending it to the Huguenots and giving them a twelve-hour deadline to answer it. The French who were with them at La Briguiterie tried to dissuade them from answering the admiral's challenge, but they did not shy away from the challenge. Asking for help "from the Spirit of Jesus

---

54. de Léry, *Viagem à terra do Brasil*, 89.
55. Calmon, *História do Brasil*, 282–83.

Christ," according to the words of the author of the *Histoire des Martyrs*, they chose Jean du Bourdel to write the confession because he was the most literate and knew Latin. After writing it, he submitted it to his companions, who signed it.

On February 9 they were taken to the fort—Pierre Bourdon stayed behind because he was sick. On introducing themselves to the admiral and reaffirming their desire to remain faithful to the confession, they experienced all the hatred of Villegagnon. The Huguenots were arrested, and terror gripped the islanders. The next morning, Friday, February 10, 1558, Villegagnon tried to get the Huguenots to renounce the confession, but they stood firm. After slapping du Bourdel violently, he ordered the executioner to handcuff the man's hands and lead him to a rock to throw him into the sea. After encouraging the other companions, he sang a Psalm, confessed his sins, and was thrown into the sea. Matthieu Verneuil was also led to the rock, and after reaffirming his desire not to recant, uttered his last words, "Lord Jesus, have mercy on me." André La Fon was considered harmless by Villegagnon who did not order his killing, and kept him at his service, for La Fon was a tailor—he needed to keep him to care for his wardrobe. Villegagnon crossed the estuary and went to the house where Bourdon, having fallen ill, had taken shelter. As Bourdon refused to deny the confession of faith, an executioner strangled him, and his body was thrown into the sea. His last words were:

> Lord God, I am also like those of my companions who with honor and glory fought the good fight for your Holy Name, so I ask you to grant me the grace not to succumb to the assaults of Satan, the world and the flesh. And forgive, O Lord, all the sins committed by me against your majesty, and this I implore you in the name of your beloved son Jesus Christ.[56]

Jacques Le Balleur was spared because he was a blacksmith.[57] This virtually marked the end of the French colony, and ended the Guanabara tragedy.

---

56. Crespin, *A Tragédia da Guanabara ou*, 55–64, 72–83.

57. Beaver, "The Genevan Mission to Brazil," 71. After managing to live in hiding, Jacques Le Balleur was arrested by the Portuguese near Bertioga. Authorities sent Jacques to Salvador, Bahia, which was the seat of the colonial government, where he was tried for the crime of "invasion" and "heresy" in 1559. In April 1567 he was burned at the stake, being an assistant

The End of the Colony

In late 1558, Villegagnon withdrew from the Fort of Coligny, returning to France. He was under the suspicion of both the Huguenots, who began to call him "Cain of America," "apostate," and "murderer," and on the part of Catholics, who suspected his Reformed inclinations. This marked the end of the French colony, which was under the supervision of Bois Le Comte. The colony was already being bedeviled by the Maracajás Indians, allies of the Portuguese, so they sent Mem de Sá to Brazil, whose orders were the expulsion of the French. In 1560 Mem de Sá left Salvador for Rio de Janeiro, with two ships, eight smaller vessels, and about 2,000 soldiers, having received more reinforcements from São Vicente. Jean Cointac betrayed the French by revealing all French positions. The fighting began on March 15. The number of Frenchmen on the island was 114, with some eight hundred Tupinambás supporting them. The fight was difficult and lasted two days. Following the capture of the gunpowder magazine, the French surrendered on Saturday, fleeing to the mainland and hiding in the forest. The following day, Sunday, March 17, 1560, amidst the celebrations of victory, the first mass was celebrated on the island.[58] The French who were not killed by the Maracajás Indians were rescued by a ship that picked them up off the coast. Thus ended the attempt to install a colony for the French Huguenots in Rio de Janeiro.

Upon his return to France, Villegagnon tried to polemicize with several Protestants. Out of this controversy came *Histoire d'un Voyage Fait en La Terre du Brésil*, written by Jean de Léry in 1578, partly to answer Villegagnon's accusations. He tried to involve Calvin, but it is recorded that Calvin threw Villeagiagnon's letter under his own feet. Until the end of his days he fought the Calvinists and Lutherans with his pen. At the Battle of Rouen in 1562, the iron ball of a Huguenot cannon crushed his leg. In 1568 he was appointed ambassador of the Knights of Malta to the French court. He died at Beauvais, near Nemours, on February 9, 1571.[59]

---

to the executioner José de Anchieta, to the consternation of the Catholics. Alvaro Reis, *The Martyr Le Balleur* (Rio de Janeiro: 1917).

58. Pombo, *História do Brasil*, vol. 1, 216, 221–23. Refer also to Holanda et al., *História geral da civilização brasileira*, 158, and Calmon, *História do Brasil*, 282–87. Cointac was sent to Portugal to stand trial before the Lisbon Inquisition on charges of heresy. When he was acquitted, he was exiled to India.

59. Beaver, "The Genevan Mission to Brazil," 72.

THE HUGUENOT TESTIMONY

According to Jean de Léry, the main objective of the Huguenot expedition to the lands of Brazil, requested by Villegagnon to Coligny and Calvin,
was to send "ministers, but also some other well-educated people in the
Christian religion, in order to better reform himself and his own and even
open the way of salvation to the savages."[60] In light of this statement we
will review the achievements of the Reformed within the limits imposed
on them and mentioned above.

MISSION TO THE FRENCH

Perhaps the most important work done among the French was preaching.
The first evangelical service held in the Americas was held at Fort Coligny
on March 10, 1557, a Wednesday. Villegagnon ordered to

> gather all his people with us in a small room in the middle of the
> island, and Minister Richier called upon God. We sang in chorus
> Psalm V and the above-mentioned minister, took as his theme the
> words from Psalm XXVII—'One thing I have asked from the LORD,
> that I shall seek: That I may dwell in the house of the LORD all
> the days of my life'—for the first message preached at the Fort of
> Coligny in America. During this occasion, Villegagnon did not cease
> to join his hands, raise his eyes to the sky, give high sighs and make
> other gestures that seemed to us all worthy of admiration. Finally,
> the solemn prayers having finished according to the ritual of the
> Reformed churches of France, and having been scheduled for them
> one day of the week, the meeting was dissolved.[61]

Villegagnon and the Geneva ministers agreed that "public prayers would
be held every night after work" and "ministers would preach twice on
Sunday and on the other days of the week for one hour; [Villegagnon] also
expressly commanded that the sacraments be administered in accordance
with the word of God and, as for the rest, discipline should be applied
against sinners."[62]

---

60. de Léry, *Viagem à terra do Brasil*, 47.
61. de Léry, *Viagem à terra do Brasil*, 77.
62. de Léry, *Viagem à terra do Brasil*, 79.

Already on Sunday, March 21, the first Lord's Supper was held, and all who would participate in it should give public confession of faith, "abjuring, before all, all papism." Shortly after this, however, the debates concerning the real presence of Christ in the Eucharist began. As we have seen, the crisis came to light on Pentecost when Villegagnon broke a previous agreement with the Genevan pastors to expect a response from Geneva about the controversy.

On April 3, two servants of Villegagnon "married at the time of the preaching, under the laws of the Reformed Church, two of the young women we had brought from France to this country." On May 17, Jean Cointac, the pivot of the bad blood over the Eucharist, himself married one of the young women, "a relative of one Laroquete, from Rouen," who had traveled to Brazil with the Huguenots, and died shortly before the wedding. The other two girls married two Norman interpreters.[63] Marriage between French and Indians was forbidden unless Indians were educated in the Reformed religion and baptized. Andrada says that "there have been numerous conversions, many of the Rouen and Paris prisoners were moved by the austere doctrine and virtues of the Protestant ministers and have accepted Christianity."[64] In favor of the Huguenots we have the fact that, led to an extreme situation, never did they take a violent stand against Villegagnon. Léry himself was arrested, but in the midst of his revolt, he was urged by Du Pont not to take a violent action that would dishonor the Reformed church. These are some of the deeds performed by the Huguenots among the French, but none of them had continuity, involved as they were with the controversies that began to plague the Reformed church of Fort Coligny.

MISSION TO THE TUPINAMBÁS INDIANS

Léry took careful notes of the rites and customs of the Brazilian Indians. These notes were recorded in his book, and were a pioneering description of colonial Brazil. He did not reproach customs and practices that were repulsive to the Europeans, nor did he condemn them for being different. He witnessed wars and cannibalism. He discovered that the Tupinambás

---

63. de Léry, *Viagem à terra do Brasil*, 86–87.

64. Andrada, *A Igreja dos Fiéis*, 66.

did not have a notion of the only true God, being only aware of the "evil spirits" that oppressed them. Notwithstanding the culture shock, Léry discovered good qualities in the Indians, such as hospitality and a willingness to listen to friends and strangers. Léry's method of evangelism was informal, taking advantage of every opportunity to evangelize.[65]

It was the absolute lack of time that prevented the conversion of the Indians, according to Pastor Richier and Léry. It is important to mention that ten Indians, ranging between nine and ten years of age, had been captured during the war by Indians who were friendly with the French, and sold as slaves to Villegagnon. These captured Indians were shipped on the same vessel to France (the "Rosée," which through one Nicolas Carmeau, took a letter to Calvin on April 1, 1557), "after minister Richier, at the end of a preaching, laid hands upon them, and we having begged God to be graceful with them in the sense of being the first of this poor people to be called unto salvation."[66] Upon arrival in France, authorities brought the boys before King Henry II, and distributed among several nobles. One of them was baptized by order of the Lord of Passy, and Léry himself recognized him at the residence of the latter upon his return home. The work ended after the return of the Reformed to France. There were no permanent fruits, but, Léry said, "I am of the opinion that had Villegagnon not abjured the Reformed religion, and had we been able to stay longer in the country, we would have called some of them to Jesus."[67]

THE CONFESSION OF FAITH

The greatest testimony of the Huguenots in Guanabara is the Confession of Faith (*Confessio Fluminensis*). This and the case brought by Villegagnon against Jean du Bourdel, Matthieu Verneuil, and Pierre Bourdon were handed over to Du Pont, about four months after his arrival in France, by "trusted people we have left in this country." They were eyewitnesses of the Huguenot martyrdom at Fort Coligny.[68] Du Pont then handed over the Confession of Faith and the proceedings to Léry, who felt it was his duty

---

65. de Léry, *Viagem à terra do Brasil*, 197–98.
66. de Léry, *Viagem à terra do Brasil*, 85.
67. de Léry, *Viagem à terra do Brasil*, 198.
68. de Léry, *Viagem à terra do Brasil*, 198.

to have this account "in the book of those who in our day have been martyred in defense of the Gospel." In 1558 he handed the manuscripts to Jean Crespin, who inserted it in his book.[69]

Jean du Bourdel was able to produce these answers, despite the most extreme circumstances, and this is a testimony to his mental fortitude. The main features of this clearly Reformed confession of faith are: loyalty to the old creeds, the importance placed on the study of the fathers of the church, and the enviable knowledge of the Scriptures and doctrine that Christians of the past possessed. It was the first confession of faith written in America, in the first Church of Brazil.

CONCLUSION

The Reformed mission in Rio de Janeiro ended in a melancholic manner. Perhaps their biggest problem was precisely their motivations. While for Calvin, Coligny, and the rest of the Huguenots, the expedition was the best way to find a refuge for the persecuted Protestants, as well as a place to freely spread the Reformed faith, for the king of France, Henry II, it was simply a way to obtain more colonies. And Villegagnon, who was later called "Cain of America," what was this man after anyway? At the very least, personal ambition—and in the midst of this conflict of interest the mission was aborted. The French Huguenots, under the leadership of the two Genevan pastors, were the first Protestants to hold a service in the Americas, with the preaching based on Psalm 27:4, on March 10, 1557, and in May of that same year, they sealed their testimony with blood—Pierre Bourdon, Jean du Bourdel, and Mathieu Verneuil were killed by Villegagnon after confessing their faith. They were the seed of the Reformed church that returned to the country about four hundred years later.

Reformed churches have a high regard for their martyrs in Brazil. The mission that lived for a short time had no statistical conversion fruits; but it bears historical importance. When the church was confronted with doing missions, it responded immediately. Circumstantial evidence points to Calvin's approval. There was no hostility to the concept or practice of missions. The Swiss did not

69. *Confessio Fluminensis*, in *Confessions of the 16th and 17th Centuries in English Translation: Volume 2, 1552–1566*, ed. James T. Dennison Jr. (Grand Rapids: Reformation Heritage, 2010).

have colonies to direct the Genevans to faraway places. The French government supported only Roman Catholic missions in its colonial territories, and after a period of tolerance, the Reformed church was strongly persecuted. Then, historical circumstances, at another time, challenged the Calvinists of Holland and New England, and they responded positively [by doing missions], both practically and theologically.[70]

In conclusion, we can highlight the original intention of this missionary effort. It was common for explorers to regard the natives as nothing more than brute and wild animals, and therefore, in relation to civilized whites, necessarily of inferior status or even liable to slavery. But it was not so with Jean de Léry and his comrades, who demonstrated that the inhabitants of the New World were worthy of the greatest consideration, not only because they were created in God's image, but because in many humanitarian ways they were well ahead of the inhabitants of the Old World. For French Huguenots, the expedition was not aimed at the commercial expansion of a colonizing country. Instead, they saw it as a means to plant new churches and have freedom of worship—and it was solely for this purpose that the reinforcement expedition organized by Calvin himself was prepared.

Such are the essential concerns of the factors of the first Calvinist colonizing expedition. They show well that, for these Reformers, reconciliation in Christ unites all human beings in one body, above the differences of languages, races, civilizations, and social conditions; every idea of slavery or discrimination has been abolished. These men, then, are ready to carry out an evangelization work that no racial barrier could contain.[71]

---

70. Beaver, "The Genevan Mission to Brazil," 72. For Dutch Reformed Missions in Northeastern Brazil, see Frans Leonard Schalkwijk, *Igreja e Estado no Brasil Holandês 1630-1654* (São Paulo: Cultura Cristã, 2004). For Reformed missions in New England, see Ruth A. Tucker, *Até os confins da terra: uma História Biográfica das Missões Cristãs* (São Paulo: Vida Nova, 1989), 87–100; and Stephen Neill, *História das missões* (São Paulo: Vida Nova, 1997), 230–33.

71. André Biéler, *O pensamento econômico e social de Calvino* (São Paulo: CEP, 1990), 250.

In March 1557, in the midst of the service held at the Fort de Coligny, the Reformed Christians sang the Psalm 5, metric by Clement Marot, with music by Louis Bourgeois. I close this chapter with the lyrics of this hymn.

> Answer my cry, O God, for day and night I pray to you.
> So fragile I am, so poor here!
> Hurt and lonely, my soul cries, so it begs.
>
> You are the source of life and light.
> Pour out your power unto me.
> Answer my prayer, because when the sun rises early, I intercede.
>
> You are a God who does not rejoice in the stumbling of the sinner.
> Kind and just, O Lord, you are.
> You do not tolerate the proud and the liars.
>
> In the light of your holy ways, I will walk humbly and gratefully.
> You are my God, you are my king.
> I always want to walk with you, pure and sincere.
>
> Your children have constant encouragement, always happy in your
>   peace.
> You shall keep them from all evil, for your law
> O God, they know and they obey you.[72]

BIBLIOGRAPHY

Andrada, Laércio Caldeira da. *A Igreja dos Fiéis (Coligny, no Feudo de Ville-gagnon)*. Rio de Janeiro: Centro Brasileiro de Publicidade, 1947.

Barro, Antônio Carlos. "A consciência missionária de João Calvino." *Fides Reformata* 3, no.1 (January–July 1998): 38–49.

Beaver, R. Pierce. "The Genevan Mission to Brazil." In *The Heritage of John Calvin*, edited by John H. Bratt, 55–73. Grand Rapids: Eerdmans, 1973.

Biéler, André. *O pensamento econômico e social de Calvino*. São Paulo: CEP, 1990.

---

72. "O meu clamor, ó Deus, atende," note 387, in Joan Laurie Sutton, *Hinário para o culto cristão* (Rio de Janeiro: JUERP, 1992).

Cairns, Earle E. *O Cristianismo Através dos Séculos*. São Paulo: Vida Nova, 1988.

Calmon, Pedro. *História do Brasil: As origens: século XVI*. Rio de Janeiro: Livraria José Olympio, 1959.

Courthial, Pierre. "A idade de ouro do calvinismo na França." In *Calvino e sua influência no mundo ocidental*, edited by Stanford W. Reid, 87-109. São Paulo: CEP, 1990.

Crespin, Jean. *A Tragédia da Guanabara ou: A história dos protomártires do cristianismo no Brasil*. Rio de Janeiro: Typo-Lith, Pimenta de Mello & C., 1917.

D'Aubigne, D.H. Merle. *História da Reforma do Décimo-sexto Século*. Vol. 4. São Paulo: Casa Editora Presbiteriana, n.d.

Dennison, James T., Jr., ed. *Reformed Confessions of the 16th and 17th Centuries in English Translation: Volume 2, 1552-1566*. (Grand Rapids: Reformation Heritage, 2010).

George, Timothy. *Teologia dos Reformadores*. São Paulo: Vida Nova, 1993.

González, Justo L. *Uma história ilustrada do cristianismo, vol. 7: A era dos conquistadores*. São Paulo: Vida Nova, 1990.

Holanda, Sérgio Buarque de, et al. *História geral da civilização brasileira: a época colonial*. São Paulo: Difel, 1976.

Hughes, Philip. "John Calvin: Director of Mission." In *The Heritage of John Calvin*, edited by John H. Bratt, 40-54. Grand Rapids: Eerdmans, 1973.

———. *Lefèvre: Pioneer of Ecclesiastical Renewal in France*. Grand Rapids: Eerdmans, 1984.

———, comp. *The Register of the Company of Pastors of Geneva in the Time of Calvin*. Grand Rapids: Eerdmans, 1966.

Léry, Jean de. *Viagem à terra do Brasil*. São Paulo: Livraria Martins, 1924.

Lindeberg, Carter. *As Reformas na Europa*. São Leopoldo: Sinodal, 2001.

Neill, Stephen. *História das missões*. São Paulo: Vida Nova, 1997.

Pombo, Rocha. *História do Brasil, vol. 1: O descobrimento e a colonização*. Rio de Janeiro: W. N. Jackson, 1967.

Reid, Stanford. "A propagação do calvinismo no século XVI." In *Calvino e sua influência no mundo ocidental*, edited by Stanford W. Reid, 35-59. São Paulo: CEP, 1990.

Reis, Alvaro. *The Martyr Le Balleur*. Rio de Janeiro: n.p., 1917.

Schalkwijk, Frans Leonard. *Igreja e Estado no Brasil Holandês, 1630–1654*. São Paulo: Cultura Cristã, 2004.

Sutton, Joan Laurie Sutton, ed. *Hinário para o culto cristão*. Rio de Janeiro: JUERP, 1992.

Tucker, Ruth A. *Até os confins da terra: uma história biográfica das missões cristãs*. São Paulo: Vida Nova, 1989.

Viana, Hélio. *História do Brasil: Período Colonial*. São Paulo: Melhoramentos, 1994.

7

—

"THAT THERE WOULD BE ONE FLOCK UNDER ONE SHEPHERD"

Theodor Bibliander and the Role of Language for Missionary Work

Gregory J. Miller

Many surveys of Christian missions in the sixteenth century center on the great Roman Catholic missionary endeavors associated with the European voyages of exploration. By contrast, the Protestant Reformers are often seen as at best neglectful and at worst even contrary to missions in the traditional sense.[1] However, the story is more complex. Protestant missiology certainly predates the great missionary activity of the eighteenth and nineteenth centuries. Scholars of early Lutheran missions have demonstrated that cross-cultural evangelism among peoples such as the Samelats of northern Scandinavia and the Lanape in the North American colony of New Sweden date even to the early 1600s. Still, lacking the imperialist activities of a supporting secular government, early Reformers had no practical means of evangelizing those beyond their borders.

---

1. In general, missiologists, including Gustav Warneck, Julius Richter, Wilhelm Oehler, K.S. Latourette, and Walther Köhler have argued that the Reformation had no concept of missions in the modern sense. It is correct that Luther and Melanchthon considered the Great Commission to have been already fulfilled. However, a significant minority of scholars led by Karl Holl have argued that the structure of Reformation theology was missionary—but the "heathens" it sought to convert included all non-Christians, even those in the visible church. See Robert Kolb, "Mission and Evangelism," in *Dictionary of Luther and the Lutheran Traditions*, ed. Timothy J. Wengert (Grand Rapids: Baker, 2017), 506–11.

The lack of sustained missiological action does not mean the lack of reflection, however. Among the most sustained reflections on missions by an early Reformer was done by the Swiss teacher and exegete, Theodor Bibliander (1509–1564). Alongside Heinrich Bullinger, Bibliander is the most important successor to Zwingli and the Zürich Reformation. Bibliander was an heir to the Erasmian-Zwinglian Humanist strain of the Swiss Reformation, and like Erasmus, was concerned equally with concord as with reform. Bibliander was a staunch Protestant with an emphasis on the authority of Scripture and strong antipathy to the Roman church. However, he was opposed to the strongly predestinarian emphasis that he saw beginning to dominate the second generation of Swiss Reform.

Bibliander's interest in languages (especially biblical languages), his commitment to concord, and his belief in God's universal desire that all might be saved, are the triad of impulses behind the publication of one of his most important works, *De ratione communi omnium linguarum et literarum commentarius Theodori Bibliandri* [*On the Common Nature of All Languages and Letters*] (1548).[2] This book provided what Bibliander considered to be a universal overview of all world languages. Although it is highly dependent on the work of the French linguist Guillaume Postel, the scope of the book is impressive for his day.[3] It covers both the origins of language and writing as well as the causes of their mutations and development. He also treats the anatomy of speech, acoustics, sound, and the technology of printing. In what might be called a "linguistic theology," his basic narrative is a linguistic declension from primordial unity and simplicity to diversity that parallels the social and spiritual declension of humankind in Genesis. For Bibliander, the plurality of languages is related to the plurality of religions, and that as there are underlying foundational principles of grammar, so too are there foundational religious principles that can serve as the basis for religious union. This does not mean that Bibliander was a proponent of religious toleration in the modern sense.

---

2. Hagit Amirav and Hans-Martin Kirn, trans. and eds., *Theodore Bibliander. De ratione communi omnium linguarum et litterarum commentarius* (Geneva: Droz, 2011).

3. Guillame Postel (1510–1581) had an enduring influence on Bibliander. Like Bibliander, Postel believed that Hebrew was the ur-language of mankind and that the common linguistic origins of humanity pointed to the ultimate unity of all things. The classic study on Postel in English is William J. Bouwsma, *Concordia mundi: The Career and Thought of Guillaume Postel* (Cambridge, MA: Harvard University Press, 1957).

For example, in *On the Common Nature of All Languages* he referred specifically to Islam as a heresy and utilized the most negative language to describe Muhammad.

However, Bibliander believed that Muslims, and all other diverse believers around the world, could indeed become Christians as a result of a true presentation of the faith. It was Bibliander's stated desire that "there be one flock and one shepherd," that is, Jesus Christ. As this chapter will demonstrate, Bibliander had a genuine missionary impulse rooted in his commitment to the theological position of human free will, and the demonstration of the truth of Christianity proceeding from universally shared positions. This truth was analogous to the universal grammatical principles underlying the diversity of languages. A central step in the reversal of human linguistic and theological disunity is the missionary task of learning of what others believe in their own language in order to draw them to the underlying truth, and therefore to Christ.

BIOGRAPHICAL CONTEXT

After the death of Ulrich Zwingli at the Battle of Kappel in 1531, ecclesiastical leadership in Zürich passed to Heinrich Bullinger. Not all of Zwingli's responsibilities were given to Bullinger, however. The responsibility for the continuance of public lectures on Scripture begun by Zwingli was given to Theodor Bibliander.[4] Although Bullinger was clearly the more important, contemporaries viewed Bibliander as a partner in leadership. The importance of Bibliander's position is evidenced by the high level of financial support for his work. He was given Zwingli's house in which to live and an annual stipend from the income of the Grossmünster. The selection of Bibliander as Zwingli's successor was a high honor for the young scholar, then only in his twenties.[5] He was a home-grown product,

---

4. Bibliander referred to himself as the "Nachfolger Zwinglis für theologishe Vorlesungen im Dienste der Kirche Zürich." Emil Egli, *Analecta Reforrnatoria II. Biographien: Bibliander, Ceporin, Johannes Bullinger* (Zürich: Zürcher und Furrer, 1901), 15. See also Christine Christ-v. Wedel, "Theodor Bibliander in seiner Zeit," in *Theodor Bibliander (1505-1564): Ein Thurgauer im gelehrten Zürich der Reformationszeit*, ed. Christine Christ-v. Wedel (Zürich: Neue Zürcher Zeitung, 2005), 19–60.

5. It is unclear whether Bibliander was born in 1504, 1505, or 1509, although scholarly consensus is leaning now toward 1505, as seen in Christian Moser's *Theodor Bibliander: Annotierte Bibliographie der gedruckten Werke* (Theologischer Verlag Zürich, 2009). Bibliander's most important biographer, Egli argues for 1509. Egli, *Analecta*, 4.

however, and had some teaching experience. Bibliander's father was a manager of church property in nearby Bischofszell, and his older brother was a minister in the greater Zürich area. Bibliander had studied Greek and Hebrew in Zürich under Oswald Myconius and Jakob Ceporin, and in Basel under Konrad Pellican and Johannes Oecolampadius. As a result of a recommendation from Zürich, he had been appointed to serve as teacher in a new Protestant foundation in Liegnitz, Silesia, a position, which he held for two years. He had returned to Switzerland and was working on a Hebrew grammar for publication when the call came to take up public responsibilities in Zürich. Bibliander served as a central exegete in the Zürich scriptural teaching institution known as the *Prophezei*. His lectures were greatly admired and were sometimes transcribed and circulated to pastors throughout the canton. He has been described as the father of exegetical theology in Switzerland.[6] Over the course of his career, he published twenty-four books and left thirty volumes of unpublished materials (now located in the archives of the Zentralbibliothek Zürich). Bibliander's primary reputation, however, was as an expert in languages. No less a luminary than Guillaume Postel held him in the highest regard, and even expressed the desire to relocate to Zürich so that the two could collaborate on research projects.

His public career ended in an unusual way. As Bibliander was consistently an outspoken opponent of the doctrine of predestination, it was perhaps inevitable that eventually there would be a serious confrontation between him and Peter Martyr Vermigli, a strong proponent of absolute double predestination, who had been brought to Zürich as a professor in 1556. The two teachers began attacking the opposing position publicly in 1557, and the rhetoric escalated over the next three years. There is a story that the conflict came to a head when Bibliander, evidently suffering a mental breakdown, challenged Vermigli to a public duel with pole-axes as a definitive test to see whom God had "chosen."[7] Bullinger was forced

---

6. This praise is from a founding father of Swiss church history, Johann Heinrich Hottinger. See Emil Egli, "Bibliander" in *Realencyclopadie für protestantische Theologie und Kirche*, vol. III (Leipzig: JC Hinrichs'sche Buchhandlung, 1897), 185–87.

7. Although this conjures up an interesting mental image, the earliest documentary evidence for it does not appear until the 1700s. Joachim Staedtke, "Der Zürcher Praedestinationsstreit von 1560," *Zwingliana* 9:9 (1953): 536–46.

to intervene to preserve the unity of the Zürich church, and Bibliander was relieved of his duties as a professor. However, Bullinger claimed that Bibliander was suffering from the consequences of over-work, and in light of his many years of faithful service to Zürich, ensured that Bibliander was given a pension and a place to live. Bibliander continued to publish, but died of the plague four years later in 1564.

DE RATIONE COMMUNI OMNIUM LINGUARUM ET LITERARUM (ON THE COMMON NATURE OF ALL LANGUAGES AND LETTERS)

Although Bibliander is perhaps best known for his 1543 compendium on the Turks and Islam, which included the first ever printed Latin Qur'an, the *De ratione communi omnium linguarum et literarum* ranks among his most significant contributions, and is the first of his publications to have been published in a scholarly edition. In its original edition, *On the Common Nature of All Languages* was a sizeable volume of nearly 250 pages with sections ranging across the field of linguistics, including on the origin of language, linguistic mutations, morphology, and etymology. In the introduction, Bibliander began by championing the study of languages, drawing his support from a range of patristic and medieval authorities, especially Augustine, and rhetorically concluded with the ultimate authority of Scripture, especially referring to the gift of tongues from Paul's first letter to the Corinthians in chapters 12 and 14.

In what may be considered unusual for a Reformer, Bibliander emphasized the linguistic decrees of the Council of Vienne (1311–1312), which locate language study as a missionary endeavor. About the unity of all truth and the importance of language study for missions, Bibliander is spiritual kin to the medieval missionary and linguist Ramon Llull.[8] For Bibliander, the study of languages is not important primarily for commercial or instrumental purposes, but because it is a way to reverse the human divisions caused by Babel. He believed that the resultant diversity in languages (he stated that there are seventy-two languages in the world) is a

---

8. On Ramon Llull, see Mark D. Johnston, *The Evangelical Rhetoric of Ramon Llull: Lay Learning and Piety in the Christian West Around 1300* (New York: Oxford, 1996) and *The Spiritual Logic of Ramon Llull* (New York: Oxford, 1987).

prime cause of discord of all kinds, especially religious. However, *On the Common Nature of All Languages* is filled with hope. Bibliander paraphrased Zephaniah 3:9 as, "Then I shall restore the chosen language for the use of the nations, so they all invoke the name of God and serve him together as one person." Bibliander claimed that Hebrew was the ur-language and presumably the universal language of the eschatological near future.[9] His vision is universal and profound:

> It means that, with divine help, the confusion of languages origi-
> nally introduced in the Babylonian undertaking will be cancelled
> and that in some way from the multitude of languages only one
> language will be created. Moreover, it means obstacles and impedi-
> ments found in human society will be torn down and the removal of
> all hostilities in people's minds. The holy bond and commerce in all
> people will be reinstituted, reunited, supported and strengthened.
> It means that all the people around the world will be led back into
> a single fold and to the only eternal shepherd, who gave away his
> own life for the sake of the sheep. In order that the only God who,
> through his Son, created the world with the help of the Holy Spirit
> which emanates from both, shall be worshipped in one language
> and speech and by everybody at the same time, as the holy proph-
> ets of God once predicted.[10]

Theology, missiology, and linguistics are all linked in Bibliander's vision of a unified human race under Christ.

ON THE COMMON NATURE OF ALL LANGUAGES AND MISSIONS TO ISLAM

Because of the military campaigns of Suleiman the Magnificent, the Ottoman Turks became a frequent theme in early sixteenth century lit-erature. Throughout Europe "Turk" became a catchword for popular fear and anxiety.[11] Although Zürich was far from directly threatened by the

---

9. Amirav and Kirn, *Bibliander*, *De ratione*, xxv.

10. Original publication: Theodor Bibliander, *De ratione communi omnium linguarum et literarum commentarius* (Zürich: Frosch, 1548), d3(a), 29.

11. For the broader context of medieval and early modern Western understandings of Islam, see especially: Nancy Bisaha, *Creating East and West: Renaissance Humanists and the*

Ottomans, scholars there also discussed the meaning of the Turkish threat and permissible responses to it. Islam particularly intrigued Bibliander, possibly as a result of his early experience in Silesia during a period of Turkish aggression. Following the Turkish offensive, which culminated in the siege of Vienna in 1529, Bibliander seems to have sought sources on Islam and even had studied some Arabic.

Bibliander's interest in Islam was twofold. He believed that the Turks were a real threat, both militarily and religiously.[12] In this regard, he maintained that an accurate knowledge of Islam is the best weapon against it. However, Bibliander also held a missionary motive about Islam. In general, he maintained that there was hope for those outside of the visible church, based on the expressed desire of God that all would be saved. According to Bibliander, damnation depends on the choice of individuals themselves. "It is his own fault and his just desserts if one falls under the judgment of God after despising the grace of God."[13]

An essential key was the proclamation of the gospel. Bibliander's position was that the legitimate elements in all religions serve as a *preparatio evangelii*. A central theme of *On the Common Nature of All Languages* is that there were remnants in each contemporary language of a once-universal language. In addition, analogously, so are the vestiges of belief in the one true God in pre-Christian religions and in Islam, that is, where it has not been totally obscured by Muhammad. This is separate from but linked to a common grace given by a good heavenly father that is at the root of all wisdom and eloquence wherever it may be found. In opposition

---

Ottoman Turks (Philadelphia: University of Pennsylvania Press, 2004); John Victor Tolan, *Saracens: Islam in the Medieval European Imagination* (New York: Columbia University Press, 2002); Margaret Meserve, *Empires of Islam in Renaissance Historical Thought* (Cambridge, MA: Harvard University Press, 2008); David R. Blanks and Michael Frassetto, *Western Views of Islam in Medieval and Early Modern Europe: Perception of Other* (New York: St. Martin's, 1999); Samuel Chew, *The Crescent and the Rose* (New York: Octagon Books, 1937); Norman Daniel, *Islam and the West: The Making of an Image*, 2nd ed. (Oxford: Oneworld, 1993); Clarence Rouillard, *The Turk in French History, Thought, and Literature* (Paris: Boivin, 1941); Edward Said, *Orientalism* (New York: Vintage Books, 1978); and Richard Southern, *Western Views of Islam in the Middle Ages* (Cambridge, MA: Harvard University Press, 1962).

12. In addition to his compendium on Islam, Bibliander published one short work specifically on the war against the Turks: *Ad nominis christiani socios consultatio, quanam ratione Turcarum dira potentia repelli possit* (1542).

13. Quoted in Egli, *Analecta*, 74.

to Zwingli,[14] Bibliander based salvation not on election, but rather in *"der universal Hilfswille Gottes."* Since God places the heart of man *semina religionis et sapientiae*, it is possible for some to become the "friends of God" without carrying the name of Jesus. A partial revelation of God could come from a consideration of creation, the teaching of angels, by a special work of the Holy Spirit, or by being part of the *ecclesia primitivorum*. There were precious elements in all religions; Bibliander regarded these as gifts of a common heavenly father and not borrowings or thefts. However, I have not found any explicit statement in Bibliander that this *preparatio evangelii* is sufficient for salvation. Rather, Bibliander repeatedly asserts that the pious aspirations of all peoples could not be satisfied except in the fuller revelation of Christ as the Son of God. Therefore, in Bibliander's mind missionary work was imperative.

On the question of possible salvation for Muslims, Erasmian humanism in particular significantly influenced Bibliander.[15] Erasmus's doctrinal simplification of Christianity had the consequence that the boundary between the *philosophia Christi* and natural law morality was obscured, to the advantage of devout pagans.[16] For Erasmus, the noble pagan possessed a *religio naturalis*, and therefore, it was possible that some moral and pious Turks were perhaps already part of the true church and that others could be converted. However, as he wrote in the introduction to his 1518 edition of the *Enchiridion*, this evangelization should be by example, not conquest.[17] In a similar way, Bibliander also championed the possibility of the conversation of Muslims.

---

14. Zwingli had broad views of pagan salvation based on primordial election. He saw virtue as *signa electionis*, even in pagans. George Williams, "Erasmus and the Reformers on Non-Christian Religion and Salus Extra Ecclesiam," in *Action and Conviction in Early Modern Europe*, ed. Theodore K. Robb and Jerrold E. Siegel (Princeton: Princeton University Press, 1969), 357–59.

15. Williams, "Non-Christian," 360–61; Rudolf Pfister, "Das Türkenbüchlein Theodor Biblianders," *Theologische Zeitung* 9 (1953): 451–52; Henry Clark, "The Publication of the Koran in Latin: A Reformation Dilemma," *Sixteenth Century Journal* 15:1 (1984): 6.

16. Williams, "Non-Christians," 336–67; see also Rudolf Pfister, "Reformation, Türken und Islam," *Zwingliana* 10:6 (1956): 345–75.

17. "Es gehe nicht darum, viele Türken zu töten, sondern viele zu retten." Quoted in Rudolf Mau, "Luthers Stellung zu den Türken" in *Leben und Werk Martin Luthers von 1526 bis 1546*, ed. Helmar Junghans (Göttingen: Vanderhoeck und Ruprecht, 1983), 647. See also Williams, "Non-Christian," 328.

It appears that on at least one occasion, Bibliander intended to go to Egypt personally as a missionary, but was dissuaded by Bullinger. Bullinger had received information from some merchants who had advised him that Bibliander's plan was very unworkable and would likely result in a quick death.[18] Bibliander's interest in missions to Muslim lands was strengthened by his strong eschatological expectations. Bibliander believed that according to the Islamic calendar, AD 1553 was the one-thousandth Muslim year since Muhammad's public entrance as prophet, and that Muhammad himself had prophesied that the Qur'an would perish after 1,000 years.[19] For Bibliander, the end was near, and God had ordained this time for a proclamation of the gospel in Muslim lands. Muslims, Turks, and others could become the sons of God simply if they cast off their beliefs in Muhammad the false prophet. Bibliander was optimistic enough to believe that some were not so committed that this would be impossible.[20] For Bibliander, the Great Commission remained directive. It was still valid and not restricted to the time of the apostles.[21]

Although Martin Luther was also concerned about the Turks, his views on missions to Islam were significantly different. The contrast between the two can illustrate the distinctiveness of Bibliander's positions. It should be noted that Luther's statements were strongly contextual and developed over time. Luther's "early" position on missions to Islam was developed primarily in relation to the conflict with the papacy. In the early 1520s, Luther accused the pope of always wanting to make war against the Turks, but never sending them preachers of the gospel.[22] Luther also expressed a desire that before the last judgment, the gospel would be spread throughout the entire world, including Muslim lands.

---

18. On April 1, 1546, a report from Stadtschreiber Georg Fröhlich in Augsburg to Bullinger warned that although one could indeed travel to Muslim lands and hold one's Christian faith, one word spoken against Islam would likely be lethal. Egli, *Analecta*, 88–89.

19. Egli, *Analecta*, 93.

20. Similar positions were adopted by other thinkers influenced by humanism, including Juan Luis Vives, Martin Bucer, and Heinrich Bullinger. Gustav Warneck, *Abriss einer Geschichte der protestantischen Missionen von der Reformation bis auf die Gegenwart*, 7th ed. (Berlin: Verlag Martin Warneck, 1901), 18–19.

21. Amirav and Kirn, *Bibliander, De Ratione*, xxiv.

22. Erasmus made similar suggestions. See Hartmut Bobzin, "Martin Luthers Beitrag zu Kenntnis und Kritik des Islam," *Neue Zeitschrift für Systematische Theologie* 27:3 (1985): 268.

After the first siege of Vienna in 1529, Luther became directly concerned with the actual Turkish threat and its effect on Germans. With the growing eschatological identification of the Turk and the devil, it became impossible to conceive of wholesale conversions of Turks. However, it was still possible for a few individuals to be converted. Citing the biblical examples of Joseph and Daniel, Luther suggested that any Turkish conversions would not take place through professional missionaries, Scripture, or preaching, however, but only through the example of Christian captives.[23]

In one of his most important pamphlets on the Turks, the *Muster Sermon Against the Turks* (1530), Luther offered counsel to those who might be captured: "be patient in your imprisonment (this may be God's will), serve your master well, do not commit suicide, suffer your bondage as a cross."[24] Luther concluded that since biblical evidence demands that slaves be obedient to their masters, if Christians disobeyed their Turkish lords, they shamed the name of Christ and only encouraged the Turks in their faith.[25] However, "if the [captive] Christians are a true, obedient, pious, humble, diligent people, this will shame the Turkish faith and perhaps convert many."[26] Even women could participate in this missionary work by submitting to their Turkish masters "at bed and table" for Christ's sake. They were not to think that they were damned for doing so: "the soul can do nothing about what the enemy does to the body."[27] There was only one qualification to this absolute obedience. Captives were to resist the command to fight against Christians, even resisting to the point of death. Cooperation with the Turkish army would put an individual on the wrong side of the eschatological battle and would damn them with the rest of the devil's minions.[28] There was no mention of any sending mission to the Turks.

Late in life, Luther was even more pessimistic. In his translation of Ricoldo de Monte Croce's *Confutatio Alcorani*, Luther changed his earlier

---

23. Martin Luther, *Heerpredigt wider den Türken* (1529), Weimar Ausgabe (hereafter WA) 30II, 192–95. See also Walter Holsten, *Christentum und nichtchristliche Religion nach der Auffassung Luthers* (Gütersloh: Bertelsmann, 1932), 144.

24. Luther, *Heerpredigt*, 194.

25. Luther, *Heerpredigt*, 194.

26. Luther, *Heerpredigt*, 195.

27. "[N]icht verzweifeln, als weren sie verdampt. Die Seele kan dazu nichts, was der Feind an dem Leibe thut." Martin Luther, *Vermahnung zum Gebet wider den Türken* (1541), WA 51, 621.

28. Luther, *Heerpredigt*, 196–97.

opinion and stated that Turks and Saracens could not be converted because they were so hardened.[29] "How can one be converted if they reject the entire scriptures, both Old Testament and New Testament and permit no argument from scripture?"[30]

Although Bibliander shared much of Luther's negative perspective on the Turks, he never foreclosed the possibility of Muslim conversions. In contrast to Luther, Bibliander argued that the Qur'an had some positive value, included some genuine Scripture, and that it contained nothing more false than many heathen philosophies.[31] Like Ramon Llull before him, Bibliander placed the highest hope and stress on the study of the Arabic language. If there were a common linguistic understanding between Christians and Muslims, many would be soon converted. Bibliander considered ignorance of the religion of the Turks to be the chief barrier both of defending Christendom against them as well as to proclaiming the gospel to them. His 1543 compendium that included the first published Qur'an, a veritable sixteenth century encyclopedia of Islam, was his effort to instruct Christian scholars for both tasks.[32]

BIBLIANDER'S UNDERSTANDING OF THE COMMON GROUND AMONG RELIGIONS FROM ON THE COMMON NATURE OF ALL LANGUAGES

As Bibliander began to conclude his linguistic analysis in *On the Common Nature of All Languages*, he inserted an important statement on comparative religion. The section is titled, "In what account doctrinal and religious disputes may rage and what may stand between Christians, Jews, Turks, Tartars, Saracens, and other nations," but it is fundamentally an exposition

---

29. Martin Luther, *Verlegung des Alcoran Bruder Richardi Prediger Ordens* (1542), WA 53, 276. For an exceptional discussion of this, see Adam Francisco, *Martin Luther and Islam: A Study in Sixteenth-Century Polemics and Apologetics* (London: Brill, 2007), 175–210.

30. Luther, *Verlegung*, 274. See also Bobzin, 283.

31. Walter Holsten, "Reformation und Missions," *Archiv für Reformationsgeschichte* 44 (1953): 24, 28.

32. Gregory J. Miller, "Theodor Bibliander's *Machumetis saracenorum principis eiusque successorum vitae, doctrina ac ipse alcoran* (1543) as the Sixteenth Century 'Encyclopedia' of Islam," *Islam and Christian-Islamic Relations* 24:2 (2013): 241–54.

of beliefs held in common by *all* religions.[33] His numerated list consists of the following ten items and merits a full paraphrased description:

1. Christians, Jews, and Muslims, as well as Indians (who are considered worshipers of Satan), believe that a person is composed of body and soul, and that the soul is the most important part.

2. All believe that at death a person does not perish entirely, but that there is life after death, a place and a condition into which they go after they depart this world.

3. All believe that there are spiritual beings with much greater faculties than humans, and that there are good angels, messengers, and administering blessing to humans, and demons who torture and execute God's judgments.

4. All believe that there is one true God, eternal, most wise, the best, omnipotent, who created the heaven and the earth, and the sea and everything to do with the world, and that he cares for it and rules it, providing especially for humans. Bibliander states that although the Indians and the Scythians are unaware of the names Christian, Jew, or Muslim, and allegedly worship stars, snakes, representations of animals, and even devils, they are actually monotheists who worship the one God of heaven and earth who they call "diatha."[34]

5. All believe that God will judge human actions along with all thoughts, words, and deeds. God approves what is right, good, true, laudable, and worthy of distinction, and detests what is depraved, evil, and turpid.

6. All believe that God has made known to all generations his will and judgments, and that this has been achieved by different methods, including the use of people particularly receptive

---

33. Bibliander, *De ratione*, 538.

34. It is unclear to what Bibliander was referring with this term. I have been unable to identify the source of his knowledge.

towards the godly mind, and who in writings unfolded their knowledge of divine will, judgments, and nature.

7. All believe that God's commands are to be observed in both public and private things. For God will rightly honor with ample reward in this world and the next those who do right, but will inflict tortures upon the evil.

8. All agree that religion and worship of the divine is by far the most important of human activities.

9. All believe that those who rightly embrace religion and worship become the friends of God, and together constitute a sacred society, the people of God. On the other hand, those who reject the true God are enemies and collectively compose the impious faction and conspiring mob against God.

10. All peoples and nations believe that God will provide for all eternity some ruler of the people of God who will govern according to divine law. In contrast, at the end of the world's time, impious and wicked humans will get an imitation of the legitimate ruler created by God, a monstrous freak of nature, an abominable scourge of the civilized world. This enemy of God is called by the Jews and by the Turk, Tartar, and Saracen disciples, Muhammad "Gog," and his savage battalions are called "Magog." "We, however, being educated by our Lord Jesus Christ and his most holy apostles call him the antichrist or the pseudochrist."[35]

According to Bibliander, the tenth thesis is the most controversial: "If this were resolved there would be no obstacle to a general concord amongst people as to the other points."[36] What he means is that the key question is: Who ultimately speaks for God? Muhammad? Jesus? Someone else?

There was no doubt in Bibliander's mind. He concluded his book with an apology for Christianity: "So that the inhabitants of the whole world

---

35. Amirav and Kirn, *Bibliander, De ratione*, 543 (original publication 206, C3[b]).
36. Amirav and Kirn, *Bibliander, De ratione*, 545 (original publication 207, C4[a]).

will one day be led to true concord, in which there should be one flock and one shepherd, I will now provide you with a precise explanation as to who the chief ruler of the people of God and the holy religion is."[37] Bibliander believed that the truth of Christianity could be proven by ample evidence and convincing arguments, but that it cannot be forced upon anyone by way of threat, acts of terror, the tools of the executioner, or wars. He argued that the truth of Christianity was so powerful that, presented properly with divine help, God himself "attracts, occupies, binds, stirs, and rules the minds of people."[38]

As evidence of the truth of Christianity, Bibliander started with secular portents at Rome traditionally connected to Emperor Augustus, and simply applied them to Christ. He emphasized natural phenomenon, such as the darkness when Christ died (which he stated was reported by "Pliny in Italy, Phlegon in Greece, and Apollophanes the friend of Dionysius in Heliopolis, Egypt"[39]). This is clearly an attempt to provide a wide-ranging evidence for the claim of Christ to be God—support that even the pagans can support. Throughout his writings, Bibliander relied heavily on the support for Christianity that he found in non-Christian writings. For example, he used a spurious letter of Pilate to Tiberius to demonstrate the resurrection of Christ, and quoted Josephus from the *Antiquities* as an authoritative testimony to the resurrection.

As one would expect, significant attention was paid to Islam: "And what shall I say about Mohammad and his followers and of how magnificently they speak of Christ? For we should be less ashamed of them [Muslims] than of some semi-Arian Christians."[40] His treatment was not entirely positive, however. He went on to summarize Muslim's views of Jesus in contrast to Christian ones (centering on the Islamic denial of the crucifixion), and emphasized that "churches, however, must not ignore what the enemies have declared about their prince, Jesus Christ." However, his treatment of Islamic views of Jesus centered on common places rather than divergences. According to Bibliander, the Qur'an "attributes to Him [Jesus] the

---

37. Amirav and Kirn, *Bibliander, De ratione*, 545 (original publication 207, C4[a]).
38. Amirav and Kirn, *Bibliander, De ratione*, 547 (original publication 208, C4[b]).
39. Amirav and Kirn, *Bibliander, De ratione*, 553 (original publication 211, D2[a]).
40. Amirav and Kirn, *Bibliander, De ratione*, 561; (original publication 214, D3[b]).

highest degree of truth, to be commensurate with the Word of God. What is it then if not admitting, albeit through negation, that Jesus is God and the Son of God?"[41] In support, Bibliander added several Qur'anic passages about the virgin birth and about Christ, although all of them are from poor translations that de-emphasize Islamic distinctives. In his concluding section on Islam, he quoted a pseudo-Muslim prophecy that Islam will fall under a Christian sword and that Christianity will triumph. His source was Bartholomew Georgijevic and the so-called Red Apple Prophecy.[42] Bibliander believed that this prophecy concurred with Revelation chapter 10 and referred to the end of time.

The last section of *On the Common Nature of All Languages* was a summary of Bibliander's understanding of the basics of the Christian faith, which included that Christ is the light of the world, the only way to God, the way to eternal life, and a summary of the Eucharist. "Moreover, Christ revealed a crystal clear and most simple doctrine about the duty of man. He, being their teacher, ordered them to imitate Him ... people should cultivate their virtue ... they should strive to do good ... whereby the whole duty of a Christian is encapsulated in one word that is mutual love."[43] He concluded with "the philosophy which is necessary for the eternal salvation of all people on earth," in several languages. This philosophy focused on the Apostles' Creed and the Lord's Prayer.[44]

CONCLUSION

Increasingly, Bibliander's missiological views were pushed aside as sixteenth century Reformed theology centered in Geneva became increasingly dominant. Bibliander had no true successor and Zürich sent no missionary to the Muslim world. In many ways, he represents a path not taken in the Erasmian-Zwinglian Reform that contrasted with the developing

---

41. Amirav and Kirn, *Bibliander, De ratione*, 561 (original publication 214, D3[b]).

42. Bibliander mistakenly calls it the "Golden Apple" prophecy. The legend is derived from an ancient Byzantine pseudo-prophecy that Muslims would one day capture the "Red Apple" (generally thought to represent Constantinople) but would hold it only for a definite period of time after which a Christian ruler would drive them out and destroy all Muslims who did not convert to Christianity. On Georgijevic, see Gregory J. Miller, *The Turks and Islam in Reformation Germany* (New York: Routledge, 2018), 151–75.

43. Amirav and Kirn, *Bibliander, De ratione*, 579 (original publication 222, E3[b]).

44. Amirav and Kirn, *Bibliander, De ratione*, 581 (original publication 223, E4[a]).

covenantal theology of Heinrich Bullinger and the Reformed tradition centered in Geneva.

Yet, because he had no direct successors among the early Reformers does not mean that his contribution was unimportant. In a distinctive way, Bibliander connected the Renaissance emphasis on rhetoric and language as the focus of Christian education with a genuine missionary impulse. In fact, the entirety of Bibliander's Reformation theology was decisively shaped by an Erasmian emphasis on practical piety (*pietas*) combined with literary knowledge and linguistic skills (*eruditio*), directed towards a peaceful unification of humankind (*pax et concordia mundi*) conveyed by successful universal communication in the "harmony of languages" (*harmonia linguarum*).[45]

It is important to note that Bibliander was more than a precursor to deistic enlightenment concepts of the unity of all religions, as Hagit Amirav and Hans-Martin Kirn infer in their introduction to the scholarly edition.[46] Bibliander's distinct theological humanistic perspective in *On the Common Nature of All Languages* is clear. However, this was a book with a wider purpose: to defend Christian faith and to encourage the proclamation of the gospel in non-Christian lands with *modestia* (restraint and temperateness). In order for this to be done successfully, it must be preceded by real knowledge, including real linguistic knowledge.

In Norman Daniel's essential study, *Islam and the West: The Making of an Image*, he wrote that sixteenth-century Christian engagement with Islam largely reiterated the medieval image of Islam without significant variation.[47] In Bibliander's *On the Common Nature of All Languages*, evidence for this argument is easily found in anti-Islamic sentiments and the overall framework of Christian apologetics.[48] However, when we examine texts like this more carefully, we discover a high level of ambiguity.[49] Renaissance humanism, traditional Christian apologetics against Islam, missions'

---

45. Amirav and Kirn, *Bibliander, De ratione*, xxii.

46. Amirav and Kirn, *Bibliander, De ratione*, xli.

47. Daniel, *Islam and the West*, especially 271–307.

48. Amirav and Kirn, *Bibliander, De ratione*, xxiii.

49. I reach the same conclusion in a recent re-evaluation of the first English Qur'an (1649), generally attributed to Alexander Ross. See Gregory J. Miller, "Views of Islam in Early Modern Britain: Insight from the First Translation Qur'an in English," in *The Islamic Quarterly*, 61:4 (2017): 483–504.

impulses, and a respect for Islam and the Arabic language are all inter-twined. Early modern European engagement with Islam and other religious traditions is not as unambiguous as conventional scholarship would suggest. This ambiguity opens up space for new and different approaches while supporting, simultaneously, the received tradition.[50] And for this, the Swiss linguistic missiologist Theodor Bibliander is one of the most important exemplars.

BIBLIOGRAPHY

Amirav, Hagit and Hans-Martin Kirn, trans. and eds. *Theodore Bibliander. De ratione communi omnium linguarum et litterarum commentarius.* Geneva: Droz, 2011.

Birchwood, Matthew. *Staging Islam in England: Drama and Culture, 1640–1685.* Rochester, NY: DS Brewer, 2007.

Bisaha, Nancy. *Creating East and West: Renaissance Humanists and the Ottoman Turks.* Philadelphia: University of Pennsylvania Press, 2004.

Blanks, David R., and Michael Frassetto. *Western Views of Islam in Medieval and Early Modern Europe: Perception of Other.* New York: St. Martin's, 1999.

Bobzin, Hartmut. "Martin Luther's Beitrag zu Kenntnis und Kritik des Islam." *Neue Zeitschrift für Systematische Theologie* 27:3 (1985): 262–89.

Bouwsma, William J. *Concordia mundi: The Career and Thought of Guillaume Postel.* Cambridge, MA: Harvard University Press, 1957.

Burton, Jonathan. *Traffic and Turning: Islam and English Drama, 1579–1624.* Newark: University of Delaware Press, 2005.

---

50. This line of argument is congruent with a host of recent studies in the field of early modern British literature relating to the Turks. See especially Matthew Birchwood, *Staging Islam in England: Drama and Culture, 1640–1685* (Rochester, NY: DS Brewer, 2007); Jonathan Burton, *Traffic and Turning: Islam and English Drama, 1579–1624* (Newark: University of Delaware Press, 2005); Gerald MacLean, *Looking East: English Writing and the Ottoman Empire before 1800* (New York: Palgrave, 2007); Matthew Dimmock, *New Turkes: Dramatizing Islam and the Ottomans in Early Modern England* (London: Ashgate, 2005); and Daniel Vitkus, *Turning Turk: English Theater and the Multicultural Mediterranean, 1570–1630* (New York: Palgrave, 2003). Several of these studies put at the center of their interest the rhetorical use of Islam for internal purposes. In fact, a central argument of Burman's *Reading the Qur'an* is that medieval European engagements with Islam are more complex and problematic than has been previously understood.

Chew, Samuel. *The Crescent and the Rose*. New York: Octagon Books, 1937.

Christ-v. Wedel, Christine. "Theodor Bibliander in seiner Zeit." In *Theodor Bibliander (1505-1564): Ein Thurgauer im gelehrten Zürich der Reformationszeit*, edited by Christ-v. Wedel, 19-60. Zürich: Neue Zürcher Zetitung, 2005.

Clark, Henry. "The Publication of the Koran in Latin: A Reformation Dilemma." *Sixteenth Century Journal* 15:1 (1984): 3-12.

Daniel, Norman. *Islam and the West: The Making of an Image*. 2nd ed. Oxford: Oneworld, 1993.

Dimmock, Matthew. *New Turkes: Dramatizing Islam and the Ottomans in Early Modern England*. London: Ashgate, 2005.

Egli, Emil. *Analecta Reforrnatoria II. Biographien: Bibliander, Ceporin, Johannes Bullinger*. Zürich: Zürcher und Furrer, 1901.

———. "Bibliander." In *Realencyclopadie für protestantische Theologie und Kirche*. Vol. III. Leipzig: JC Hinrichs'sche Buchhandlung, 1897: 185-87.

Francisco, Adam. *Martin Luther and Islam: A Study in Sixteenth-Century Polemics and Apologetics*. London: Brill, 2007.

Holsten, Walter. "Reformation und Missions." *Archiv für Reformationsgeschichte* 44 (1953): 1-32.

———. *Christentum und nichtchristliche Religion nach der Auffassung Luthers*. Gütersloh: Bertelsmann, 1932.

Johnston, Mark D. *The Evangelical Rhetoric of Ramon Llull: Lay Learning and Piety in the Christian West Around 1300*. New York: Oxford, 1996.

———. *The Spiritual Logic of Ramon Llull*. New York: Oxford University Press, 1987.

Kolb, Robert. "Mission and Evangelism." In *Dictionary of Luther and the Lutheran Traditions*, edited by Timothy J. Wengert, 506-11. Grand Rapids: Baker, 2017.

Luther, Martin. *Heerpredigt wider den Türken* (1529). Weimar Ausgabe (hereafter WA) 30II: 149-97.

———. *Verlegung des Alcoran Bruder Richardi Prediger Ordens* (1542). WA 53: 272-76.

———. *Vermahnung zum Gebet wider den Türken* (1541). WA 51: 585-624.

MacLean, Gerald. *Looking East: English Writing and the Ottoman Empire before 1800*. New York: Palgrave, 2007.

Mau, Rudolf. "Luthers Stellung zu den Türken." In *Leben und Werk Martin Luthers von 1526 bis 1546*, edited by Helmar Junghans, 647–62. Göttingen: Vanderhoeck und Ruprecht, 1983.

Meserve, Margaret. *Empires of Islam in Renaissance Historical Thought*. Cambridge, MA: Harvard University Press, 2008.

Miller, Gregory J. "Views of Islam in Early Modern Britain: Insight from the First Translation Qur'an in English." *The Islamic Quarterly* 61:4 (2017): 483–504.

———. "Theodor Bibliander's Machumetis saracenorum principis eiusque successorum vitae, doctrina ac ipse alcoran (1543) as the Sixteenth Century 'Encyclopedia' of Islam." *Islam and Christian-Islamic Relations* 24:2 (2013): 241–54.

———. *The Turks and Islam in Reformation Germany*. New York: Routledge, 2018.

Moser, Christian. *Theodor Bibliander: Annotierte Bibliographie der gedruckten Werke*. Zürich: Theologischer Verlag Zürich, 2009.

Pfister, Rudolf. "Das Türkenbüchlein Theodor Biblianders." *Theologische Zeitung* 9 (1953): 438–68.

———. "Reformation, Türken und Islam." *Zwingliana* 10:6 (1956): 345–75.

Said, Edward. *Orientalism*. New York: Vintage Books, 1978.

Rouillard, Clarence. *The Turk in French History, Thought, and Literature*. Paris: Boivin, 1941.

Southern, Richard. *Western Views of Islam in the Middle Ages*. Cambridge, MA: Harvard University Press, 1962.

Staedtke, Joachim. "Der Zürcher Praedestinationsstreit von 1560." *Zwingliana* 9:9 (1953:1): 536–46.

Tolan, John Victor. *Saracens: Islam in the Medieval European Imagination*. New York: Columbia University Press, 2002.

Vitkus, Daniel. *Turning Turk: English Theater and the Multicultural Mediterranean, 1570–1630*. New York: Palgrave, 2003.

Warneck, Gustav. *Abriss einer Geschichte der protestantischen Missionen von der Reformation bis auf die Gegenwart*. 7th ed. Berlin: Verlag Martin Warneck, 1901.

Williams, George. "Erasmus and the Reformers on Non-Christian Reli-
    gion and Salus Extra Ecclesiam." In *Action and Conviction in Early
    Modern Europe*, ed. Theodore K. Robb and Jerrold E. Siegel, 319–70.
    Princeton: Princeton University Press, 1969.

8

—

CHARACTERISTICS OF ANABAPTIST MISSION IN THE SIXTEENTH CENTURY

James R. Krabill

In the summer of 1990, Anabaptists from across the globe gathered in Winnipeg, Manitoba, Canada, for the twelfth Mennonite World Conference assembly.[1] As a resource for the worship services at that gathering, a book of songs was compiled, including one new piece entitled, "We are people of God's peace." The text of this song was inspired and translated by Esther Bergen from the writings of Dutch Anabaptist church leader, Menno Simons (1496–1561), based on some of his favorite biblical texts—Romans 14:19, 2 Corinthians 5:17–19, and Ephesians 2:14–18. Bergen's original three-stanza hymn will have a fourth verse added in the upcoming *Voices Together* hymnal to be published by MennoMedia in November 2020. The text of the hymn makes this declaration:

> We are people of God's peace as a new creation.
> Love unites and strengthens us at this celebration.
> Sons and daughters of the Lord, serving one another,
> A new covenant of peace binds us all together.
>
> We are heralds of God's peace for the new creation;
> And by grace the word of peace reaches ev'ry nation.

---

1. Beginning in 1925 and for the next fifty years, these gatherings took place in either Europe or North America. In the past five decades, international settings have been chosen where large Anabaptist populations are located, in Brazil, Zimbabwe, India, Paraguay, and Indonesia.

Though we falter and we fail, Christ will still renew us.
By the Holy Spirit's pow'r, God is working through us.

We are children of God's peace in this new creation,
Spreading joy and happiness, through God's great salvation.
Hope we bring in spirit meek, in our daily living.
Peace with ev'ryone we seek, good for evil giving.

We are servants of God's peace, of the new creation.
Choosing peace, we faithfully serve with heart's devotion.
Jesus Christ, the Prince of peace, confidence will give us.
Christ the Lord is our defense; Christ will never leave us.

This hymn brings together a number of themes important to sixteenth-century Anabaptists and to the one and a half million global members of the Mennonite World Conference body today.[2] Anabaptists clearly identify themselves as participants in God's reconciling mission in the world, "spreading joy and happiness, through God's great salvation." They are "heralds of God's peace" for the new creation that God is bringing about. Achieving God's purposes will not happen by the mighty forces of human effort. Rather, it is by God's grace that "the word of peace reaches ev'ry nation." Despite human faltering and failing, "Christ will still renew us." For "by the Holy Spirit's pow'r, God is working through us."

The communal sense of belonging to God's people is a deep value for Anabaptists. *We* are heralds. *We* are servants. *We* are children. *We* are people of God's peace. God has called forth *a people* to be the primary model and messenger of a cosmic project to reconcile all things in Christ (Col 1:20), recruiting and naming members of this people as nothing less than "ministers of reconciliation" and "ambassadors of Christ" (2 Cor 5:18, 20).

If reconciliation is the *message* of God's project, it is also its *method* of delivery, characterized—as the song text affirms—by faithful service, meekness of spirit, devoted hearts, lives of peace, generosity toward evil

---

2. As of 2018, MWC membership included one international association and 107 Mennonite and Brethren in Christ national churches from fifty-eight countries, with baptized believers in about 10,000 congregations. Over 80 percent of these believers are African, Asian, or Latin American, with less than 20 percent located in Europe and North America. See: "Mennonite World Conference" website, https://mwc-cmm.org/content/about-mwc.

doers, and confidence in Christ's abiding presence at all times and in all places.

For the first generation of sixteenth-century Anabaptists, there was a seamless relationship between mission *thinking* and *practice*. Many members of the movement were simple folk with limited education, "sons and daughters of the Lord," bringing hope in daily living, and "serving one another," in "a new covenant of peace" that "binds us all together."

SIXTEENTH-CENTURY ANABAPTIST MISSIOLOGY: IN THOUGHT

If we were to take a closer look at how early Anabaptists understood their mission calling, we would be well served by the helpful insights of Ross Langmead, a newer generation Australian Christian "with Anabaptist leanings."[3]

Before identifying some of the missiological themes in Anabaptist thought, Langmead reminds us of the complexities we face in speaking of "Anabaptism" because of the great variety the movement represents in its early years, ranging from political engagement to withdrawal, from militant activism to pacifist commitments, and "positioned on nearly all points of the theological spectrum on many major doctrines."[4]

Despite these many differences, there did exist, according to Langmead, an emerging unity that became clearer by the mid-sixteenth century. It rejected the clericalized and territorially based church of Christendom and focused instead on the baptism and "priesthood" of all believers, the vocation of peacemaking, and a desire for the church to live communally, separately, and different from the world, following the New Testament pattern and under Jesus' authority.

---

3. Ross Langmead, "Anabaptist Perspectives for Mission," in *Prophecy and Passion: Essays in Honour of Athol Gill*, ed. David Neville (Adelaide: Australian Theological Forum, 2002), 328–45.

4. Langmead, "Anabaptist Perspectives," 329. Scholars have variously identified differing tendencies within the movement as "inspirationalist," "rationalist," "anti-trinitarian," "spiritualist," "radicalized reformers," and mainstream "Anabaptist," as well as, categorizations acknowledging variations based more on the regional differences existing between Swiss Brethren, South German Anabaptists, and Frisian and Dutch members of the movement. For more detail on this matter, see James Stayer, Werner Packull, and Klaus Deppermann, "From Monogenesis to Polygenesis: The Historical Discussion of Anabaptist Origins," *Mennonite Quarterly Review* 49 (1975): 83–121.

According to Langmead, Anabaptist fervor for mission "flows from aspiring to live as Christ lived." And "in their enthusiasm of evangelism the early Anabaptists foreshadowed the modern Protestant missionary movement by over two hundred years."[5]

Langmead proposes six major missiological emphases in early Anabaptism. These include: "kingdom theology" (or in Langmead's words, the multi-dimensional commonwealth of God), mission as discipleship, a cruciform mission, peacemaking, mission from the margins, and mission in community.

THE MULTI-DIMENSIONAL COMMONWEALTH OF GOD

Central to an Anabaptist understanding of mission is God's invitation to cooperate "in ushering in a new order" of "justice, peace, and covenant community." The nature of this kingdom is its "upside-down" character, its small beginnings, and its mysterious, yet steady and surprising growth. It is not the church's job to *build* the kingdom, but rather to *witness* to what God is bringing forth in the world.

God's kingdom is not a socio-political or territorial realm; rather, it is God's dynamic and saving presence, "a new reign," "a new order," and "a new set of relationships in God's creation." To capture the full scope and comprehensive meaning of what God is bringing forth, all aspects of Christian engagement are required—"evangelism, caring for our neighbors, community development, justice seeking, peacemaking, social action, living in a welcoming community, environmental action," and "praying in hope for God's kingdom to come." God's action grows out of a cosmic vision to reconcile and transform *all things*. God expresses this action through "embodiment" and ongoing presence in the created order, in history, and ultimately, "in the person of Jesus Christ" and "the life of church." It is God alone who builds and ushers in this "multi-dimensional commonwealth." The task of the church, then, is "only to respond to God's Spirit within us and point to God at work."[6]

---

5. Langmead, "Anabaptist Perspectives," 329–30.

6. The preceding two paragraphs include direct quotes, paraphrased expressions, and summary statements from Langmead's "Anabaptist Perspectives," 330–32. In presenting the remaining five missiological emphases in early Anabaptism, we will proceed in a similar manner for "mission as discipleship" in Langmead, 332–37; "mission shaped by the cross,"

MISSION AS DISCIPLESHIP

The Christian life, according to Anabaptists, requires a voluntary "full-bod-ied discipleship." The church is a community gathered around Jesus. It is a body of *believers*, certainly. But it is also a body of *followers*. And to follow Jesus means responding to his call to bear witness to the gospel's power in the life of the believers. Discipleship and mission are, thus, *one*, as mission is none other than a "natural dimension of the lives of ordinary believers in the course of following Jesus." Every believer is, in that sense, a mis-sionary—called to preach and practice the gospel as a living sign of God's reign. *Discipleship* for followers of Jesus is a lived-out social alternative to the world's values, ways, and priorities. And *mission* is thought of and practiced as full-bodied, incarnated discipleship.

On the continuum of withdrawing from society or adopting the Christendom model where church and society live symbiotically with each other, Anabaptists have been more inclined to withdraw. For "the church's mission is primarily to be the church and act in ways that point to a new order, not compromising with the old order." Discipleship for Anabaptist followers of Jesus has no need, then, to be called *radical* disci-pleship, as some observers are wont to do, since for Anabaptists, "there is no other type."

MISSION SHAPED BY THE CROSS

A commitment to following Jesus for Anabaptists inevitably leads to the cross. The path of discipleship is cruciform. "Anabaptist missiology calls Christians to face issues of suffering, cost and possible death on the [road] to new life and the experience of resurrection." A missiology shaped by the cross rejects language and approaches emphasizing conquest, victory, triumphalism, and strategies centering on power. Anabaptists *do* celebrate the spiritual victory, joy, and power of the risen Christ. But the resurrection is understood as God's *Yes* to Jesus' "sacrificial, world-challenging life and consequent death" and calls believers to follow Jesus as master, model, and guide in leading self-giving lives of obedience to God's kingdom purposes.

337–38; "peacemaking," 339–40; "mission from the margins," 340–43; and "mission in com-munity," 343–44.

Christ's resurrection is central to Anabaptist faith, hope, and power. But "the path to resurrection is through the cross." Suffering is not only— or even primarily—the believer's inward wrestling with sin. "It is the end of a freely chosen path after counting the cost" and the expected result in a rebellious world of representing God's present and coming reign.

PEACEMAKING

Aside from a few exceptions in the early years of the Anabaptist movement, the call to renounce violence, to turn the other cheek, and to love one's enemies has been understood and practiced by Anabaptists as a direct consequence of following Jesus and the way of the cross. "Jesus' arrest and death flowed from his decision at every major point in his life to live and teach the way of suffering servanthood rather than to take up the sword." As disciples of Jesus, the call to peacemaking and peacekeeping has been a prominent characteristic of the Anabaptist understanding and approach to mission.

Ironically, this key conviction emerged and grew ever stronger in the sixteenth-century context where violent means were employed against the Anabaptists in an effort to contain and ultimately suppress the movement. Not surprisingly, however, this was interpreted by adherents of the movement as the natural cost of faithful discipleship and the way of the cross. Non-violent love and forgiveness are understood by Anabaptists as the way that followers of Jesus become Christ's ambassadors of reconciliation (2 Cor 5:18–20) and participate in God's reconciling mission to the world.

MISSION FROM THE MARGINS

The region of Galilee where Jesus lived and worked was a backwater region on the margins of Judaism. In that context, Jesus focused much of his ministry on the disenfranchised—publicans, lepers, poor, prostitutes, women, children, foreigners, and neighboring Samaritans living just to the south. Jesus' home and ministry location, along with his economic and social teachings, are instructive for understanding who he was and how he modeled for his disciples living out the reign of God.

Early Anabaptist missionaries, mostly poor and uneducated, did not theologize much about "heading to the margins" since "that's where they found themselves anyway." They did believe, however, that their mission should be shaped by the mission of Jesus. "They read the Bible through the eyes of the poor and saw a Jesus who challenged the powers and included the outcast." In the alternative communities they formed, Anabaptists refrained from using titles and hierarchies, shared common goods, practiced the priesthood of all believers, included the poor, and "expected to see Christ in the hungry and homeless."

MISSION IN COMMUNITY

Early Anabaptists held to a high ecclesiology. They saw the body of Christ, modeled after the first-century New Testament church depicted in the Acts of the Apostles, as a covenanted faith community, following Jesus, and living as a sign of God's reign in the midst of the world. *Mission* for Anabaptists, then, as a natural outworking of these convictions, was intrinsically communal. "It is not," writes Langmead, "that *I* partially embody the risen Christ in my life, but that *we* partially embody the risen Christ in our life together."[7]

Anabaptists set the bar high for Christ followers by calling for all aspects of daily life to be submitted to Christ's lordship, by viewing mission as cruciform and shaped by suffering, by committing themselves to renouncing and overcoming violence, by engaging mission from the margins, and by aspiring to life in an alternative society as a visible expression of God's reconciling work in the world. These represent some of the core beliefs and commitments of early Anabaptists with regard to the church and its participation in God's mission.

SIXTEENTH-CENTURY ANABAPTIST MISSIOLOGY: IN PRACTICE

In some circles, Anabaptism has earned a reputation of de-emphasizing theological reflection in deference to holy or righteous living.[8] In the preceding section, we have attempted to nuance that view by highlighting

---

7. Langmead, "Anabaptist Perspectives," 343.

8. Various branches of the Anabaptist movement approach this matter differently. According to Mennonite historian, John S. Oyer, the Amish—one of the historic sub-groups of the broader Anabaptist family—have no formal, "explicit" systematic theology. And the "implicit" theology that one *does* find comes through talking with Amish people, rather than reading written treatises. See Oyer's chapter, "Is There an Amish Theology?" in *Les amish: Origine et particularismes*, ed. Lydie Hege and Christoph Wiebe (Ingersheim, Germany:

some of the missiological thinking that stands behind the mission practice for which Anabaptists are known and for which they died in the early sixteenth century.

At a time when the major Protestant Reformers in their writings and actions did manifest some understanding and commitment to mission, Anabaptists went further in passionately believing that the Great Commission remained binding on all Christians and setting about to actively evangelize their society.[9] "My heart trembles in me," wrote Menno Simons; "all my joints shake and quake when I consider that the whole world, lords, princes, learned and unlearned people … are so estranged from Christ Jesus and from evangelical truth and from eternal life."[10]

This statement clearly illustrates the Anabaptists' dispirited attitude toward sixteenth-century Christendom and their desire for *restitution*— restoring the life, faith, and practice of the early church, the "Golden Age" of Christian history—instead of *Reformation*, based on their utter despair over the possibility of ever effectively reforming the church of their day. The Anabaptists' critique of Roman Catholic Christianity essentially mirrored the criticisms they leveled at the Protestant Reformers themselves, condemning them as half-way men for failing to introduce a thoroughgoing reformation of church life. Three among many alarming concerns held by Anabaptists were Christendom's full amalgamation of church and state, the prevailing formalism and spiritual laxity of both members and leaders within the church, and the baptism of infants "before their understanding was mature enough to give the association any content."[11]

The continent of Europe, for Anabaptists, had once again become an open, urgent mission field requiring a missionary response. "In their

---

Mennonitischer Geschichtsverein/Association Française d'Histoire Anabaptiste-Mennonite [AFHAM], 1996), 278–302.

9. John H. Yoder has identified seventeen potential explanations as to why mission thought and activity was not high on the agenda of Magisterial Protestant Reformers in his chapter, "Reformation and Missions: A Literature Survey," in *Anabaptism and Mission*, ed. Wilbert R. Shenk (Scottdale, PA: Herald Press, 1984), 40–50. For a review and summary of this matter from a mainline Protestant perspective, see David J. Bosch, in "The Reformers and Mission," *Transforming Mission: Paradigm Shifts in the Theology of Mission* (Maryknoll, NY: Orbis, 1991), 243–52.

10. In *The Complete Writings of Menno Simons c. 1496-1561*, ed. J. C. Wenger and trans. Leonard Verduin (Scottdale, PA: Herald Press, 1956), 293.

11. Franklin H. Littell, in *Anabaptism and Mission*, ed. Shenk, 18.

understanding," says Bosch, "there was no difference between mission in 'Christian' Europe and mission among non-Christians."[12] And in contrast to Roman and dominant Protestant policies of *cuius regio, eius religio* ("as the prince, so the religion"), Anabaptists disregarded territorial designations of religion, emboldened as they were by the Psalmist's declaration that the entire "earth is the Lord's, and the fullness thereof" (Ps 24:1). In defiance, therefore, of Christian rulers who attempted to dictate the religious affiliation of those they ruled, Anabaptists sent their missioners across politico-religious boundaries to anywhere and everywhere they could find an audience. "Krakau, Aachen, Stockholm, and probably Venice and Salonica," notes Franklin H. Littell, "would appear on our map of the movement. Wanderings and exile, for individuals and whole families, fill the annals of the movement. And in their defeat, they triumphed [... confessing] themselves strangers and pilgrims upon the earth. They elaborated a theology of martyrdom [and] developed what we might call a 'concept of mobility' in analyzing their doctrines of the church and its world mission."[13]

As they went, Anabaptists perceived their missionary activity as the principal alternative to the approach taken by Christendom's Magisterial Reformers. In the view of Mennonite historian, C. J. Dyck, "Not coercion but persuasion, not primary emphasis on reforming society but on establishing a new society, not individualistic or sacramental salvation, but personal experience and corporate faith were their alternatives."[14]

The extraordinary missionary movement carried out by Anabaptists was dynamic, spontaneous, and characterized by the full participation of both lay men and women. This does not indicate, however, an absence of planned intentionality about their activities. In August 1527, in fact, a group of some sixty Anabaptist leaders gathered in Augsburg, Germany, to determine how best to proceed in evangelizing Europe and beyond. Details of the meeting are scant, but representatives from various and dispersed Anabaptist communities are thought to have been present. "The threat of persecution, and possibly death, was no deterrent to these leaders," writes

---

12. Bosch, *Transforming Mission*, 247.

13. Littell, in *Anabaptism and Mission*, ed. Shenk, 17.

14. C. J. Dyck, in *Anabaptism and Mission*, ed. Shenk, 12.

Wilbert R. Shenk. "This has been called the Martyrs' Synod because many of the delegates died within a short time as martyrs."[15]

Mennonite Brethren mission historian Hans Kasdorf has described in considerable detail the goals, timing, locations, audiences, methods, agents, and Holy Spirit power employed by early Anabaptists in their witness to the sixteenth-century European context in which they found themselves.[16] A summary of Kasdorf's findings identify the following features of the movement's missiological commitments and practices.

SETTING DEFINABLE GOALS

The primary missionary objectives for Anabaptists were determined less by numbers than by seeing people become true disciples of Jesus. This goes to the heart of why so much emphasis was placed on the order of the Lord's directives in Matthew 28:18-20 to go and make believing disciples—first, *going*; then, *making disciples* of all nations; followed by the two subsequent activities of *baptizing* the new Jesus followers and *teaching* them to observe all things. The order here given by Jesus mattered to the Anabaptists. It was of central significance and occurred repeatedly in their sermons, writings, testimonies, court records, and faith confessions. It shaped the way they witnessed to their neighbors and preached to gathered audiences. And perhaps most importantly, it put into serious question the practice of infant baptism by substantiating their firm conviction that making believing disciples could only take place in the hearts and lives of assenting adults, and not in newborn babies, still far too young to understand, receive teaching, believe, and obey "all things" commanded by Jesus. "While mainline Reformers rediscovered the great Pauline term *Glaube* (faith)," notes Kasdorf, "the Radical Reformers rediscovered the evangelists' word *Nachfolge* (discipleship). People cannot, they maintained, call Jesus Lord unless they are his disciples indeed, prepared to follow him

---

15. Wilbert R. Shenk, in *Fully Engaged: Missional Church in an Anabaptist Voice*, ed. Stanley W. Green and James R. Krabill (Harrisonburg, VA: Herald Press, 2015), 21.

16. Hans Kasdorf, in "The Anabaptist Approach to Mission," *Anabaptism and Mission*, ed. Shenk, 51-69. The author admits the somewhat anachronistic nature of this list of categories, but still contends on page 52 that "although these terms were not used [by Anabaptists], the principles they expressed ungirded the entire Anabaptist mission program. Thus, the application of contemporary mission concepts will enhance our understanding of—and appreciation for—the dynamic mission movement of sixteenth-century Anabaptism."

in every way. This was the message they preached, the code they lived by, and the faith they died for."[17]

SELECTING RESPONSIVE POPULATION GROUPS

In many instances, Anabaptist missionaries naturally found themselves sharing the gospel with people of similar socio-economic standing. There is also some indication, though, that this approach was intentionally adopted for increased effectiveness so that, according to Kasdorf, "the lay missionary was sent to rural areas, winning whole family units to Christ; the artisan evangelists were sent to people of their profession, leading them to profess Jesus as Savior and Lord; the educated were sent to the cities where they were bound to meet the sophisticated and secular elite, introducing them to Christ."[18] Because, however, of the Anabaptists' general disregard for the territorial realms fixed by Roman and Magisterial Protestant leaders, Anabaptists were often forced to select times, places, and audiences out of sight and control of the ruling politico-religious establishment. Many early Anabaptist meetings took place, thus, "at night, in the forest, on remote farms, in isolated mills or sheltered in huge rock caves, far from authorities, and in hushed tones to avoid being detected."[19] Punishable consequences for failing to comply with existing civil and ecclesiastical laws included eviction from the territory, property repossession, trial, torture, incarceration, or death at the hands of the church or state.

APPLYING RELEVANT METHODS

The first few years of the Anabaptist movement, 1525–1527, can best be characterized by spontaneous expansion not unlike that of the early apostolic church. Kasdorf identifies four particular evangelistic approaches employed by Anabaptists during this early period.

Preaching pilgrims. Leaders of the movement initially wandered clandestinely, fled persecution, called people to repentance, and offered pastoral care to emerging faith communities along the way. As persecution

---

17. Kasdorf, *Anabaptism and Mission*, ed. Shenk, 53.

18. Ibid., 54.

19. Janie Blough and James R. Krabill, in *God's People in Mission: An Anabaptist Perspective*, ed. Stanley W. Green and Rafael Zaracho (Bogota, Colombia: Mennonite World Conference, 2018), 121–22.

intensified, whole groups of migrant families began to form, traveling toward more secure communities in Moravia further east.

House meetings. The goal for many Anabaptist missioners was to see entire family units hear and accept the gospel message. Some such gatherings took place in the form of simple, spontaneous household visits; others were organized by new members of the movement. In some instances these gatherings resembled revival meetings resulting in conversions, adult baptisms, and the celebration of the Lord's Supper.

Bible reading and lay evangelism. "Since the leaders of the awakening were quickly arrested and banned," writes Kasdorf, "the responsibility of spiritual care and continued evangelism was transferred to local farmers and artisans. Those who could read began to read the Word of God to nonliterates as they met in homes and barns and village churches. When people confessed Christ, lay brothers performed the rite of baptism."[20]

Persecution. Opposition to the Anabaptist movement was fierce. New converts and leaders were tracked down, imprisoned, or put to death by burning, beheading, drowning, or hanging.[21] By 1527 all of the movement's founding leaders in Switzerland had either been expelled from the territory or put to death. Women and children were generally kept alive, but carefully monitored. In the duchy of Württemberg, government authorities felt the need to chain women in their homes "to keep them from going to their relatives and neighbors to witness to their faith."[22] Not unlike what happened during the first centuries of the Christian movement, the courageous and defenseless posture of Anabaptist martyrs proved a powerful witness to both their executioners and to those witnessing their earthly demise, and in many cases attracted more people to the movement than it drove away.

---

20. Kasdorf, *Anabaptism and Mission*, ed. Shenk, 56.

21. According to John H. Yoder and Alan Kreider, "Anabaptists were put to death *by fire* in the Catholic territories" and "*by drowning and the sword* under Protestant regimes" (italics mine); see their chapter, "The Anabaptists," in *The History of Christianity: A Lion Handbook*, ed. Tim Dowley (Herts, England: Lion Publishing, 1977), 399–403, esp. 402.

22. Donald F. Durnbaugh, *The Believers' Church: The History and Character of Radical Protestantism* (New York: Macmillan, 1968), 231–32.

SENDING RESPONSIBLE AGENTS

Immediately following the 1527 Augsburg Missionary Conference, also known as the Martyr's Synod, Anabaptists became more intentional about their mission efforts with "a grand map of evangelical enterprise."[23] They "systematically divided Europe into sectors for evangelistic outreach and sent missionaries out into them in twos and threes."[24] Operating on the biblical principle of the priesthood of all believers, lay people served as primary missionary agents making use of family connections, neighborhood relationships, and occupational contacts. According to Kasdorf, these agents possessed five key characteristics—they were *compelled* by the Great Commission, *convicted* by a deep sense of calling, *committed* to a high view of discipleship, *called* to carry out the apostolic task, and *commissioned* by a supporting church.[25] Procedures for commissioning outgoing missionaries often took place in ordinary worship services where "candidates gave testimony to their calling and received prayer, counsel, and encouragement for the dangers ahead."[26] In one remarkable twenty-five stanza commissioning hymn from the early years of the movement, Anabaptists recognized the likely chance that those going forth might "taste sword and fire" and never return:

> And if thou, Lord, desire
> And should it be thy will
> That we taste sword and fire
> By those who thus would kill
> Then comfort, pray, our loved ones
> And tell them, we've endured
> And we shall see them yonder—
> Eternally secured.[27]

---

23. Durnbaugh, *The Believers' Church*, 233.

24. Yoder and Kreider, "The Anabaptists," 400.

25. Kasdorf, *Anabaptism and Mission*, ed. Shenk, 61–65, italics mine. See also the important chapters by Wolfgang Schäufele ("The Missionary Vision and Activity of the Anabaptist Laity," 70–87) and Hendrik W. Meihuizen ("The Early Missionary Zeal of the Early Anabaptists," 88–96) in *Anabaptism and Mission*, ed. Shenk.

26. Blough and Krabill, *God's People in Mission*, 122. For more on early Anabaptist worship patterns and their missional impact, see the full chapter ("Worship and Mission," 113–25) where this citation is found.

27. Wilhelm Wiswedel, "Die alten Täufergemeinden und ihr missionarisches Wirken," *Archiv für Reformationsgeschichte* 41 (Part 2, 1948): 121–22. Translation by Kasdorf.

MEASURING THE RESULTING HARVEST

The price paid by Anabaptists for their missionary zeal was enormous. The names of over 2,000 Anabaptist martyrs are known and recorded, though some estimate that number to be much higher, as many as 4,000 to 5,000. Despite the devastating losses experienced by the early movement, German historian and theologian, Ernst Troeltsch, reports that "the whole of Central Europe was soon covered with a network of Anabaptist communities, loosely connected with each other, who all practiced a strictly scriptural form of worship. The chief centers were Augsburg, Moravia, and Strassburg, and later on, in Friesland and the Netherlands."[28] Kasdorf completes the picture by noting that by the mid-1500s, Anabaptist preachers could be found carrying out mission efforts throughout Germany, Austria, Switzerland, Holland, France, Poland, Galicia, Hungary, Italy, and reaching as far as Denmark, Sweden, Greece, and Constantinople.[29] There was reportedly even consideration among Anabaptists in Switzerland of going "to the red Indians across the sea."[30]

THE CONTRIBUTION OF ANABAPTIST MISSION

The legacy of the sixteenth-century missionary movement as envisioned and modeled by early Anabaptists is a rich and fruitful one, though until now insufficiently examined by most missiologists. What productive reflection and research might potentially come, for example, from exploring ways in which the free church impulse championed by Anabaptists shaped Protestant mission efforts in recent centuries? Church historian Kenneth Scott Latourette made the observation already in the 1940s, in fact, that the worldwide expansion of the Christian faith was increasingly a function of Protestantism's "left wing" with signs of a faith less and less dependent on racial and national lines than either Roman Catholic or Protestant Christendom of the sixteenth century. "From the radical wing," he noted, "come a majority of the missionaries who are propagating Christianity in other lands. This means that the worldwide Protestantism of the decades ahead is probably to depart further from the Christianity

---

28. See Troeltsch's *The Social Teachings of the Christian Churches*, 2 vols., trans. from the German by Olive Wyon (London: George Allen and Unwin, 1950), 2:704.

29. Kasdorf, *Anabaptism and Mission*, ed. Shenk, 66–67.

30. John Allen Moore, *Der Starke Joerg: Die Geschichte Georg Blaurocks, des Täuferführers und Missionars* (Kassel, Germany: Oncken Verlag, 1955), 35.

of pre-Reformation days than has that of Western Europe and the British Isles. Presumably, the trend will be augmented as the 'younger churches' in non-Occidental countries mount in strength."[31]

Other historians, like Franklin H. Littell, express the same sentiment concerning the impact the free church tradition played in shaping particularly nineteenth-century mission efforts. Writes Littell, "The way in which the Great Century has authenticated the faith and testimony of the free churches is clearly indicated in the record. ... The maintenance and implementation of a missionary worldview are more a mark of the voluntary religious associations than of the ancient geographical centers of 'Christian civilization.'" In addition, notes Littell, "Reformation Europe once had its chance to embrace a pattern of free religious association and rejected it. ... Both Rome and dominant Protestantism were committed to the medieval parish pattern, and determined to suppress the independent congregational and freely conceived evangel of the party of the Restitution."[32] It is this resolute commitment to independent church life, free from state and establishment authority, that prompts Donald Durnbaugh to credit the Anabaptists with sowing the seeds, though perhaps unintentionally, for what we today recognize as religious liberty. Writes Durnbaugh, "The Anabaptists did not have the cause of religious liberty in the commonwealth in mind when they demanded freedom from the state to worship, but their suffering witness helped to establish it."[33]

What shape the newer churches in the Majority World will take is still emerging and not totally clear. But even here, some observers see the Anabaptist legacy in evidence. Mission historian Andrew F. Walls was one of the first to point out the striking similarity between Anabaptists and African-initiated churches. He goes so far as to claim, in fact, that "it is helpful to think of the independent churches as Africa's Anabaptists. Profusion of variety, the eccentricity of their wilder manifestations, and a spirituality and radical Bible-centredness are essential to them at their best. They relate to older Reformed churches as the sixteenth-century Anabaptists did to the Reformed. They are a response to Christianity in

---

31. Kenneth Scott Latourette, "A Historian Looks Ahead: The Future of Christianity in the Light of the Past," *Church History* 15 (1946): 3–16, esp. 12 and 14.

32. Littell, in *Anabaptism and Mission*, ed. Shenk, 15.

33. Durnbaugh, *The Believers' Church*, 241.

African terms, 'a place to feel at home'; and also, a witness to the fact that there is here no 'abiding city.'"[34]

As we move increasingly in the West toward postmodern, post-Christendom, and ultimately post-Christian realities, the potential contribution of Anabaptist understandings of church and mission become even more evident. Many observers have already made this point. Brian McClaren, for example, states that "believing as I do that modernity is slowly but surely being replaced by a new postmodern ethos—and believing that in this postmodern milieu Christians will have neither the dominating position they had through the Middle Ages nor the privileged position they had during much of modernity—I believe we have a lot to learn at this juncture from the Anabaptists."[35] Darrell Guder, one of the leading voices in the missional church movement, further declares that "neither the structures nor the theology of our established Western traditional churches is missional. They are shaped by the legacy of Christendom. ... The obvious fact that what we once regarded as Christendom is now ... a mission field stands in bold contrast today with the apparent lethargy of established church traditions in addressing their new situation both creatively and faithfully. Yet this helpfully highlights the need for and providential appearance of a theological revolution in missional thinking that centers the body of Christ on God's mission rather than post-Christendom's concern for the church's institutional maintenance."[36] Anabaptists would certainly find resonance in Guder's assessment.

Responses to this dilemma are beginning to emerge in the thought and writings of "newer Anabaptists" like Stuart Murray in the United Kingdom. "The end of Christendom," says Murray, "marks the collapse of a determined but ultimately futile attempt to impose Christianity rather than inviting people to follow Jesus. The fourth-century decision to transfer from the margins to the centre in one enormous leap for power resulted in coercive but nominal Christianity. ... The marginality of post-Christendom churches [today] holds out the enticing prospect of recovering the power

---

34. Andrew F. Walls, "African Independent Churches," in *The History of Christianity: A Lion Handbook*, 628.

35. Brian McLaren, *A Generous Orthodoxy* (Grand Rapids: Zondervan, 2004), 206.

36. Darrell L. Guder, ed., *Missional Church* (Grand Rapids: Eerdmans, 1998), 5, 7.

and appeal of subversive Christianity and getting the missional movement back on track."[37]

One might add yet another contribution that sixteenth-century Anabaptists could make to challenges that twenty-first-century churches are facing, that of faithful and respectful engagement with people of other faiths. For, rather remarkably, according to Mennonite missiologist David W. Shenk, "It is within the 16th century context of conflict between Christendom and the Islamic Dar al-Islam that the Anabaptist movement was formed. The Christian-Muslim conflict helped to form the theology of mission of the Anabaptists. ... The Anabaptist yearning for a non-violent engagement and witness among Muslims is most remarkable. They would share the Gospel with the Turks; they would never kill them."[38] With Christians and Muslims today comprising over half of the world's population, is there a word of wisdom here that followers of Jesus might do well to heed?

MENNO SIMONS: THE GOSPEL OF CHRIST'S PEACE, THE TRUE NATURE OF GOD'S LOVE

As the Anabaptist movement expanded northward into Holland, it attracted to its ranks a young Catholic priest named Menno Simons. In 1536 Menno was ordained to Anabaptist ministry and began his lifelong clandestine ministry as a Reformer and leader, teaching, writing, and organizing congregations throughout northern Europe. Though hunted by the authorities his entire career, he was amazingly never apprehended. As a part of his literary legacy, Menno leaves us these words describing his passion for sharing the gospel of God's peace in Jesus Christ:

> We preach, as much as possible,
> Both by day and by night,
> In houses and in fields,
> In forests and wastes,
> Hither and yon,
> At home or abroad,

---

37. Stuart Murray, *Church after Christendom* (Waynesboro, GA: Paternoster Press, 2004), 148–49.

38. David W. Shenk, in his important chapter, "Anabaptists and Muslims: Commitment to the Kingdom of God," in *Anabaptism and Mission*, ed. Wilbert R. Shenk and Peter F. Rempel (Schwarzenfeld, Germany: Neufeld Verlag, 2007), 85–108, esp. 100.

In prison and in dungeons,
In water and in fire,
On scaffold and on the wheel,
Before lords and princes,
Through mouth and pen,
With possessions and blood,
With life and death.

We have done this these many years,
And we are not ashamed of the Gospel of the glory of Christ.
For we feel His living fruit and patience and willing sacrifices
Of our faithful brethren and companions in Christ Jesus.
We could wish that we might save all mankind
From the jaws of hell,
Free them from the chains of their sins,
And by the gracious help of God
Add them to Christ by the Gospel of His peace.
For this is the true nature of the love which is of God.[39]

BIBLIOGRAPHY

Blough, Janie, and James R. Krabill. "Worship and Mission." In *God's People in Mission: An Anabaptist Perspective*, edited by Stanley W. Green and Rafael Zaracho, 113–25. Bogota, Columbia: Mennonite World Conference, 2018.

Bosch, David J. *Transforming Mission: Paradigm Shifts in the Theology of Mission*. Maryknoll, NY: Orbis, 1991.

Durnbaugh, Donald F. *The Believers' Church: The History and Character of Radical Protestantism*. New York: Macmillan, 1968.

Dyck, C. J. Front matter quotation. *In Anabaptism and Mission*, edited by Wilbert R. Shenk, 12. Scottdale, PA: Herald Press, 1984.

Guder, Darrell L., ed., *Missional Church*. Grand Rapids: Eerdmans, 1998.

Langmead, Ross. "Anabaptist Perspectives for Mission." In *Prophecy and Passion: Essays in Honour of Athol Gill*, edited by David Neville, 328–45. Adelaide: Australian Theological Forum, 2002.

---

39. In Wenger, ed., *The Complete Writings of Menno Simons*, 633.

Latourette, Kenneth Scott. "A Historian Looks Ahead: The Future of Christianity in the Light of the Past." *Church History* 15 (1946): 3–16.

Littell, Franklin H. "The Anabaptist Theology of Mission." In *Anabaptism and Mission*, edited by Wilbert R. Shenk, 13–23. Scottdale, PA: Herald Press, 1984.

Kasdorf, Hans. "The Anabaptist Approach to Mission." In *Anabaptism and Mission*, edited by Wilbert R. Shenk, 51–69. Scottdale, PA: Herald Press, 1984.

McLaren, Brian. *A Generous Orthodoxy.* Grand Rapids: Zondervan, 2004.

Meihuizen, Hendrik W. "The Early Missionary Zeal of the Early Anabaptists." In *Anabaptism and Mission*, edited by Wilbert R. Shenk, 88–96. Scottdale, PA: Herald Press, 1984.

Mennonite World Conference. Homepage statistics. https://mwc-cmm. org/content/about-mwc.

Moore, John Allen. *Der Starke Joerg: Die Geschichte Georg Blaurocks, des Täuferführers und Missionars.* Kassel: Oncken Verlag, 1955.

Murray, Stuart. *Church after Christendom.* Waynesboro, GA: Paternoster Press, 2004.

Oyer, John S. "Is There an Amish Theology?" In *Les amish: Origine et particularismes*, edited by Lydie Hege and Christoph Wiebe, 278–302. Ingersheim: Mennonitischer Geschichtsverein/Association Française d'Histoire Anabaptiste-Mennonite [AFHAM], 1996.

Schäufele, Wolfgang. "The Missionary Vision and Activity of the Anabaptist Laity." In *Anabaptism and Mission*, edited by Wilbert R. Shenk, 70–87. Scottdale, PA: Herald Press, 1984.

Shenk, David W. "Anabaptists and Muslims: Commitment to the Kingdom of God." In *Anabaptism and Mission*, edited by Wilbert R. Shenk and Peter F. Rempel, 85–108. Schwarzenfeld: Neufeld Verlag, 2007.

Shenk, Wilbert R. "Why Missional and Mennonite Should Make Perfect Sense." In *Fully Engaged: Missional Church in an Anabaptist Voice*, edited by Stanley W. Green and James R. Krabill, 19–28. Harrisonburg, VA: Herald Press, 2015.

Stayer, James, Werner Packull, and Klaus Deppermann. "From Mono-
    genesis to Polygenesis: The Historical Discussion of Anabaptist
    Origins." *Mennonite Quarterly Review* 49 (1975): 83–121.

Troeltsch, Ernst. *The Social Teachings of the Christian Churches.* 2 vols.
    Translated by Olive Wyon. London: George Allen and Unwin, 1950.

Walls, Andrew F. "African Independent Churches." In *The History of
    Christianity: A Lion Handbook,* edited by Tim Dowley, 626–28.
    Herts: Lion Publishing, 1977.

Wenger, J. C., ed. *The Complete Writings of Menno Simons, c. 1496–1561.*
    Translated by Leonard Verduin. Scottdale, PA: Herald Press, 1956.

Wiswedel, Wilhelm. "Die alten Täufergemeinden und ihr missionar-
    isches Wirken." *Archiv für Reformationsgeschichte* 41 (Part 2, 1948):
    115–32.

Yoder, John H. "Reformation and Missions: A Literature Survey." In *Ana-
    baptism and Mission,* edited by Wilbert R. Shenk, 40–50. Scottdale,
    PA: Herald Press, 1984.

Yoder, John H., and Alan Kreider. "The Anabaptists." In *The History of
    Christianity: A Lion Handbook,* edited by Tim Dowley, 399–403.
    Herts: Lion Publishing, 1977.

9

THE AUGSBURG "MISSIONS CONVENTION" OF AUGUST 1527 AND EARLY ANABAPTIST OUTREACH

Charles E. Self

Historians and missiologists are increasingly discovering the Anabaptist streams that feed the evangelical missions river.[1] The Pietist movements and Moravian communities of the late seventeenth and early eighteenth centuries deserve honor as William Carey's predecessors. However, the sixteenth-century Anabaptists have been largely ignored. Mennonite scholar, Hans Kasdorf, summarizes this phenomenon:

> One of the most misrepresented facets in the history of the expansion of the Christian faith is that of the Anabaptist movement during the sixteenth-century Protestant Reformation. Their extension of the Gospel through planned evangelism and church planting across linguistic, cultural, and national boundaries is still a missing chapter in mission history. During the last few decades, writers like Franklin H. Littell, Roland H. Bainton, Donald F. Durnbaugh, and (in Europe) Wilhelm Wiswedel, Walther Koehler, and Wolfgang Schaeufele have made noble efforts to bring to light the expansion of the Anabaptists. But histories of Christianity and of missions

---

1. "Evangelical" in this context refers to the diverse, multidenominational movement arising out of three historical streams: the Protestant Reformation(s) of the sixteenth century, the Pietist and early Protestant missionary movements of the seventeenth and early eighteen centuries, including the Moravians, and the revivals of the mid-eighteenth century in Great Britain and the North American colonies.

either wholly ignore or barely mention the subject. Kenneth Scott Latourette, however, devotes two chapters to the Radical Reformation and points out that the "missionaries of the movement were numerous." The question naturally arises why the records of mission history bypass the missionary activities of the Anabaptists. This silence becomes even more puzzling when one compares the tremendous mission emphasis of the Roman Catholic Church with the almost total absence of mission thinking among the Protestant Reformers (Martin Luther, Huldrych [Ulrich] Zwingli, Jean Calvin). One would think that Protestant mission historians of the nineteenth and twentieth centuries would have searched out those within the Protestant movement who were concerned about bringing Christ to all the world.[2]

This chapter will explore the reality that Great Commission thinking permeated the Anabaptist movement from the beginning. The subversive activity of some Anabaptist groups (especially those influenced by Jan of Leyden of Munster fame and his calls for a violent overthrow of the social order), alienated many sympathetic Protestants, and led to even more severe persecutions. Yet, the communities that remained biblically rooted understood that faithfulness to Christ included sharing the true gospel with everyone.

I will examine the Augsburg (in Swabia, Bavaria, Southern Germany) Convention that shaped the early beliefs and practices of the Anabaptists, and chronicle some of the missionary highlights that flowed from those convictions. The Jesuits and other monastic orders offered missionary zeal for Roman Catholics reeling from Protestant expansion, with their call to re-evangelize (restore to Roman Catholic allegiance) Europe and bring the church's message and structure to Asia and the New World. The Anabaptists were the only Reformation stream consciously and consistently reflecting on missionary work (that resulted in new churches) across communities,

---

2. Hans Kasdorf, "Anabaptists and the Great Commission in the Reformation," *Direction* 4, no. 2 (April 1975): 303. See directionjournal.org/4/2/anabaptists-and-great-commission-in. html. Kasdorf's work is the foundation of much of the content and basic arguments of this chapter. For a tribute to his work, see Henry J. Schmidt, "Hans Kasdorf's Contribution to Mission Theology" *Direction* 28, no. 1 (Spring 1999): 6–17. Schmidt places Kasdorf alongside George W. Peters, Jacob A. Loewen, and Paul G. Hiebert as the vital voices of mission history and missiology in the Anabaptist tradition.

countries, and cultures. Reformed advocates argue that Calvin and others led similar efforts from Geneva toward France and parts of the Holy Roman Empire, but these efforts were in the context of Magisterial Reform.[3]

Anabaptist beliefs about believer's baptism, the separation of church and state, peacemaking, and Christian holiness in both personal character and social engagement are influential throughout contemporary evangelical Christianity. What is fascinating about this ethos is that it is consistent with other historical-global Christian missionary successes that are divorced from military-political power. The progress of the gospel along the Silk Road for a millennium and many contextually fruitful outreaches of Roman Catholic and Eastern Orthodox leaders display the power of the message, and the receptivity of both leaders and common folk when the church is not a part of a conquering empire.[4]

The Anabaptist story of Great Commission passion and strategy underscores the importance of valuing all global Christian narratives, from the millennium of non-Chalcedonian missionary efforts to current Majority World missiology. The Anabaptists represent the marginal groups often being closer to the center of God's mission than the powerful are willing to admit. Caricature and generalization arising from the extremists in Anabaptist circles have often prevented the gospel-centered insights of these diverse movements from being heard.

In today's global competition between missionary Christianity, Islam, and the pagan-secular forces of various nations, the integral vision of the early Anabaptists offers insights for faithful exilic witness in a post-Christendom West, and the newly evangelized Global South. These principles can be sources of renewal for vibrant Christian nations watching the coming generation be less enthusiastic about the gospel and mission. Malcolm

---

3. Narratives concerning the foci of the various streams of the Reformation are found in all major church history works, from Philip Schaff's *History of Christianity*, vols. 7 and 8, along with the major historians cited in Kasdorf. Justo González' *The Story of Christianity, Volume 2* is more empathetic toward the radical side of the Reformation. See John D. Woodbridge and Frank A. James III, *Church History, Volume Two: From the Pre-Reformation to the Present Day* (Grand Rapids: Zondervan, 2013), 107–218. Alec Ryrie's *Protestants: The Faith That Shaped the Modern World* (New York: Penguin Random House, 2017), 61–84, offers a critique of the limits of Magisterial Reform. Steven Ozment, *Protestants: Birth of a Revolution* (New York: Doubleday, 1991), 116–47, offers insights into this period not found in most other books.

4. Philip Jenkins, *The Lost History of Christianity: The Thousand-Year Golden Age of the Church in the Middle East, Africa, and Asia—and How It Died* (New York: Harper One, 2009), 1–96.

Yarnell affirms the importance of Anabaptist efforts as he addressed church leaders in 2018:

> The Great Commission was given to the church in order to prepare humanity for the second coming of Jesus Christ. On the coming day of the Lord, the nations will be required to give an account of their conduct. Human beings will be judged for the sinful deeds we have done and the good deeds we have left undone.
>
> The Great Commission was understood by our theological cousins, the Continental Anabaptists, in ways very similar to those exposited in the preaching and practice of our direct forefathers, the English Baptist, [including] the General Baptists of the early 17th century. The Particular Baptist Benjamin Keach, popularized and regularized the term Great Commission. And the evangelical Baptists (Andrew Fuller, William Carey) revolutionized our own understanding of this passage in the late 18th century, thereby launching the modern missions movement which has shaped Southern Baptist life and thought in significant ways, compelling us to obey Jesus like never before.[5]

THE CONTEXT OF AUGUST 1527

Historians debate the best way of organizing early Anabaptist history, with some seeing 1527 as the critical watershed that begins the coalescence of a movement. Others note the work of Menno Simons in the 1540–50s as the vital moment of codification. Still others see the stability of the 1650–60s as the moment when ferment gives way to institutional formation.[6]

From the moment Lutheran and Reformed ideas began spreading in the early 1520s, theological disputes grew exponentially as Protestants, freed from captivity to the Roman Catholic systems, debated the many ways of restoring biblical and apostolic Christianity. Over the course of time, Luther admitted that many were not ready for complete reform—a

---

5. Malcolm Yarnell, "The Anabaptists and the Great Commission," *Intersect*, October 8, 2018. See https://intersectproject.org/faith-and-culture/malcolm-yarnell-anabaptists -great-commission/.

6. These debates are summarized in Kasdorf, 305–15. See the *Christian History*, issues 5 and 118 for more methods of ordering this era.

gradualist approach on key ideas and structures was best (except for the vital issues of *Sola Scriptura, Sola Fide*, unity of church and civil authority, and the Lord's Supper). Ulrich Zwingli and later Reformed leaders believed that change was best instituted with the cooperation and leadership of the civil authority—hence his deep aversion to the "anarchy" of emerging Anabaptist groups. Other pastors and scholars allowed greater liberty and moved toward faith as a matter of conscience and not conformity, with a variety of mediating positions.[7]

The years 1523–1527 represent formative ones as Anabaptist leaders emerge, baptizing each other, and evangelizing throughout parts of Austria, Germany, and Switzerland. These dynamic voices are challenging the new Protestant movements and Roman Catholic authorities with their free-church convictions and polity. Our modern lens of freedom of conscience and religious toleration make this historical moment difficult since imposing our vision on leaders emerging from a millennium of Roman Catholic Christendom is unfair. Conversely, the Magisterial Reformers were aware of the contradictions of their positions, advocating for gospel liberty while suppressing dissent from their vision of a transformed church. It is probably too much to ask of the modern reader to embrace the entire Anabaptist ethos, especially pacifism, and disengagement from most facets of civil authority. Yet, allowing these communities to peacefully assemble and proclaim the truth as they saw it, would have advanced global missionary efforts, and perhaps lessened some of the religious and political tensions culminating in the destructive Thirty Years War, with its secularizing aftermath.[8]

For my purpose, 1527 represents a decisive moment in ecclesiological and missiological history as widely disparate leaders gathered at Schleitheim in the canton of Schaffhausen (on the southern border of modern Germany) on February 24, 1527, and agreed on Seven Articles for the "Brotherly Agreement of Some of the Children of God." These articles

---

7. All the magisterial leaders saw themselves as reforming a single church that would be the foundation of civil society. Toleration of other non-Roman Catholic religious communities (other than the marginalized, and often persecuted Jewish synagogues) developed gradually, and only truly flowered after the exhaustion brought on by the Thirty Years War (1618–1648). See Justo González, *The Story of Christianity: Volume 2*, 2nd ed. (New York: HarperOne, 2010), 37–86.

8. The tragedy of Protestant factionalism is spelled out in my dissertation, *The Tragedy of Belgian Protestantism: Subversion and Survival* (PhD diss., University of California, 1995).

provide the ecclesial-theological foundations for the work later that year at Augsburg, when many of the same leaders will meet for missionary purposes as well as resolving other disputes. Here are the articles:

- Article One affirms that baptism is only for true regenerate believers, who commit to a holy life.

- Article Two imposes the infamous "ban" on unrepentant members of the church. After two private warnings, there is a public condemnation, and then a ban from fellowship until full repentance is in place.

- Article Three, in partial agreement with Zwinglian theology, declares that communion is a memorial meal, with the focus on the faith of the recipient, with dire consequences for eating unworthily.

- Article Four asserts the separation of church and state, with voluntary local church attendance and membership.

- Article Five bestows on each local congregation the selection and support of its ministers (described as shepherds).

- Article Six calls for all believers to reject "the sword." Government law enforcement is needed for unbelievers; however, Christians should not be soldiers or engage in any part of government where violence may ensue.

- Article Seven prohibits believers from taking any oaths and swearing of any kind.[9]

In Zurich, Zwingli and other leaders vehemently opposed these affirmations, seeing ecclesial and social anarchy as the consequences. Anabaptists themselves, likewise, were not uniform on the application of these principles, and many Protestant leaders were hesitant to impose harsh penalties

---

9. There is much research on the Schleitheim Confession. In addition to Kasdorf and Anabaptist summaries, see Michael D. Wilkinson, "Bruderliche Vereiniging: A Brief Look at Unity in the Schleitheim Confession," *Southwestern Journal of Theology* 56, no. 2 (Spring 2014): 199–213. Further insights on Michael Sattler's influence are found in Sean F. Winter, "Michael Sattler and the Schleitheim Articles," *Baptist Quarterly* 34, no. 2 (1991): 52–66.

on nonviolent citizens. The legacy of the Peasants' Revolt of 1525–1526 and the violence of Munster pushed many otherwise kind leaders to severe opposition.[10] The suppression of the peasant rebellions by both Roman Catholic and Protestant authorities opened many to the Anabaptist message of gospel holiness and separation, community accountability, and nonviolence. The enthusiasm of the missionaries and joyful fellowship of the communities were a vital part of building an endurance under persecution.

The social and political implications of Anabaptist ecclesio-theological innovations troubled those in power, even while being part of the progress toward political and religious liberty in the West. Reformed Christianity from Switzerland influenced the rise of representative civil government, with their inherent distrust of monarchial ecclesial and political structures. Protestantism engendered economic and social equality, and ultimately, liberty of conscience. Gradually, these movements brought religious variety to nations willing to embrace freedom.[11]

THE MARTYRS' SYNOD OF
AUGSBURG (AUGUST 20–24, 1527)

This historic meeting of Anabaptist leaders—most of whom would be dead by 1530—took place on the heels of Zwingli's published reactions to Anabaptist assertions from Schleitheim and subsequent activities. This gathering of over sixty leaders offers a window into the missionary vitality of the early Anabaptist movement. With its historic leadership in finance and trade, vibrant Lutheran community, and relative proximity to Switzerland, Swabian Augsburg was a fine choice as a hub for spreading the Anabaptist message.

There are no minutes or official declarations of the meetings. We must reconstruct the debates and decisions based on later court testimonies and other scattered writings. We do know the fruit of these deliberations, however, as specific missionary efforts issued from this gathering, and a

---

10. Ulrich Zwingli's early ambivalence and subsequent violent resistance to Anabaptist rejection of a state church and pacifism is described by Leland Harder, "Zwingli's Reaction to the Schleitheim Confession of Faith of the Anabaptists," *The Sixteenth-Century Journal* 11, no. 4 (Winter 1980): 51–66.

11. See Ben Hawkins, "Do Baptists Spring from Anabaptist Seed?" July 3, 2017, bpnews. net/49158/do-baptists-spring-from-anab-seed.

paradigm for the next century of expansion was established. The attendees were a varied lot, with several followers of the eschatologically and prophetically minded Hans Hut in attendance. Hut was convinced that the return of Christ was immanent and shared his calculations for possible dates. By the end of the Synod, Hut agreed to limit his speculations to private conversations in the interest of ecclesial unity. Other attendees included such notables as Johannes Denck, Ludwig Hatzer, Konrad Huber, Hans Schlaffer, Leonhard Schreme, and Balthasar Hubmaier.[12]

The attendees were united on matters of discipleship and mission. They affirmed three baptisms: in water (for believing adults), in the Spirit (a combination of regeneration, sanctification, and empowerment), and suffering (based on Jesus asking Peter if he can truly follow his example, Matt 20:22-23 and Luke 12:50). There was some debate on the relationship of Scripture and the inner light of the Holy Spirit (John 1:4-9). In these debates, we see a proto-Pentecostal[13] ethos, and unconscious connections with ecstatic elements of Eastern Orthodoxy, the Churches of the East, and a few mystical streams within Roman Catholic tradition. They challenged the implicit cessationism[14] of the post-Augustinian era, and this is a point of concern for the Magisterial Reformers as they sought to ground all their beliefs and practices in Scripture. The later Quaker movement would build on the concept of the inner light in ways unforeseen by the Anabaptists of the sixteenth century.[15]

ANABAPTIST MISSIONARY METHODS

All the delegates agreed on the model of sending pairs of emissaries to specific locations to share their version of the gospel with as many people as possible before the immanent return of Jesus. Evangelizing in this context

---

12. Hans Kasdorf, "The Anabaptist Approach to Mission." In *Anabaptism and Mission*, ed. Wilbert R. Shenk (Scottdale, PA: Herald Press, 1984), 51–64.

13. By "proto-Pentecostal" I am referring to the openness of some Anabaptist groups to the manifestation gifts of the Spirit enumerated in 1 Corinthians 12.

14. Cessationism was less a dogma than an observation. Eastern Orthodox and other Churches of the East continued affirming ecstatic experiences and signs and wonders. See Stanley Burgess, *Christian Peoples of the Spirit: A Documentary History of Pentecostal Spirituality from the Early Church to the Present* (New York: New York University Press, 2011), 4–96.

15. Kasdorf, 61–64; see also Jessamyn West, ed., *The Quaker Reader* (Wallingford, PA: Pendle Hill Publications, 1992), especially the essay, "The Message of George Fox," 39–106.

involved: (1) sharing a message of salvation by grace through faith, apart from Roman Catholic rituals; (2) offering water baptism to repentant adherents; (3) dedication to a holy life in a community of believers separated from state churches; (4) creating new voluntary churches led by godly shepherds; and (5) pacifism that rejects any civilian or military violence. Here are some of the teams commissioned from the gathering:

- Peter Scheppach and Ulrich Trechsel were sent to Worms (in the Rhineland-Palatinate region and the setting for Martin Luther's famous affirmation of the supremacy of God's Word and conscience over church tradition at the Diet of Worms in 1521).[16]

- Hans Denck and Hans Beck went to Basel and the area around Zurich.

- Leonhard Spörler and Leonhard Schiemer were commissioned to Berne.

- Eukarius Binder and Joachim Mertz pioneered Anabaptist churches in Salzburg (in modern Austria).[17]

The initial efforts were unsuccessful. This was not from a lack of zeal or unresponsiveness on the part of the hearers. Severe persecution led to the deaths of most of the missionaries within a short period of time and led most groups to withdrawal from public engagement and evangelization.

Hans Kasdorf asserts that the Anabaptists were energetically involved in missionary work for decades, and more than any other group since the first century, they were successful in creating local churches. In the words of Swedish historian Gunnar Weston, this reflected the "individual minority fellowships" that were characteristic of the first-century church. These missionaries repeated the first-century strategy of beginning with the synagogue and then assembling elsewhere. When the local parishes

---

16. Luther at the Diet of Worms is well documented. See Roland H. Bainton, *Here I Stand* (Nashville: Abingdon Press, 2013).

17. Kasdorf, *Anabaptism and Mission*, 55–60.

rejected their beliefs, they assembled in houses and fields, rented halls and even gathered in caverns to avoid persecution.[18]

Here are some of the principles and strategies, which characterize the first century of Anabaptist missionary efforts:

- An urgent eschatology among many leaders. This varied from highly speculative, immanent apocalyptic expectations to reified premillennial ideas of pre-Augustinian Christianity. The persecuted Anabaptist communities greeted the extremists with skepticism. Roman Catholic and Magisterial Protestant authorities confronted them with exile and martyrdom.

- Sending out missionaries in pairs for preaching and planting churches.

- Evangelizing in concentric circles of culture and relationships. In simpler terms, directly and indirectly referencing the words of Jesus in Acts 1:8, these apostolic emissaries began to evangelize within local kinship groups, expanded to regions already open to reform, and then moved to areas under Roman Catholic or Magisterial Protestant rulers.

- Church planting—in this case, house fellowships—began with preaching and calls to conversion. Water baptism follows for all believers ready for a lifetime of cruciform obedience. Then elders and/or leaders are established as overseers of the fellowship. Many of these communities were quite small, though some, especially in more isolated or tolerant areas, were several score in number.

- Personal piety, congregational worship, discipleship, and mission were not separate spheres of life, but an integrated whole; a life lived in the light of the grace of the cross and the discipline of the Sermon on the Mount (Matt 5–7).

- Finally, burgeoning fellowships would send out missionaries to neighboring hamlets.

---

18. Kasdorf, *Anabaptism and Mission*, 53–54.

The following is a summary of Anabaptist lay missionaries:

> A peasant carting his onions to market; a furrier plying his craft
> in north German towns; a housewife or nun to whom some new
> word about Christ or the saints raised questions about religious
> practice; a weaver or a shearer joining with fellow cloth makers in a
> Lowlands town; a schoolteacher whose natural theological curiosity
> pressed him to re-examine both Scripture and the Latin fathers—
> all of these and many more found themselves open to the new and
> strange words of itinerant Anabaptist missionaries. They spoke
> plainly to the common people and moved on to other towns and
> villages after only a few days of instructing new converts. Many
> peasants bitterly resented restrictions on hunting and fishing, and
> the enforced payment of tithes to a church that they considered cor-
> rupt. Townsfolk were caught in economic cycles with downturns
> that no one understood. They all resented the wealth and privileges
> of their local clergy and especially of monasteries near at hand.[19]

This kind of earthy vitality is reminiscent of the early days of Luther. It evokes the enthusiasm of the colporteurs (itinerant booksellers) that peddled Protestant books, and the optimism that the first decade of the Reformation engendered everywhere. Alas, powerfully entrenched forces of Catholic governments and emerging Protestant structures had no room for any kind of religious non-conformity that upset the social order.

The Anabaptist challenges and successes of the sixteenth century reveal the powerful success of Christian missions disconnected from political power and the interests of the empire. This is confirmed by the work of Philip Jenkins in his work detailing the progress of non-Chalcedonian and Monophysite Christianity along the Silk Road from the fifth to fifteenth centuries.[20] Further examples are enumerated by historian Justo González, especially the contrast in Roman Catholic missionary strategies

---

19. See Walter Klaassen and John Oyer, "A Fire That Spread," *Christian History* 118 (2016): 28–32. christianhistoryinstitute/magazine/article/urban-reformation-a fire-that-spread. See also issue 5 in the same journal: "The Anabaptists: A Gallery of Factions, Friends, and Foes," christianitytoday.com/history/issue/issue5/anabaptists-gallery-of-factions-friends-and-foes.html.

20. Philip Jenkins, *The Lost History of Christianity*, 1–96.

in Asia and Latin America. The former had no military and political power behind their efforts, while the latter were intertwined with the imperial ambitions of Portugal and Spain.[21]

AFTERMATH OF THE MISSIONS CONVENTION

Early on April 12, 1528, members of the Anabaptist congregation in the German city of Augsburg gathered in the home of Susanna Doucher, for an Easter Sunday sunrise service. The congregation had grown to include between seven hundred and one thousand people, despite the fact that they were forced to meet in secret. By 1527, the group had developed its own organization for poor relief, a regular Bible study for members, a rudimentary job-placement program for immigrants, and a plan for training evangelists.

At the same time, however, resistance to the Anabaptist movement from Augsburg and elsewhere was growing. After the Martyrs' Synod, during the fall of 1527, most of the leaders of the Augsburg congregation are arrested, tortured, and banished, with the city issuing dire warnings against anyone caught baptizing or meeting in secret.

Yet, on that April morning of 1528, the beleaguered congregation of Augsburg gathered to celebrate the resurrection of Christ. Early in the service, Hans Leupold, who had received a warning that authorities might disrupt the meeting, encouraged anyone who was afraid to leave. At 7:00 a.m., the police arrested all eighty-eight members who had remained. The foreigners were immediately banished, and the locals were imprisoned, tortured, and forced to flee upon their release. By the early 1530s, there were no Anabaptist congregations in Augsburg.[22]

CONCLUSION

In the summers of 1992 and 1993, while doing doctoral research in Belgium, I had the honor of conversing with Jules Lambotte, *Fils*, the chief archivist of Anabaptist and Mennonite history in the Low Countries. His small house and office, located near Louvain in Wallonia, was jammed with

---

21. Justo González, *The Story of Christianity, Volume 1: The Early Church to the Dawn of the Reformation*, 2nd ed. (New York: HarperOne, 2010), 447–90.

22. John D. Roth, "The Anabaptist Martyrs Are Not Dead" in *The Mennonite* (June 1, 2013): the Mennonite.org/opinion/anabaptist-martyrs-dead.

documents and books chronicling the suffering of Protestants in general, and Mennonites in particular. Though my academic focus was on the general history of Belgian Protestantism, the persecution of the Anabaptists-Mennonites in the Low Countries from the 1520s to the 1640s revealed the challenges of this era, especially the subversion of Protestant progress caused by infighting among the non-Roman Catholic traditions. There were more than 100,000 martyrs during this period; their deaths almost equally shared between Catholic and Protestant authorities.[23]

The historical progress of religious toleration and the Great Commission are interwoven, for it is the sacrificial efforts and zeal of the smaller communities of beleaguered believers who paved the way for the expansion of gospel missions in the past three centuries. The seeds sown in 1527 by the Anabaptist movement are bearing eternal fruit, and it is gratifying that historians, missiologists, and pastors are open to the contributions of these important communities. There are Christians from many traditions discovering the breadth and depth of Anabaptist influences upon twentieth and twenty-first century global Christianity. I believe that true ecumenical understanding and cooperative mission can only be enhanced by these connections.[24]

BIBLIOGRAPHY

Alexander, Paul. *Peace to War: Shifting Allegiances in the Assemblies of God.* Telford, PA: Cascadia Publishing House, 2009.

"The Anabaptists: A Gallery of Factions, Friends, and Foes." *Christian History* 5 (1985). christianitytoday.com/history/issue/issue5/anabaptists-gallery-of-factions-friends-and-foes.html.

Bainton, Roland H. *Here I Stand: A Life of Martin Luther.* Nashville: Abingdon Press, 2013.

---

23. See Charlie Self, *The Tragedy of Belgian Protestantism*, 1995.

24. See Michael Grenholm and his work with the Charismactivism mission and website (www.charismactivism.com), where the emphases are "signs, wonders, peace, and justice. Jerry Kennell's article, "Guatemalan Pentecostals Are Drawn to Anabaptism," in *Mennonite World Review*, September 3, 2018, reveals the convergence of maturing liberation theology, vitality of grassroots Pentecostal communities, and deepening desire for justice. Paul Alexander, *Peace to War: Shifting Allegiances in the Assemblies of God*, vol. 9, C. Henry Smith Series series, edited by J. Denny Weaver, 9 vols. (Telford, PA: Cascadia Publishing House, 2009).

Burgess, Stanley M. *Christian Peoples of the Spirit: A Documentary History of Pentecostal Spirituality from the Early Church to the Present*. New York: New York University Press, 2011.

González, Justo. *The Story of Christianity*. Rev. ed. 2 vols. New York: HarperOne, 2010.

Grenholm, Michael. www.charismatvism.com.

Harder, Leland. "Zwingli's Reaction to the Schleitheim Confession of Faith." *The Sixteenth Century Journal* 11, no. 4 (Winter 1980): 51–66.

Hawkins, Ben. "Do Baptists Spring from Anabaptist Seed?" https://bpnews.net/49159/do-baptists-spring-from-anab-seed.

Jenkins, Philip. *The Lost History of Christianity: The Thousand-Year Golden Age of the Church in the Middle East, Africa, and Asia—and How It Died*. New York: HarperOne, 2009.

Kasdorf, Hans. "Anabaptists and the Great Commission in the Reformation." In *Direction* 4, no. 2 (April 1975): 303–15.

Kennel, Jerry. "Guatemalan Pentecostals Are Drawn to Anabaptism." *Mennonite World Review* (September 2018): 1–2.

Klaassen, Walter, and John Oyer. "A Fire That Spread." *Christian History* 118 (2016): 28–32. christianhistoryinstitute/magazine/article/urban-reformation-a fire-that-spread.

Ozment, Steven. *Protestants: Birth of a Revolution*. New York: Doubleday, 1991.

Roth, John D. "The Anabaptist Martyrs Are Not Dead." *The Mennonite* (June 2013): 1–2.

Ryrie, Alec. *Protestants: The Faith That Shaped the Modern World*. New York: Penguin Random House, 2017.

Schaff, Phillip. *History of Christianity*. Vols. 7 and 8. Hendrickson, 2006.

Schmidt, Henry J. "Hans Kasdorf's Contribution to Mission Theology." *Direction* 28, no. 1 (Spring 1999): 6–17.

Self, Charles Everitt. "The Tragedy of Belgian Protestantism: Subversion and Survival." PhD diss., University of California, 1995.

Shenk, Wilbert R. *Anabaptism and Mission*. Scottdale: Herald Press, 1984.

Trueblood, D. Elton. *The Incendiary Fellowship*. New York: Harper and Row, 1967.

West, Jessamyn, ed. *The Quaker Reader*. Wallingford, PA: Pendle Hill Productions, 1992.

Wilkinson, Michael D. "Brüderliche Vereiniging: A Brief Look at Unity in the Schleitheim Confession." *Southwestern Journal of Theology* 56, no. 2 (Spring 2014): 199–213.

Winter, Sean F. "Michael Sattler and the Schleitheim Articles." *The Baptist Quarterly* 2 (1991): 52–66.

Woodbridge, John D., and Frank A. James III. *Church History, Volume Two: From the Pre-Reformation to the Present Day.* Grand Rapids: Zondervan, 2013.

Yancey, Philip. "The Lure of Theocracy." *Christianity Today* (July 2006): 64–66. https://www.christianitytoday.com/ct/2006/july/24.64. html.

Yarnell, Malcolm. "The Anabaptists and the Cross." *Intersect*, November 27, 2018. https://intersectproject.org/faith-and-culture/Malcolm-yarnell-anabaptists-cross.

———. "The Anabaptists and the Great Commission." *Intersect*, October 8, 2018. https://intersectproject.org/faith-and-culture/malcolm-yarnell-anabaptists-great-commission/.

Part Two

—

ROMAN CATHOLIC MISSION

10

—

THE *SPIRITUAL EXERCISES*

Ignatian Spirituality in Sixteenth-Century Mission in China

Luisa J. Gallagher Stevens

In the mid-sixteenth century, Ignatius of Loyola (1491–1556) founded the Society of Jesus, drawing together likeminded Catholic intellectuals who sought spiritual renewal. Loyola advocated for a new order that balanced spiritual imagination along with intellectual rigor, and situational flexibility in conjunction with obedience to papal authority. The influence of the Society, also called the Jesuits, spread throughout the sixteenth to eighteenth centuries, with a twofold purpose of mission and education.

Core to the Jesuit approach to education and mission was Loyola's foundational work and practice, the *Spiritual Exercises*. These exercises notably encompass the Jesuit daily examination of conscience, an imaginative approach to prayer, and the practice of "finding God in all things." The influence of the life and spiritual practices of Ignatius of Loyola, particularly through the *Spiritual Exercises*, is prominent in sixteenth-century Jesuit mission in China. This is keenly visible in the emphasis on accommodation and the adaptive mission style of regional manager Alessandro Valignano (1539–1606) and missionary Matteo Ricci (1552–1610). To best understand the insights of Jesuit mission in the sixteenth century, I will first review the life of its founder, Ignatius of Loyola, the training he instated in the *Spiritual Exercises*, and overarching purpose of mission and education of the Society of Jesus.

IGNATIUS OF LOYOLA

Originally a Spanish soldier, Ignatius of Loyola had a radical conversion to Christ while recovering from wounds he received during the battle of Pamplona, Spain, against the French in 1517. Through reading about the Catholic saints in *The Golden Legend* by Jacopo da Voragine and *The Life of Christ* by Ludolph of Saxony during his recovery, he was inspired to live his life in an altogether different way. "Here it will be to ask for an intimate knowledge of our Lord, who has become human for me, that I may love him more and follow him more closely."[1] Once recovered, Loyola journeyed to the Benedictine Monastery in Monserrat in 1522 and gave up his sword and dagger, turning from his past towards a life of service to God.[2]

Desiring to do mission work in Jerusalem, Loyola left Monserrat and journeyed to Manresa, near Barcelona, Spain.[3] It is here that Loyola encountered God in deeply emotional and vibrant avenues, describing the experience in terms of consolation and desolation.[4] Loyola compiled his reflections on his time at Manresa and developed the *Spiritual Exercises*, written between 1522–1524, which later became the foundation of spiritual education for the Society of Jesus. Ignatius of Loyola eventually arrived in Jerusalem in 1523 anticipating the beginning of his illustrious mission work. Loyola wrote, "My great desire was to 'help souls' ... to tell people about God and His grace and about Jesus Christ, the Crucified and Risen, so that their freedom would become freedom of God."[5] Following one month in Jerusalem, however, Loyola was quickly ordered by the Franciscans in Jerusalem to leave Palestine as many Christians in the region had been

---

1. Ignatius Loyola, *Spiritual Exercises and Selected Works*, trans. George E. Ganss, S.J. (New York: Paulist Press, 1991), 89.

2. Monserrat is located in Catalonia, in Northern Spain.

3. However, he was delayed in Manresa for ten months to a year by issues such as the onset of the plague.

4. Loyola attended mass daily, upheld ascetic practices of simplicity and penance, and spent each day in many hours of prayer. Ignatius of Loyola describes his experience of consolation as a quiet, gentle, peaceful, and joyful encounter with God; in consolation he was drawn towards God and deeds of loving service. However, Loyola also experienced periods of desolation, or discouragement, fear, and agitation that disturbed and discouraged him from seeking after God and the greater good.

5. Loyola in Karl Rahner and Paul Imhof, *Ignatius of Loyola* (London: Collins, 1979), 11.

captured and ransomed.[6] A failed mission attempt, Loyola returned home determined to be trained and receive an education.

At the age of thirty-three, Loyola began his education among school children in Barcelona, Spain, learning the basics of Latin.[7] In the midst of his studies, Loyola began giving the *Spiritual Exercises*. However since he had not completed his theological education, and had begun to give the *Spiritual Exercises* without approval, he attracted the attention of the Spanish Inquisition, and was imprisoned multiple times. To gain distance from the suspicions of the Inquisition, Loyola left Spain and continued his studies, eventually receiving his master's degree from the University of Paris at the age of forty-three.

Seventeen years following his initial encounter with God at Manresa, with six fellow students at the University of Paris, including Peter Faber and Francis Xavier, Loyola formed the Society of Jesus. September 27 in 1540, with just ten men in the Society, Pope Paul III (1468–1549) gave a papal bull in approval for its formation as an order based on education and mission. In the newly formed order, the Jesuits took four vows, including the three typical vows of poverty, chastity, and obedience. The additional fourth vow contained a promise of "a special obedience to the sovereign pontiff in regard to the missions, according to the same Apostolic Letters and the Constitutions."[8] The Apostolic Letter, or the papal bull, *Regimini Militantis Ecclesiae,* noted the key directives of Jesuits: "to strive especially for the progress of souls in Christian life and doctrine and for the propagation of the faith by the ministry of the word, by *Spiritual Exercises* and works of charity, and specifically by the education of children and unlettered persons in Christianity. He should further take care to keep always before his eyes first God, and the nature of this Institute which is his pathway to God."[9] Central to the purposes of the Jesuit order was the "progress of

---

6. Loyola was so adamant in his desire to do mission work that he left Jerusalem only when threatened by the Franciscans with excommunication.

7. He continued his education in Alcala, Spain, and Salamanca, Spain.

8. Ibid., 205, note 527. The introduction of this new Jesuit order was not universally appreciated. Some rival Catholic orders were concerned that the inclusion of this fourth vow was political, and that the Jesuits would function as the pope's army.

9. Ignatius of Loyola, *The Constitutions of the Society of Jesus and Their Complementary Norms,* ed. John W. Padberg, S.J. (St. Louis: The Institute of Jesuit Sources, 1996), 3–4.

souls in the Christian life"[10] and the engagement of the *Spiritual Exercises*. Eventually, with papal approval, *Spiritual Exercises* was published for the official use of the Society of Jesus in 1548.

SPIRITUAL EXERCISES: AT THE HEART OF JESUIT EDUCATION AND MISSION

The *Spiritual Exercises* are composed of prayers, meditations, and contemplative practices focused on the life and journey of Christ. For Loyola, the intent of the *Spiritual Exercises* was for the Jesuit novice "to overcome oneself, and to order one's life, without reaching a decision through some disordered affection."[11] In other words, the desired outcome of participating in the *Spiritual Exercises* was for the individual to develop a heartfelt commitment to God.

Led by a Jesuit spiritual director, all new novices would undertake the *Spiritual Exercises* over a thirty-day silent retreat, or over a four-week period. The *Spiritual Exercises* are like a manual for the soul, they are intended to be interpreted by a Jesuit spiritual director, like an expert tennis player would read an instruction manual to direct another individual "how to play tennis."[12] The exercises contain a balance of intellect and emotion, a combination of head knowledge and an inner experience of heart encounter with God. They facilitate an ongoing conversation with God to discern his will.

The first week of the *Spiritual Exercises* focuses on the individual's life in light of God's love, reviewing possible patterns of sin, and ending with a meditation on Christ's call to follow him. The second week addresses the novice's need to follow Christ as his disciple. The individual is led through imaginative reflections on Christ's birth and baptism, and his ministry of healing and teaching. The third week addresses the Last Supper, and the passion and death of Christ. Individuals are encouraged to use their imagination to contemplate Christ's suffering and the gift of the Eucharist. The final week, novices meditate on Jesus' resurrection and his appearance to his disciples. Individuals participating in the *Spiritual Exercises* are encouraged to have actionable steps to serve Christ and commit to follow him.

---

10. Ibid.

11. Ibid., 129, note 21.

12. Loyola, *Spiritual Exercises and Selected Works*, 50.

Central to the *Spiritual Exercises* is a love and reverence for God. Loyola begins his *Spiritual Exercises* with *The First Principle and Foundation*:

> The Goal of our life is to live with God forever. God, who loves us, gave us life. Our own response of love allows God's life to flow into us without limit. All the things in this world are gifts from God, presented to us so that we can know God more easily and make a return of love more readily. As a result, we appreciate and use all these gifts of God insofar as they help us to develop as loving persons. But if any of these gifts become the center of our lives, they displace God and so hinder our growth toward our goal. In everyday life, then, we must hold ourselves in balance before all of these created gifts insofar as we have a choice and are not bound by some obligation. We should not fix our desires on health or sickness, wealth or poverty, success or failure, a long life or a short one. For everything has the potential of calling forth in us a deeper response to our life in God. Our only desire and our one choice should be this: I want and I choose what better leads to God's deepening his life in me.[13]

The foundation of the Jesuit order is focused on love for and service to God. The purpose of the Jesuit's life in the *Spiritual Exercises* is viewed in relation to God and others, noting that if something promotes love in God, it may continue, whereas if anything gets in that way, it should be removed. The cultivating of the internal spiritual life is foundational to Jesuit mission as evidenced in the continued work of the *Spiritual Exercises* in the daily lives of Jesuit priests.

Three key tenants of the *Spiritual Exercises* include: (1) the examination of conscience, (2) imaginative prayer, and (3) "finding God in all things." The examination of conscience is used daily to prepare individual priests to develop attentiveness, openness, and responsiveness to God.[14] For Loyola, the purpose of the examination of conscience, or the daily Examen, was "to purify oneself and make a better confession."[15] The daily Examen can be expressed as follows:

---

13. Ignatius of Loyola, "The First Principle and Foundation," translated by David L. Fleming, in *Heart on Fire: Praying with the Jesuits*, ed. Michael Harter, S.J., 7–8, note 23.

14. Loyola, *Spiritual Exercises and Selected Works*, 118, note 261.

15. Ibid., 132, note 32.

1. "To give thanks to God our Lord for the benefits I have received.

2. To ask grace to know my sins and rid myself of them.

3. To ask an account of my soul from the hour of rising to the present examen, hour by hour or period by period; first as to thoughts, then words, then deeds, in the same order as was given for the particular examination.

4. To ask pardon of God our Lord for my faults.

5. To resolve, with his grace, to amend them."[16]

Like an imaginative daily confession, the examination of conscience provided Jesuit priests with prayerful engagement with God, a time to see God in all aspects of daily life. The practice involved recollecting moments during the day and reflecting on how God was present at those times, followed by a decision to act in response to God's presence.

Imaginative prayer, or Ignatian contemplation, is integrated throughout the *Spiritual Exercises*. It involves a strong use of personal imagination and exploration. In the second week of the *Spiritual Exercises*, individuals are encouraged to imagine themselves in the gospel story with Christ, to explore their emotions, to pay attention to details with their senses, and to witness Christ's life in a personal way, and feel drawn closer towards Christ in consolation. Lastly, the *Spiritual Exercises* assumes that God is active in our world. Through the use of the *Spiritual Exercises*, Jesuits seek "to find God in all things." The ability to find God at work in all areas of society and life enabled Jesuit priests to have an experiential education and mission praxis, and to engage in imaginative freedom in their daily ministry and lives.

TWOFOLD PURPOSE OF THE JESUIT ORDER: EDUCATION AND MISSION

Following the death of Pope Paul III, in the first year of his rule in 1550, Pope Julius III asserted, "The Company [Society of Jesus] is founded to employ itself entirely in the defense and the spread of the holy Catholic faith, and to help souls in Christian life and doctrine by preaching, public

---

16. Ibid., 134, note 43.

reading of the Scriptures and other means of teaching the word of God, by giving *Spiritual Exercises*, teaching Christian doctrine to children and the ignorant, hearing confessions, and administering the sacraments."[17] Similarly, Loyola professed, "What [the Jesuits] should especially seek to accomplish for God's greater glory [the Jesuit motto is *ad majorem dei gloriam* (AMDG), to the greater glory of God] is to preach, hear confessions, lecture, instruct children, give good example, visit the poor in the hospitals, exhort the neighbor according to the amount of talent ... so as to move as many as possible to prayer and devotion."[18] Towards this end, the Jesuit order engaged in work with the poor, with prostitutes, and orphans, yet particularly, the Society of Jesus focused on education and mission.

Drawn from Loyola's own learning experience, education became an important component of every Jesuit's training, and eventually a key aspect of Jesuit mission. Education was not only to acquire information, but was intended for transformation, and the very process of Jesuit education mirrored the flexibility, creativity, and imagination of Ignatius of Loyola.

JESUIT EDUCATION

Education was a core element of the establishment of the Society of Jesus, and became a central part of Jesuit purpose and mission. Loyola noted the important role of educating future influencers: "From among those who are now merely students, in time some will depart to play diverse roles: one to preach and carry on the care of souls, another to the government of the land and the administration of justice, and others to other callings. Finally, since young boys become grown men, their good education in life and doctrine will be beneficial to many others, with the fruit expanding more widely every day."[19]

Since their founding, the Jesuit approach to education and cycle of action and reflection is overwhelmingly experiential. Figure 1 is a diagram of Jesuit teaching pedagogy.[20]

---

17. Paul Van Dyke, *Ignatius Loyola: The Founder of the Jesuits* (New York: Charles Scribner's Sons, 1926), 175.

18. Ignatius of Loyola in Norman O'Neal, S.J., "The Life of St. Ignatius of Loyola," 2000, 65. https://www.luc.edu/mission/archivedjesuitpages.

19. Loyola in O'Neal, "The Life of St. Ignatius of Loyola," 19.

20. Rebecca S. Nowacek and Susan M. Mountin, "Reflection in Action: A Signature Ignatian Pedagogy for the 21st Century," in *Exploring More Signature Pedagogies: Approaches*

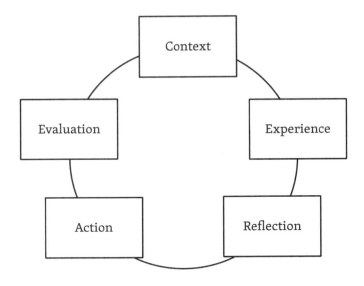

FIGURE 1: JESUIT PEDAGOGY

In the Jesuit tradition academic activity is coupled with reflection to develop meaning from action. In Ignatian pedagogy, "participants must attend to and recollect the *experience* of the day fully, then they must *reflect* on that experience, to formulate a course of *action,* which they can later *evaluate.*"[21] The Jesuit pedagogy listed in Figure 1 is a continuous cycle, beginning with the concept of *context,* proceeding through each stage clockwise, before entering back into the learning experience.

An example of *context* in the *Spiritual Exercises* utilized by Loyola encourages the spiritual director to "adapt to the condition of the one who is to engage."[22] *Context* includes: "The real context of a student's life ... the socioeconomic, political and cultural context within which a student grows ... the institutional environment of the school or learning center ... and previously acquired concepts students bring with them to the start of the learning process."[23] Following *context,* in Ignatian pedagogy, *reflection* means "a thoughtful

to *Teaching Disciplinary Habits of Mind,* ed. Nancy L. Chick, Aeron Haynie, and Regan A. R. Gurung (Sterling: Stylus, 2012), 134.

     21.   Ibid.

     22.   Ignatius of Loyola and Louis J. Puhl, S.J., *The Spiritual Exercises of St. Ignatius: Based on Studies in the Language of the Autograph* (Chicago: Loyola University Press, 1951), 7.

     23.   International Commission on the Apostolate of Jesuit Education (ICAJE), "Ignatian

reconsideration of some subject matter, experience, idea, purpose or spontaneous reaction, to grasp its significance more fully ... the process by which meaning surfaces in human experience."[24] The hope of Jesuit education is that students would move from reflection towards action.

Action is the goal of the learning process, to move students to engage with new knowledge they have experienced and appropriated. *Action* refers to "internal human growth based upon experience that has been reflected upon as well as to its manifestation externally."[25] *Action* is a two-step process, involving the interior, such as a shift in attitude, or perspective, and external choices, such as a physical action "to do something consistent with this new conviction."[26]

Jesuit educators were looking not only to influence individuals, but also to create leaders who would influence the world for the common good. Duminuco writes,

> If truly successful, Jesuit education results ultimately in a radical transformation not only of the way in which people habitually *think* and act, but of the very way in which they live in the world, men and women of competence, conscience and compassion, seeking the *greater good* in terms of what can be done out of a faith commitment with justice to enhance the quality of peoples' lives, particularly among the poor, oppressed and neglected.[27]

Jesuit pedagogy is not just intended as a method of learning, but rather, as a transformational way of proceeding in the world.

JESUIT APPROACH TO MISSION

Similar to the purposive approach of educating future leaders, Ignatius's mission strategy purported: "preference ought to be shown to the aid, which is given to the great nations, such as the Indies, or to important cities, or to universities, which are generally attended by numerous persons who by being aided themselves can become laborers for the help of

---

Pedagogy: A Practical Approach," in *The Jesuit Ratio Studiorum, 400th Anniversary Perspectives*, edited by Vincent J. Duminuco (New York: Fordham University Press, 1993), 253–54.

24. Ibid., 257.
25. Ibid., 260.
26. Ibid., 261.
27. Ibid., 243.

others."[28] The Jesuits continued to educate young boys and men in Europe, yet similar to Loyola's initial call to save souls in Jerusalem, there was a drive to take the gospel of Christ to the far reaches of the world. "By 1556 [the year of Loyola's death] the Society of Jesus had well over 3,000 members, dispersed in many countries of Western Europe [Italy, Spain, France, Germany, and Ireland] as well as in India, Japan, Brazil, and other exotic places [Malacca and the East Indies]."[29]

Jesuit mission was marked by obedience to authority; however, it was matched also by flexibility. The Constitutions note,

> Although it is the part of those who live under the Society's obedience not to involve themselves, directly or indirectly, with how they are sent on mission, either by His Holiness or by their own superior in the name of Christ our Lord, nevertheless, someone who is sent to a large territory such as the Indies or other provinces, and for whom no particular region is assigned, may remain for longer or shorter periods in one place or another, going off to whatever places he deems after having weighed the various factors, found himself indifferent as to his will, and made his prayer to be more expedient for the glory of God our Lord. From this it is clear that, without swerving from the chief and primary obedience due to His Holiness, in missions of this type the superior will be all the more able to direct a member to one place rather than another as he judges in the Lord to be expedient.[30]

Sixteenth-century Jesuit missionaries approached their work with a flexibility and accommodating spirit which was unique at the time.[31] The intent of Jesuit mission was to listen to the Spirit's voice, and to the voices of those they were seeking to reach.

The Jesuit philosophy of mission was led from Loyola's foundational approach to the spiritual life with God. In the inner life of the Jesuit priest,

---

28. Loyola, *The Constitutions of the Society of Jesus*, 74.

29. John W. O'Malley, *The First Jesuits* (Cambridge: Harvard University Press, 1993), 51.

30. Loyola, *The Constitutions of the Society of Jesus*, 296, note 633.

31. In contrast, Franciscans and Dominicans orders in the sixteenth century appear "less accommodating, less elite-oriented, less involved with the sciences, and, less tolerant towards local ritual traditions" (Nicolas Standaert, "Matteo Ricci: Shaped by the Chinese," *China Heritage Quarterly* no. 23 [Sept 2010]: para. 10).

the *Spiritual Exercises* played a significant role of shaping and inspiring a life of commitment to Christ. Imaginative prayer and a daily examination of conscience likewise encouraged the Jesuit priest and missionary to "find God in all things." Jesuit mission in sixteenth-century China reveals an openness and flexibility outlined in Ignatian imagination and implemented through practices of accommodation.

ACCOMMODATION IN CHINA

The methodology of early Jesuit mission in China came from the core convictions of the Ignatian *Spiritual Exercises* and from the detailed Jesuit governance of the Constitutions. The Constitutions, written and edited by Loyola over a fifteen-year period, served as a "guiding spirit of the education work of the Jesuits" as well as Jesuit mission from 1551.[32] Jesuit mission during the Ming Dynasty in China exemplifies the approach of Loyola and his early followers, who promoted an adaptive and flexible approach to spiritual life and to mission."[33] "The belief that God labors directly in the individual and that the individual must then be accommodated was the fundamental premise of the [*Spiritual*] *Exercises*."[34] Directed by the regional manager, Visitor Alessandro Valignano and implemented by Matteo Ricci, the Jesuit mission to China provided accommodation for the cultural beliefs and values of the Chinese.

In 1573 Alessandro Valignano, was instated as Visitor, or regional supervisor, over the Portuguese dominated Macau, and was granted a wide range of influence over the region, which included the area from Cape of Good Hope

---

32. Francesco C. Cesareo, "Quest for Identity: The Ideals of Jesuit Education in the Sixteenth Century," in *The Jesuit Tradition in Education and Missions: A 450 year Perspective*, ed. Christopher K. Chapple (Scranton: University of Scranton Press, 1993), 834.

33. The Jesuit Constitutions suggest developing a posture of attentiveness, reverence, and devotion, noting that "finding God in all things" develops devotion, or "the singularly moving way in which God works in that situation, revealing goodness and fragility, beauty and truth, pain and anguish, wisdom and ingenuity" (George W. Traub, *An Ignatian Spirituality Reader* [Chicago: Loyola Press, 2008], 254). Three themes emerge from the Constitutions: an enduring love for God, a strong Christian formation and outlook, and the preparation of future leaders to meet society's needs (Loyola, *The Constitutions of the Society of Jesus*). The Constitutions, along with the *Spiritual Exercises*, underline the importance of imaginative, flexible, emotionally aware, and creative spiritual formation.

34. Stephen Schloesser, "Accommodation as a Rhetorical Principle: Twenty Years after John O'Malley's The First Jesuits (1993)," *Journal of Jesuit Studies* 1, no. 3 (2014): 356.

in South Africa to Japan.[35] Valignano arrived in Macau via Goa, India, in 1578, eventually showcasing his skills in administration and organizing, as well as his ability to advocate for Jesuits in the political realm of the papal courts.[36] Yet, his area of lasting influence was in the application of the Jesuit ideals of adaptation and accommodation to local culture and customs.[37] In his new role, Vaglinano set about cleaning house throughout the region. In Japan, he removed Cabral, the superior who had been serving in Japan, and introduced the study of language as a precursor for service.[38] In Japan, Valignano also sought to change the approach to Jesuit mission as it currently stood, noting the importance of treating the Japanese converts as fellow Christians with full dignity. He devoted efforts to nurturing Japanese Christians to become priests and brought reform to the treatment of the local Japanese.

At his arrival in Macau, Valignano established St. Paul Jesuit College, and began the clear shift toward accessing mainland China.[39] Valignano's mission strategy included seminary reform and the study of the local language.[40] To rectify the situation in Macau, and to prepare for entering

---

35. The history of Jesuit engagement in mission reveals an accommodating spirit through missionaries like Pierre Favre and Francis Xavier. Pierre Favre went to Germany and instead of war, advocated for reconciliation with the Protestants. Francis Xavier likewise oversaw this region from 1551 until his death in 1552 and advocated for language learning for Jesuits in Goa, India. Although Loyola had been dead for twenty-two years, his vision of a flexible mission model persisted when Valignano was appointed as Visitor in 1573 and was instated as Visitor in Macau.

36. In 1582 Valignano traveled to Rome to promote Japan and the region he oversaw. He took four Japanese converts with him to showcase the success of Japanese mission in the East. These youths met with both the pope as well as with Phillip II of Spain.

37. Valignano promoted language learning and accommodation to cultural values as modeled by Francis Xavier. Xavier was dismayed that the Indian Christians had little understanding of the gospel when he arrived in Goa, India, the priests had no knowledge of the local language, and Xavier raised questions about the accuracy of the gospel interpretation by translators.

38. Discipline was instilled in the Jesuit order by the founder of the Society of Jesus. Loyola addressed a letter to the members of the society in Portugal in 1553 to directly discipline the Jesuit priests that had drifted away from his focus of flexible and adaptive mission and education. Loyola had heard of Jesuits in Portugal who were disobedient, sought power, practiced prayer observations regimentally, and asceticism. In the letter, the Jesuits in Portugal were instructed to be more flexible and less austere. He removed the person in charge of Portugal as they showed too much restraint in prayer, regimen, and asceticism.

39. The Jesuits arrived in Macau in 1563 because mainland China during the Ming Dynasty was closed to foreigners. The first attempt by the Jesuits to reach China was made in 1552 by Francis Xavier. Unfortunately, Xavier never reached the mainland, dying after only a year on the Chinese island of Shangchuan.

40. At the time, Macau was a stepping-stone for the Portuguese traders, and the early Jesuits in Macau did not learn Chinese. Their missionary work could reach only the very

China, Valignano sought out Michele Ruggieri (1543–1607) who arrived in 1579 to embark on language education and begin an intentional entry into mainland China, he was later followed by Matteo Ricci in 1582.[41]

Following intensive language learning in Macau, Matteo Ricci, entered China in 1583, where he spent the remainder of his life working until his death in Beijing in 1610. Implementing Valignano's top-down mission strategy of connecting with key influencers, Jesuit missionaries like Ricci invested energy in reaching the literate elite of China, hoping to create an open posture towards Christianity and a larger influence within the Chinese landscape. Ricci commented on the political status of the Chinese literati stating boldly, "While it is quite true to say that the literary class, known as the philosophers, do not govern the empire, it must be admitted that they exercise a wide influence over its rulers."[42] Although the Jesuits initially lacked the necessary *guanxi* or relationships to secure the social capital for their goals, the literati soon became key allies of Ricci, helping him enter a level of prominence and freedom in China unknown to foreigners at the time.[43] Based on his Jesuit education as a novitiate in 1572, Ricci utilized his learning resources and cultivated a lasting and impactful connection with the Chinese literati (*wrenren*), or scholar-officials (*shidafu*).[44] Ricci wrote a letter to a friend in Europe expressing his approach of building friendships in mission work: "Little by little we shall win the confidence of this people and remove all their suspicions, and then we will deal with their conversion."[45]

---

small number of Chinese who spoke Portuguese. Valignano ordered all Jesuits in Macau, aside from Ricci, to enter a two-year language course where they would read, write, and speak in the Chinese language.

41. Ruggieri was one of first Jesuits to adeptly learn Chinese and began to translate the Ten Commandments into Chinese in 1582.

42. Matteo Ricci, *China in the Sixteenth Century: The Journals of Matthew Ricci 1583–1610*, trans. Louis J. Gallagher, S.J. (New York: Random House, 1953), 26.

43. Once relationships with the literati were built by Ricci and early Jesuits, they had access to live in key cities, travel, and set up outposts in China.

44. This strategy did not create many converts; however, it did open doorways for the Jesuits to move about freely in China and gain influence in the Ming Dynasty where foreigners had previously been denied access. Matteo Ricci did not worry about lower numbers at the beginning of his mission. See Ronnie Po-chia Hsia, *Matteo Ricci and the Catholic Mission to China, 1583–1610: A Short History with Documents* (Cambridge, England: Hackett Publishing, 2016), 120.

45. Ricci in Albert Chan, S.J., "Late Ming Society and the Jesuit Missionaries," in *East Meets West: The Jesuits in China, 1582–1773*, ed. Charles E. Ronan and Bonnie B. C. Oh (Chicago: Loyola University Press, 1988), 169.

Ricci spent much of his time with the Confucian literati, engaging with them as they planned and studied for their examinations to become Chinese officials. Literati were a highly motivated group whose desire to enter government service in provincial administrations was considered a high and noble calling. In a letter to Francesco Pasio, vice-provincial in the Japan Jesuit mission, Ricci notes that "by nature [the Chinese are] intelligent and clever, which can be seen in their books, discourses, in the elaborate clothing they make, and in their governance, which is the envy of all of the Orient. If we can teach them our science, they would not only succeed in being eminent men, but we could also easily induce them to embrace our holy law."[46] The Jesuit humanist approach to education included rigorous study of the sciences and Western technology, and along with Ricci's incredible aptitude for memorization, Ricci was prepared for life debating with, eating with, and living among the educated elite of China.

The mission strategy implemented by Ricci in China was responsive to Chinese culture, and influenced by Chinese individuals, a key use of Jesuit imagination and creativity. This is evidenced in the use of science and technology to connect with the literati, as well as the way the early-Jesuit missionaries adapted imagery to reflect Chinese culture, and highlighted Christian messages that the Chinese found more desirable while avoiding more problematic areas.[47] Another distinct area of adaption and flexibility in mission came in the form of dress. Initially, the Jesuits in China, such as Ricci, chose to blend into the Chinese culture by dressing like Buddhist monks.[48] However, the Buddhist monks were considered of low social value in China, and this dress was despised by the top literati scholars. Confucian literati Qu Taisu (Qu Rukui) encouraged Ricci to change attire

---

46. Ricci in Hsia, *Matteo Ricci and the Catholic Mission to China*, 120.

47. Ignatius of Loyola had the Jesuit artist Jerónimo Nadal draw 153 scriptural images for teaching and to support the *Spiritual Exercises*. Ricci and the Jesuits adapted this book to a Chinese audience by removing shadows from the images as Chinese did not include these, and included Ming dynasty households and Chinese landscape. In displaying imagery and in written form, the exclusive nature of Christ continued to be an issue for the Jesuits in China as the Chinese did not like the crucifixion and resurrection of Jesus, so Ricci chose not to focus on these areas. He avoided displaying the crucified Christ or discussing the incarnation of Jesus, instead highlighting the mother of Jesus with child.

48. Buddhism was practiced by over 90 percent of the Chinese population and had proved helpful to mission in Japan. Valignano wrote a manual of how priests were to live in rank as Buddhists, and act and dress like those they were engaging with.

from Buddhist to Confucian dress to be accepted. After nearly fifteen years of experience and dressing as a Buddhist monk, Ricci adapted to the new lifestyle and etiquette of the Confucian literati.

In accommodating Chinese culture, Ricci had a tolerant attitude towards Confucian rites, such as ancestor worship and the veneration of Confucius. However, Ricci and the Jesuits did not accept all aspects of Chinese culture. The Jesuits still rejected polygamy, did not adapt to wearing long nails, and did not adopt customs that would go against biblical ideals and laws. Ricci decried slavery, infanticide against female babies, selling of children into slavery, suicide, and the castration of male children.[49] Ricci was not without resistance in his accommodations, nor in his cultural views. He wrote and spoke against Buddhist religious thought, which angered some Buddhist thinkers while also endearing him to many Confucian literati. A Buddhist layman Huang Zhen wrote the following about the Jesuits, "The fact that Ricci and his gang have come successively to China is nothing but a plan by their whole country to subvert the Chinese with barbarian ways, and to grab the two supreme powers of ruling and teaching. Now their country has secretly studied our language and books, and has obtained the right to emend the calendar; it is a cunning and profound stratagem to select and reward with riches their people who can teach in our realm."[50] In areas that did not go against biblical values and ideals, Ricci continued to adapt and respond to the interests of the literati and the Chinese culture.

In the Jesuit residence in Zhaoqing, Ricci had a small Italian map on the wall which gained attention from Chinese officials. The Western map included many areas that the Chinese maps did not include, and at the request of the governor Wang Pan, Ricci created a Chinese version.[51] In the midst of adapting to interest in Western technology and science, Ricci drew attention towards God. Ricci declared that the map offered testimony "to the supreme goodness, greatness and unity of Him who controls heaven

---

49. Ricci in Chan, "Late Ming Society," 86–87. Ricci particularly did not like the eunuchs of the royal courts. There were over 100,000 eunuchs in the Ming Dynasty court at the time who served as intermediaries between Ricci and the emperor.

50. Huang Zhen in Hsia, *Matteo Ricci and the Catholic Mission to China*, 124–25.

51. "The James Ford Bell Library to Unveil Ricci Map on January 12," 2009, para. 1–2, https://www.lib.umn.edu/bell/riccimap. Eventually, the Western maps made by Ricci gained recognition, and even the emperor requested copies of maps to display and to give as gifts.

and earth."[52] In mission in China, Ricci utilized the humanist Jesuit education he received as a novitiate by the Jesuit order, including the training of sciences, technology, and literature.[53] Ricci translated works on mathematics and astronomy in response to requests from converts such as Xu Guangqi. He brought his interest of science, incredible memory, and adaptable spirit, and he opened up a dialogue between Western and Eastern scholars.

Writing and scholarship had long been important in Chinese culture as it was during the Ming Dynasty.[54] Ricci published over twenty books in Chinese throughout his lifetime; among these books were religious, moral, and philosophical treatises, astronomical and mathematical works, books on music, and books covering various Western classics.[55] Initially the approach of the Jesuits was to publish mostly religious tracts, however, interest among the Chinese literati dictated the publishing direction Ricci and the Jesuits chose to pursue.[56] Ricci translated Confucian classics into Latin with Xu Guangqi, favorably comparing Confucius with Seneca and Confucians with Epicureans.[57] "The True Meaning of the Lord of Heaven" is one of Ricci's most Christo-centric works written in Chinese, as it explains the concepts of heaven and hell, connects with Confucian thought about human nature, adopts the idea of a heavenly king, and attempts to win people towards Christ by displacing Buddha. In this book, there is seen an attempt towards the Jesuit ideal to "find God in all things." Ricci used existing Confucian and Chinese concepts to explain Christianity, highlighting

---

52. Rothstein, "A Big Map That Shrank the World," *The New York Times*, January 19, 2010, para. 17.

53. Ricci may have had a photographic memory as he was able to retain word for word many of the classical books that he had learned in his formative education in Rome. He knew the work of Greek stoic philosopher Epictetus by heart, including his *Enchiridion*.

54. The Chinese Emperor Cao Pi (187–226) extolled the virtues of literature in his influential "Essay on Literature," noting the Confucian idea that literary writing was good for wellbeing, and as important as ruling the state, noting the immortal influence and everlasting nature of literature (Maria Kaikkonen, "Becoming Literature: Views of Popular Fiction in Twentieth-Century China," in *Literary History: Towards a Global Perspective*, vol. 1, ed. Anders Pettersson [Berlin: Walter de Gruyter, 2006], 68).

55. Ricci noted the importance of utilizing the cheap published option of books. See Hsia, *Matteo Ricci and the Catholic Mission to China*, 120.

56. Ibid.

57. Paul Rule, *K'ung-tzu or Confucius? The Jesuit Interpretation of Confucianism* (Sydney: Allen & Unwin, 1986), 28–29.

the similarities between Confucian and Catholic thinking, using the term "Lord of Heaven" to describe God, although there is typically a traditional Chinese worship of heaven. Ricci utilized the curiosity in areas of Western science and technology to attract interest in Christianity and to enter the dialogue already happening in China at the time.

Matteo Ricci was well respected by scholars in his day, and even in centuries beyond.[58] Towards the end of his work in China, Ricci began to be called *Xiru*, or Western scholar, an individual of worth and value to the literati and to Chinese society as a whole. Matteo Ricci died in 1610, and while most foreigner's remains were sent to Macau, Ricci was so deeply respected among the literati that many lobbied on his behalf and his remains were buried in Beijing, China.

CONCLUSION

Based on a rich spiritual life of imagination, early Jesuit missionaries in China practiced mission with their eyes attuned to the work of God through the *Spiritual Exercises*. From the First Principle of the *Spiritual Exercises*:

> For everything has the potential of calling forth in us
> A deeper response to our life in God.
> Our only desire and our one choice should be this:
> I want and I choose what better leads
> To God's deepening his life in me.[59]

As evidenced in sixteenth-century Jesuit mission in China, the Jesuits made accommodations other orders considered ludicrous, remaining open to influence from "the other" while developing mission methodology and praxis. The Jesuit spiritual practice of "finding God in all things" gave freedom to mission strategists like Alessandro Valignano and practitioners like Matteo Ricci to engage with people and culture with creativity, flexibility, and with compassion. The early Jesuit missionaries serve as a model that might be utilized in mission praxis today.

---

58. Over two hundred years later, in a list compiled by Chinese scholars, over twelve of Matteo Ricci's work are included. These are mostly scientific works. Included in the list are "On Friendship" and "The True Meaning of the Lord of Heaven."

59. Loyola, "The First Principle and Foundation," 7–8, note 23.

BIBLIOGRAPHY

Cesareo, Francesco C. "Quest for Identity: The Ideals of Jesuit Education in the Sixteenth Century." In *The Jesuit Tradition in Education and Missions: A 450 year Perspective*, edited by Christopher K. Chapple, 17–33. Scranton: University of Scranton Press, 1993.

Chan, Albert S.J. "Late Ming Society and the Jesuit Missionaries." In *East Meets West: The Jesuits in China, 1582–1773*, edited by Charles E. Ronan and Bonnie B. C. Oh, 153–72. Chicago: Loyola University Press, 1988.

Hsia, Ronnie Po-chia. *Matteo Ricci and the Catholic Mission to China, 1583–1610: A Short History with Documents*. Cambridge, England: Hackett Publishing, 2016.

Ignatius of Loyola. *The Constitutions of the Society of Jesus*. Translated by George E. Ganss, S.J. St. Louis: The Institute of Jesuit Sources, 1970.

———. *The Constitutions of the Society of Jesus and Their Complementary Norms*. Edited by John W. Padberg, S.J. St. Louis: The Institute of Jesuit Sources, 1996.

———. "The First Principle and Foundation." Translated by David L. Fleming, S.J. In *Heart on Fire: Praying with the Jesuits*, edited by Michael Harter, S.J., 7–8. Chicago: Loyola Press, 1993.

———. *Spiritual Exercises and Selected Works*. Translated by George E. Ganss, S.J. New York: Paulist Press, 1991.

———, and Louis J. Puhl, S.J. *The Spiritual Exercises of St. Ignatius: Based on Studies in the Language of the Autograph*. Chicago: Loyola University Press, 1951.

International Commission on the Apostolate of Jesuit Education (ICAJE). "Ignatian Pedagogy: A Practical Approach." In *The Jesuit Ratio Studiorum, 400th Anniversary Perspectives*, edited by Vincent J. Duminuco, 231–93. New York: Fordham University Press, 1993.

Kaikkonen, Marja. "Becoming Literature: Views of Popular Fiction in Twentieth-Century China." In *Literary History: Towards a Global Perspective*, vol. 1, edited by Anders Pettersson, 36–70. Berlin: Walter de Gruyter, 2006.

Nowacek, Rebecca S., and Susan M. Mountin. "Reflection in Action: A Signature Ignatian Pedagogy for the 21st Century." In *Exploring More Signature Pedagogies: Approaches to Teaching Disciplinary Habits of Mind*, edited by Nancy L. Chick, Aeron Haynie, and Regan A. R. Gurung, 129–42. Sterling: Stylus, 2012.

O'Malley, John W. *The First Jesuits*. Cambridge: Harvard University Press, 1993.

O'Neal, Norman, S.J. "The Life of St. Ignatius of Loyola." *Jesuit Community at Loyola University Chicago*, 2000. https://www.luc.edu/mission/archivedjesuitpages.

Rahner, Karl, and Paul Imhof. *Ignatius of Loyola*. London: Collins, 1979.

Ricci, Matteo. *China in the Sixteenth Century: The Journals of Matthew Ricci 1583-1610*. Translated from the Latin by Louis J. Gallagher, S.J. New York: Random House, 1953.

Rothstein, Edward. "A Big Map That Shrank the World." *The New York Times*. January 19, 2010.

Rule, Paul. *K'ung-tzu or Confucius? The Jesuit Interpretation of Confucianism*. Sydney: Allen & Unwin, 1986.

Schloesser, Stephen. "Accommodation as a Rhetorical Principle: Twenty Years after John O'Malley's *The First Jesuits* (1993)." *Journal of Jesuit Studies* 1, no. 3 (2014): 347–72.

Standaert, Nicolas. "Matteo Ricci: Shaped by the Chinese." *China Heritage Quarterly* (The Australian National University), no. 23, September 2010. http://www.chinaheritagequarterly.org/features.php?searchterm=023_standaert.inc&issue=023.

"The James Ford Bell Library to Unveil Ricci Map on January 12." James Ford Bell Library. Minneapolis: Regents of the University of Minnesota, 2009. https://www.lib.umn.edu/bell/riccimap.

Traub, George W. *An Ignatian Spirituality Reader*. Chicago: Loyola Press, 2008.

Van Dyke, Paul. *Ignatius Loyola: The Founder of the Jesuits*. New York: Charles Scribner's Sons, 1926.

11

ACCOMMODATING CHRISTIANITY TO CONFUCIAN CULTURE

Matteo Ricci and the Early Jesuit Mission to China (1582–1610)

Alice T. Ott

The sixteenth-century Jesuit missionary to China Matteo Ricci (1552–1610) attempted to accommodate Christianity to Chinese Confucian culture in a way that was virtually unheard of in his era. Yet his path toward cultural accommodation did not emerge straightaway but was a gradual process. Ricci was born to a prosperous family in Macerata, Italy, in 1552. When the Society of Jesus established a college in the town, his father Giovanni promptly entrusted his nine-year-old son to the Jesuits for seven years of classical preparatory education. This early association with the order provided an excellent education; it also bore spiritual fruit in the young student. In August 1571, several months before his nineteenth birthday, Matteo Ricci joined the Jesuit order, despite his father's strong objection. The six years Ricci then spent as a Jesuit novice in Rome (1571–1577) were foundational for his future life. He completed his formal studies in liberal arts and philosophy at the Jesuit Roman College (*Collegio Romano*). He developed important and influential friendships, among others, with Alessandro Valignano (1539–1606), who supervised first his novitiate and later his mission work. Additionally, in 1576, Ricci responded to the call for missionary candidates for the order's Asian fields.[1] After a ten- month stay in Portugal, Ricci and thirteen other missionary recruits set sail from Lisbon for the treacherous six-month journey to India. They arrived at the Portuguese colony of Goa on the coast of western India in September 1578. Goa was a fortified trading post, which, along with Malacca in the Spice Islands, Macau in the Pearl River delta of China, and Mozambique, formed part of an expansive Portuguese trading network transporting people and goods between Europe, Africa, and Asia.[2]

Ricci would spend four years in Portuguese India (1578–1582). While there, he completed his theological training, was ordained to the priest-hood, and taught Greek at the Jesuit colleges in Goa and nearby Cochin. Then in 1582, Alessandro Valignano, now the Visitor (or superintendent) of the Jesuit missions to India, Japan, and China, assigned the young missionary to a new post. Ricci was to join his older colleague Michele Ruggieri in Macau to prepare for a lifelong mission to mainland China.[3] On Valignano's orders, this mission, as well as that to Japan, was to differ significantly from the mission efforts common in the Portuguese settle-ments. In such enclaves, "the great majority of Portuguese clergy ... were there to tend to the spiritual needs of the Portuguese" and not to reach out to the local populations.[4] This stood in sharp contrast to Valignano's man-date that both Ruggieri and Ricci pursue evangelistic goals. However, the Visitor insisted that the China missionaries not rush headlong into minis-try until they had learned the Chinese language well. Without a high-level of proficiency in the Mandarin language, he argued, evangelistic effective-ness would be thwarted, and true accommodation of the Christian mes-sage to Chinese culture could not be achieved. Ricci not only embraced Valignano's vision of cultural accommodation, but later, as head of the Jesuit China mission, he would expand that vision even further.

---

1. No writings from Ricci exist from his Roman novitiate, therefore, his motivation for missionary service is unknown. R. Po-Chia Hsia, *A Jesuit in the Forbidden City: Matteo Ricci 1552-1610* (Oxford: Oxford University Press, 2010), 23.

2. R. Po-Chia Hsia, *Matteo Ricci and the Catholic Mission to China, 1583-1610: A Short History with Documents* (Indianapolis: Hackett Publishing, 2016), 3.

3. Ruggieri had arrived in Macau three years before Ricci, and despite his linguistic limitations and lack of study aids, had made good progress in Chinese. Hsia, *Ricci and the Catholic Mission to China*, 22-23.

4. Hsia, *Ricci and the Catholic Mission to China*, 22.

Ricci's cultural accommodation was controversial from the outset. Even today there are a wide spectrum of scholarly evaluations of his mission approach. In this chapter, I will first briefly portray representative viewpoints of some contemporary scholars. Then I will unpack what key sixteenth-century Jesuits meant by the concept of accommodation. Against this backdrop, I will examine why Ricci abandoned the early-Jesuit missionary approach, initiated by Ruggieri, of identification with Buddhism (1583–1586). Ricci's mature mission method, most clearly revealed in a letter he wrote to Francesco Pasio in 1609, a year before his death, will then be discussed. This method aimed to accommodate Christianity as much as possible to Chinese Confucian culture. I will argue that Ricci's approach was revolutionary and innovative, a sharp contrast to the *tabula rasa* (erased like a "clean slate") mindset so common in that era. However, the outcomes of his mission approach were not what Ricci intended. He achieved acceptance by some key Confucian elites including the Chinese emperor, but few high-class Chinese converted. Instead, the Jesuit mission reaped a harvest among the usually illiterate and frequently Buddhist middle and lower classes, among whom an indigenous Catholic Church was established.

SCHOLARLY EVALUATIONS OF RICCI'S CULTURAL ACCOMMODATION

Scholarly evaluations of Ricci's accommodation to Chinese Confucian culture have been varied. Jesuit and other scholars from the 1950s and 1960s on have often championed the China Jesuits as progressive "forerunners of 'modern' or 'tolerant' attitudes" of enculturation. They "possessed an enlightened ability to distinguish between essential and non-essential cultural and doctrinal concerns."[5] Representative proponents of this view are George H. Dunne in *Generation of Giants* (1962) and Andrew Ross, *A Vision Betrayed* (1994). Dunne argues that Ricci "was destined to write … one of the most glowing chapters in the history of cultural relations and missionary enterprise." He was able to "achieve a synthesis of Chinese and Christian culture, with respect for and understanding of the former and without

---

5. Liam Matthew Brockey, *Journey to the East: The Jesuit Mission to China, 1579–1724* (Cambridge, MA: Harvard University Press, 2007), 15.

injury to the latter."[6] For Dunne, Ricci was an exemplary model of appropriate enculturation. Ross contends that the Jesuit missions in Japan and China should be viewed as "one story" and "one missionary effort," rooted and shaped by the thinking of one group of predominantly Italian Jesuits, led by one man, Alessandro Valignano. Valignano found in Ricci "the perfect instrument to carry out and indeed lead and develop his [mission] programme" in China. Nevertheless, "those who have tried to explain Ricci without Valignano inevitably present an incomplete picture of the Jesuit effort."[7] The progressive vision of Valignano and Ricci, however, was ultimately "betrayed" in the debacle of the Chinese Rites controversy.

On the other side of the scholarly spectrum lies Jacques Gernet's *China and the Christian Impact* (1985). His approach was to collect and analyze sixteenth- and seventeenth-century Chinese reactions, both positive and negative, to the early Jesuit mission. Gernet concludes that the Jesuit mission from its inception was an "enterprise of seduction" (his subsection title of chapter 1). Ricci not only falsely represented himself as a philosopher, rather than what he actually was—"a priest who had come to preach the true God to pagans."[8] He and other Jesuits intentionally deceived the Chinese by remaining silent concerning certain Christian doctrines, most notably Christ's death on the cross. Furthermore, the missionaries made egregious "errors of interpretation ... when examining the concepts of the Chinese."[9] For instance, they misunderstood the nature of God in Confucianism.

Numerous mediating positions occupy the realm between Gernet's castigations and the unmitigated praise of Dunne. Mary Laven in *Mission to China* (2011) rejects Gernet's unnuanced simplification of Ricci's mission method. In her view, Ricci was "neither a saint nor a con man, but someone who was working to adapt himself to the values of an alien world."[10]

---

6. George H. Dunne, *Generation of Giants: The Story of the Jesuits in China in the Last Decades of the Ming Dynasty* (Notre Dame, IN: University of Notre Dame, 1962), 17, 368.

7. Andrew C. Ross, *A Vision Betrayed: The Jesuits in Japan and China, 1542–1742* (Maryknoll, NY: Orbis Books, 1994), xv and xvii.

8. Jacques Gernet, *China and the Christian Impact*, trans. Janet Lloyd (Cambridge: Cambridge University Press, 1985), 17.

9. Gernet, *China and the Christian Impact*, 2.

10. Mary Laven, *Mission to China: Matteo Ricci and the Jesuit Encounter with the East* (London: Faber and Faber, 2011), 22.

Ricci's mission was not a "triumphant success," rather "it was in reality ... more vexed and complicated." The Jesuits achieved little success through the numerous "learned texts" (both philosophical and apologetic), which they produced for Confucian elites. Rather, more converts were won among Chinese commoners, who were generally Buddhist, who were reached when the Jesuits appealed to the emotional "world of rituals, images and objects."[11] In contrast, R. Po-Chia Hsia in *Matteo Ricci and the Catholic Mission to China* (2016) argues that "Ricci's remarkable career was a spectacular success. ... By accommodating himself to Chinese culture, Ricci enabled Christians in the Late Ming and early Qing dynasties to express their own understanding of this foreign religion in a synthesis of Chinese learning and western doctrines."[12] Although, "Ricci was especially keen to understand the religious rituals and beliefs of the Chinese" he was "not without prejudice and subjectivity."[13] This was seen most clearly in his "complete repudiation of Buddhism" in favor of Confucianism.[14]

Both Nicholas Standaert, S.J., in his writings, and Liam Brockey in *Journey to the East* (2007), shift the focus in varying degrees from the Jesuit missionaries to the Chinese recipients of the Christian message. Standaert contends that Ricci's mature mission method was not a reflection of "Jesuit corporate culture." Rather, "the heavy influence of the Other," the Chinese, was found in the "Jesuit strategy of accommodation. The Chinese made the Jesuits adapt to the particularly Chinese situation."[15] Brockey repositions attention away from Ricci and the "interactions of missionaries and mandarins at court" in Beijing, and unto "the centers of the proselytizing activity in the Chinese provinces." He argues that the Jesuits fashioned the Chinese mission church "in its own image" and according to "the Society's organizational templates." Nevertheless, their "importation of elements of early modern Catholic piety into the late imperial Chinese

---

11. Laven, *Mission to China*, 24, 30.

12. Hsia, *Ricci and the Catholic Mission to China*, 35–36.

13. Hsia, *Ricci and the Catholic Mission to China*, 11.

14. Hsia, *Jesuit in the Forbidden City*, 135.

15. Nicholas Standaert, S.J., "Jesuit Corporate Culture as Shaped by the Chinese," in *The Jesuits: Cultures, Sciences, and the Arts, 1540–1773*, eds. John W. O'Malley et al. (Toronto: University of Toronto Press, 2015), 357. Cf. Ibid., *Chinese Voices in the Rites Controversy: Travelling Books, Community Networks, Intercultural Arguments* (Rome: Institutum Historicum Societatis Iesu, 2012), 217–18.

context" resonated with local Christians and enabled them to maintain Christianity in China long after "the Jesuit mission faded into memory."[16] Ultimately, he argues, the Chinese Christians transformed the new faith into a culturally appropriate model.

JESUIT CONCEPT OF ACCOMMODATION

The Jesuit terms "accommodation" or "adaptation" are not commonly used in contemporary missiological circles. Instead, terms such as "encultura-tion" or "contextualization" are more commonly employed. It is beyond the scope of this chapter to discuss these contemporary terms. Our focus is to understand what some key sixteenth and early seventeenth century Jesuit missionaries understood when they used the virtually synonymous terms accommodation or adaptation in their writings.[17] What did accommodation mean to the likes of Alessandro Valignano and Matteo Ricci? Liam Brockey aptly expresses the crux of accommodation. It referred to a "typically Jesuit or, more specifically, Ignatian spirit that subsumed the means of spark-ing conversions ... to the ends," in order to accomplish the "ultimate goal of their mission: the conversion of the Chinese to Christianity."[18] In other words, on one level, accommodation was essentially a practical mission-ary strategy to clear away unnecessary cultural hindrances to conversion by the target population. To use Loyola's words quoted more fully below, accommodation was necessary *in part* in order to "meet with better [evan-gelistic] success."[19]

It is significant that Ignatius Loyola (1491–1556) founded the Society of Jesus in the era of Renaissance humanism when openness and respect for native cultures was on the rise. Loyola insisted that Jesuit missionaries learn the language of the country in which they served, an approach that

---

16. Brockey, *Journey to the East*, 19, 20, 21.

17. Roberto de Nobili, Jesuit missionary to Hindu Brahmins in South India, titled his defense of an accommodational mission method *Adaptation* (1619). His principles of adap-tation were very similar to the accommodation espoused by Valignano and Ricci. Cf. the four principles of adaptation in Roberto de Nobili, *Adaptation*, ed. by S. Rajamanickam, S.J. (Palayamkottal: De Nobili Research Center, 1971), 7–71; and Francis X. Clooney, S.J. "Roberto de Nobili, Adaptation and the Reasonable Interpretation of Religion," *Missiology* 18, no. 1 (Jan. 1990): 25–36.

18. Brockey, *Journey to the East*, 44.

19. St. Ignatius of Loyola, "Letter 1," http://www.library.georgetown.edu/woodstock/ignatius-letters/letter1#letter.

was not universally practiced at that time. He also gave an early description of accommodation in a letter written in September 1541. "Whenever we wish to win someone over and engage him in the greater service of God our Lord," the missionary should do the following:

> He enters with the other, not by opposing his ways but by praising them. He acts familiarly with the soul, suggesting good and holy thoughts that bring peace to the good soul. Then, little by little, he tries to come out his own door, always portraying some error or illusion under the appearance of something good, but which will always be evil. So, we may lead others to good by praying or agreeing with them on a certain good point, leaving aside whatever else may be wrong. Thus, after gaining his confidence, we shall meet with better success. In this sense, we enter his door with him, but we come out our own.[20]

Duarte de Sande (1547–1599), Jesuit missionary and mission superior of China, defended accommodation in 1595 in distinctly Ignatian terms. He noted that:

> In truth, among these nations that are so different from ours, and have laws and customs so different, it is necessary to enter with theirs to come out with ours, *accommodating ourselves* to them in what our Holy Faith permits, in this way to divulge and teach our holy doctrine, which they would receive in no other way.[21]

Both Loyola and de Sande argued that it was imperative for missionaries to adapt as much as possible to foreign cultures in order to successfully evangelize them. Only when they entered fully through the door of the receiving culture, would they be able to entice members of the target population to follow them into the Christian faith. It is important to note that Loyola and de Sande are not stating that Christian converts would retain all aspects of their native culture, or that their Christian faith would be wholly dissimilar to that of the missionaries. After all, the converts "come out our own" (European) Christian door. In practice, accommodation meant that the similarities between the Christian faith and the major world religions,

---

20. St. Ignatius of Loyola, "Letter 1."
21. Quoted in Brockey, *Journey to the East*, 44. Emphasis added.

whether Confucianism, Hinduism, or Buddhism, were stressed. All customs, "unless they are clearly against divine law," should be followed completely. "When preaching the Gospel, we should avoid mixing in European customs not needed for the salvation of souls," advised Valignano.[22]

Valignano's admonition above brings us to a second aspect of accommodation: an intentional "style of mission that attempted to break free from both European political imperialism and, what was even more powerful and longer lived, Europeanism—the belief that the European experience is the Christian experience and is definitive for all humanity."[23] Contemporary proponents of European ethnocentricity asserted that indigenous cultures needed to be eliminated, erased clean like a blank slate (*tabula rasa*), in order to be replaced with European Christian culture. This approach was common in Spanish and Portuguese territories regulated by patronage (Portuguese *Padroado*; Spanish *patronatus*) agreements. In a series of papal bulls in the late fifteenth and early sixteenth centuries, the Iberian monarchs were given the right to colonize and rule over lands they discovered, as long as they supported Christianization efforts among the locals. "The whole crusading experience of recent Spanish—and to a lesser degree Portuguese—history meant that it was difficult for Spaniards and Portuguese to conceive of an expansion of Christianity that did not mean the expansion of Iberian political authority and Iberian culture."[24] China belonged to the Portuguese *Padroado*. In 1585, Pope Gregory XII gave the Jesuits the exclusive right to send missionaries to China. This arrangement gave Valignano, at least temporarily, the freedom to develop his own mission method, independent of a Christendom concept.[25]

Ricci embraced the vision of cultural accommodation expounded by Loyola and Valignano. In two letters sent to his friends from the Roman College in autumn 1585, he candidly wrote about his commitment to accommodation, and the challenges that such accommodation could entail. Ricci admitted in a letter to his former professor, Ludovico Maselli, dated October 20, 1585, "How different it is for me now to be in the midst of people inimical

---

22. Hsia, *Ricci and the Catholic Mission to China*, 66.

23. Ross, *A Vision Betrayed*, xv.

24. Ross, *A Vision Betrayed*, xii.

25. N.B. This arrangement only lasted until the early seventeenth century. Nicholas Standaert, ed., *Handbook of Christianity in China: Volume 1, 635–1800* (Leiden: Brill, 2001), 296.

to God." Yet, Ricci hoped that "I will finish my earthly existence, in the few days that God will grant me, *in accommodating myself and loving this land as much as I can.*"[26] A month later, Ricci wrote a letter to his college friend Guilio Fuligatti about his experience in China. "As you already know we have become Chinese in dress, mien, ceremony and all outward appearances. ... I think I have become a barbarian for the love of God."[27] These letters portray a very human side of Ricci—fully committed to adapting himself to Chinese culture and loving China and its people, all the while intimately aware of the personal sacrifice such accommodation could require.

RICCI'S EARLY MISSION METHOD (1583–1595)

The mission method employed by Matteo Ricci was not static but evolved over time. His older colleague, Michele Ruggieri, had launched the mission on the Chinese mainland, and secured permission for himself and a companion to reside in Zhaoqing, the capital of Guangdong province. This in and of itself was an accomplishment, since the residence of foreigners within the Ming Empire was seldom allowed. After a short stay in Zhaoqing in 1582, at which time Francesco Pasio was Ruggieri's companion, the two men were ordered back to Macau. Later, in September 1583, Ruggieri, this time with Ricci in tow, was allowed to return to Zhaoqing. There the two Jesuit missionaries enjoyed the patronage of Wang Pan, a local magistrate. Wang encouraged them to adopt the dress of Chinese Buddhist monks, something Ruggieri readily agreed to, since he had already for some time identified himself as a monk from India. A plaque was placed at the entrance to the Jesuit residence with the words "temple of the Flower of the Saints" in Chinese, thus confirming their identification with Buddhism.[28]

This identification with Buddhism would prove to be both a benefit and a liability. One positive benefit was that it provided protection for the Christian mission in these early years. Association with Buddhism, a very popular and accepted religion in China, meant that Christianity avoided "outright confrontation" in the religious sphere. Furthermore, Roman Catholicism paralleled some Buddhist practices and doctrines

---

26. Quoted in Hsia, *Jesuit in the Forbidden City*, 106.

27. Hsia, *Jesuit in the Forbidden City*, 106; Michela Fontana, *Matteo Ricci: A Jesuit in the Ming Court* (Lanham, MD: Rowman and Littlefield, 2011), 67–68.

28. Ross, *A Vision Betrayed*, 123.

(monasticism, fasting, rosary beads, images of saints, heaven and hell).[29] It is not surprising that the vast majority of the eighty Christian converts in Zhaoqing were former Buddhists. Identification with Buddhism was also a liability. It is questionable whether the Buddhist-background converts in Zhaoqing clearly differentiated Christianity from their former religion, in part because Buddhist terminology abounded in the first Christian catechism in the Chinese language, prepared by Ruggieri.[30]

During his years in Zhaoqing (1583–1589), Ricci acquired an astonishing level of competency in the written and spoken Chinese language, surpassing the ability of his older colleague Ruggieri. Valignano had commissioned Ricci to translate the Four Books (Confucian classics) into Latin to improve both his language skills, and to deepen his understanding of Chinese Confucianism.[31] This exercise would contribute to Ricci's growing conviction that the Jesuit association with Buddhism was a serious mistake and a hindrance to conversion. In 1589, a new magistrate in Zhaoqing requisitioned the Jesuit residence, forcing Ricci and fellow Jesuit Almeida to relocate to a provincial town in northern Guangdong, Shaozhou, where Ricci remained until 1595. There he became the lifelong friend of the scholar Qu Rukei. Rukei advised him to abandon his association with Buddhism, arguing that Buddhist clergy, in contrast to Ricci himself, had low social status and intellectual ability. He would be better served by associating with and dressing like the Confucian literati. In time Ricci's aversion to Buddhism would grow to outright hostility, which he expressed in his apologetic as well as specifically anti-Buddhist writings.

Ricci's years in Guangdong province convinced him that the future of the Jesuit mission lay elsewhere. Anti-European feeling was rife in the province due to the ongoing presence of foreigners at the Guangzhou (Canton) trading fairs, as well as its proximity to Macau, where the Portuguese still exerted political influence.[32] On several occasions the Jesuit residence in Zhaoqing was barraged with stones. In Shaozhou, the missionaries were the victims of sporadic acts of violence and vandalism. The need for

---

29. Hsia, *Ricci and the Catholic Mission to* China, 23–24.
30. Hsia, *Ricci and the Catholic Mission to* China, 23–24.
31. Ross, *A Vision Betrayed*, 118, 126.
32. Brockey, *Journey to the East*, 35.

protection for the mission was an important factor in the development of mission strategy. According to Dunne, "To win for Christianity a position in the empire safe from the danger of sudden destruction had been in Ricci's conception the primary objective of the mission" in the early years.[33] This objective could only be achieved by promoting good relationships with local magistrates, and later with the Chinese imperial court in Beijing. Thus the need for protection for the mission ultimately resulted in a radical change in mission policy.

RICCI'S MATURE MISSION METHOD (1595–1610)

The year 1595 was a pivotal one in the development of the Jesuit China mission. In that year Ricci was asked to accompany a high-ranking Confucian magistrate to Beijing. Though he left the magistrate before reaching Beijing, he settled in the important second capital city of Nanjing. This northward movement from Guangdong was viewed as a godsend. Already in late 1592 Ricci had met personally with Valignano in order to discuss the next stages of the China mission. The two men agreed that it was imperative for the success of the mission to move away from Guangdong and closer to the centers of political power. Ricci explained to his superior, Duarte de Sande, in a letter: "Until we have a foothold in one of these two royal cities [Beijing or Nanjing] we will always live in fear of losing this mission to China."[34] At the 1592 meeting with Valignano, Ricci also raised the issue of changing his dress from that of a Buddhist monk to that of the Confucian educated elite, the literati. *Literati* is the term given to those scholars who sat for at least one of the three triennial examinations on the Confucian classics, even if they did not pass the exam. These examinations were a prerequisite for holding an official office in the local, provincial, or the imperial government. Thus, the literati were a large elite group of scholars, many of whom were also magistrates.[35] Valignano consulted with other Jesuit missionaries, with the Superior General (or head) of the order in Rome, and with the pope himself.[36] Ricci received the green light to identify himself with

---

33. Dunne, *Generation of Giants*, 226.
34. Brockey, *Journey to the East*, 43.
35. Standaert, *Handbook*, 474.
36. Ross, *A Vision Betrayed*, 126–27.

the Confucian literati. So on his way north in 1595 Ricci donned the robes of the mandarins and grew his hair and beard to emulate the Chinese elite. "Ricci and his successors ... attempted to benefit from the social prestige of the literati ... by talking and dressing like them; at the same time, they bore a religious message, something not ordinarily the province of the *ru* (scholars)." Thereby, they "blurred the visual distinctions between the religious and social spheres of Chinese society."[37] This change of dress and move to an imperial capital, Nanjing, was the first step in his "ascent to Beijing," as it is often called, where Ricci arrived in January 1601. It also was the culmination of his developing missionary strategy.

A year before his death, on February 15, 1609, Ricci wrote a letter to his colleague Francesco Pasio, then the Vice Principal of the Jesuit Japan mission. In the letter Ricci outlined in eight points the key elements of his mature mission method. These eight points revealed his conclusions on the best way to evangelize the Chinese drawn from his nearly thirty years of experience. The points overlap one another considerably, with the result that some modern scholars have combined them differently into fewer points, as shall I.[38]

The first key element of Ricci's mature mission method was his identification with the Confucian literati. After 1595, when Ricci distanced himself and the Jesuit mission from Buddhism, these elite scholars and magistrates became the mission's principal evangelistic target group. In his letter to Pasio, Ricci rejoiced that the Jesuit missionaries had "all gained the names of learned and virtuous men," in other words, they were viewed as literati, something Ricci "hope[d] we will continue to be considered ... until the end."[39] In practice, this focus on the literati had monumental consequences for the day-by-day activities of the missionaries. Much of the missionaries' time was occupied nurturing social relationships with the literati through the obligatory rounds of visiting and hosting one another.

---

37. Brockey, *Journey to the East*, 43.

38. Ross, *A Vision Betrayed*, 143–45, has four points. My list is most similar but not identical to the four characteristics of the Jesuit mission found in Standaert, *Handbook*, 310–11, and Standaert, "Jesuits in China," in *The Cambridge Companion to the Jesuits*, ed. Thomas Worcester (Cambridge: Cambridge University Press, 2008), 172f., although Standaert does not link the characteristics to the Pasio letter.

39. Text of the letter found in Hsia, *Ricci and the Catholic Mission to China*, 119–22, here 119, 121.

During these visits, the literati desired primarily to discuss philosophical and scientific topics. Thus, focus on the scholarly class frequently served to distract from the task of preaching, and "the work of conversion that was the goal and primary fruit for which we had come," as Jesuit missionary Feliciano da Silva (1579–1614) frankly admitted.[40] Both Valignano and Ricci were taking a long view of the China mission. Ricci's task was not "to build up worshipping communities" or "initiate ... [a] mass conversion movement." Rather, the goal was to carefully "lay the foundation" for a "truly Chinese and Christian Church" in the future.[41]

A second element of Ricci's mature mission method, and a clear corollary of the first element, was a top-down evangelistic approach. By 1609 when the Pasio letter was written, Jesuits were at the two imperial courts of Beijing and Nanjing, where they "conversed" regularly with the Confucian elite. Since scholarship was "highly esteemed" in China, Ricci was convinced that "it will thus be easy to persuade the leaders of the realm that the things of our holy faith are confirmed with rational evidence. With the most important of the leaders agreeing with us, it will be easy to convert the rest of the people."[42] This method held that if the "leaders of the realm," ideally the Chinese emperor and his court, converted, then the entire country would ultimately be won for the Christian faith. In reality, it was considerably more difficult to win Chinese elites to the gospel than anticipated, and a mass conversion of the Chinese never occurred. Nevertheless, Ricci's "ascent to Beijing," and his growing network of relationships with members of the Chinese governmental bureaucracy, provided credibility and protection for Catholicism in China. His residence at the capital "also permitted the geographic expansion of the Jesuit enterprise" in the provinces.[43] This occurred naturally when members of the Confucian bureaucracy, who had befriended the Jesuits, were transferred to a new government post, something that transpired with regularity. While the handful of literati converts were widely and publicly celebrated by the Jesuits, Brockey reminds us that "it is clear from their writings that the Jesuits sought to make new

---

40. Brockey, *Journey to the East*, 60.

41. Ross, *A Vision Betrayed*, 135.

42. Hsia, *Ricci and the Catholic Mission to China*, 120.

43. Brockey, *Journey to the East*, 50.

Christians from all ranks of Chinese society and that they proselytized the lower orders whenever it was possible for them to do so."[44]

The third key element of Ricci's mature mission method is the so-called "scientific apostolate." This refers to the use of western knowledge, particularly mathematics, astronomy, and cosmography, to interest Chinese intellectuals initially in a relationship with the Jesuits, ultimately in conversion to Christianity. This method can be viewed as an indirect approach to the propagation of the faith. Chinese intellectuals were first drawn to the Jesuits as purveyors of exotic western knowledge that they desired to acquire. Then, ideally, once an ongoing relationship of dialogue and discussion of more secular topics had been established, an interest in the Christian message would develop. Ricci was convinced of the efficacy of the scientific apostolate. He wrote Pasio: "We have opened the blind eyes of the Chinese" through "teaching on the natural science of mathematics. What would they say if they knew about the more abstract subjects such as physics, metaphysics, theology, and the ... supernatural? If we can teach them our science, they would not only succeed in being eminent men, but we could also easily induce them to embrace our holy law."[45] The Jesuit mission was committed to the scientific apostolate as a valid and effective means of evangelizing Confucian Chinese intellectuals. Throughout the seventeenth century, they would recruit well-trained Jesuit mathematicians, astronomers, and scientists to serve at the imperial court in Beijing.[46]

The writing and translating of books on both scientific and apologetic/religious topics were an important aspect of the indirect method of evangelization that the Jesuits pursued among the literati. An "apostolate through books became one of the major means of spreading Christianity among the elite."[47] During the seventeenth century, roughly 120 texts on science and the West were published in Chinese by missionaries and Chinese Christians. During the same century, 470 texts on apologetics and religious or moral topics were printed.[48] In the letter to Pasio, Ricci listed some of the advantages of print medium. "Books ... can travel everywhere without hindrance

---

44. Brockey, *Journey to the East*, 48.

45. Hsia, *Ricci and the Catholic Mission to China*, 120.

46. Standaert, *Handbook*, 312.

47. Standaert, *Handbook*, 600.

48. Standaert, *Handbook*, 600.

... reach more people, more often, than we can, and can provide greater detail and precision than we can orally."[49] The written word could also be read by speakers of various Chinese dialects.

The fourth key element of Ricci's mature mission method was accommodation to Chinese Confucian culture and religion. True accommodation, according to Ricci, required an in-depth knowledge of the Chinese language. Early on, a strategic decision was made to learn Mandarin, the language of the literati, rather than Cantonese or another Chinese dialect. Mastering the language was essential, since, as he stressed to Pasio, "knowing our own language [Italian] without knowing theirs accomplishes nothing." Unfortunately, however, as Ricci freely admitted, the majority of Jesuit missionaries had not "achieved even a mediocre command of Chinese letters."[50] During Ricci's tenure as leader of the China mission, new Jesuit recruits for the mission underwent a two-phased program of study: the first phase focused on spoken Mandarin; the second was dedicated to a serious study of the Four Books of Confucianism.[51]

A second aspect of accommodation was to Confucianism itself. The issue of whether Confucianism is an ethical and social philosophy or a religion is debated by scholars and is beyond the scope of this chapter. In the Pasio letter, however, Ricci gave a nod to this issue. On one hand, "the literati sect [Confucianism] does not speak about supernatural things," but primarily of "ethics [that] are almost entirely in concordance with ours." On the other hand, Ricci at times does refer at times to this "sect" in religious terms. Of the "three sects in this realm," Daoism, Buddhism, and Confucianism, the first two, in Ricci's estimation, were clearly "idolatrous."[52] In contrast, Ricci held that "the most ancient and most authoritative ... books of the literati," what he calls *original* Confucianism in contrast to neo-Confucianism, was not. The Chinese people from antiquity were "little given over to idolatry; and the idols they adored were not as destructive as those adored by our Egyptians, Greeks and Romans." "No worship" of polytheistic gods was found in the ancient Confucian canon. Instead, "they

49. Hsia, *Ricci and the Catholic Mission to China*, 120.

50. Hsia, *Ricci and the Catholic Mission to China*, 121.

51. Brockey, *Journey to the East*, 252.

52. Hsia, *Ricci and the Catholic Mission to China*, 122.

venerate only Heaven, Earth and the Lord of both." Confucian "natural philosophers [were] second to none—and we can hope that with divine mercy, and through the grace of God's love, many of the Chinese ancients who observed natural law were saved."[53]

In the Pasio letter and in his book of Christian apologetics entitled *The True Meaning of the Lord of Heaven*, Ricci argued that original Confucianism was essentially monotheistic and not polytheistic, since it was free of the idolatrous, Buddhist accretions prevalent in neo-Confucianism. The transcendent Lord of Heaven in the ancient Confucian canon was none other the Christian God of the Bible. Certainly, the divine truth found in early Confucianism was incomplete, and only a prelude to the fuller revelation found in Christianity. Nevertheless, Ricci and his compatriots gave high value to the Truth content (with a capital T) about God and morality in original Confucianism, making a synthesis of this ancient system with Christianity possible. It is in this light that Ricci's bold statement concerning the salvation of ancient Chinese philosophers must be read. Furthermore, Ricci believed that ancestor veneration was a legitimate expression of filial piety for Chinese Christians, since such rites were not idolatrous nor superstitious. Filial piety was the foundation of all Confucian morality, was consistent with Christian ethics, and therefore should be allowed.

UNEXPECTED OUTCOMES

The reality was that, despite a well-thought-through mission method focused on winning the Confucian literati to Christianity, only a very small number of them converted. There was a "profound mismatch between the Jesuits' stated aims" and the type of converts. "It was not that the Jesuits were failing to make converts; rather they were making the wrong sort of converts."[54] Standaert's research indicates that during the seventeenth century the number of literati converts (including their family members) was roughly 1 percent of the Chinese Catholic population.[55] The reason for this disconnect was largely because of the negative impact that Christian

---

53. Hsia, *Ricci and the Catholic Mission to China*, 121.

54. Laven, *Mission to China*, 196, 52.

55. Standaert, *Handbook*, 387. In addition, a small group of non-converted literati and officials existed, who were sympathetic to the Jesuits (474f).

conversion could have on the lives and careers of the educated elite. They would need to repudiate their concubines, adopt a foreign religion, and undergo some offensive Christian ritual practices.[56] The actual social background of Chinese converts was quite different from the intended target group. Ninety percent of the newly baptized were illiterate. The vast majority were not only uneducated, but common people with an "idolatrous" Buddhist background. They adopted the Christian faith, not because it convinced them rationally, but because it met their emotional and spiritual needs. Healing from illness, freedom from evil spirits, and miraculous events involving images of Christ, the Virgin Mary, or a crucifix were common reasons for conversion.[57] Nevertheless, a focus on the Confucian elites was not entirely ill-conceived. The Jesuit network of contacts with the literati ensured not only protection and credibility for the mission, it also aided the conversion of commoners in the provinces.

A second unintended outcome of Ricci's mature mission method was an anti-Christian backlash launched by Chinese intellectuals against his understanding of Chinese religions and his presentation of Christianity. The Jesuits had learned early along that certain key Christian doctrines, particularly Christ's salvific death on the cross, were offensive to the Chinese. For this reason, Ricci omitted the cross of Christ in his key apologetic work, *The True Meaning of the Lord of Heaven*. This omission would come back to haunt Ricci's successors after his death in 1610. A group of Chinese intellectuals in the seventeenth century argued, independently of one another, that Christianity, Confucianism, and Buddhism were all misrepresented by Ricci and the Jesuit mission. Shen Que petitioned the emperor in 1616 against the Jesuit missionaries for encouraging the people to worship an executed criminal. Yang Guangxian stated it more pointedly in 1664: "In his books, Ricci took very good care not to speak of the lawful execution of Yesu. Thus all the literate elite have been duped and deceived."[58] Zhang Chao, who had been a friend and collaborator of some prominent Jesuits, called into question Ricci's understanding of Confucianism. Zhang rejected the conflation of the personal Christian God, the Lord of Heaven (*Tianzhu*),

---

56. Brockey, *Journey to the East*, 48.

57. Standaert, *Handbook*, 390–91; Standaert, "Jesuits in China," 175f.; and Laven, *Mission to China*, 55, 227f.

58. Laven, *Mission to China*, 224.

with the impersonal Confucian Heaven (*Tian*).[59] Finally, Ricci made little attempt either to understand Buddhism or to accommodate Christianity to it. In *The True Meaning of the Lord of Heaven*, Ricci launched a "direct attack" on Buddhism. Hsia notes that he "ridicule[d] the Buddhist teaching of reincarnation and karma, and dismisse[d] the idea of non-killing and vegetarianism."[60] In response to this attack, Yu Chunxi, a Mandarin and devout Buddhist, wrote an open letter, in which he faulted Ricci for his obvious lack of familiarity with the Buddhist sutras, and his prejudicial attitude against Buddhism.

These contemporary Chinese critiques have some validity. Ricci was silent on the cross in apologetic writings and in evangelistic contexts. Often it was only when a prospective convert had become a catechumen that the full range of Christian doctrines were revealed. Furthermore, Ricci's construct of "original Confucianism" is quite arbitrary. All religion is fluid and changing, and it is highly questionable whether sixteenth-century Chinese separated "original Confucianism" from its later accretions. Ricci's impulse to choose an indigenous name for God, rather than a foreign, Western name was laudable. Ultimately, however, the ensuing debates over which term for God was appropriate for Roman Catholicism was decided by papal decree in 1742 (*Tianzhu*). Finally, given the large number of Buddhist-background converts, hindsight suggests that Ricci's aversion to Buddhism and lack of accommodation to it were regrettable.

There was a third unintended outcome of the Jesuit mission to China. Ricci and the Jesuit mission initially attempted to import a contemporary form of Roman Catholic and Jesuit spirituality, the confraternity, into the Chinese context with its European form intact. However, lay participation in a similar sort of local associations was common in both Buddhist and Daoist sects. In time, a new form of confraternity emerged, which fused both "traditional Chinese and Christian elements," mixing a "Chinese type of social organization" with "European-inspired congregations."[61] These confraternities presented a Chinese face to their communities. The congregations were led and sustained by lay Chinese catechists, who provided

---

59. Laven, *Mission to China*, 223.
60. Hsia, *Ricci and the Catholic Mission to China*, 32.
61. Standaert, "Jesuits in China," 176. See further Brockey, *Journey to the East*, 332f.

oversight for the group and spiritual care for its members. They catechized the children, exhorted the faithful, baptized converts, and preached occasionally. Since a priest would only visit the congregations once or twice a year to administer the Eucharist and hear confession, it is no exaggeration to state that the catechists "were responsible for maintaining Christianity in China during the eighteenth century, as the Jesuit mission faded into memory."[62] The Chinese church had become indigenous.

Despite these unexpected outcomes, Ricci's mature mission method and the accommodation it promoted truly was ground-breaking and innovative. It demonstrated a high-level of interaction with and appreciation for Chinese Confucian culture. In order to win the right to share the Christian faith, Ricci and his followers, for the most part, adapted themselves to the Chinese people, rather than expecting the Chinese to conform to them. They immersed themselves in the Confucian canon and were willing to affirm truth content in early Confucianism. This approach was revolutionary in the era of the Portuguese *Padroado*, when a *tabula rasa* mindset toward indigenous cultures and a disdain for non-Christian religions was the norm. Ricci's method validated the other. In essence, it proclaimed that it was possible to be authentically Chinese and truly Christian. Such an approach was rarely found among the Roman Catholic mendicant orders (Franciscans and Dominicans) in the sixteenth century or among Protestant missionaries until at least the eighteenth century.

BIBLIOGRAPHY

Brockey, Liam Matthew. *Journey to the East: The Jesuit Mission to China,*
    1579–1724. Cambridge, MA: Harvard University Press, 2007.

Clooney, Francis X., S.J. "Roberto de Nobili, Adaptation and the Reasonable Interpretation of Religion." *Missiology* 18, no. 1 (Jan. 1990):
    25–36.

Dunne, George H. *Generation of Giants: The Story of the Jesuits in China in the Last Decades of the Ming Dynasty.* Notre Dame, IN: University of Notre Dame, 1962.

Fontana, Michela. *Matteo Ricci: A Jesuit in the Ming Court.* Lanham, MD: Rowman and Littlefield, 2011.

62. Ibid., 20, 330.

Gernet, Jacques. *China and the Christian Impact.* Translated by Janet Lloyd. Cambridge: Cambridge University Press, 1985.

Hsia, R. Po-Chia. *A Jesuit in the Forbidden City: Matteo Ricci, 1552–1610.* Oxford: Oxford University Press, 2010.

———. *Matteo Ricci and the Catholic Mission to China, 1583–1610: A Short History with Documents.* Indianapolis: Hackett Publishing, 2016.

Laven, Mary. *Mission to China: Matteo Ricci and the Jesuit Encounter with the East.* London: Faber and Faber, 2011.

Nobili, Roberto de. *Adaptation.* Edited by S. Rajamanickam, S.J. Palayam-kottal: De Nobili Research Center, 1971.

Ross, Andrew C. *A Vision Betrayed: The Jesuits in Japan and China, 1542–1742.* Maryknoll, NY: Orbis Books, 1994.

St. Ignatius of Loyola. "Letter 1." Woodstock Theological Library. http://www.library.georgetown.edu/woodstock/ignatius-letters/letter1#letter.

Standaert, Nicholas, S.J. *Chinese Voices in the Rites Controversy: Travelling Books, Community Networks, Intercultural Arguments.* Rome: Institutum Historicum Societatis Iesu, 2012.

———. *Handbook of Christianity in China: Volume 1, 635–1800.* Edited by Nicholas Standaert, S.J. Leiden: Brill, 2001.

———. "Jesuit Corporate Culture as Shaped by the Chinese." In *The Jesuits: Cultures, Sciences, and the Arts, 1540–1773*, edited by John W. O'Malley et al. Toronto: University of Toronto Press, 2015.

———. "Jesuits in China." In *The Cambridge Companion to the Jesuits*, edited by Thomas Worcester. Cambridge: Cambridge University Press, 2008.

12

—

THE JESUIT MISSION TO THE KINGDOM OF KONGO (1548–1555)

John Thornton

In 1548 Jesuit missionaries landed in the kingdom of Kongo. It would be the first time that the Jesuits sent a mission to an extra-European (African in this case) Catholic country. The mission to Ethiopia, which began a few years later in 1555, would also go to a Christian African country, but one that had joined the Eastern Church in not accepting the rulings of the Council of Chalcedon in 451. The two missions operated in parallel, and the Kongo mission soon failed. Understanding this failure helps to contextualize both the Jesuit approach to Catholic Reform and its outlook on non-Western countries. A careful examination of the evidence can help to determine the causes for this failure.

The kingdom of Kongo had begun the process of conversion when its king Nzinga a Nkuwu was baptized in 1491 as João I, and Christianity became the official state-sponsored religion of the country during the reign of his son Afonso I Mvemba a Nzinga (1509–1542). During Afonso's reign the church gained not only state support and financing but built a country-wide and extensive program of schools designed to spread the religion systematically throughout the realm.[1]

Because Kongo was not a colony of any European country, it had molded the religion it accepted to extend and modify its traditional religion. In

---

1. John Thornton, "The Development of an African Catholic Church in the Kingdom of Kongo, 1491–1750," *Journal of African History* 25 (1984): 147–67; and Thornton, "Afro-Christian Syncretism in the Kingdom of Kongo, 1491–1600," *Journal of African History* 54 (2013): 53–77.

this way, it might be seen as a variant on the medieval church that the Jesuits, and other orders born of the Counter-Reformation encountered. The Jesuits were therefore not in Kongo to convert the heathen, but to reform a new but vibrant Catholic Church. But the mission failed, and by 1555 the last Jesuit left Kongo, seven years after it started.

The first Jesuit mission to Kongo (a much more successful one followed in 1619) has not received very much attention in either literature on the Jesuits, or on the kingdom of Kongo. Jesuit historians, like Francisco Rodrigues, have seen its failure in the attitude of King Diogo I, ruler of Kongo at the time toward Jesuit reforms and his unwillingness to support their Christianization plans.[2] Portuguese historians, especially those working in the colonial period, cast the events in light of African cultural resistance to Portugal's historic mission to elevate Africa to civilization.[3] Historians of Kongo, notably Jan Vansina, who have dealt with the mission in any specificity, have seen the Jesuits as having too many connections to São Tomé–based merchants and their ecclesiastical allies.[4] Graziano Saccardo, primarily a historian of the Capuchins (and a Capuchin himself), has sought to incorporate the problem of Portuguese interests, the slave trade, and Jesuit difficulties most fully.[5]

The only full treatment of the mission is Carlos Almeida's excellent article in 2004. Almeida's overall assessment was that the Jesuits brought negative attitudes about African culture with them to the mission and this poisoned their relationship with the king, while also giving attention to both the role of the slave trade and confliction between São Tomé and Kongo over trade and authority.[6]

---

2. Francisco Rodrigues, *História da Companhia de Jesus na assisstência de Portugal*, 7 vols. (Porto: Apostolado da Imprensa, 1931-1950), Tome I, part 2, 543-56.

3. Ralph Delgado, *História de Angola*, 2nd ed., 4 vols. (Luanda: Edição do Banco de Angola, 1971 [first edition, 1946]), 1:211-29.

4. Jan Vansina, *Kingdoms of the Savanna* (Madison: University of Wisconsin Press, 1968 [original French, 1965]), 58-61. Other Africanists have only made off-hand use of the mission in context of using their reports as primary sources for arguments unrelated to the specifics of the mission, for example, W.G. L. Randles, *L'ancien royaume du Congo des origèns à la fin du XIXème siècle* (Paris: Mouton, 1968), 105; Anne Hilton, *The Kingdom of Kongo* (Oxford: Oxford University Press, 1985), 66.

5. Graziano Saccardo, *Congo e Angola con la storia dell' antica missione dei Cappuccini*, 3 vols. (Venice, 1982-1983), 1:50-52.

6. Carlos Almeida, "A primeira missão da Companhia de Jesus no Reino do Congo (1548-1555)," in *João III e o Império: Actas do Congresso internacional commemorative de seu nacimento* (Lisbon: CHAM, CEPCEP, 2004): 865-88.

As will be revealed here, the Jesuits faced great difficulties from the minute they arrived in Africa, facing a delicate situation in Kongo and aggressive activities of some of the Portuguese players in the economics and politics of the time, but that there would be a way to work through them. Rather, it was as much the faults and conflicts of (political and material) interests of the missionaries themselves, and their inability to reconcile them that led to the mission's collapse.

THE KONGO CATHOLIC CHURCH IN 1548

It may never be clear why the kings of Kongo took so quickly and whole heartedly to Christianity. When the first Portuguese navigator to reach Kongo, Diogo Cão, landed at the mouth of the Congo River in 1483, he was well received. After an exchange of hostages, in 1487 King Nzinga a Nkuwu sent a high-level member of the Kongo aristocracy named Kala ka Mfusu (subsequently baptized as João da Silva) as head of a mission to Portugal to learn more.[7] The mission to Portugal included both adults and children (who could be taught to speak Portuguese as native speakers). While in Lisbon, they learned Portuguese, taught at least one priest their own language (Kikongo), studied Christianity, interacted with the Portuguese elite, and were baptized. In 1491 they returned to Kongo, and on May 3, 1491, Nzinga a Nkuwu was himself baptized as João along with members of his court.

Documentation on what happened for the next few years is scant, and what documentation there is emanated from the lengthy correspondence of João Nzinga a Nkuwu's son Afonso Mvemba a Nzinga. Afonso represented himself as dedicated to Christianity, and the occasional account of priests who served in Kongo confirmed it, dubbing him the "Apostle of Congo." His task was to establish Christianity, and so he began to construct the system of schools, sent significant numbers of the nobility to study in Europe, including even sending representatives to study at the University of Paris.[8]

---

7. The earliest sources on these first few years are vague, see Carmen Radulet, "As viagens de Diogo Cão: ainda uma problema em aberta," *Revista da Universidade de Coimbra* 34 (1988): 105–19, for a carefully argued reconstruction. The ambassador's name is given in the earliest source (in Italian) as "Chracanfusus," and the orthography here is my attempt to make it fit the Kikongo language.

8. John Thornton, "King Afonso I of Kongo: The Making of an African Christian King and His Kingdom," in Dana Robert, ed. *Dictionary of African Christian Biography* (Pietermaritzburg,

At the same time, Afonso developed a mass local educational establishment, which began with European clergy and a few educated Kongolese teaching in schools established in the capital. By 1516, the graduates of these schools were operating in the provinces, and eventually the whole country was full of schools. The teachers in these schools (*mestres de escola*), members of the Kongolese nobility, provided a basic religious education throughout the country.[9] Diogo was confident that this portion, the basic conversion to Christianity and a certain knowledge of its tenets, was well established in the country. Writing to the pope in 1547, he contended that the Portuguese had provided their teachers with sufficient knowledge that they "have already taught our own people, so that Christianity has come, through divine grace and bounty, to spread throughout the country."[10]

Afonso had been anxious that his newly organized church receive its full due in Europe, and to that end, he dispatched his son, Henrique, to Portugal in 1507 to study and subsequently attached him to a mission led by Pedro de Sousa, with the aim of paying homage to the pope and thus joining officially the community of Christian nations. This obedience was done, not by anyone from Kongo, it seems, but on Kongo's behalf by a Portuguese mission in 1513–1514.[11] Following that, Henrique was ordained as a priest, and in 1518 made a bishop, *in partibum infidelum*, of Utica, a North African See that the Vatican used to create free-floating bishops.[12]

Afonso definitely intended to have a fully functional church in Kongo under his control. In 1526 he proposed that Henrique be joined by two other bishops, Afonso's nephews, who were going to Rome to be consecrated. In due order, they would then ordain the best qualified teachers of the school

South Africa: Cluster Publications, 2018).

9. Thornton, "Afro-Christian Synthesis," 61–63; for a fuller study Inge Brinkman, "Kongo Interpreters, Traveling Priests, and Political Leaders in the Kongo Kingdom," *International Journal of African Historical Studies* 49 (2016): 255–76.

10. Diogo to Pope, 1547, *MMA* 15: 146. This letter, intended to accompany a mission that did not take place, was never actually sent.

11. Sebastien Kikoula Meno, "Autour de l'ambassade de Mbanza Kongo, 1514," *Annales Aequatoria* 18 (1997): 471–88. For an overview of Kongo's diplomatic relations with Rome, Teobaldo Filesi, *Le Relazioni tra il Regno di Congo e la Sede Apostolica nel XVI secolo* (Como: Instituto Italiano per l'Africa e l'Oriente, 1968), 35–40 (on the 1513–1514 mission).

12. François Bontinck, "Ndoadidiki ne-Kinu a Mubemba, premier évêque du Congo (c. 1495–1531)," *Revue africaine de théologie* 2 (1979): 149–69; Arsène Francoeur Nganga, *Monseigneur Dom Henrique Ne Kinu A Mvemba (1495–1531): Premier noir évêque de l'église catholique*, 2nd ed. (Saint-Denis: Edilivre, 2018).

system as priests.[13] He was greatly disappointed when Henrique died in
1531, that the Papacy decided in 1534 to create, at Portugal's request, an
episcopal see in its newly colonized island of São Tomé, and to put Kongo
under its jurisdiction.[14]

There were a certain number of complications in actually getting a
bishop to take up the position, and for a few years the church in São Tomé
was under various forms of vicars.[15] One of the tasks of the new episco-
pate, however, was to remove and replace clergy who were not under their
authority or another recognized authority as well as those judged unfit to
be priests.[16] Because Afonso's priests came from a wide range of places
and without much systematization, his church was hit hard by this, and
numerous priests were forced to leave.

Thus, Afonso was faced with a dual disappointment. Not only had he
not succeeded in getting his own church organized using priests he favored,
whether Portuguese or Kongolese, but even the priests he did have were
being taken away. While they might be replaced, they would not be his and
would answer to a different authority, located on an island out of his jurisdiction under leadership that would not have his, or Kongo's, interests in mind.

Afonso had spent much of his time as king dealing with the problem
of ecclesiastical authority. From very early in his reign he had complained
about the quality and loyalty of the priests in his country. Often this clergy
were connected to São Tomé, and even the priests of St. Eloi, of whom he
was particularly fond, were accused of trading illegally with São Tomé in
1532 and again in 1535.[17]

---

13. Afonso to João III, undated fragment (ca. 1526 per editor), *MMA* 4: 141 (see António
Brásio, "Um fragmento precioso," in António Brasio ed. *História e Missiologia: Ineditos e Esparsos*
(Luanda: Instituto de Investigação Científica de Angola, 1973 [original 1953]), 326–28; Afonso
to João III, March 18, 1526, *MMA* 1:459–64.

14. Saccardo, *Congo e Angola*, 1:39–40.

15. Jean Cuvelier and Louis Jadin, *L'ancien Congo d'après les archives romaines* (Brussels:
Academie Royale des Sciences Coloniales, 1954), 31–33, 40–42.

16. The original document, from João Bautista's "constitutions," is lost and only summarized in a survey of documents (most of which are now lost) of the priest Diogo Rodrigues
in 1558, *MMA* 1:435.

17. Biblioteca Pública de Braga, MS 924, Jorge de São Paulo, "Epilogo e compendio da
origem de congregação de S João Evangelista … & outros memorias" (1658), 229 (making use
of church documents that are no longer extant). This scandal was addressed in a Papal brief
as well. François Bontinck, "Un document inédit concernant un missionaire portugais au
Royaume de Congo (1536)," *Nouvelle revue de science missionaire* 33 (1977): 58–66.

Afonso died in 1542 at some eighty-five years of age. The last years of his life were full of jockeying as his descendants began to position themselves to succeed him when he died. His son and heir-designate Pedro I Nkanga a Mvemba duly accepted the crown, but after a three-year rule, was overthrown by Afonso's grandson, Diogo. Although overthrown, Pedro had managed to reach a church in the capital city and sought sanctuary there, and in spite of the political danger, Diogo did not seek to break the sanctuary and seize his rival. Diogo's act of loyalty to church law was costly, for it was soon obvious that Pedro was busy plotting with a variety of people in the kingdom to get back the throne.[18]

Diogo became king in 1545 and soon afterward decided to regularize his relationship with Portugal. He immediately ran into problems with the Dominican bishop, João Bautista, who had come to São Tomé in 1543 and visited Kongo soon after, where he began to clash with the new king.[19] Diogo complained that the bishop had been "much trouble and hardly courteous"; he did not teach, say mass, or carry out his duties. He described his tenure as "against our service" and that the bishop was not as virtuous as he was held to be.[20] The bishop ordered all clergy out of Kongo that did not have an episcopal license, apparently with the intention of replacing them with his own people.

The ecclesiastical affairs of Kongo were wrapped up in the larger way in which the Portuguese empire was run. Much of the way offices and incomes were given was through patronage, in which a powerful man would grant position and powers under his authority to clients of his. But this patronage was itself complicated because the crown allowed several powerful men to operate at the same time. On São Tomé, which was the center for Portugal in this period, there were the captains, but also the

---

18. For a transcription, English translation, and contextualization of the plot see John Thornton and Linda Heywood, "The Treason of Dom Pdro Nkanga a Mvemba against Dom Diogo, King of Kongo," in Kathryn Joy McKnight and Leo J. Garofalo, eds. *Afro-Latino Voices: Narratives from the Early Modern Ibero-Atlantic World, 1550–1812* (Indianapolis: Hackett Publishing, 2009), 2–29.

19. João Bautista was not the bishop, but rather the "ring bishop" that is acting as a vicar of the actual bishop who had renounced his office; like Henrique before him, he was bishop of Utica. However, in contemporary correspondence he was usually referred to as simply a bishop.

20. Diogo I to Diogo Gomes, December 12, 1546, and Diogo I to João III of Portugal, February 25, 1547, both in António Brásio, ed. *Monumenta Missionaria Africana* [henceforth *MMA*], 1st ser., 15 vols. (Lisbon: Agência Geral do Ultramar, 1952–1988), 2:150, 155–56.

bishops, and beyond them, sometimes royal judges sent from Portugal to handle specific problems. Commerce and income were in turn often dominated by the clients of these men, so that in many ways there was no such things as a simple merchant, as anyone doing international business needed a patron.

The kingdom of Kongo complicated the problem because the kings were powerful men in their own right, and moreover not under the authority of Portugal. They had their own clients within the country, but also among the Portuguese, who did business there, resided there, or served in their government or the church. This way, the Portuguese community in Kongo was fundamentally divided between people who were clients of Diogo, as opposed to those who were clients of the captain of São Tomé, and yet again, those who were clients of the new bishop of São Tomé and Kongo, and those priests who were clients of the king. If that were not enough, in Diogo's day, there were Kongolese nobles and priests who supported him, and others who still supported Pedro in his plots. While many of these struggles between them were local, many others appealed to the king in Portugal as a central authority or mediator. It created a documentary puzzle in which it seemed everyone was denouncing everyone else, as patrons defended their clients and attacked their opponents.[21]

When Diogo went for someone to send as his ambassador to Portugal in 1546, he reached for the Portuguese community, choosing the one that suited him best. He choice fell on the 27- or 28- year-old Diogo Gomes, who was born in Kongo "of a Portuguese father & mother." No contemporary document relates to the specifics of his descent; this statement was made in 1647 by the noted Jesuit chronicler, Baltazar Telles.[22] While there were quite a few Portuguese men living in Kongo, there were very few Portuguese women, and so it is difficult to imagine that a married couple would have been there in or around 1520.[23] It seems much more likely that he was of

---

21. John Thornton, "Early Kongo-Portuguese Relations: A New Interpretation," *History in Africa* 8 (1981): 183–204, especially 194–97.

22. Balthezar Telles, *Chronica de Companhia de Iesu na Provincia de Portugal*, 2 vols. [2 partes] (Lisbon: Paulo Craesbeeck, 1647), Pt II, Cap 5.4, 273. Jorge Vaz, who interviewed him shortly after his arrival in Lisbon, called him simply a "Portuguese priest," Jorge Vaz to the Jesuits of Coimbra, September 18, 1547, *MMA* 2:166–67.

23. Portuguese families did go to Kongo in 1491, ostensibly to help train the Kongolese in agriculture and making bread.

mixed race, but the Jesuits, whose order Gomes eventually joined, found it very difficult to admit non-whites to their order worldwide. Therefore, it seems likely that Telles's statement was a quiet way of denying his mixed ancestry, even stressing this point by describing both parents.[24]

Whether Portuguese by descent or not, he was certainly bilingual and bicultural, familiar with the language and customs of Portugal, yet fully enmeshed in Kongolese life. He was, as far as can be told, also educated in Kongo, presumably in one of the schools that had been built in Afonso's reign. Finally, he had been ordained a priest and was Diogo's personal confessor, effectively the head of Kongo's church, and could be counted on to be loyal to his patron. In many respects, he would be the perfect ambassador to Lisbon.

Diogo enjoined his ambassador to clear his name in Portugal, as Bishop Bautista had already begun denouncing the king as a weak Christian, and also to have one of King Diogo's favorite and most reliable priests, Master Gil, returned from Portugal. It was Gil's young nephew, raised in Kongo, that Afonso had wished to send to Paris to study. In order to ensure that the negative report that the bishop had sent would be countered, he also sent his personal secretary as a parallel mission.[25]

Once in Portugal, King João III recognized Gomes as a person of high social standing in Kongo and provided him with both an income and title as a noble of his house.[26] When it came time to discuss ecclesiastical affairs, Gomes brought up the question of clergy and particularly the charges of João Bautista. We do not know how the king decided on the question of Diogo's complaints about João Bautista, or if Master Gil was returned, but the king did answer the question that was framed as obtaining better clergy. He summoned Simão Rodrigues, Jesuit leader in Lisbon, and asked him if they could supply some priests. Rodrigues was very pleased to comply with no shortage of passionate volunteers, and the Jesuit mission to Kongo was

---

24. See, for example the question of mixed race clergy in Peru, described in Sabine Hyland, *The Jesuit and the Incas: The Extraordinary Life of Blas Valera, S.J.* (Ann Arbor, MI: University of Michigan Press, 2004). Here, of course, it is a colonial setting with stronger racial ideas and divides, but it was also true in non-colonial settings, such as Japan and China, see C. R. Boxer, *The Portuguese Seaborne Empire, 1415–1825* (London: Penguin, 1973).

25. Diogo to Gomes, December 12, 1546, *MMA* 2:150.

26. Almeida, "Primeira missão," 867; Vaz to College of Coimbra, 18 September 1547, *MMA* 2:166–67.

born.[27] Perhaps more important, though, while in Portugal, Gomes had what he described as a spiritual calling to join the Jesuit order himself, a calling which Jorge Vaz, who would become the leader of the mission to Kongo, happily reported to his peers.[28] It would ultimately prove to be the fatal flaw in the Jesuit mission.

The Jesuits arrived in Kongo on March 18, 1548.[29] They were received with a tremendous show of support and were quite overwhelmed with the numbers of people that came to see them, both when they landed and especially when they approached the capital city of Mbanza Kongo. But they were also entering a zone of great problems that would require a good deal of skillful diplomacy to manage.

Diogo had hopes for them to engage in higher studies, presumably to teach the elite among his own teachers, and as a foil against, or at the very least a supplement, to João Bautista and the vicars he had in mind. Since Diogo still entertained the idea of having his own bishop, he realized he would need higher studies to be strengthened in Kongo, and not simply come in Portugal. He hoped that his own prized client, Diogo Gomes, would work to assist him in furthering his church.

The initial efforts of the Jesuits, reported in the middle of 1548, showed a promising beginning. They began erecting churches, proposed that the king allow women to hear mass, something which they had not been allowed to do previously, and conducted classes for them at the church that had been earlier built on the pre-Christian burial ground. In addition to teaching the women, the Jesuits conducted regular classes for some six hundred students that had been *mestres* and were *mestres*-to-be as its students.[30]

True to the Counter-Reformation views of religious life, they found faults in the faith of the rank and file Kongolese parishioners. Also consistent with the attitudes that Jesuits had to all secular clergy, they blamed the

---

27. Melchior Nunes to Martinho de Santa Cruz, September 27, 1547, *MMA* 2:171–73.

28. Vaz to the College of Coimbra, September 18, 1547, *MMA* 2:166.

29. Saccardo, *Congo e Angola* 1:50–52 for an overview of the mission. A thorough but rather prejudiced description can be found in Rodrigues, *História* Tome I, part 2, 543–56.

30. Italian translations of their letters were published in 1558, and are presented in *MMA* 2: 177–88. The more complete original Portuguese versions of their letters, dated July 13 or August 1, 1548, are in *MMA* 15:148–63.

continuation of these practices on them, and hoped that they could reform the country through retraining the seculars.[31] Although rather vaguely mentioning "superstition," which probably meant the well-established custom of making use of pre-Christian methods to petition the Other World, they mentioned one interesting idea and a far more subtle problem.[32]

As the Jesuits understood them, the Kongolese regarded themselves as "immortal," or they "rose up" upon death, and that it was a great insult to say to someone that their mother or father were dead, as to the Kongolese death could only be caused by witchcraft or in warfare.[33] While the context for this is missing, it seems probable that they were grappling with the different understandings that Kongolese had of the afterlife, one that the earliest development of Christianity had not addressed.

In traditional or European Christianity, a person who dies is resurrected, that is, they are reborn in some other space, but located in the Other World. This might be Heaven, Hell, or Purgatory, depending on an act of divine judgment, the nature of which was being hotly debated in Europe. The terms were known in Kongo, although apparently they had been reinterpreted. In Kongo, those who died entered the Other World directly and without judgment and did not go to a distant place but rather remained nearby, generally near their graves. There, as ancestors, they intervened actively in the affairs of their living descendants.[34]

However that may be, the Jesuits believed that their "errors" could be corrected by teaching, and at least as they told the story, they were successful in this. Beyond what they saw as correctible errors, the Jesuits admired the genuine enthusiasm that the Kongolese showed Christianity. When

---

31. Letter of Cristovão Ribeiro, August 1, 1548 *MMA* 15:161–63.

32. Almeida, "Primeira missão," 871–74, for some underlying ideas.

33. Jacome Dias, August 1, 1548; Cristovão Ribeiro, 1 August 1548, *MMA* 15:155, 163.

34. Reconstructing the pre-Christian religion is all but impossible, as there are no early or pre-Christian descriptions of it. This reconstruction has been done using several sources: accounts of illicit practices (according to priests) of the Kongolese during or after this period; studying descriptions of religions of Kikongo-speaking people who were not converted, especially in the neighboring kingdom of Loango (but also in the related Kimbundu-speaking neighbors to the south); and finally by work done in recent times by ethnographers, anthropologists, and missionaries, see for this John Thornton, "Religious and Ceremonial Life in the Kongo and Mbundu Areas, 1500–1700," in Linda Heywood, ed. *Central Africans and Transformations in the American Diaspora* (Cambridge: Cambridge University Press, 2002), 71–90. For a different interpretation, Almeida, "Primeira missão," 879–83, based largely on the work of Ann Hilton and Wyatt MacGaffey.

they began their teaching, the Jesuits asked them who created them, and all answered "*Nzambi nkwa Mpungu*," a phrase which both Kongolese tradition and the Jesuits had already determined was equal to the Christian God. They met very little resistance; one young man, the son of "fetishers" had learned from his parents that the new teaching was all lies, but he was already defying his parents and joining the church.[35]

The Jesuits all but ignored the role of the local school system in instructing the mass of the population. They were appalled to see the priests doing mass baptisms of children and even older people through aspersion using a hyssop, without any preliminary instruction.[36] This practice emerged because of the shortage of clergy and the Kongolese acceptance of the idea that the sacraments could only be administered by an ordained priest. The priest was primarily present to perform the sacrament and not for education, save perhaps for the most elite of the believers, while basic religious training remained in the hands of the *mestres de escola*, and that instruction was deemed sufficient so that the priest could administer baptism without doing his own instruction.

It is hardly a surprise that Diogo Gomes, who became a Jesuit in 1552, knew about the school system, since he himself had been raised through it, though he thought it inadequate. This is why, on the road to Mbanza Kongo in 1553, he decided to baptize a young boy whose father insisted that he had gone to a "good school," presumably one that Gomes recognized as one that he might have gone. Otherwise, he made it a point, as his colleagues had earlier, not to baptize anyone over the age of seven who had not been fully instructed according to the Jesuit system of education. His strategy greatly irritated most of the lay people in Kongo.[37]

It was not matters of theology that would overthrow the mission, however; it was the Jesuits' serious missteps in the political realm. They were walking into a situation that was fraught with political problems: first, they were going to be opposed by the secular clergy, especially those who had been avoiding the bishop's deportation order successfully by being clients of the king. Diogo was patron to these people who he knew and trusted,

35. Chistovão Ribeiro, August 1, 1548, *MMA* 15:162–63.

36. Cristovão Ribeiro, July 31, 1548, *MMA* 15:149.

37. Cornelio Gomes [Diogo Gomes's Jesuit name] to Diego Mirón, October 29, 1553, *MMA* 15:296–97.

and it was this battle in particular that caused Diogo to send Gomes to Portugal in the first place. But once Gomes became a Jesuit, he was held to their policy which put them squarely in the camp of the bishop.

A second problem was the question of the rights of Portuguese authorities based in São Tomé to regulate the lives of all people of Portuguese ancestry residing in Kongo. This often took on the form of commercial disputes, especially since virtually the entire external trade of Kongo went through the island, and the governors and bishops sought to get special treatment for their clients, vicars, and interests in Kongo. Often Diogo's clients were "new Christians," that is, Jews who had converted to Christianity after they were ordered to convert or leave in 1529.[38] This lower status made them valuable to Diogo who could count on their loyalty, and low in the eyes of the higher-status Portuguese. The Jesuits therefore also sided with the captain of São Tomé and wanted traders (i.e., those from São Tomé who were clients of the captains) to be exempt from Kongo law, to have free passage through the country, and to be free of other taxes. They also wanted all the Portuguese in Kongo to fall under Portuguese jurisdiction, including Diogo's clients.[39]

This battle over commerce, taxation, and rights of the captain's clients was waged during the period of the Jesuits' residence. Francisco de Barros de Paiva, the captain of São Tomé, wrote to Portugal to complain that Diogo's soldiers and his clients harassed the merchants that were loyal to him, at times beating them and stealing their goods. Moreover, Diogo also closed markets and prevented them from trading in the northern markets (*pumbos*), all this clearly to protect his own clients that dealt in them.[40]

In these battles of jurisdiction and patronage, the Jesuits, from the time they left Portugal, were plainly under the instructions to support the interests of the bishop. In anticipation of trouble on this score, they asked that the king give them a brief addressed to João Batista, telling him not to "vex" them.[41] Whatever issues might emerge from the question of authority and

---

38. Belchoir de Sousa Chicorro to King, July 18, 1553, *MMA* 2:285–86.

39. These issues were implicit from the start, after his entering the Jesuits, Diogo (now Cornelio) Gomes wrote them out explicitly, "Apontamentos que dyó el P^e Cornelio al Rey de Congo," ca. 1552, *MMA* 15:164–66.

40. Francisco de Barros de Paiva to João III, February 18, 1549, *MMA* 2:231–37.

41. Jorge Vaz to the Jesuits of Coimbra, September 18, 1547, *MMA* 2:165.

hierarchy, effectively they moved squarely into the camp of João Bautista and his clergy with regards to Kongo.[42]

Diogo retaliated by limiting the income the Jesuits received, so at least Cristovão Ribeiro and Jacome Dias began conducting regular commerce themselves with São Tomé. While they might have initially done so to support their work, as it appears they did, they also diverted some of the funds they acquired from the slave trade to personal projects, causing a scandal, at least in Portugal if not in Kongo.[43] More to the point, the Jesuits became closely connected to the captain of the island, and thus working contrary to Diogo's clients even in the secular sphere.[44]

Priests engaging in trade were probably not as much a scandal for Diogo as for the Jesuits, although it did reveal their intentions and connections to him. For Diogo, the question of João Bautista was critical: he was very committed to having an independent church and in reversing the 1534 decision to place Kongo under São Tomé. There was no middle ground for him; he wanted unequivocal support for an independent church. In 1547 he was preparing a mission to Rome, repeating more or less exactly what Afonso had proposed in 1539. He was also demanding all the rights appropriate to any other king in Christendom, which would include his own bishop and right of patronage.[45] Although the mission did not go, Diogo would repeat the effort in 1553, so this was a consistent priority of his.

These issues were compounded by a certain arrogance on the part of the Jesuits themselves. Like many other European groups of the era, they had definite ideas about the hierarchy of humanity, and such matters as eating bread and drinking wine, living in stone houses, and wearing specific types of clothing in particular designs, were markers of superior status. They were concerned that cannibals lived in the vicinity, and that some of these

---

42. Almeida, "Primeira missão," 868.

43. Inacio de Azevedo to Inacio de Loyola, December 7, 1553, *MMA* 15:167–72; Juan Alfonso Polanco, *Chronicon Societatis Iesu* (Madrid, 1894), excerpt in *MMA* 2:311–14 (the chronicle was written in 1573–1574, its author was fully in touch with both the documentary base of the period and a witness to it).

44. Cristovão Ribeiro to Francisco de Barros de Paiva, January 25, 1549, *MMA* 2:220–25.

45. The draft of a letter, based directly on a version created by Afonso I in 1533, shows his intentions, see *MMA* 2:174–76 (and the explanatory note of Brásio in footnote on 176); a second version is found in *MMA* 15:143–44, and a draft of an explanatory letter at *MMA* 15:146–47.

cannibals had been recruited into Kongo service.[46] All this gave them a sense of superiority that was probably discretely prominent even among long-standing Portuguese residents including perhaps Gomes himself. A key display of this arrogance was revealed when they intervened to support a white slave owner when a princess of Kongo was beating his slave for disrespecting her, and she in turn scratched the priest, creating a scandal. To make matters worse, Gomes publicly berated Diogo during a sermon, calling him an ignorant dog, and pointing at him in an accusatory way.[47]

Further complicating the matter of attitude, Gomes, who Diogo assumed would be his trusted ambassador, turned to support the Jesuits as he wished to become one himself. Although he could not immediately join the order, he was admitted to the novitiate. Given the Jesuit concept of obedience, he was thus linked to their policies and leadership, and thrown into the choices that leadership (exercised by Vaz) made. Ultimately, Diogo felt Gomes sufficiently disrespectful for "dishonoring me from the pulpit" that he sent him out of the country within months of his arrival, though writing a letter to him expressing his regret and remembering the service Gomes had done for the country.[48]

Even these were petty matters, however, compared to what was going on in the larger field of Kongo. Diogo had managed to be crowned king but was not yet in control of the whole country, and there were many provinces which were held by appointees of Pedro that he did not feel strong enough to take over, even if it were his constitutional right. His enemy, the former king Pedro, was living in a church in the capital and whether for religious respect of the right of sanctuary or for fear that seizing him would lead nobles who were wavering in their support to oppose him we cannot say, but Diogo simply did not seize him.

Among the areas that Diogo was not in control of was a region called Chamgalla in the documents of the time.[49] Diogo made obtaining a brief

---

46. Almeida, "Primeira missão," 869-71.

47. Diogo to João III, March 10, 1550, *MMA* 2:242-45.

48. Diogo to Diogo Gomes, November 13, 1548, *MMA* 2:207-08.

49. Jean Cuvelier glossed this term as "Kiangala" in Kikongo, a term which implies a previous class seven noun; it might also be respelled as "Nsi a Ngala" (in the São Salvador dialect, "nsi" is pronounced "nshi" as reflected in the term "Moxicongo" for *Mu-nsi-Kongo* in sixteenth century documents) or the country of Ngala (meaning not necessarily a defined province, but a region).

to destroy this district an important request for Diogo Gomes's mission, and wrote about it in nearly apocryphal terms, being "a principal enemy of our Holy Catholic Faith," persecutor of Christians. Without the brief he could not proceed against it, and "this capital enemy could not be punished according to his idols and fetishes."[50]

Near-contemporary maps put it on the south coast of Kongo, in an area that included Musulu, a territory that Afonso had only claimed lordship over in 1535, rather than as being an integral part of the kingdom. Its location allowed it to block the movement of *nzimbu* shells, Kongo's money, from their "mine" on the island of Luanda to the Kongolese capital. The Jesuits noted that the absence of these *nzimbus* was causing economic hardship, and it is no surprise that Diogo was in the process of mounting a military campaign against it when the Jesuits arrived. Two powerful nobles, the Mwene Kabunga and Mwene Kiova (each said to be able to raise 10,000 to 15,000 troops), accompanied the Jesuits to the capital for fear that someone from Chamgalla would capture them.[51]

Diogo was particularly worried about the security of Luanda Island and its *nzimbu* shells because Portuguese merchants had been visiting the Kwanza River since the 1520s, primarily from São Tomé, in defiance of Portuguese royal orders and agreements made with Kongo. But they had been able to flourish because they had made an alliance with the growing power of the king of Ndongo, whose main base was in the mountainous interior east of the coast, but accessible via the Kwango River.

Afonso had declared that Ndongo, which he called Angola after the title of its ruler, was a tributary as early as 1535, but it was clear that it was not truly obedient. The Portuguese sent a mission to convert the king in 1520, and although they had had some success, Afonso had intervened in 1526 and replaced the missionaries Portugal had sent with priests of his own. But that same year, he also complained that Portuguese vassals, surely the community in Ndongo, had been capturing his people and dealing in illegal goods.[52]

---

50. Diogo to Diogo Gomes, August 15, 1546, *MMA* 2:147–48.

51. Letter of Cristovão Ribeiro, July 13, 1548; letter of Jacome Dias, August 1, 1548, *MMA* 15:148–49; 154.

52. Linda Heywood and John Thornton, *Central Africans, Atlantic Creoles and the Foundation of the Americas* (Cambridge: Cambridge University Press, 2007), 67–84.

Diogo led his armies against Chamgalla in 1548 and won a decisive victory over it. But he also found that Portuguese, perhaps linked to São Tomé, were living there, and although he wished to punish them, he let them go because they were Portuguese subjects.

The Portuguese commercial connection with Ndongo through São Tomé continued even after the victory over Chamgala. Violating Kongo's monopoly on the slave trade was a great problem to Afonso and it would be to Diogo as well. In addition to the support they had given Chamgalla, the merchants around the Kwanza had been drawing Kongolese shipping from São Tomé to them. In 1548, as the Jesuits were arriving, Diogo had an inquest done among the primary shippers in Mpinda, his own port on the mouth of the Congo River. They reported being unable to find shipping to carry slaves that they wished to sell away, and this report made clear to João III that his agreements with Kongo were being violated.[53]

If Diogo's campaign against Chamgalla had relieved any of the problems of the Portuguese community in Ndongo, it had not alleviated his own political problems at home. Pedro was actively plotting against the king, sending messages out by visitors. These visitors were proposing that various nobles support the ex-king against their ruler.

In 1550 Diogo ordered another inquest to determine the nature of the plot. What it revealed would be troubling to any political leader. Many of the governors of eastern provinces were actively interested in the plot, although some were clearly not. Pedro felt confident enough that the plot had reached the point of active planning to raise armies in the provinces with the goal of capturing the capital and dethroning Diogo. Beyond that, the plotters had allies outside the country. Among them was Rodrigo de Santa Maria, a Kongolese noble and nephew of Afonso I, who resided in São Tomé. His part in the plot was to work to get a Papal Bull to support Pedro, and presumably to obtain further support in São Tomé and Portugal. A copy of this inquest was sent to Portugal in 1552, in part to support the extradition of de Santa Maria from São Tomé.[54]

Thanks to Diogo's pressure, the Jesuits abandoned Kongo, Ribeiro, and Dias, the last to go, went to São Tomé, pursuing their commercial enterprise

---

53. Act of Inquest, November 12, 1548, *MMA* 2:197-206.
54. Act of Inquiry, 1550, ed. Thornton and Heywood.

around mid-1550, where the scandal of their slave trading worked out.[55] Thus, although the mission was no longer staffed, João III still had an interest in keeping it going. He turned to Diogo Gomes, who had officially become a Jesuit in 1549, to lead the new mission to Kongo, and to also clear up affairs with the scandal in São Tomé along the way. This was in spite of the fact that Gomes, who had now taken the religious name of Cornelio, was deeply at odds with his old friend Diogo.[56]

Gomes probably knew of the plot against Diogo even before he left Kongo in 1548. By late 1552, before returning, he wrote to Ignacio Loyola that he believed he had a way to get the Jesuits' problems relieved. He had heard, he intimated, that the king of Kongo would be overthrown, and that the one most likely to succeed him was "totally ours," meaning, at the least, a friend of the Jesuits.[57] While not being explicit that this new king was Pedro, he almost certainly meant it would be.

Gomes was extremely unlucky in the second mission. The other Jesuit who accompanied him was already fatally ill by the time he reached Mbanza Kongo. More to the point, Diogo was certainly aware that the plot involved people on São Tomé, and implicated Gomes in it. He accused Gomes of being a spy for the Portuguese king, and moreover in playing a part in a plan to send an army from São Tomé to overthrow him.[58] In his formal letters to the order, Gomes maintained that this was not true, and it was probably not likely to be executed successfully, but it was also clearly something that was being discussed and that Gomes knew about.[59]

Diogo refused to have very much to do with Gomes, and systematically blocked his work, refusing to allow him to preach, to teach, or even to say masses for the soul of Afonso. Isolated, Gomes sought some help in the Portuguese community that had links to the governor and to the bishop.

As for the king, Gomes now opted to criticize him for his domestic life. He pointed out that Diogo, as well as other nobles in the court, was practicing polygamy; and that Diogo's desire to marry a relative that would have

---

55. Polanco, *Chronicon*, in *MMA* 2:311–12.

56. Polanco *Chronicon* in *MMA* 2:277–78.

57. Cornelio Gomes to Ignacio Loyola, July 18, 1552, *MMA* 2:275–76.

58. Cornelio Gomes to Diego Mirón, May 9, 1554, *MMA* 15:178.

59. Cornelio Gomes to Diego Mirón, October 29, 1553, *MMA* 15:298.

been too close for standard rules to apply was forbidden.[60] Of course, such marriages were common among the European elite and the normal rules were often lifted by the Vatican. In fact, Diogo was already petitioning for an exemption for this marriage.[61] Gomes's strictures hardly mattered to Diogo, who had priests in his court besides Gomes and they were willing to do what he wished.

On April 1, 1554, Diogo made a move against his enemies. He arrested and almost immediately killed a large number of nobles, including close relatives and men with high titles. Their wives were likewise arrested and some of them were also executed. Gomes wrote a pained letter about this and confronted the king with the lack of legal process.[62] It is likely, too, that once this stroke had been laid, the idea that Diogo could be overthrown was gone. Gomes wished to leave Kongo at this point, but the Portuguese authorities demanded he remain, which he did, though he eventually relocated to Mpinda and ministered to the Portuguese merchants there.

Diogo's purge of opponents continued, for he decided to expel a significant number of Portuguese from his kingdom and dispatched several thousand soldiers to accomplish that. Given that we know a number of others remained, the expelled Portuguese were probably implicated in the larger plot to overthrow the king, or simply clients of João Bautista or the captain of São Tomé. In 1553, the Portuguese king issued an order allowing the Portuguese community to govern itself, effectively eliminating at least the formal control that the captains of São Tomé exercised against Diogo's clients.[63] Gomes was back in Lisbon in August 1555, and the Jesuit mission was over.[64]

The Jesuits would be back in Africa soon, accompanying Paulo Dias de Novais in a new mission, this time to Ndongo, and to follow up the diplomatic leads that that country had been developing since the 1520s. That mission would subsequently lead to the new mission, this one of explicit conquest that Dias de Novais led in 1575 that founded the colony of Angola.

---

60. Cornelio Gomes to Diego Mirón, March 26, 1554, *MMA* 15: 180–88.

61. Regimento of Diogo (ca. 1553) *MMA* 2: 326 (the date is established by reference to Cornelio Gomes being in Kongo and his Jesuit companions being dead).

62. Cornelio Gomes to Diego Mirón, April 10, 1554, *MMA* 15: 190.

63. João III Alvara to Diogo of Kongo, 1553, *MMA* 2: 321–22.

64. Cornelio Gomes to Ignacio Loyola, September 4, 1555, *MMA* 2: 374–76.

Jesuits from Angola visited Kongo during those early years, and it was not until 1619 that a formal mission to Kongo was established again. This mission was far more successful, and while its story lies outside the scope of this work, was much more skillful in diplomacy and in approaching the politics of Kongo and of the Portuguese colony.

In the end, it was the Jesuits of the first mission's insistence on backing the interests of the bishop and the captain of São Tomé over the interests of Kongo that did them in. That they were quite likely to have actually been a party to the plot to overthrow Diogo was a final, fatal step. This would contrast with how the Jesuits reacted, years later, when the Portuguese governor of Angola invaded Kongo in 1622, a few years after the Jesuits had re-established their mission there. This time, they firmly denounced the governor, and took the side of the local Portuguese community that backed Kongo interests. When the governor retaliated by harassing them, they managed, using their influence and allies, to get him removed.[65]

Would the 1548 mission have gone better if the Jesuits had not been so quickly aligned with the bishop and São Tomé? Could they have managed by remaining neutral in those disputes given the interest that the Portuguese crown had in their supporting the bishop? And finally did the negative attitudes they had about African people in general, which troubled the first but not the second mission to Kongo, ultimately lead to their flawed decisions on how to deal with a powerful African ruler?

BIBLIOGRAPHY

Almeida, Carlos. "A primeira missão da Companhia de Jesus no Reino do Congo (1548–1555)." In *João III e o Império: Actas do Congresso internacional commemorative de seu nacimento*, 865–88. Lisbon: CHAM, CEPCEP, 2004.

Bontinck, François. "Ndoadidiki ne-Kinu a Mubemba, premier évêque du Congo (c. 1495–1531)." *Revue Africaine de Théologie* 2 (1979): 149–69.

Boxer, C. R. *The Portuguese Seaborne Empire, 1415–1825*. London: Penguin, 1973.

---

65. For this event and its aftermath, John Thornton and Andrea Mosterman, "A Re-interpretation of the Kongo-Portuguese of 1622 According to New Documentary Evidence," *Journal of African History* 51 (2010): 235–48.

Brásio, António, ed. *Monumenta Missionaria Africana*. 1st ser., 15 vols. Lisbon: Agência Geral do Ultramar, 1952–1988.

———. "Um fragmento precioso." In *História e Missiologia: Inéditos e Esparsos*, edited by António Brasio, 326–28. Luanda: Instituto de Investigação Científica de Angola, 1973 [original 1953].

Brinkman, Inge. "Kongo Interpreters, Traveling Priests, and Political Leaders in the Kongo Kingdom." *International Journal of African Historical Studies* 49 (2016): 255–76.

Cuvelier, Jean, and Louis Jadin, eds. and trans. *L'ancien Congo d'après les archives romaines*. Brussels: Academie Royale des Sciences Coloniales, 1954.

Delgado, Ralph. *História de Angola*. 2nd edition, 4 vols. Luanda: Edição do Banco de *Angola*, 1971 [first edition, 1946].

Filesi, Teobaldo. *Le Relazioni tra il Regno de Congo e la Sede Apostolica nel XVI secolo*. Como: Instituto Italiano per l'Africa e l'Oriente, 1968.

Heywood, Linda, and John Thornton. *Central Africans, Atlantic Creoles and the Foundation of the Americas*. Cambridge: Cambridge University Press, 2007.

Hilton, Anne. *The Kingdom of Kongo*. Oxford: Oxford University Press, 1985.

Hyland, Sabine. *The Jesuit and the Incas: The Extraordinary Life of Blas Valera, S.J.* Ann Arbor: University of Michigan Press, 2004.

Meno, Sebastien Kikoula. "Autour de l'ambassade de Mbanza Kongo, 1514." *Annales Aequatoria* 18 (1997): 471–88.

Nganga, Arsène Francoeur. *Monseigneur Dom Henrique Ne Kinu A Mvemba (1495–1531): Premier noir évêque de l'église catholique*, 2nd ed. Saint-Denis: Edilivre, 2018.

Polanco, Juan Alfonso. *Chronicon Societatis Iesu*. Madrid, 1894. Excerpt in *MMA* 2:311–14.

Radulet, Carmen. "As viagens de Diogo Cão: ainda uma problema em aberta," *Revista da Universidade de Coimbra* 34 (1988): 105–19.

Randles, W. G. L. *L'ancien royaume du Congo des origèns à la fin du XIXème siècle*. Paris: Mouton, 1968.

Rodrigues, Francisco. *História da Companhia de Jesus na assisstência de Portugal*. 4 tomes in 7 vols. Porto: Apostolado da Imprensa, 1931–1950.

Saccardo, Graziano. *Congo e Angola con la storia dell' antica missione dei Cappuccini*. 3 vols. Venice, 1982–1983.

Telles, Balthezar. *Chronica da Companhia de Iesu na Provincia de Portugal.* 2 vols [2 partes]. Lisbon: Paulo Craesbeeck, 1647.

Thornton, John. "Afro-Christian Syncretism in the Kingdom of Kongo, 1491–1600." *Journal of African History* 54 (2013): 53–77.

———. "Early Kongo-Portuguese Relations: A New Interpretation." *History in Africa* 8 (1981): 183–204.

———. "The Development of an African Catholic Church in the Kingdom of Kongo, 1491–1750." *Journal of African History* 25 (1984): 147–67

———. "King Afonso I of Kongo: The Making of an African Christian King and His Kingdom." In *Dictionary of African Christian Biography*, edited by Dana Robert. Boston, 2018.

———, and Andrea Mosterman. "A Re-interpretation of the Kongo-Portuguese of 1622 According to New Documentary Evidence." *Journal of African History* 51 (2010): 235–48.

———. "Religious and Ceremonial Life in the Kongo and Mbundu Areas, 1500–1700." In *Central Africans and Transformations in the American Diaspora*, edited by Linda Heywood, 71–90. Cambridge: Cambridge University Press, 2002.

———, and Linda Heywood. "The Treason of Dom Pedro Nkanga a Mvemba against Dom Diogo, King of Kongo." In *Afro-Latino Voices: Narratives from the Early Modern Ibero-Atlantic World, 1550–1812*, edited by Kathryn Joy McKnight and Leo J. Garofalo, 2–29. Indianapolis: Indiana University Press, 2009.

Vansina, Jan. *Kingdoms of the Savanna.* Madison: University of Wisconsin Press, 1968 [original French, 1965], 58–61.

13

—

TERESA OF AVILA AND MARY WARD

Spirituality and Re-imagining Mission

Amanda J. Kaminski

In 1560, after a series of mystical revelations, Teresa Sánchez de Cepeda y Ahumada (1515–1582) began her pioneering work, first founding a convent in her hometown of Avila and then expanding her mission to establish fourteen houses for nuns and friars throughout Spain.[1] Her renewed commitment to the Carmelite Rule centered on vibrant practices of meditation and contemplation with the purpose of praying for the evangelistic efficacy of the Church and living in service to the poor. The dynamic foundress garnered favor with Philip II, king of Spain and Portugal, and son of Charles V. However, her opponents leveled harsh theological attacks against her, published slanderous pamphlets, and undermined her reforming work. At the request of her detractors, a papal delegate arranged to travel to Spain with the authority to deal with Teresa as he saw fit. She quickly took refuge in Avila, retreating from her apostolic endeavors. She wrote that she felt herself "a kind of prisoner" in the cloister, knowing from an intellectual vision that God had commissioned her to itinerant ministry.[2] The papal nuncio made Teresa one of the targets of his campaign to root out heterodoxy and disorder, calling her a "restless gadabout."[3] The

---

1. Kieran Kavanaugh, "Introduction," in Teresa of Avila, *The Interior Castle*, eds. Kieran Kavanaugh and Otilio Rodriguez (Mahwah, NJ: Paulist Press, 1987), 5.

2. Kavanaugh, "Introduction," 17, quoting Teresa.

3. Kavanaugh, "Introduction," 17, quoting Papal Nuncio Felipe Sega.

Inquisition deliberated over her writings and reviewed her doctrine for any hint of heresy. With their audience in mind, Teresa edited her *Vida* even as disciples hid away copies of her original writings, not knowing what would come of the investigation. Ultimately, her fledgling movement developed into a dynamic order, and her legacy eventually earned her the title Doctor of the Church.

A generation later, Englishwoman Mary Ward (1585–1645) found herself similarly under magisterial scrutiny. Mocked for her audacious imagination and her "manly" missional pursuits, she found herself labeled "a Jesuitess," "a heretic and a schismatic," the ringleader of the so-called "galloping girls," and the instigator of a sect of "wandering nuns."[4] Mary's radically egalitarian theological anthropology earned her the bitter opposition of some in the Roman hierarchy. In 1631 Pope Urban VIII signed a Bull of Suppression against her Institute.[5] Suddenly, in the middle of the night, papal militants descended on her, arrested her, and imprisoned her in a dank, dark cell in a German cloister of Poor Clares. There she was inhibited from speaking to the women in the nunnery through solitary confinement. Cut off from all communication with her co-workers as they labored in the schools their movement had established for educating girls in more than eight cities in Europe, the indefatigable leader began secretly encoding messages to her partners using lemon juice on laundry paper. Twenty-three of these "lemon juice letters" survive as part of the fragmented collection of Mary's extant writings. Though she died surrounded by sisters still mourning the closure of their educational facilities and the confiscation of their houses, she believed that God would continue the work they had begun. On her deathbed, she comforted her companions saying, "O, fie, fie! What? Still look sad? Come let us sing and praise God for all his lovingkindness,"[6] for "God will assist and help you; it is no matter the who but the what."[7] She tes-

---

4. Laurence Lux-Sterritt, "An Analysis of the Controversy Caused by Mary Ward's Institute in the 1620s," *British Catholic History* 25, no. 4 (2001): 624; M. Immolata Wetter, *Mary Ward under the Shadow of the Inquisition* (Oxford: Way Books, 2006), 21.

5. *Pastoralis Romani Pontificas.*

6. Mary Catherine Elizabeth Chambers, *The Life of Mary Ward*, vol. 2 (London: Burns and Gate, 1885), 496.

7. "Letter from Mary Poynzt to Barbara Babthorpe in Rome, 31 January 1645," *Till God Will: Mary Ward through Her Writings* (hereafter, *Mary Ward through Her Writings*), ed. M. Emmanuel Orchard (London: Darton, Longman and Todd, 1985), 121.

tified with total confidence that God would vindicate their innocence and reestablish their mission. Despite its delay, the divine promise was fulfilled when the Roman Catholic Church approved a version of her Institute in 1877, acknowledged her as foundress of the Congregation of Jesus in 1909, and granted her sisters the use of the Jesuit Constitutions in 1978.[8]

How did these two women persist in their evangelical ministries while navigating the political terrain of a church in the midst of monumental schisms? How did Teresa in 1560 and Mary in 1611 imagine and enact itinerant, public, apostolic lifeforms just as the Council of Trent (1546–1563) sought to more strictly enforce mandatory enclosure for religious sisters? And how did these pioneers navigate the systematic attempt to isolate, confine, mitigate, and censor their devotional material and theological teaching? A historical and literary analysis of the documents attesting to their revelatory encounters with God sheds light on these questions. An intertextual reading begins to evidence a spirituality that can be qualified as mystico-missional, indicating an emphasis on personal connection to God through Jesus by the Spirit resulting in a mystical consciousness that unveils a vocational call expressed in evangelical outworking.

In 1560, Teresa received a vision in prayer which catalyzed an apostolic dimension of her ministry. This Christophany led to a newly prophetic identity and launched her radical renewal of Carmelite religious life. Teresa's encounter with the glorified Christ empowered her to hold tightly to her divinely ordained calling, even under the scrutiny of the Inquisition. Devotional literature, like Teresa's spiritual writings, greatly influenced English Catholic women in the next generation as they recused themselves from state-mandated Protestant worship. In this chapter, I examine how the mystical revelations of Mary Ward demonstrate similar characteristics to the vision of Teresa sketched in her magisterial work *The Interior Castle*. I seek to demonstrate a unitive phenomenology that connects Teresa and Mary despite their differing responses and, consequentially, their distinct ministerial foci. The link between the mystical and the missionary suggests an interesting intersection that has gone largely unstudied in historical treatments of sixteenth- and seventeenth-century

---

8. Christine E. Burke, *Freedom, Justice and Sincerity: Reflections on the Life and Spirituality of Mary Ward* (Hindmarsh, S. Australia: ATF Press, 2009), 130.

movements. Using the mystico-missional analytic to connect these figures suggests (1) a historical unity with exciting research possibilities, particularly as it resists the trend to silo figures by confessional or institutional identity, and (2) the importance of religious practices that create space for the epistemic rupture needed to disrupt and dismantle dysfunctional homogenizing narratives and spiritual disciplines that foster resilience in agents reforming defunct structures.

TERESA OF AVILA

Born in the city of Avila on March 28, 1515, Teresa lived under Spanish rule as the country rose to the height of its greatest power. Led first by Catholic monarchs Ferdinand and Isabella and then expanded under the emperorship of Charles V, Spain asserted its political and military dominance in every known territory in the European world. This ascendency and dominance developed in strategic unity with the spread of Catholicism. Militaristic enforcement ensured allegiance to both the crown and the faith through conquest and forced conversions. When Charles's son Philip II inherited the Spanish throne, he used the defense of the faith to legitimize his war campaigns against the Ottoman Empire, Protestants in England and Ireland, French Calvinists, Morisco rebels, and natives in the "New World." As political strife threatened the "Golden Age" of Spain's rule, homogenizing the practice of religion offered a seemingly effective way to bind together Castilians, Aragonés, and Catalans. The Spanish Inquisition sought not only to quash cryptic reversions of Jewish *conversos* and Muslim *moriscos* to their original religious devotions but also to stamp out unauthorized movements of reform, dissent, and mystical spirituality among Catholics.

A prophetic spirituality fecundated reforms in the first half of the sixteenth century manifested in the development of a resistant mystical imagination encoded in devotional literature taking many forms: prayer guidebooks, vitas, and treatises on ways to perfection. The writings of these religious innovators, at first known singularly as *alumbrados*, or illuminists, made possible the flowering of mysticism in the second half of the century. The influence of the printing press cannot be overstated, as the duplication and dissemination of this literature circulated widely carrying inspiration and training, first in differing linguistic editions for Catholics and later in revised editions aimed at Protestants.[9]

The Inquisition's deep suspicion of the *alumbrados* may have been exacerbated by Fernando de Valdés y Sala, the overseer of the Valdés Index of Forbidden Books, whose personal mission involved rooting out heterodoxy, especially branches that encouraged spirituality sympathetic to the projects of Erasmus or Luther. In 1524, the Inquisition condemned forty-eight illuminist propositions. Shortly thereafter, the same body condemned the heresies of Luther. In the political campaign to tamp down on dangerous new measures, official teaching caricatured women as particularly weak and susceptible to the misleading enthusiasms of inward inspiration, accused mystics of predilection to possession by the devil or demonic voices, and altogether denounced passive, apophatic forms of prayer.[10] The censorship forbade many texts that Teresa had come to cherish, use, and recommend for formation. Later Indices investigated and renounced some of her own writings, causing her self-presentation to employ certain features of gender essentialism and to object through anticipation the main accusations that she and her confessors expected could discredit her or endanger the Carmelite reform she led, particularly through the elevation and endorsement of enclosure.[11]

The most exemplary connection between her interior life of mysticism and her active life of itineracy emerged after her mystical encounter in 1560. In June, she experienced her first intellectual vision of the humanity

---

9. See Jeanne Cover, *Love: The Driving Force* (Milwaukee: Marquette University Press, 1997), 31–44, 64–76.

10. Teresa's larger oeuvre features a strategic if not unsettling acknowledgement and play off of this caricature. She frequently outlined techniques for determining whether inner revelations and voices come from demonic or divine origins.

11. Here perhaps more than anywhere an intertextual reading of Teresa and Mary shows a glaring divergence between the two. Teresa's emphasis on the need for enclosure directly conflicts with Mary's apostolic mission of public service through education. However, Teresa's own itinerancy and external ministry activity evidences her own mercurial relationship with the withdraw from society required for contemplative sisters which she endorsed. Nevertheless, the theological anthropology of both figures demonstrates a radically egalitarian notion of personhood. Further both women's leadership challenged gendered expectations of performed piety and defied the institutionalization of hierarchy by sex. For more on Teresa's literary self-presentation see Gillian T. W. Ahlgren, *Teresa of Avila and the Politics of Sanctity* (Ithaca, NY: Cornell University Press, 1998), 15–21.

of Christ.[12] Then in January of 1561, she encountered Christ in risen form through an imaginative vision.[13] For the next two and half years, she frequently received this spiritual grace.[14] Consequently, Teresa recommitted to her vows and insisted upon the foundation of a new manner of Carmelite practice. She established a small community of eleven nuns living by the Carmelite Rule but devoted to unceasing prayer and commitment to the poor. As she set about to establish the foundations for this new religious lifeform at St. Joseph's, she received clarification about the purpose of her mission from God in prayer: the contemplatives in this movement would draw near to God, becoming intimate friends in prayer; and through this ministry, they would live in service to the Church by praying for the missional efficacy of evangelistic campaigns in the crown's outer territories of influence, like the Indies.

By 1567, the General of the Carmelites visited Spain to meet Teresa and authorized her apostleship, instructing her to continue founding new monasteries of discalced nuns and commissioning her to establish similar communities for friars. This new post, which she took up with John of the Cross, paved the way for an incredible political and religious career through which she met not only Philip II, inquisitors, nuncios, bishops, dukes, duchesses, and all manner of nobility, but also professors, theologians, "spiritual men," vowed women, and common people who had been influenced by her writings. Her spiritual maturity and reputation also earned her invitations to participate in negotiations to avoid wars, to ease tensions between Rome and the crown, to calm regional and ethnic hostilities, and to resolve family crises and other such disputes. The vitality of her ministry and the profundity of her teaching depended upon her dynamic life of imaginative and intellectual prayer. Her re-imagination of mission came in the wake of her mystical experiences, expanding her spiritual influence and unleashing her institutional innovation.

What did Teresa mean by intellectual and imaginative visions? What significance did this differentiation make for her project? Teresa's oeuvre

---

12. "The Book of Her Life" (hereafter *Vida*), *The Collected Works of St. Teresa of Avila*, vol. 1, rev. ed., trans. Kieran Kavanaugh and Otilio Rodriguez (Washington, DC: ICS Publications, 1987), 93.

13. Teresa of Avila, *Vida*, 227-36.

14. Teresa of Avila, *Vida*, 237.

frequently shifts between the two, and she insisted upon the importance
and spiritual value of both. But distinguishing between the imaginative
and intellectual showed the way that these differing modes of prayer and
their revelations related to doctrine and authority. In parsing the distinctive content of an imaginative vision in the Sixth Dwelling of the *Interior
Castle*, Teresa emphasized that images remain operative. In such experiences, she received discursive knowledge of God. At times, she used the
beatific visionary convention of saying she had "seen" the risen Jesus; at
other times, she employed the language of locution to express having heard
the voice of the Lord. She metaphorically likened this type of revelation
to a spark that passes on so quickly that it does not create a fire.[15] She
evaluated its worth as sublime and called it an awakening, emphasizing
the spiritual efficacy of such phenomena. However, these prayers engage
mental activity and human faculties like senses, rationality, and feelings
and thus do not fully reach the height of mystical union. She warned that
the careful person must analyze these imaginative visions by testing their
authority against Scripture, evaluating their consequences, and apprais-
ing their longevity in memory.[16] She assured her readers that they could
discern when their imaginations or when the devil had deceived them in
prayer by leading them far from the teaching of Scripture, by producing

---

15. Teresa of Avila, *Interior Castle*, "Sixth Dwelling," 116–17.

16. Recollection, or *recogimiento*, plays a key role in the work of Teresa. This term referred
to the disciple's turn inward in order to open the soul to reception of divine self-giving. A
general term for prayer, *recogimiento* included both vocal prayer and mental prayer, that
is quiet, internal communion with God accompanied by discursive patterns of knowledge.
However, *recogimiento* as a prayer process aims to allow the soul to still first outer, then
inner, faculties in increasingly passive reception to a God whose mystery transcends images,
thoughts, and language. Eventually, recollection leads to a profound spiritual awakening and
continually deepening knowledge of God through intensified moments of acute awareness
as the soul is infused with wisdom beyond rational understanding. In other words, it moves
the practitioner from utilizing human faculties, first vocal, then intellectual or imagistic, into
the stillness of divine union, which defies linguistic expression and operates pre-rationally
as an epistemic phenomenon. The way of recollection fuses the affective with the intellectual
and the active with the passive even as it aims for a total immersion in the divine recollection, therefore, relates intrinsically to memory. She recognized the anamnestic tendency of
Christianity. In approaching prayer as a remembrance, she linked it to the central narrative
act of the faith, that is the remembrance and proclamation of the passion of Jesus. But she also
included in the practice the intentional remembrance of God's revelations in the experience of
the practitioner. Thus, God's carving of God's revelations into the memory of the person and
the person's practice of rehearsing these moments through meditation and prayer activates
anew the power of the awakening and testifies to God's presence, calling upon the Spirit to
make effective the insight and its effect again.

something other than meaningful recollection and desire for praise of God, or by passing quickly from the memory.

Teresa taught that intellectual visions also happen by "flashes of lightning" in the soul or through locution by God speaking to the soul. However, the revelation comes when the soul is in a passive state with the faculties of imagination, reason, and affection stilled. The non-discursive giving of Godself to the receiver effects inexplicable, self-authenticating, transformative knowledge of God and union between the one praying and her Holy Spouse. Lack of doubt, inability to have fabricated such truth, immediate effect, and inexplicable or unutterable revelation characterize these mystical phenomena. She labored to pen the texture of such graces asking: "If there is no image and the facilities do not understand how can the visions be remembered?" "If the faculty are so absorbed that we can say they are dead, and likewise the senses, how can a soul know that it understands the secret?"[17] She answered her rhetorical objections metaphorically using the image of her Seven Dwellings of the Interior Castle to symbolize that different layers of revelation take place in different "rooms" of the human soul. She clarified that no door stands between the final two dwellings, such that things not yet reached in the seventh room cannot yet be discovered by the ones in the sixth chamber but that the one who moves into the deepest part can move back and forth between the sixth and seventh places. This image pictures the human soul alternating between the imaginative and the passive, the articulate and the ineffable. In the prayer of quiet, God absorbs the soul, unhindered from human weaknesses and rational limitations, to pass into the mercies of God's grace. Engraved forever in the heart of the earthly spouse, the vision etches itself onto the memory and harbors the gift of God's self-communication, accessed later by practices of recollection. Neither in the first event nor in later moments of remembrance can words fully capture the grandeur of the deepest grace of the seventh dwelling, for the unitive encounter of the soul with Godself remains an experience of unspeakable glory.[18]

---

17. Teresa of Avila, *Interior Castle*, "Sixth Dwelling," 127.

18. She made the qualification that a serious fault can cause the practitioner to lose awareness of the engraved memory, that is, that sin can inhibit the disciple from remembering rightly; Teresa of Avila, *Interior Castle*, "Sixth Dwelling," 137.

Teresa's teaching about the imaginative and intellectual transgressed the distinctions of testimony and doctrine. The authority she claimed from intellectual visions rested on her experience. Her unswerving assertion that these mystical illuminations came to her directly from the divine, unmediated, inaccessible by reason, and unauthorized by human powers, enabled her to safeguard the missional manifestations effected by these revelations from the policing power of gendered conventions and institutional censorship. Teresa's imaginative visions of the glorified Christ and intellectual visions of her prophetic identity functioned like the theophany of Moses at the burning bush, the Christophany of Paul on the Damascus Road, and the locution of the Father alongside the descent of the dove on Christ at his baptism.[19] These mystical phenomena effected apostolic careers for these biblical characters with transformative political, spiritual, narrative, theological, and historical import. Thus, Teresa set herself in the lineage of those whose revelations included a commissioning ordained by the One who granted the revelation and who included with it supernatural and supra-institutional authority. She assured her readers that "many of the things I write about here do not come from my own head, but my heavenly Master tells them to me."[20] She did not shrink back, even in the face of accusations of her association with heretical groups, even under the threat of the Inquisition. She politically positioned herself in conversation with the learned men of the Church whose doctrinal savvy could undo her entire apostolic career and threatened the method of prayer she felt certain God had commissioned her to develop. She wrote, "The mystery of the Blessed Trinity and other sublime things are so explained that there is no theologian with whom [the soul] would not dispute in favor of the truth of these grandeurs."[21] And while she continued to differentiate her project from the excesses of her milieu, she embraced the caricature attributed to mystics. She inverted the suspicion cast upon mystics as evidence of insanity and exalted the holy mania of union with the divine as

19. Sandra Schneiders, "Jesus Mysticism of Teresa of Avila: Its Importance for Theology and Contemporary Spirituality," *Berkeley Journal of Religion and Theology* 2, no. 2 (2016): 47.

20. Teresa of Avila, *Vida*, 329–42.

21. Teresa of Avila, *Vida*, 227–37.

the goal of the spiritual life: "Oh what blessed madness, Sisters! If only God would give it to us all!"[22]

In the midst of ecclesiastical upheaval and diametrically opposed schools of mystical thought and practice, Teresa established a middle way between the mental and the passive, between the utterable and the ineffable. She embraced cognitive meditations on the humanity of Christ and championed the value of imagining oneself in conversation with Jesus. However, just as quickly as she heralded this Christological prayer posture, she averred that in entering into the One known in history as Christ, the soul finds deeper still the mystery of the Trinity, the indescribable, mystical God. Nowhere more beautifully does she express this tension between the discursive and non-discursive, the Christological core and Trinitarian paradox of faith than in her sixth and seventh dwellings of the *Interior Castle*. A truly mystical encounter with the divine changes one's sense of identity, shifts perspective, births new imagination, and elicits missional activity in the world. For Teresa, her revelatory encounters with God inspired her reform, nourished her spiritual perseverance amidst the anxiety of Inquisitional investigations, and granted her the wisdom and humility both to carefully edit and boldly proclaim the insights of her spiritual experiences.

MARY WARD

The extant writings of Mary Ward do not provide nearly the detailed picture that remains of Teresa of Avila. Born on January 23, 1585, in Yorkshire, England, Mary grew up during the reign of Elizabeth I. The Protestant monarch established Recusancy Laws in 1559 that made "outward conformity" to the state church's Reformed faith obligatory for all English subjects. Both of Mary's parents were listed in the 1590 roll of recusants, and, as landed gentry, they eventually succumbed to the seizure of their property. Thus, Mary spent her childhood passing between the houses of friends and family as her father broke up the household to avoid persecution.[23] While a full rehearsal of the narrative of Mary's early life falls outside

---

22. Teresa of Avila, *Interior Castle*, "Sixth Dwelling," 142.

23. Many of Mary's relatives, including her paternal grandmother, served prison sentences for their faith. Her paternal grandfather was executed, while two of her uncles, Thomas and Christopher Wright, joined militant resistance by attempting to blow up the Parliament

the boundaries of this chapter, the remarkable narrative of her spiritual maturation and the manifestation of her call, like Teresa's, followed a pattern of unfolding mystical revelations. The context of her upbringing in recusant England and her fascination with devotional writings suggest the historical probability of Teresa's direct influence.[24] However, the content of Mary's mystical revelations did not mimic the Christophanies of Teresa. Neither did her public ministry take the form of the Discalced Carmelite foundress. Looking beyond the literary expression and the historical particularities of each woman's experiences enables a unifying phenomenology to emerge. Mary's explication of her key visions captures the difficulty she, like Teresa, found in expressing how the beatific experiences themselves began to manifest the historical realities foreshadowed or imaged in discursive reflection on the events. An intertextual investigation highlights the importance of direct, unmediated divine encounter for each foundress's cultivation of a prophetic Christian imagination. The ongoing spiritual recollection of key visionary moments empowered them to withstand pressure to submit to clerical reinterpretation or erasure of their revelatory insights.

Mary recorded four mystical encounters that disclosed crucial insights about her missionary project and offered her divine permission for her Ignatian reformulation. She traced the first to 1609. She had recently completed the *Spiritual Exercises* of Ignatius on retreat with a group of Poor Clares she had established in Gravelines. None of the women had yet formally joined the order while they awaited the oversight of their professions by the bishop of Flanders. At ten o'clock in the morning on May 2, on the feast of Athanasius, while making religious

---

building in London in response to anti-papist laws. For more on her family history, see M. Margarita O'Connor, *That Incomparable Woman* (Montreal: Palm Publishers, 1962).

24. Jeanne Cover suggests three influential spiritual resources in the early life of Mary: the inspiration of the martyrs and the likening of Catholic martyrdom to the suffering of Christ; the religious practices of recusant Catholics, especially the ongoing celebration of mass and the prayer practices taught by Jesuits, who were often secretly harbored in the households where she stayed; and, finally, devotional literature. While displaced from her parents and siblings after the breakup of her household to avoid persecution, Mary treasured the stories of the martyrs, developing a spirituality that gave meaning to their suffering and reifying her Catholic allegiance in the midst of great confessional fluidity. Mary recorded specific written works lent to her by her Jesuit confessor that influenced her thinking. One of her spiritual directors noted also that he gifted her a copy of Teresa's *Vida*. Cover, *Love*, 32.

cords for the local Franciscan brothers and reciting the litanies of the Blessed Lady on behalf of whomever would wear the work of her hands, Mary experienced

> a thing of such a nature that I knew not, and never did know, how to explain. It appeared wholly divine, and came with such force that it annihilated and reduced me to nothing ... there was no operation in me but that which God fulfilled in me; the sight—intellectually ... to see that God willed to make use of me in what pleased him more. Here it was shown me that I was not to be of the Order of St. Clare; some other thing I was to do, what or of what nature I did not see, nor could I guess, only that it was to be a good thing, and what God willed.[25]

She painfully discerned with her Jesuit confessor that she should not take the habit of the Poor Clares and that she should depart from the convent she had spent two years building.[26] The same year, as she attempted to understand and picture what God's will might be for her instead, she considered joining the Discalced Carmelite order of Teresa. She recommitted to perpetual chastity, vowed obedience to her confessor, and made a temporary commitment to return to England to do as much good to those suffering as she could while she waiting for God to reveal the divine will.

She left the continent for London, where she immediately took up visiting those in prison and organizing benevolence for Catholics in need. Soon a group of young female companions joined her. They lived together around a rhythm of spiritual practices in a fashionable part of London called the Strand. Mary shared the texts and practices of her upbringing and her formation in Europe to lead the community in a life of contemplation and service. One morning after "coldly" meditating, she purposed to

25. Mary Ward, Christina Kenworthy-Browne, and Mary Poyntz, *Mary Ward (1585-1645): A Brief Relation—with Autobiographical Fragments and a Selection of Letters* (hereafter Mary Ward Fragments) (Woodbridge: Published for the Catholic Record Society by the Boydell Press, 2008), 136.

26. In 1607, she jumped at the opportunity to move to Flanders to establish a new convent of Poor Clares at Gravelines for English Catholic women in diaspora. Despite the success of her venture and the clear entrepreneurial gifts she exercised in fundraising, managing the construction of the convent, and forming a group of novices, Mary continued to feel trapped in cloistered life and restless under the community's Rule. However, she maintained obedience to her abbess from St. Omer as she discerned her vocation with her Jesuit confessor.

go out to aid a woman who wanted to join vowed religious life but lacked the dowry to enter a convent. She began dressing herself in the customary fashion of the day, and while looking in the mirror fixing her hair, she received her Glory Vision:

> Something very supernatural befell me similar to that already related on the day of St. Athanasius, but more singular, and, as it appears to me, with greater impetuosity, if there could be. I was abstracted out of my whole being, and it was shown to me with clearness and inexpressible certainty that I was not to be of the Order of St. Teresa, but that some other thing was determined for me, without all comparison more to the glory of God than the entrance into that holy religious Order. I did not see what the assured good thing would be, but the glory of God which was to come through it, showed itself inexplicably and so abundantly as to fill my soul in such a way that I remained for a good space without feeling or hearing anything but the sound: Glory, Glory, Glory.[27]

Just as Teresa described, this intellectual vision left Mary with absolute confidence in its divine origin. And like in the innermost dwelling of the *Interior Castle*, Mary encountered a non-discursive Reality that subsumed her faculties in glory. The language of the spirituality of the senses could not describe the surety of the revelation: she did not see; she could not hear. With her faculties stilled, she slipped into ecstasy awaking after what seemed a moment to find that two hours had passed.[28] Despite the lack of a concrete alternative to the Teresian lifeform, Mary knew for certain that God did not want her to enter the Carmelites either. She remained uncertain about what lifestyle, commitments, qualities, and practices would cultivate the charism that the Spirit had begun disclosing to the would-be foundress and her co-laborers. The Glory Vision did not grant her discursive knowledge: no form or image of a rule; no inspiration provided her insight about how to move in another direction; no economic or political plan took shape. Rather, she presciently experienced the delight of God that would accompany her pursuit of the greater thing that God had set

---

27. Ward et al., Mary Ward Fragments, 139.

28. Ward, *Mary Ward through Her Writings*, 27.

out for her. She transcended the immanent and rational concerns of leadership; these urgencies faded, as did time and all faculties, as she felt herself completely immersed in the indescribable glory of God to which she had singularly committed.

Between 1609 and 1611, Mary and her so-called "English Ladies" grew their apostolic ministry by developing an educational curriculum for girls. This project would come to characterize the movement and garner for the women social clout, land, income, political allies, and ecclesial enemies. The group moved to St. Omer to minister to the English community in diaspora, where they opened a school for girls, many of whom had brothers in the local college for boys run by the Jesuits. There they encountered incredible pressure from "divers spiritual and learned men" to take up a rule from one of the Church-approved orders appropriate for women.[29] As they developed an uncloistered life of contemplation, sisterhood, and public ministry, they prayed and labored without direct oversight by a priest even while discerning the distinct contours of their religious lifeform under the spiritual direction of Jesuit Roger Lee with the support of the bishop of Flanders.

In 1611, after recovering from a serious case of the measles, Mary encountered her next divine encounter on a pilgrimage to our Blessed Lady of Sichem.[30] She and her ladies had been operating their school and ordering their contemplative lives according to the rhythms Mary had adopted from her experience among the Poor Clares. However, the manner of their community suddenly and altogether changed after her experience in Zichem. She heard the words, "Take the same of the Society." She

---

29. Ward, *Mary Ward through Her Writings*, 28.

30. This pilgrimage site is more commonly known as Our Lady of Sherpenheuval and resides fifteen miles beyond Louvain in Zichem, Belgium. The Marian cult revolved around a small, wooden statue of the Holy Mother that hung from a holy oak tree on top of a hill, thus the term *sherpenheuval*, which means sharp hill in Dutch. Devotion at the site centered on intercession by the Virgin on behalf of the pilgrim and the thaumaturgic power of the wood of the tree on which the statue hung. Upon official approbation by Mathias Hovius, archbishop of Mechelen, in 1606, the tree was cut down and a chapel built nearby to house the statue. A large section of the wood remained for use in the chapel dedicated to Our Lady of Sherpenheuval; two large pieces were gifted to Archduke Albert of Austria and his wife, Isabella, the daughter of King Philip II of Spain; the remainder were carved into statues and pieces distributed among princes, nobles, influential patrons, and clergy to propagate the cult.

qualified the way she heard this insight using words similar to Teresa's own intellectual visions:

> Being alone in some extraordinary repose of mind, I heard distinctly, not by sound of voice but intellectually understood, these words: "Take the same of the Society," so understood as that we were to take the same, both in matter and manner, that only excepted which God by diversity of sex hath prohibited. These few words gave so great measure of light in that particular Institute, so much comfort and strength, and so changed the whole soul that it was impossible for me to doubt but that they came from him whose words are works. … All is as done by me: it only remains that I be faithful on my part.[31]

This intellectual vision employed an Ignatian grammar to give form and expression to the unspeakable but certain revelation unfolding to Mary. A female order that followed the Jesuit lifeform, that is one with a Christo-centric contemplative spirituality, an evangelical, public ministry, and independent governance responsible only to the pope, defied social and institutional precedent. Through this phenomenon, she understood that God had commissioned her to found a female order patterned after the Society of Jesus, though such a vision defied social customs, gendered expectations, and ecclesial possibilities. Mary's mystical insight revealed that she should take up the customs, practices, and organizational structure founded by Ignatius exclusively for men. Thus, the revelation's content went beyond rationality and against political norms. However, she drew upon her Ignatian formation. John Gerard had provided Mary a copy of the Society's *Formula Instituti* (1550), which she used to begin drafting her own Institute,[32] despite the opposition of the Society and the moderating cautions of her advisor.

Aptly, while on an eight-day Ignatian retreat in 1615, Mary received her last key revelation. She set about her intentional time of withdraw to discern the traits required of one who would lead the community God

---

31. Burke, *Freedom, Justice, and Sincerity*, 19. Emphasis mine.

32. In the third version of the Institute for the English Ladies penned in 1621 and entitled *Institutum,* Mary composes her most complete and bold iteration of the plan for her community and the missionary project of her English Ladies. Lux-Sterritt claims that 85 percent of its language, structure, and ideation comes directly from the 1550 Jesuit *Formula Instituti,* 2.

had shown her. The vision that she received detailed qualities that would characterize her order. Taking more of the form of an imaginative vision in Teresa's schema, this encounter left Mary with a picture of the "just soul." This impression pulled upon concrete discursive knowledge, historical exemplars, biblical images, and spiritual topoi from the Ignatian tradition that allowed Mary to articulate the attributes revealed to her by God.[33] The first quality, which she called "singular freedom," drew upon the Ignatian principle of detachment, or indifference. This feature emphasized the state of uninhibited pursuit of God grounded in the love of the divine and thus loosed from the bondage of affections, values, desire, appetites, and habits that compete with the singular goal of following Christ. This liberty also enables a "disposition to all good works" regardless of the cost or the suffering.[34] The second essential, implicit in the descriptor of the exemplary soul, came to Mary in the word "justice." She imagined this as an active state of labor accompanied by a posture of innocence that imbued the person with an orientation to righteousness. Lastly, the vision imaged the women to "appear and appear such as we are."[35] Scholars and members of the Congregation of Jesus have focused the meaning of this part of the revelation on spiritual authenticity, or sincerity. However, I suggest that the notion had equally as much to do with the economic manner of the women, meaning that they would not don a habit but would wear clothes that presented them appropriately and modestly as members of the society to which they ministered.[36]

She persisted in drafting versions of her community's rule that incrementally adopted language and form from the Jesuit's Constitutions, despite the controversy it stirred. The fame of the English Ladies' innovative liberal arts education, which included the traditional curriculum offered to boys but added practical training in household management, sewing, and other necessary competencies necessary for young ladies, soon resulted in a flood of invitations to found colleges in neighboring cities. Mary and

---

33. Burke, *Freedom, Justice, and Sincerity*, 23.

34. Burke, *Freedom, Justice, and Sincerity*, 23.

35. Burke, *Freedom, Justice, and Sincerity*, 23.

36. Mary repeatedly refers to how she dressed and issues of appearance throughout her autobiographical writings, noting specifically the freedom she embraced outside of the Poor Clares when she began to dress "in the custom of the day."

her companions began opening new sites, first at Liege, then in Cologne, and Trèves. In 1621, Mary and some of her partners made a pilgrimage to the Holy City to receive official confirmation of their Institute, which had already been received and affirmed in Rome.[37] By the time the Bull of Suppression circulated in 1631, papal nuncios had already begun closing branches of Mary's movement in Rome, Naples, Vienna, and Prague. Before Mary's death, Pope Urban VII granted her request to remove the charges of heresy leveled against her in the Bull, released her imprisoned co-workers, and agreed to allow a single Roman site where the sisters' ministry and common life could resume under papal supervision.

CONCLUSION

This era of shifting political confessions, flowering movements of mysticism, and innovating new communities of spiritual practice warns against dysfunctional narratives of exceptionalism and superiority that bolster violent homogenizing religious forces seeking to root out diversity. Studies of this period frequently emphasize how a few key elites exchanged political, social, religious, and economic capital to insulate and guarantee ecclesial and state power. However, recovery of female-authored sources and texts cataloguing popular piety offer missiologists opportunity to uncover how people outside of centers of power nourished a resistant imagination. The mystico-missional spirituality of Teresa and Mary demonstrated how vital prayer lives can awaken prophetic consciousness that births imaginative new social and religious movements. Focusing on the spiritual

---

37. In 1616, an English friend, Thomas Sackville, carried one of the first two versions of Mary's Institute to Rome for approval. According to Mary's Appeal to Pope Urban VIII and the Cardinals from March 25, 1629, Sackville achieved success: he presented the document to Pope Paul V who referred it to the cardinals of the Holy Council of Trent who weighed the matter and reported back, after which the Pope gave approval and promised to consider confirmation. By the time Mary arrived in Rome in 1621, Pope Gregory XV had succeeded the late Pope Paul V. By the time she wrote her appeal in 1625, Pope Urban VIII had succeeded the late Pope Gregory XV. The 1612 draft of the Institute, entitled *Schola Beatae Mariae*, sketched a version of the rule that focused on the educational missionary work of the women and emphasized the nuns' salvation and spirituality. Written by Roger Lee, Mary's confessor and spiritual advisor, this first version imaged the order as an enclosure and thus did not represent the community Mary truly envisioned. However, the revised version, *Ratio Instituti*, which Mary wrote with her own hand in Latin after the mystico-missional vision on the pilgrimage to Zechem, took up the governance structure and manner of the Society of Jesus for women. Presumably this is the document she entrusted to Sackville to carry to Rome on her behalf.

practices used by Teresa and Mary and the liminal spaces they occupied as they sought to exercise agency and gain credibility in the midst of Tridentine reform emphasizes the ongoing need to recover narratives of female Catholic practice in early modern Europe that demonstrate how women "negotiated their lives within the parameters of patriarchy, social status, gender expectations, and Catholic religious reform."[38]

BIBLIOGRAPHY

Ahlgren, Gillian T. W. *Teresa of Avila and the Politics of Sanctity*. Ithaca, NY: Cornell University Press, 1998.

Burke, Christine E. *Freedom, Justice and Sincerity: Reflections on the Life and Spirituality of Mary Ward*. Hindmarsh: ATF Press, 2009.

Chambers, Mary Catherine Elizabeth. *The Life of Mary Ward*. Vol. 2. London: Burns and Gate, 1885.

Cover, Jeanne. *Love: The Driving Force*. Milwaukee: Marquette University Press, 1997.

Laqua-O'Donnell, Simone. *Women and the Counter-Reformation in Early Modern Munster*. Oxford: Oxford University Press, 2014.

Lux-Sterritt, Laurence. "An Analysis of the Controversy Caused by Mary Ward's Institute in the 1620s." *British Catholic History* 25, no. 4 (2001): 626–47.

O'Connor, M. Margarita. *That Incomparable Woman*. Montreal: Palm Publishers, 1962.

Schneiders, Sandra. "Jesus Mysticism of Teresa of Avila: Its Importance for Theology and Contemporary Spirituality." *Berkeley Journal of Religion and Theology* 2, no. 2 (2016): 43–74.

Teresa of Avila. *The Collected Works of St. Teresa of Avila*. Translated by Kieran Kavanaugh and Otilio Rodriguez. Vol. 1. Washington, DC: Institute of Carmelite Studies, 1987.

———. *The Interior Castle*. Introduction by Kieran Kavanaugh. Edited by Kieran Kavanaugh and Otilio Rodríguez. Mahwah, NJ: Paulist Press, 1979.

---

38. Simone Laqua-O'Donnell, *Women and the Counter-Reformation in Early Modern Munster* (Oxford: Oxford University Press, 2014), 12.

Ward, Mary, Christina Kenworthy-Browne, and Mary Poyntz. *Mary Ward (1585–1645): A Brief Relation—with Autobiographical Fragments and a Selection of Letters*. Woodbridge: Published for the Catholic Record Society by the Boydell Press, 2008.

Ward, Mary. *Till God Will: Mary Ward through Her Writings*. Edited by M. Emmanuel Orchard. London: Darton, Longman and Todd, 1985.

Wetter, Immolata M. *Mary Ward under the Shadow of the Inquisition*. Oxford: Way Books, 2006.

14

BARTOLOMÉ DE LAS CASAS

Defender of the Indians, Defender of the Word

Allen L. Yeh

LATIN AMERICA'S *MESTIZO* CONTEXT

Latin America, like its people, is a hybrid. On the one hand it is obviously Western: it was colonized by Spain and Portugal, which are Western European nations, bringing their language and cultures with all their implications. On the other hand, it is strikingly non-Western, having Asian physiological features carried over from across the Bering Strait, African influences in its music and food, and indigenous roots in race and religion. This *mestizo* identity is most prominently identified in the Virgin of Guadalupe, who not only has Indian features but has the maternal nurturing spirit, making her the mother of the Americas.

If there were a father of the Americas, however, this chapter is arguing that it would be Bartolomé de las Casas. Many people may think the best claim might be laid by Hernán Cortés, who—along with his Aztec mistress La Malinche—produced the first *mestizos* in their offspring, in the Aztec capital of Tenochtitlan (today Mexico City). However, most Mexicans, despite the fact that they are *mestizo*, regard both Cortés and La Malinche not so much as their Adam and Eve, but as their Judases. La Malinche gave Aztec secrets to Cortés so that the latter could conquer the Aztec Empire. Thus, *mestizo* identity is complicated:[1] the indigenous are often seen as the

---

1. Allen Yeh and Gabriela Olaguibel, "The Virgin of Guadalupe," *International Journal of Frontier Missiology* 28, no. 4 (Winter 2011): 169–77.

"good guys" and the Spaniards as the "bad guys," even though *mestizo* identity is comprised of both. And yet, fairer-skinned people in Latin America are regarded as more beautiful and of higher social status. So, *mestizos* want to be white with all its benefits, while simultaneously resenting whites for their oppression. Bartolomé de las Casas—being a white European and simultaneously the hero/rescuer of the Indians—thus makes a better "father" of the Americas as his contribution was not so much DNA "life" for the Indians, but liberation "life."

One of the key geographical locations that bears Las Casas's name is the city of San Cristóbal de las Casas. This is a beautiful colonial town, and originally the capital city of the state of Chiapas in southern Mexico. It was designated a "Pueblo Mágico" (Magical Village)[2] in 2003; in fact, it was considered "the most magical of the Pueblos Mágicos" by President Felipe Calderón in 2010.

The name of the city appears to encapsulate "strange bedfellows": is this combining the names of the (inadvertently) xenocidal Columbus with the abolitionist Las Casas? Perhaps we might be better served emulating the recent efforts in the United States to turn Columbus Day into Indigenous Peoples Day. But the "San Cristóbal" (St. Christopher) in question is not Christopher Columbus as many suspect, but rather a third-century saint, famous for being the patron saint of travelers. But the "de las Casas" in the name is indeed referencing Bartolomé de las Casas, the subject of this chapter.

As is typical of some Mexican cities, the latter part of the city name was added later, such as Oaxaca which later became Oaxaca de Juarez, named after the beloved Mexican President Benito Juarez who hailed from that city. When San Cristóbal became San Cristóbal de las Casas in 1848, it was cementing the legacy of a man who, in his later years, became an icon of Latin America, and ended his career as the Catholic bishop of Chiapas. But he was not originally from Mexico; he came there from Spain by way of Peru.

---

2. The name granted by the Mexican government to eighty-three of the most welcoming, charming, historical, gustatory, artistic, and cultural towns in Mexico worthy of promotion of tourism.

During his eighty-two years on earth, Las Casas's contributions are inestimable. This paper will address his abolition of Indian slavery and his evangelistic methods, thus the title: "defender of the Indians, defender of the Word." It will argue that he was a proto-Reformer, by virtue of his Dominican leanings as well as his holistic ministry. In fact, in many ways he might even be viewed as a proto-evangelical as he was characterized by (admittedly anachronistically) both the Bebbington Quadrilateral (biblicism, conversionism, activism, crucicentrism)[3] and the Wesleyan Quadrilateral (Scripture, reason, tradition, experience).

EXPERIENCE: BARTOLOMÉ DE LAS CASAS'S EARLY LIFE

Bartolomé de las Casas was born November 11, 1484, and died on July 18, 1566. His birthplace, Seville, Spain, was famous for being the gateway to the Americas: the location of the Archivas de las Indias (the repository of all documents pertaining to the "discovery of the New World"), and Christopher Columbus's tomb. So the irony—as complicated as *mestizaje* (mixing ancestries)— still remains, that there is still a link between this "Defender of the Indians"[4] (Las Casas) and the "pillager" or "rapist" of the Americas (Columbus). In fact, as a nine-year-old boy, Las Casas was initially inspired by Columbus when the latter returned from his first voyage to the Americas in 1493, bringing back native Taínos from Hispaniola (today, the island which is occupied by the two modern nations of the Dominican Republic and Haiti). Las Casas's own father, Pedro, joined Columbus on his second journey to the New World and brought back a Taíno servant for his son. So, the fascination and indoctrination of the Western hemisphere beckoned Las Casas from a young age. He would soon join his father on the westward journey himself, landing in Hispaniola in 1503 on the expedition of thirty ships commanded by Nicolás de Ovando, who would become Spanish governor of the Indies and cruelly subjugate the natives by developing the *encomienda* system. Included on this expedition was Francisco Pizarro, who would be Cortés's counterpart in South America, conquering

---

3. David Bebbington, *Evangelicalism in Modern Britain* (London: Unwin Hyman, 1989), 2–3.

4. Ondina E. González and Justo L. González, *Christianity in Latin America: A History* (Cambridge: Cambridge University Press, 2008), 31.

the Incas the same way Cortés conquered the Aztecs. Las Casas's personal role models were people like Columbus, Ovando, and Pizarro, so it was no surprise he was molded in their vein. In fact, he ended up even editing Columbus's diary of his four journeys to the Indies.[5] He quickly established himself as an *encomendero* (both in Hispaniola and later Cuba) upon arrival in the Western hemisphere in 1502, even while being the first Spanish priest ordained into the secular priesthood in the Americas in 1507, not experiencing any internal conflict within himself about his dual roles.[6]

The *encomienda* system[7] was one in which lands and people in the Americas were taken by a conquistador if the natives would not submit to the Spanish crown after a decree, the *Requerimiento*,[8] was read to them. This document included an explanation of the Christian faith, the creation story, the "superior" anthropology of the Spaniards, the papacy, and a statement of the Spanish "right" to invade them if they did not submit (with the understanding that the natives had no one to blame but themselves if they did not respond "appropriately"). Most of the time, the natives responded with inaction or resistance, simply because they did not understand Spanish. This, then, gave the conquistadors the "justification" to claim the land and the people for themselves. In theory, the *encomendero* was supposed to be a beneficent master over his land and people, by protecting them and Christianizing them. But in reality, the *encomienda* system was tantamount to slavery, with forced labor.[9] The *Requerimiento* absolved the conquistadors of any sin, and the conquest became just war for the cause of the spread of Christianity. Las Casas wrote in his *History of the Indies*, "slaves were the primary source of income for the Admiral (Columbus) with that income he intended to repay the money the Kings were spending in support of Spaniards on the Island. They provide profit and income to the Kings." In

---

5. Edwin Williamson, *The Penguin History of Latin America* (New York: Penguin, 1992), 148.

6. González and González, *Christianity in Latin America*, 31.

7. Williamson, *The Penguin History of Latin America*, 14.

8. "The Requerimiento (1513)," in *A History of Christianity in Asia, Africa, and Latin America, 1450–1990*, ed. Klaus Koschorke, Frieder Ludwig, and Mariano Delgado (Grand Rapids: Eerdmans, 2007), 288–89.

9. González and González, *Christianity in Latin America*, 29.

addition, the Indians were forced into communities called *Congregaciones* or *Reducciones* where they could be easily evangelized.[10]

MISSION IN THE IBERIAN WORLD

Here we will turn to the larger missiological context within which Las Casas lived. Much has been made about who started the modern mission-ary movement. Often the credit is given to William Carey, who wrote *An Enquiry* in 1792 and advocated for mission societies, demographic studies, and the application of the Great Commission to all Christians. Some point to Count Nikolaus Ludwig von Zinzendorff, the leader of the Moravians, as he preceded Carey and launched not only missionaries but a prayer movement all over the world. But an argument could also be made for St. Ignatius of Loyola, founder of the Jesuit order.

Michael Stroope, in his book *Transcending Mission*, talks about the Latin church, but uses that word in the original sense of the word, namely the language Latin which was spoken by the Roman Empire (i.e., the Latin church is referring to the Catholic Church, which carries with it certain implications, including a top-down power structure and non-separation of church and state). He discusses the first person in history to use the word "mission" in the Christian sense in which we use it today, namely St. Ignatius. A Spanish priest, Ignatius had much impact on the continent of Latin America, and even today Pope Francis—heralded because he is the first-ever Latin American pope—often goes unrecognized that he is also the first-ever Jesuit pope. The Jesuits were radical contextualizers and the most missional of the Catholic monastic orders. So the word "mis-sion" made its way early on into Latin America and various other parts of the world via the Spanish language. In fact, etymologically the word "mission" comes from Romance languages (*misión* in Spanish and *missão* in Portuguese, "terms in wide use to describe the diplomatic and military activities of Iberians in foreign lands"[11]) and not from English (which has Germanic roots). So, mission was not invented by Anglo colonial powers but by Iberian ones. But this is part of why Stroope is so uneasy with it:

---

10. Ibid., 31.

11. Michael W. Stroope, *Transcending Mission: The Eclipse of a Modern Tradition* (Downers Grove, IL: IVP Academic, 2017), 246.

the unholy marriage of the cross and the sword represents conversion by conquest, power, and destruction.

But the missionaries were a different sort from the conquistadors, even though the latter purported to bring Christianity as well. The physical manifestations of such help to illustrate these starkly. The conquistadors set up presidios (military forts), while the missionaries set up mission stations. As an example par excellence of Spain's Catholic ministry in the New World, in the state of California (originally *Alta California*, or Upper California), the Franciscans established twenty-one mission stations, which have been restored by the U.S. government and are a key part of the history and legacy of the state. However, less well known are the thirty *Baja California* (Lower California) missions, set up by the Jesuits and the Dominicans, which preceded the Alta California missions and acted as a model for them. Time has not been as kind to the Baja California missions, as the Mexican government has not restored them the same way the ones in Alta California were, so some are nothing more than a hole in the ground or a pile of rubble. Yet, some still stand strong as a physical testimony to the work of these three monastic orders. The eleven Dominican missions occupy the northern half of Baja California.[12] Essentially, these mission stations functioned centripetally (drawing people in) rather than centrifugally (going out to the people).

TRADITION: THE DOMINICAN ORDER

It is helpful to compare and contrast these three monastic orders that dominated missions in the Iberian colonies of the Americas. The Franciscans were well known for their ministry to the poor and love of nature, as befitting followers of St. Francis of Assisi. As mentioned above, the Jesuits were

---

12. In chronological order, the Dominican missions of Baja California are:

Misión Nuestra Señora del Santísimo Rosario de Viñadaco, founded in 1774
Visita de San José de Magdalena, founded in 1774
Misión Santo Domingo de la Frontera, founded in 1775
Misión San Vicente Ferrer, founded in 1780
Misión San Miguel Arcángel de la Frontera, founded in 1787
Misión Santo Tomás de Aquino, founded in 1791
Misión San Pedro Mártir de Verona, founded in 1794
Misión Santa Catarina Virgen y Mártir, founded in 1797
Visita de San Telmo, founded in 1798
Misión El Descanso (Misión San Miguel la Nueva), founded in 1817
Misión de Nuestra Señora de Guadalupe del Norte, founded in 1834

the most radical contextualizers and thus recognized for their missionary work perhaps above all others. They also classically have had a link to the pope, carrying out his will directly.

But the Dominicans are often forgotten (in fact, this is the only Dominican-focused chapter in this book). Known as the "Order of Preachers," in many ways they are the most Protestant of all the Catholic orders. Not only do they focus on the Word, but they often engaged in holistic ministry (in Spanish, *misión integral*). Named for St. Dominic (1170–1221), they are roughly contemporaneous in their foundation with the Franciscans, as St. Francis lived from 1181–1226. Less is known about Dominic than about Francis (because the latter is perhaps the most beloved of all Catholic saints), but the two men were not altogether different. Both advocated vows of poverty, chastity, and obedience, and often in a context of itinerancy. The main difference, of course, is the Dominicans' focus on homiletics. The modern-day order says that they "preach with the Sacred Scripture in one hand and the newspaper in the other. In this way their preaching is to bring the Word of God into dialogue with the complexities and challenges of our world."[13] This is reminiscent of the saying by neo-orthodox Swiss-German theologian Karl Barth that one should "read the Bible in one hand, and the newspaper in the other."[14] In other words, their sermons were never simply theoretical, they always linked practically to real-world issues and concrete situations.

The Franciscans and Dominicans approached the Indians quite differently. The former often did mass conversions, baptizing thousands simultaneously (some records indicated 8,000, 10,000, or even 14,000 in a single day).[15] The latter were appalled by this practice, because their emphasis on preaching meant that they cared about discipleship as a precursor to evangelism. This conflict was exemplified in microcosm by Toribio de Benavente (a.k.a., Motolinía, from an Aztec [Nahuatl] word meaning "poor")[16] and

---

13. "Four Branches of the Dominican Order," *Being Dominican*, http://www.domlife.org/BeingDominican/WhoWeAre/BeingDominicanIndex.htm.

14. Not actually ever found in this direct form, but Barth used versions of this quote throughout his life: "About CBS," *Center for Barth Studies*, https://barth.ptsem.edu/frequently-asked-questions/.

15. Ruth A. Tucker, *From Jerusalem to Irian Jaya: A Biographical History of Christian Missions*, 2nd ed. (Grand Rapids: Zondervan, 2004), 61.

16. Williamson, *The Penguin History of Latin America*, 148.

his debate with Las Casas. Las Casas argued that trying to convert anyone without a sufficient understanding of the faith was premature, exasperating Motolinía who felt that quantity was more important than quality and that Las Casas was not aggressive enough in his evangelistic efforts. At its heart, this really was a debate about anthropology and how the Spaniards viewed the Indians. Both Motolinía and Las Casas ended up writing outstanding (though agenda-oriented) histories of the Indies to justify their views of the Indians' humanity.[17] Las Casas firmly made his case in the pamphlet *De unico vocationis modo* ("On the only way of conversion"). Pope Paul III eventually sided with Las Casas on this matter, issuing the papal bull *Veritas Ipsa* (a.k.a., *Sublimis Deus*) on June 2, 1537, arguing for full rationality of the Indians: "They are to have, to hold, to enjoy both liberty and dominion, freely, lawfully. They must not be enslaved. Should anything different be done, it is void, invalid, of no force, no worth. And those Indians and other peoples are to be invited into the faith of Christ by the preaching of God's word and the example of a good life."[18] This papal support was a huge boon to Las Casas's discipleship approach, complementing his view that Indians "are very clean in their persons, with alert, intelligent minds, docile and open to doctrine, very apt to receive our holy Catholic faith, to be endowed with virtuous customs, and to behave in a godly fashion."[19] Likewise, Emperor Charles V was persuaded by Las Casas, inviting him to a conference in Spain in 1519, appointing him "Protector of the Indians," and leading the Emperor to issue the short-lived New Laws "for the good treatment and preservation of the Indians" on November 20, 1542.[20] While the New Laws initially freed the Indians from slavery, they were met with such opposition that they were repealed the following year. Thus, Las Casas still had to fight on—and would eventually see success, though he had to wait even longer to see its fruits.

In many ways, the characteristics of the Dominicans exemplified how Las Casas carried out his life's ministries: he waged a battle of words, using the

---

17. Ibid., 148–49.

18. "Pope Paul III on the Human Dignity of the Indians (1537)," in Koschorke et al., 290–91.

19. Bartolomé de las Casas, *The Devastation of the Indies* (1565), in Timothy L. Hall, *Religion in America* (New York: Facts on File, 2007), 354.

20. Eric Williams, *From Columbus to Castro: The History of the Caribbean 1492-1969* (New York: Vintage, 1970), 35.

pen over the sword and sermons to change the heart. Though this may have been less efficient in the short term, it was more effective in the long term.

CONVERSIONISM AND BIBLICISM/ SCRIPTURE: LAS CASAS'S REBIRTH

Bartolomé de las Casas experienced a radical Christian conversion—in fact, one might almost say that he was "born again" despite this being more characteristic of evangelical Christians. One aspect of his conversion was from a sermon, and the other was from the Bible. In the first instance, he heard the preaching of Antonio de Montesinos (1475-1545), a Dominican friar, on the Sunday before Christmas in 1511, saying:

> You are in mortal sin, and live and die therein by reason of the cruelty and tyranny that you practice on these innocent people. Tell me, by what right or justice do you hold these Indians in such cruel and horrible slavery? By what right do you wage such detestable wars on these people who lived mildly and peacefully in their own lands, where you have consumed infinite numbers of them with unheard of murders and desolations? ... Are they not men? Do they not have rational souls? Are you not bound to love them as you love yourselves? ... Be sure that in your present state you can no more be saved than the Moors or Turks who do not have and do not want the faith of Jesus Christ.[21]

In addition to this powerful sermon, the Dominicans denied communion to any slave holders, including Las Casas. These so convicted Las Casas that he joined the Dominican order in 1523.

In the second instance, Las Casas himself was preparing a sermon for the Feast of Pentecost and read a passage from the Apocrypha, namely Ecclesiasticus (Sirach) 34:18-20, which states, "He that sacrificeth of a thing wrongfully gotten, his offering is ridiculous; and the gifts of unjust men are not accepted. The Most High is not pleased with the offerings of the wicked; neither is he pacified for sin by the multitude of sacrifices. Whoso bringeth an offering of the goods of the poor doeth as one that

---

21. Robert M. Buffington and Lila Caimari, eds., *The Colonial Era*, vol. 1 of *Keen's Latin American Civilization* (New York: Routledge, 2018), 110.

killeth the son before his father's eyes"[22] (KJVA). In vernacular parlance, it is saying that offering sacrifices from the poor is as bad as killing a son in front of his father.

This two-part conversion moved Las Casas to have a change of conscience, renounce his *encomienda*, preach vehemently against the entire institution, and thereafter work to abolish slavery. He realized that individual conversion of people's hearts was not sufficient or always effective. As such, he had to return to Europe in 1515 to argue in the courts of Spain to enact legislative changes, accompanied by Montesinos himself and his prior, Friar Pedro de Córdoba. This is similar to the experience of John Newton (author of the famous song "Amazing Grace") who was a slaveholder, experienced a dramatic conversion, became an abolitionist, and influenced others for the cause such as William Wilberforce who worked through the British government to change the laws to abolish slavery in England.

Las Casas rejected the *Requerimiento* on two grounds: Indian rationality, and social justice. In his own words:

> Supposing that the Indians understood our language and its words, and the meaning of each ... what feelings would they have—what love and reverence toward the God of the Spaniards would it inspire in their hearts, especially in the kings and lords—to hear that by God's order, St. Peter or his successor the pope had given their lands to the king of the Spaniards, while they believed themselves and their ancestors to be true kings and free and the ancient owners of the land from many years before; and that they and their slaves were being asked to accept as lord someone they had never seen or known or heard, not knowing whether he was evil or good, or whether he intended to rule them well or rob or destroy them. ... [also,] Is it customary and right, in reason and natural law, to ask them to swear obedience to a foreign king without establishing a treaty or contract or covenant with them regarding the good and just way in which the king would rule them, and regarding the service that they are required to render, which treaty would establish

---

22. Ibid., 34

from the beginning their choice and acceptance of the new king, or of a new successor if it is an ancient state?[23]

Clearly, winning people through the transformation of the mind was Las Casas's primary means of effecting social change.

ACTIVISM AND REASON: ABOLITIONISM

In a kingdom in which there was theoretically no separation of church and state, ironically theologians and the crown came into conflict with one another. The Salamanca[24] school of theology (championed by Francisco de Vitoria, its dean)[25] argued for natural law, meaning the rights of the Indians for their life and land. This delegitimized the monarch's right to colonize and enslave at will. Natural law only permitted evangelization of the New World. Therefore, Las Casas went so far as to advocate for not only the abolition of slavery, but for the total withdrawal of Spain from all New World territories.[26] Of course the latter did not actually happen, but at least Las Casas was effective in his advocacy of the former.

Yet, there were still complexities. The crown realized it needed conscripted Indian labor to maintain its empire, yet the subhuman designation of the Indians was called into question. The former idea that Indians were barbarians, or like children, or half human, fell apart in the light of Christian theology, even as Christianity was the justification for divine right of Spain to conquer the Americas. The *encomienda* system (purportedly one of economic transactions between two nations—the Indians and the Spaniards) was found to be a straw man in its obvious guise of justification of slavery.[27]

The most symbolic incident to characterize the two opposing opinions found within the church was the debate between Las Casas and Juan Ginés de Sepúlveda, a Spanish humanist scholar. This famous debate occurred

---

23. "Bartolomé de las Casas: Criticism of the Requerimiento (ca. 1526)," in Koschorke et al., 289–90.

24. The University of Salamanca, in Spain, was one of the four "leading lights" (ancient universities) of Europe, along with Bologna in Italy, the Sorbonne in Paris, and Oxford in England.

25. González and González, *History of Latin America*, 43.

26. Williamson, *The Penguin History of Latin America*, 64–65.

27. Ibid., 110.

in August 1550 in Valladolid, Spain. Sepúlveda was not actually arguing for slavery (very few were so bald-faced) but for a paternalism based on the "childlike" qualities of the Indians who needed Spanish guidance to flourish, and in fact needed conversion (utilizing just war theory to support their reasoning). He stated that the Indians "are as inferior to the Spaniards as children are to adults, women are to men, the savage and ferocious to the gentle, the grossly intemperate to the continent and the temperate and finally, I shall say, [are] almost as monkeys are to men."[28] Las Casas pushed back using a justice argument as well, but contending that the Indians were actually the just ones, having to defend their lives and their lands from invading Spaniards. In addition, while the Spaniards did have just cause in fighting against atrocities such as cannibalism or human sacrifice, the collateral damage of innocent Indian lives lost was so great that it was not worth it. Finally, he also excused their initial resistance to conversion, claiming that they had an "invincible ignorance."[29]

Their arguments consisted of Aristotelian vs. biblical principles. Sepúlveda, as a humanist, employed the Greek philosopher to justify his hierarchical perspective, that some were "natural slaves" and others were "natural masters."[30] Las Casas used the *imago Dei* as found in the Bible to lend dignity to the Indians as equally valuable as the Europeans. Both argued for Spain to have some measure of responsibility over the Indians, but for Las Casas it was limited to evangelistic efforts, whereas for Sepúlveda it justified a feudalistic system. Although neither man definitively "won" the debate, history does lean toward Las Casas's perspective as having had the greater influence.[31]

In addition to this debate, Las Casas's publication of *A Short Account of the Destruction of the Indies* in 1552 really helped to shed light on the subject. He offered what he claimed to be (though some doubted their accuracy) hard statistics about the numbers of the genocide, against the prevailing opinion that the Spaniards had not caused much harm. History, to him,

---

28. Juan Ginés de Sepúlveda, *Democrates segundo, o de las justas causas de la guerra contra los indios*, ed. Angel Losada (Madrid: CSIC, 1951).

29. González and González, *History of Latin America*, 46.

30. Ibid., 42.

31. Williamson, *The Penguin History of Latin America*, 112.

was not merely facts; it was persuasive for a purpose, namely that of compassion and peace.

CRUCICENTRISM: EVANGELISM

This is, admittedly, the most tenuous link between Las Casas and the Bebbington/Wesleyan Quadrilaterals. Though he definitely respected the authority of the Bible, had a spiritual rebirth, stood on tradition, enacted social justice, had his worldview informed by his experiences, and employed reason, can he be said to have focused on the cross as the center of his faith? The conquistadors infamously brought the "cross and the sword" to the New World in their religious justification for their militaristic conquests. But this was obviously not the intent of the true cross of Christ.

Las Casas's own words are instructive in his *The Only Method of Attracting All People to the Truth Faith*: "First, preachers should make clear to hearers that they have no intention of acquiring power over them through their preaching. Second, preachers should make clear to the hearers that they have no desire for riches. Third, preachers should be mild, humble, courteous, and of goodwill. Fourth, preachers should display love for all men in the world. Fifth, preachers must be holy."[32] Though he was not explicit about it, the cross is evident in his fivefold call to powerlessness, poverty, humility, love, and holiness. Ultimately the cross, to Las Casas, was Jesus' identification with the humble poor, for Jesus was subjected not just to death but also to oppression. Las Casas took the side of the poor, and denounced the conquest and the colonization of the Indians. As Paul Chung notes, Gustavo Gutiérrez found that "there was a close link in Las Casas' thought regarding salvation and social justice. ... Las Casas saw in the Indian the poor one of the gospel, Christ himself. This aspect is at the heart of Las Casas' spirituality and theology."[33]

He also worked to plant churches, such as in Puerto de Plata (his first church plant after joining the Dominicans), or in 1537 in Verapaz amongst

---

32. Terry Muck and Frances Adeney, *Christianity Encountering World Religions: The Practice of Mission in the Twenty-First Century* (Grand Rapids: Baker Academic, 2009), 134.

33. Paul S. Chung, *Reclaiming Mission as Constructive Theology: Missional Church and World Christianity* (Eugene, OR: Wipf & Stock, 2012), 48.

the Tuzulutlan Indians.[34] His method of conversion was always peaceful, thus his naming of Verapaz ("True Peace") which ultimately pointed to peace in Christ. Paul Chung observed that "Las Casas emphasizes the gospel of peace by relating missionaries as the lovers of peace and messengers of peace."[35] Peace, to Las Casas, was the full meaning of the Hebrew word *shalom*: it was holistic, encompassing all that comprises the fullness of life, including churches, farms, hospitals, schools, and indigenous communities, which met the spiritual, physical, mental, and social needs of the people.

CRITICISMS OF LAS CASAS

To avoid hagiography, we must also analyze the weaknesses of Las Casas's approaches, despite the great achievements of his life. These are in the areas of black slavery, historical accuracy of reporting, and allowing his passion to overcome his wisdom of tone.

One of the biggest blind spots of Las Casas was his initial disregard for Africans; or perhaps it is better said that he regarded Africans as less than Indians. Eric Williams points out that Las Casas

> consented, however, to sacrifice the well-being of the Negroes to the preservation of the Indians. What he gave to humanity with one hand, he took away with the other. ... In order to protect the Indians from the excessive labour imposed on them, Las Casas accepted the solution proposed by the Dominican monks in an approach to the King in 1511, to the effect that, "as the labour of one Negro was more valuable than that of four Indians, every effort should be made to bring to Hispaniola many Negroes from Guinea." The rationalisation of Negro slavery and the Negro slave trade had begun.[36]

How much of the blame of the African slave trade can be laid at Las Casas's feet is uncertain, but he definitely did not help quell the issue. To be fair, later in his life, he wrote in his *History of the Indies*, "I soon repented and judged myself guilty of ignorance. I came to realize that black slavery was

---

34. Manuel Giménez Fernández, "Fray Bartolomé de Las Casas: A Biographical Sketch," in *Bartolomé de las Casas in History: Toward an Understanding of the Man and his Work*, ed. Juan Friede and Benjamin Keen (DeKalb: Northern Illinois University Press, 1971), 90.

35. Chung, *Reclaiming Mission*, 42.

36. Williams, *From Columbus to Castro*, 37.

as unjust as Indian slavery ... and I was not sure that my ignorance and good faith would secure me in the eyes of God" (vol II, 257).[37]

Another area where Las Casas may be untrustworthy is in his historical data. Admittedly he was doing this for a positive agenda, but it was still an agenda nonetheless. He almost certainly overexaggerated the decimation population numbers of the Indians in the New World.[38] In reality, the population estimates ranged from 200,000 to 1.2 million. However, by 1509, there was a reduction of anywhere between 69 to 95 percent of the population, down to 62,000 people. However, Las Casas furthered the narrative with what became known as the "Black Legend": that the Spanish were murderous greedy colonists and the Indians were Edenic innocents, and the massacre of the former toward the latter caused massive unwarranted bloodshed (when in reality, lack of immunity to European diseases actually wiped out more of the indigenous population than actual murder, which is not to say that murder didn't happen in some large scale). Perhaps his exaggeration was necessary, as he was trying to "fight fire with fire" by going against the opposite exaggeration by slave advocates that this was a justifiable enterprise. But truth-telling is necessary for integrity, and trusting Las Casas's objective narrative is important as political biases may color one's trust of our "hero."

Finally, Las Casas was not as effective as he could have been due to his passionate desire to see change. Though an advocate of peace, in his eagerness he sometimes moved too harshly or too quickly to enact changes, which sometimes backfired on him. The years 1516–1522 were his most active ones. He tried to create a utopian society of Indians and Spaniards in Venezuela at Cumaná before such radical racial reconciliation was viable. He rushed to get the outward visible peace settled before ensuring that people's hearts were in the right place, and unsurprisingly sin caused inequality and racism, expressed in renewed attempts at slavery, and rebellion and murder. This only further gave fuel to Las Casas's detractors that his methods were not realistic. Also, when his efforts led to the New Laws, they were so far ahead of their time that they led to rebellion by the Spaniards,

---

37. Brian Pierce, "Bartolomé de las Casas and Truth: Toward a Spirituality of Solidarity," *Spirituality Today* 44, no. 1 (Spring 1992): 4–19.

38. Williams, *From Columbus to Castro*, 36.

eventually causing those New Laws to be repealed and Las Casas losing his bishopric in Chiapas.[39] However, these New Laws—though ineffective in their time—later became a template for international law, leading to works such as the United Nations' *Declaration of Human Rights* in his efforts at advocating for human dignity.

LEGACY OF LAS CASAS: EVANGELICAL PROTESTANTISM AND *MISIÓN INTEGRAL*

Nonetheless, despite his shortcomings, Las Casas is largely remembered as a positive figure in Latin America. His legacy included not just what he personally affected, but his influence on others who would also effect change, both in social justice and in faith.

For example, he became a hero and influencer on others who would take up the abolitionist mantle after him, such as Tomas Mercado and Alonso de Sandoval.[40] In addition, Las Casas affected others in joining the Dominican order such as Gustavo Gutiérrez,[41] the "father of liberation theology" who would fight for the rights of the poor in Peru and larger Latin America. In fact, Gutiérrez would later pen, in addition to his groundbreaking *A Theology of Liberation* (1971), his other famous work, *Las Casas: In Search of the Poor of Jesus Christ* (1992).

However, even more than being a proto-liberation theologian,[42] he was a proto-evangelical and a proto-Reformer. Similar to John Wycliffe who has been nicknamed the "morning star of the Reformation," perhaps Las Casas deserves a similar title. He is often not acknowledged as such, most likely because of his Catholicism and the fact that he labored in the Latin (as opposed to northern European/Protestant) world. But he is a sixteenth-century representative of Christianity in the Global South, and as such, our history needs to be rewritten to acknowledge such giants that come from outside the "Western" or Anglophone world.[43]

---

39. Tucker, *From Jerusalem to Irian Jaya*, 2nd ed., 62.

40. Williams, *From Columbus to Castro*, 43–45.

41. González and González, *History of Latin America*, 254–55.

42. Chung, *Reclaiming Mission as Constructive Theology*, 47–48.

43. There is starting to be such deserved acknowledgement. The ELCA (Evangelical Lutheran Church in America) lists him on their Calendar of Saints, with a feast day of July 17. And a play was written in November 2007 called "Las Casas: Defender of the Indians in a Time of Conquest," written by Irish playwright Marcus Maher Whitfield and performed at

CONCLUSION

Bartolomé de las Casas was an early Reformer/evangelical because he exemplified both the historical descriptions of Evangelicalism (as defined by David Bebbington) and the characteristics displayed by John Wesley (often thought of as the first evangelical). Timothy Larsen asserts that, though Wesley's conversion is the official timeline designation after which evangelicalism appears, nonetheless a general trajectory *toward* evangelicalism is evident:

> The inclusion of a "prehistory" of evangelical forbears was thought to be useful—those by whose work evangelicals have often been shaped and with whose examples they have been identified. The earliest figure who has been included is John Wyclif. Thus my rule of thumb for the chronological scope of the volume has always been "from John Wyclif to John Wimber" (and, I suppose one might add, "via John Wesley"). The Reformers and Puritans are the most obvious examples of individuals included because of their influence on the evangelical community, even though they were not "evangelicals" in a technical sense.[44]

This non-technical Reformation flavor was present in Las Casas, as much as it was in the reforms of the Second Vatican Council in the mid-twentieth century. This serves as ecumenical hope that Catholics and Protestants can grow to appreciate each other's ministries as there are commonalities to be focused on, not just differences.

BIBLIOGRAPHY

Bebbington, David. *Evangelicalism in Modern Britain*. London: Unwin Hyman, 1989.

Canning House in London. One memorable line from the play is: "My noble Council, I do not know what will entail from this day to next but I hope out of all this life will reach and gentler hand to the natives of the Indies, because even the deepest river flows with the least sound. You asked me about my loyalty, do you not know it is my deep love of Castille that spurs me on to write the books that I have, I say this with deep unction as not befall our country with a wrath of that of which we have exploited those very peoples I speak of."

44. Timothy Larsen, ed., *Biographical Dictionary of Evangelicals* (Downers Grove, IL: InterVarsity Press, 2003), 1.

Buffington, Robert M., and Lila Caimari, eds. *The Colonial Era.* Vol. 1 of *Keen's Latin American Civilization.* New York: Routledge, 2018.

Chung, Paul S. *Reclaiming Mission as Constructive Theology: Missional Church and World Christianity.* Eugene, OR: Wipf & Stock, 2012.

Fernández, Manuel Giménez. "Fray Bartolomé de Las Casas: A Biographical Sketch." In *Bartolomé de las Casas in History: Toward an Understanding of the Man and his Work,* edited by Juan Friede and Benjamin Keen, 67–126. DeKalb: Northern Illinois University Press, 1971.

González, Ondina E., and Justo L. González. *Christianity in Latin America: A History.* Cambridge: Cambridge University Press, 2008.

Gutiérrez, Gustavo. *Las Casas: In Search of the Poor of Jesus Christ.* Maryknoll, NY: Orbis, 1995.

Koschorke, Klaus, Frieder Ludwig, and Mariano Delgado, eds. *A History of Christianity in Asia, Africa, and Latin America, 1450–1990.* Grand Rapids: Eerdmans, 2007.

Larsen, Timothy, ed. *Biographical Dictionary of Evangelicals.* Downers Grove, IL: InterVarsity Press, 2003.

Las Casas, Bartolomé de. *The Devastation of the Indies.* 1565. In Timothy L. Hall, *Religion in America,* appendix A. New York: Facts on File, 2007.

Muck, Terry, and Frances Adeney. *Christianity Encountering World Religions: The Practice of Mission in the Twenty-First Century.* Grand Rapids: Baker Academic, 2009.

Pierce, Brian. "Bartolomé de las Casas and Truth: Toward a Spirituality of Solidarity." *Spirituality Today* 44, no. 1 (Spring 1992): 4–19.

Sepúlveda, Juan Ginés de. *Democrates segundo, o de las justas causas de la guerra contra los indios.* Edited by Angel Losada. Madrid: CSIC, 1951.

Stroope, Michael W. *Transcending Mission: The Eclipse of a Modern Tradition.* Downers Grove, IL: IVP Academic, 2017.

Tucker, Ruth A. *From Jerusalem to Irian Jaya: A Biographical History of Christian Missions.* 2nd ed. Grand Rapids: Zondervan, 2004.

Williams, Eric. *From Columbus to Castro: The History of the Caribbean 1492–1969.* New York: Vintage, 1970.

Williamson, Edwin. *The Penguin History of Latin America.* New York: Penguin, 1992.

Yeh, Allen, and Gabriela Olaguibel. "The Virgin of Guadalupe." *International Journal of Frontier Missiology* 28, no. 4 (Winter 2011): 169–77.

15

SACRIFICIAL LABORS OF COLONIZATION

Sixteenth-Century Franciscan Missions in Central Mexico and in La Florida

Viviana Díaz Balsera

GLOBALIZING THE WORD OF CHRIST IN THE MEXICAN HIGHLANDS

In the prologue to the *Colloquies* between the Mexica lords and the newly arrived Franciscans to Mexico-Tenochtitlan, eminent proto-ethnographer friar Bernardino de Sahagún affirms that after the foundation of the "primitive church," God had allowed no greater event in the world than "the conversion of the Gentiles from the Indies of the Ocean Sea since 1520."[1] This was the year when the Aztec city fell to the forces of Hernán Cortés. Four years later, twelve Franciscans arrived to spread the salvific news of Christ to multitudes who lived in a part of the globe that had been believed to be uninhabitable since Aristotle. The encounter with the new lands and peoples had disclosed the ineffability of God's designs to an astonished Christianity by showing that the world revealed by present experience did not correspond to the image handed down from the most authoritative astronomers, physicists, and cosmographers of the ecumene since classical antiquity.

---

1. Bernardino de Sahagún, *Colloquios y Doctrina christiana* [1564] in Christian Duverger, *La conversión de los indios de la Nueva España* (Mexico: Fondo de Cultura Económica, 1993), 55.

While the need to find mention of the newly found multitudes in the Scriptures would trouble if not obsess many early modern scholars and theologians, the Franciscans saw themselves as the appointed ones to labor for their incorporation into the Christian *communitas* in the new era of history that had been opened with the encounter.[2] The Friar Minors would be present in Cuba, Mexico, Peru, Florida, almost in all areas where the Spaniards attempted conquest. This essay will focus on the first two decades of missionary activity by the Friars Minor in two radically different indigenous theaters: Central Mexico and La Florida. By comparing their portrayed competence and unwavering disposition to broker unknown, heterogeneous "heathen" cultures and bring them into the fold, the resolute commitment to the imagination of a common human universality warranted by the event of the incarnation comes to the forefront as one of the forces that shaped the early modern period.

MOTOLINÍA AND THE POLITICS OF THE WORD

Fray Toribio de Benavente, one of the Twelve, wrote a foundational chronicle about the first twenty years of the evangelization endeavor in Mexico. Having disembarked in the port of Veracruz in May 13, 1524, the Twelve gave their first display of sacrificial apostolic labor to Spaniards and Indians by walking all the way to Mexico City barefoot as was their custom. When the contingent made a stop in Tlaxcala, fray Toribio heard that many among the multitudes of congregated Indians pointed at their raggedly vestments saying "*motolinia*," which meant poor or dispossessed. The friar anointed himself with this name.[3] It embodied in Nahuatl the pas-

---

2. Georges Baudot, "Amerindian Image and Utopian Project: Motolinia and Millenarian Discourse," in *Amerindian Images and the Legacy of Columbus*, ed. René Jara and Nicholas Spadaccini (Twin Cities: University of Minnesota Press, 1992), 375, 400.

3. See Marjorie Reeves, *Joachim of Fiore and the Prophetic Future* (New York: Harper and Row, 1977); Placid Hermann, O.F.M., "Introduction and Notes to *St. Francis of Assisi*," in *Writings and Early Biographies*, ed. Marion A. Habig (London: The Society for Promoting Christian Knowledge, 1979); and John L. Phelan, *The Millennial Kingdom of the Franciscans in the New World* (Berkeley: University of California Press, 1970); Jacques Lafaye, *Quetzalcoatl and Guadalupe: The Formation of Mexican National Consciousness, 1531–1813* (Chicago: University of Chicago Press, 1987); Georges Baudot, *La pugna franciscana por México* (México: Alianza Editorial, 1990); *Utopia and History in Mexico* (Niwot: University of Colorado Press, 1995); and Viviana Díaz Balsera, *The Pyramid Under the Cross* (Tucson, University of Arizona Press, 2005). See also Frank Graziano, *The Millennial New World* (Oxford: Oxford University Press, 1999) for a discussion on how the encounter with a new world reignited millennial expectations in Europe.

toral baton of poverty and detachment he trusted would be instrumental in drawing to the bosom of Christianity peoples from a very sophisticated, very developed civilization, but which had never heard anything about Jesus Christ, Israel, Islam, India, Egypt, or Europe, and about which there was nothing written or known.

In an astute political, but perhaps also somewhat contrite move, the controversial conqueror of Mexico Hernán Cortés received the Twelve with an inaugural ceremony of subordination. At the head of a cortege of the highest ranked Spanish conquerors of Mexico, the indisputably most powerful man in the land knelt in front of the humbly dressed friars and kissed their right hand. The ruthless Pedro de Alvarado known as Tonatiuh or "red sun" and the rest of the wayward Spanish soldiers did the same. Watching closely, the indigenous *tlatoque* lords and *pipiltin* or noblemen from Mexico-Tenochtitlan and prominent neighboring city-states or *alte-petl*, all followed suit. The indigenous masses looked on, beholding the new powers to which their leaders submitted, and which they were also to obey.[4]

Historian of colonial Mexico James Lockhart has pointed out that since for the Nahuas victory was "prima facie evidence of the strength of the victor's god" they hardly needed to be converted, but rather just instructed in the ways they had to serve the new deity (passive).[5] Empowered by Cortés's gesture of submission, the Twelve, soon after their arrival in Tenochtitlan, joined forces with five other friars who were already working in Mexico. They divided themselves up in four groups, each destined to a populated city in Central Mexico: Mexico-Tenochtitlan, Texcoco, Tlaxcala, and Huejotzingo. The task of teaching the Nahuas in things Catholic would be daunting but not because of indigenous resistance, incapacity, or hatred. Quite the opposite: all towns or *altepetl* would seek tenaciously to have friars residing or at least visiting their places. This was not only for their desire to be preached the ways of Christianity, however, but also for what it meant in terms of prestige, sovereignty, and social standing in the Nahua

---

4. The Franciscan Jerónimo de Mendieta narrates the encounter in book 3, chapter 12 of his *Historia eclesiástica Indiana* finished circa 1596. The *Historia* remained unpublished until 1870. I am using the 1993 edition of the text published in Mexico, Editorial Porrúa.

5. James Lockhart, *The Nahuas after the Conquest: A Social and Cultural History of the Indians of Central Mexico: Sixteenth through Seventeenth Centuries* (Stanford, CA: Stanford University Press, 1992), 203.

world. Under the guidance of the friars, now also turned master builders by necessity, the indigenous peoples from the towns and cities in which the friars would reside took in earnest to the construction of monasteries and churches, seeking to outshine other settlements. Following pre-Hispanic precedent, religious buildings for the Nahuas served as statements of the community's standing and identity.[6] In addition, even though the friars may have been aware of these aspects of altepetl politics, for them there was something uncannily epochal, breathtakingly groundbreaking about how such culturally based receptivity would blend with Franciscan eschatological missionary expectations. That the great lords of Central Mexico and their people would compete for status, sovereignty, and altepetl identity by deploying their capacity to wield and manage the material signs of Christological power, albeit all too human, was enabling indeed.

Motolinía's service of chronicling the labors of the Friars Minors in Mexico for posterity was also political, however. One year after the Franciscans in Central Mexico were constituted into the independent province of the Santo Evangelio in 1535, Motolinía's superior assigned him to write a history of the Minorite achievements in the land.[7] His *History of the Indians of New Spain* was to document and show Spanish audiences how multitudes of souls in Anahuac had been opportunely gained for Catholicism by the exemplary apostolic vocation of the indefatigable Friars Minor. The *History* was also destined to garner the support of the influential Count of Benavente for the Franciscans, since friars from other orders had challenged their streamlined baptismal practices as will be discussed below.[8] As an active participant in the events that he narrates, Motolinía would spend six years traveling and compiling information for his foundational chronicle.

Also, politically well informed was the Franciscans' use of the role model powers of Mexica nobles or *pipiltin*. Motolinía recounts how the friars first instructed and baptized the grandsons and nephews of Montezuma "out

---

6. James Lockhart, *The Nahuas after the Conquest*, 206.

7. Baudot, *Utopia and History in Mexico*, 275.

8. See Robert Ricard, *La conquista espiritual de México*, trans. Ángel Garibay K. (México: Fondode Cultura Económica, 1986), 165–71; and Baudot, *Utopia and History in Mexico*, 277–78.

of regard" for their status as principal people.[9] Indeed, rulers in Aztec culture claimed to be descendants of the Mesoamerican god Quetzalcoatl and, thus, recipients of nonhuman powers and specialized knowledge about the workings of the world.[10] Thus, the baptism first of noble children and lords was not merely a religious event marking the new life of Christianity for these individuals. The friars knew it was also a political affair because after baptizing the powerful elites it was likely that everybody else would follow suit.[11] Many lienzos and indigenous annals record the baptisms of lords as significant events for the whole community.[12] All newly baptized children and adults received a Spanish Christian name while retaining an indigenous one.[13] In this way, the sacrament both conferred to the people a modern Christian social identity and operated as a sign of their traditional corporate subordination, since nobody wanted or could afford to be left behind in their communities.

---

9. Fray Toribio de Benavente, Motolinía, *History of the Indians of New Spain*, trans. Francis Borgia Steck (Washington, DC: Academy of American Franciscan History, 1951), 174.

10. Davíd Carrasco and Scott Sessions, *The Daily Life of the Aztecs: People of the Sun and Earth* (Westport, CT: Greenwood Press, 1998), 132–33. Quetzalcoatl or the Plumed Serpent was a major deity in the Mesoamerican pantheon. One of the earliest known representations of this god appears in an Olmec stellae at the archaeological site known as La Venta, located in the present-day Mexican state of Tabasco. La Venta reached its apogee circa 900 to 400 B.C. Centuries later, an important temple dedicated to the worship of Quetzalcoatl was raised (passive verb) in Teotihuacan, the greatest city of Mexico in the Mesoamerican classical period (150 to 650 C.E.) and possibly beyond. See Michael D. Coe and Rex Koontz, *Mexico: From the Olmecs to the Aztecs* (New York: Thamesand Hudson, 2008), 101. After the fall of Teotihuacan, the Toltec city of Tula or Tollan (ca. 950–1150 C.E.) became the new axis mundi of the region. Topiltzin Quetzalcoatl, priest of Quetzalcoatl, became king of the Toltecs and the most prominent Mesoamerican Postclassic cultural hero. According to Coe and Koontz Tula translates as "Place of the Rushes" or "civilized urban space," 157. Indeed, the Toltecs were great artisans, merchants, and workers of feathers and precious stones, and therefore represented the highest levels of cultural achievement. Three hundred years after the fall of Tula/Tollan, the rulers and nobles of Mexico-Tenochtitlan claimed to be the descendants of Topiltzin Quetzalcoatl and depositaries of his priestly powers. On the figure of Quetzalcoatl and his priest Topiltzin Quetzalcoatl see especially Henry B. Nicholson, *Topiltzin Quetzalcoatl: The Once and Future Lord of the Toltecs* (Boulder: University Press of Colorado, 2001); and Davíd Carrasco, *Quetzalcoatl and the Irony of Empire: Myths and Prophecies in the Aztec Tradition* (Boulder: University Press of Colorado, 2000).

11. Charles Gibson, *The Aztecs under Spanish Rule: A History of the Indians of the Valley of Mexico, 1519–1810* (Stanford: Stanford University Press, 1964), 102.

12. Osvaldo Pardo, *The Origins of Mexican Catholicism: Nahua Rituals and Christian Sacraments in Sixteenth-Century Mexico* (Ann Arbor: The University of Michigan Press, 2004), 25.

13. Lockhart, *Nahuas after the Conquest*, 119–20.

FERVOR FOR THE WORD

Motolinía expresses amazement at the zeal with which the children took to learn the Christian doctrine and prayers. In Mexico City, he claims that they gathered on their own in small groups in the patio of the churches, chapels, and their suburbs for hours in a row singing and learning Pater Noster, the Ave Maria, and the Credo. Day and night the children recited by heart the cathecism,[14] beyond the friars' expectations. There would seem to be a surplus of piety and devotion in the air, an uncanny urgency in adopting Christianity that jibed with the friars' missionary fervor in teaching and spreading the word.

To evince what he construed as the epic, providential, if not millenarian, dimensions of the indigenous demand for Christianity and of the Minorite agency in its satisfaction, Motolinía breaks down the number of baptisms administered by the Franciscans in towns and provinces: "For Mexico and its towns, for Xochimilco and its towns on the Sweetwater Lake, for Tlalmanalco and Chalco and Cuaunahuacuc, for Cuauhquechollan and Chietla—for these more than a million. For Tetzcoco, Otompa, and Tepepulco, Tollantzinco, Cuautitlan, Tollan and Xilotepec with their provinces and towns—to these more than a million. For Tlaxcallan, the city of Los Angeles, Cholollan, Huexotzinco Calpa, Tepeyac, Zactlan, Hueytlalpan, for these more than a million. For the towns of the South Sea, more than a million."[15] In fifteen years that the Franciscans had been in Mexico, Motolinia speculates that they had baptized more than nine million Indians![16]

The Friars Minor administered the sacrament of penance for the first time in 1526. Since there were so many Indians wanting to confess,

---

14. Motolinia, *History of the Indians of New Spain*, 105.

15. Ibid., 182.

16. Ibid., 183. These hyperbolic numbers were most likely highly inflated by Motolinía in his attempt to depict the providential conversion of the native populations in Mexico under the guidance of the Minorites. However, their Dominican rivals soon denounced the massive baptisms of the Franciscans as not meeting the ritual integrity of applying salt, oil, and chrism to each individual, and thus putting at risk the efficacy of the sacrament. Of course, Motolinía decried the attack as a superfluous concern with ceremony and defended the Minorite simplified practice calling attention to the endless duties of only sixty friars tending to millions of neophytes. All this resulted in a bitter controversy that the papal bull *Altitudo divinii consilii* of 1537 finally brought to a resolution. For a discussion of the controversy, see Pardo, *The Origins of Mexican Catholicism*, 20–48.

Motolinía reports that sometimes penitents had to travel up anywhere from fifty to seventy miles trying to find an available minister who would listen.[17] Many wanted to confess not only in Lent but also in Christmas, Easter, and Pentecost. Because hundreds of Indians expected their confessions to be heard, during one Lenten season when Motolinía was in Cholula he decided to expedite the process—and narrow down the numbers—by refusing to hear confessants unless they had their sins written down in figures. No sooner had the Indians heard this than they proceeded to write or paint their sins as the friar demanded. Motolinía recounts how they would then bring their figures "and designate[d] their sins with a stick, while I helped them with another stick, and in this way they made a short confession."[18] Moreover, although painting sins and later sharing their figures with the minister entailed not an insignificant labor of self-examination, Motolinía again found himself unable to take care of the multitudes who sought to be heard and cleansed of evil.[19]

FRANCISCAN PHILOLOGISTS AND EDUCATORS: THE COLEGIO DE SANTA CRUZ DE TLATELOLCO

Very early on, however, the friars knew that the grace-producing powers of the sacraments would not be enough even in the face of the marvelous Nahua willingness to receive Christianity. To spread the Holy Word effectively the missionaries quickly set themselves to learn the languages of their charges. They would excel above all other missionary orders in Mexico in the application of the methods of Renaissance humanistic philology to understand, learn, and record the languages and cultures of their indigenous brethren.[20] Shortly after establishing their mission in New Spain, the friars set up boarding schools to train the sons of the nobles in the arts of reading and to recruit their help in learning and transcribing Nahuatl in Latin characters. In 1536, the Franciscans formally instituted the College of the Holy Cross in Tlatelolco.

---

17. Motolinia, *History of the Indians of New Spain*, 192.

18. Ibid., 198.

19. Ibid.

20. Lockhart, *Nahuas after the Conquest*, 5.

This would be the first institution of higher education in the Americas. Between sixty and one-hundred boys studied at the school as interns for three years entering at the age of ten or twelve.[21] The interns learned Latin, Spanish, and Nahuatl so that they would become effective ecclesiastical cultural brokers able to draw the indigenous masses of their altepetl to Christianity.[22] The most talented received instruction in Latin, music, logic, philosophy, and indigenous medicine by the highest educated among the Franciscan missionaries.[23] The Colegio was also to prepare the very best students to become clerics. Many secular priests as well as friars from other orders vehemently opposed this educational project claiming that it was a useless if not an extremely dangerous enterprise to have Indian nobles speaking and writing, especially in Latin.[24]

Considering the bloody religious schism in Europe, especially the Dominicans feared that misinterpretations of difficult aspects of the Bible would lead to what for them were more heresy, conflict, and division. However, much less justifiably they also dreaded how knowledge of Latin would empower the students.[25] And although by the end of the century the Colegio had been all but abandoned and its goal of producing indigenous ecclesiastics proclaimed as a failure, many of its graduates indeed became the great trilingual grammarians and Latinists without whose contributions the extensive production of Franciscan ethnographic, religious, and linguistic works would have been next to impossible.[26] Influential among

---

21. Louise Burkhart, *Holy Wednesday: A Nahua Drama from Early Colonial Mexico* (Philadelphia: University of Pennsylvania Press, 1996), 57.

22. Burkhart, *Holy Wednesday*, 55.

23. Ricard, *La conquista espiritual de México*, 336.

24. In the 1580s, the then archbishop of Mexico, Moya de Contreras, and King Phillip II would also oppose teaching the Nahuas arts other than mechanical. See Burkhart, *Holy Wednesday*, 63.

25. Ricard, *La conquista espiritual de México*, 344.

26. For a classic discussion about the Colegio, the controversies around it and its unfortunate demise, see Francis Steck, *El primer colegio de América: Santiago de Tlatelolco* (México, Centro de Estudios Franciscanos, 1944); Ricard, *La conquista espiritual de México*, 332–55; José María Kobayashi, La *educación como conquista [empresa franciscana en México]* (México: El Colegio de México, 1974), 292–407; and Burkhart, *Holy Wednesday*, 55–73. See Aysha Pollnitz on the collaboration of the humanist Nahua grammarians trained at the Colegio as editors of ancient Nahua speeches or *huehuetlatolli* published by Fray Juan Bautista in 1601 in "Old Words and the New World: Liberal Education and the Franciscans in New Spain, 1536–1601," *Royal Historical Society (London, England), Transactions of the Royal Historical Society* 27 (2017): 123–52. See David Tavárez for a discussion of the Nahuatl translations of Joseph Kempis's *Imitatio*

such works is the monumental twelve-book Nahuatl-Spanish *Florentine Codex* (1549–1579) by Fray Bernardino de Sahagún and his Nahua assistants, which is one of our major sources on Late Postclassic Mesoamerican culture in Central Mexico shortly before the arrival of the Spaniards. Other essential works produced at the Colegio are Alonso de Molina's *Vocabulario* in Spanish and Nahuatl (1555–1571), still authoritative today, his widely circulating bilingual *Doctrina Cristiana* (1546) and Andrés de Olmos's *Arte de la lengua Mexicana* of 1547, the earliest known grammar of Nahuatl.[27]

ACHIEVEMENTS AND FAILURES

By 1540, almost the entire population of Central Mexico had been baptized, with the Franciscans having the lion's share of the missions in the most populated areas of Central Mexico by virtue of having been the first to arrive.[28] The public calendrical rituals to the pre-Hispanic deities had been abolished for almost fifteen years; impressive temples to the Christian god had been erected in all-important altepetls—if only as symbols of local native capacity to wield and display the new discourses of power. Indigenous baptized lords had assumed high-sounding Spanish names as marks of distinctions, and their acceptance of Christianity were recorded as key events in the life of their communities. Altepetls competed for having resident friars, and especially the Friars Minor had produced

---

Christi as another example of co-authorships between Nahua and Franciscans scholars working in the Colegio in "Nahua Intellectuals, Franciscan Scholars, and the *Devotio Moderna* in Colonial Mexico," *The Americas* 70, no. 2 (2013): 203–35.

27. Sahagún writes that the Nahua grammarians examined everything the friars composed in Nahuatl. By virtue of being trilingual they could correct any imprecision or incongruity of expression in the indigenous language. See Sahagún, *Historia de las cosas de la Nueva España*, vol. 2, ed. Alfredo López Austin and Josefina García Quintana (México: Consejo Nacional para la Cultura y las Artes, Alianza Editorial Mexicana, 1989), 635. Antonio Valeriano of Azcapotzalco, Andrés Leonardo and Martín de Jacobita of Tlatelolco, and Antonio Vergerano and Pedro de Buenaventura of Cuauhtitlan were outstanding Nahua grammarians, essential in the composition of the Nahuatl text of the *Florentine Codex*. Valeriano also worked with Sahagún's *Colloquios* mentioned in the opening of this essay, as well as with Juan Bautista's *Huehuetlatolli* of 1606, among other works. Hernando de Ribas, another Nahua Latinist trained at the Colegio, was an essential collaborator, or even co-author of Bautista's of *Confesionario en lengua mexicana y castellana* (1599), of the aforementioned *Huehuetlahtolli* (1600) and of fray Juan de Gaona's *Diálogos de la paz y tranquilidad del alma*, among many other works. Also there are the many didactic theatrical pieces or neixcuitilli for the evangelization of the Nahuas written or transcribed by the Nahua grammarians following the general indications of the friars, many of them trained at the Colegio.

28. Lockhart, *Nahuas after the Conquest*, 119.

important philological works for preaching the word in indigenous languages in collaboration with the Nahuas they had trained. In short, by preaching and instructing in things Roman Catholic to unknown, unheard of multitudes in the new world, the missionary friars of Mexico performed an impressive, hard labor of transatlantic, intercontinental connectivity at the very cutting edge of early modern history.

Of course, not without bitter power struggles, infights, and confrontations between mendicant orders, secular ecclesiastics, and royal officials, resistance from many native quarters, a frightening, mind-bugling, catastrophic reduction of the population,[29] and a lingering indigenous attachment to the deities of the land that would not be left behind throughout the three colonial centuries. The latter also much to the bewilderment of the friars who, perhaps too naively, had expected that their onerous work in spreading the Word would have been enough to obliterate in two decades the spirit of centuries of ritual worship and service to their Mesoamerican gods. All this notwithstanding, the sheer energy of the early Franciscan human effort described by Motolinía and the evidence of the deep intercultural engagement of the friars are imposing. No matter how colonialist and problematically Eurocentric they may be to our present historical constructions, such forces left an empowering imprint in the new identities of the painfully globalized and Christianized Nahua communities of early modernity.

---

29. Three major epidemics decimated the indigenous populations because of new diseases brought by the Spaniards. The first was a smallpox epidemic in 1520–1521 during the conquest of Mexico-Tenochtitlan. The second major epidemic was in 1544–1548, and the third in 1576–1581. For a list of other epidemics that scourged the Nahua populations in Central Mexico throughout the three colonial centuries, see Charles Gibson, *The Aztecs under Spanish Rule: A History of the Indians of the Valley of Mexico, 1519-1810* (Stanford, CA: Stanford University Press, 1964), 448–51. Although estimates of the indigenous populations in Central Mexico in 1519 are unreliable, there is no question that millions of Nahuas perished in sixteenth-century Mexico because of contagions, but also because of the wars of conquest, labor abuses, droughts, and other calamities. According to sixteenth-century observers, between half and two-thirds of the native population was lost in just four decades after the fall of Mexico-Tenochtitlan. See Gibson, *The Aztecs under Spanish Rule*, 138 and Frances F. Berdan, "Trauma and Transition in Sixteenth-century Central Mexico," *Proceedings of the British Academy* 81 (1993): 179. See also William T. Sanders, "The Population of the Central Mexico Symbiotic Region, the Basin of Mexico, and the Teotihuacan Valley in the Sixteenth Century," in *The Native Population of the Americas in 1492*, ed. William M. Denevan (Madison: University of Wisconsin Press, 1992), 85–150.

STRUGGLING IN THE BARREN
LANDS OF LA FLORIDA

If some questions could nonetheless be raised about the Franciscan missions in rich, wealthy Central Mexico because of the power, prestige, and dominion they afforded the friars over vast native populations, not so much can be claimed with Minorite missionary work in La Florida which finally began to take hold towards the end of the sixteenth century. The region had been a difficult challenge for Spanish expansionism since Juan Ponce de León first made contact with the land in 1513. There had been five failed expeditions before Pedro Menéndez de Avilés established St. Augustine in 1565. This became the first permanent European settlement in the North America. Nevertheless, St. Augustine, situated in the coast, was a sandy, mosquito infested, unfertile flatland, full of swamps and with little possibility of agriculture.[30] In contrast with Central Mexico, in La Florida there were no highly organized concentrations of indigenous populations in urban formations that could provide cheap labor, no mines, no pearls, or any other riches that would attract settlers from Spain. Soon it became clear that St. Augustine would be valuable for its strategic location and little else.

Except for the religious—for there were souls to be gained in the immense land. The first to try their luck were the Jesuits. Founded in 1540, the order had no presence yet in a Spanish colony although they had placed missionaries in Brazil, India, and Japan.[31] Three Jesuits arrived in 1566 and one, Father Pedro Martínez, suffered martyrdom shortly after. In 1568 and 1570 two additional contingents mounting sixteen Jesuits arrived but they were able to gain only few converts. Worse still, eight Jesuits were slaughtered in the northern region near Chesapeake Bay, where they had founded a mission near York River in 1570.[32] The Jesuits had wanted to establish this mission far away from Spanish soldiers whom they perceived as a hindrance to the evangelizing endeavors due to the latter's harsh treatment

---

30. Paul Hoffman, "Until the Land Was Understood: Spaniards Confront La Florida, 1500–1600," in *La Florida: Five Hundred Years of Hispanic Presence*, ed. Viviana Díaz Balsera and Rachel E. May (Gainesville: University of Florida Press, 2014), 69–82.

31. Jerald T. Milanich, *Laboring in the Fields of the Lord: Spanish Missions and Southeastern Indians* (Washington, DC: Smithsonian Institution Press, 1999), 89.

32. J. Michael Francis and Kathleen M. Kole, *Murder and Martyrdom in Spanish Florida: Don Juan and the Guale Uprising of 1597*, Anthropological Papers 95 (New York: American Museum of Natural History, 2011), 31.

towards the natives. Paquiquineo or don Luis de Velasco, a Powhatan noble who had been sequestered to Spain as a child and who was raised and educated by the religious, agreed to accompany the Jesuits in their mission. Upon returning to his land almost nine years later, don Luis joined his people, and the Jesuits that had come to missionize were repudiated and killed.[33] Thus by 1572, having nine martyrs to their credit but hardly any baptism registers to show, the Jesuits withdrew from Florida, unable to bear more losses for the young order.[34]

THE FRIARS MINOR COME TO STAY

The Franciscans then took over. Three friars arrived in 1573. They immediately succeeded in baptizing the wife and main cacique of Guale—a chiefdom comprising present-day Georgia and the Sea Islands—but not without resistance. Disgusted by the conversion, a subject of the cacique refused to obey him any longer. The cacique was then killed as he and his men surrounded the former's village to inflict punishment on the rebel. Claiming that her husband had been murdered because he had converted to Christianity, the wife demanded justice to the Governor Don Diego de Velasco. Trying to appease her, he put the culprit to death. Then other caciques of the region felt slighted and the Guale rebellion of 1576 broke out.[35] The Spaniards had to withdraw from the region two years later but with the hope "that the Franciscan friars' missionary work might help to quiet the coastal Indians."[36] Namely, the missionaries on the ground were the brokers, the linguists, the workers that would be able to open up and keep the frontiers of globalization. They were the teachers and students

---

33. For a recent study on don Juan's role in the death of the Jesuits, see Anna Brickhouse, *The Unsettlement of America: Translation, Interpretation, and the Story of Don Juan Velasco, 1560–1945* (New York: Oxford University Press, 2015). She proposes that don Juan's main motives were loyalty to his ethnic community and rejection of Spanish imperial designs for La Florida.

34. Milanich, *Laboring in the Fields of the Lord*, 99.

35. These are the reasons for the uprising according to Franciscan Luis Jerónimo de Oré in his 1619 *Account of the Martyrs in the Provinces of La Florida*, ed. and trans. Raquel Chang-Rodríguez and Nancy Vogeley (Albuquerque: University of New Mexico Press, 2017), 91–95. Although there were no Franciscan casualties in this uprising, at least forty Spanish soldiers perished. Also, the Indians captured a French ship near the coast that ran aground and either killed or made prisoners of its two hundred eighty passengers. See Milanich, *Laboring in the Fields of the Lord*, 104–6.

36. Milanich, *Laboring in the Fields of the Lord*, 105–6.

of cultures who took on the risks, uncertainties, and pressures of grind-
ing daily experience with the natives of the land of heretofore unheard-of
beliefs, conceptual frameworks, and living practices. For good or ill, without the Franciscans, Spanish political and military presence in La Florida
would have been much more vulnerable. Moreover, although Indians and
friars knew the Spanish soldiers would avenge the latter, it is undeniable
that the friars had to perform their evangelizing and cultural labors with
their lives under risk.

Similar to Central Mexico, the Franciscans of La Florida soon learned
the language of their charges. The Indians also constructed monasteries
in the principal towns so that friars, usually not more than two and frequently just one, would live among the people.[37] But in contrast with the
impressive cut-stone monasteries of Central Mexico and their ample atri-
ums surrounded by walls, the Floridian monasteries consisted of a small
room next to single-nave churches, all constructed in a mixture of per-
ishable whitewashed wattle and daub.[38] The friars had to walk to sparsely
populated villages six to ten miles away to tend to the new converts and
to keep up the flow of the globalizing Word. Sometimes the missionaries
catechized the Indians for four years before giving them baptism.[39] They
taught the children of the caciques to read and speak Spanish, and even to
write the language so that they could serve as *atequi* or translators. Children
and adults had to know the Pater Noster, the Ave Maria, Salve Regina, the
Credo, and how to do the sign of the cross. Like any Spanish or Nahua
Christian, they were required to memorize or at least be acquainted with
the Ten Commandments, the Seven Sacraments, the Seven Deadly sins,
the Fourteen Articles of Faith, the Three Theological Virtues, the myster-
ies of the Trinity, the incarnation, and a long list of other doctrinal items.[40]

---

37. John E. Worth, *The Timucuan Chiefdoms of Spanish La Florida* (Gainesville: University
of Florida Press, 1998), 1:113.

38. According to John Worth, the size of mission churches was sixty to seventy-five feet
long by thirty-five to forty-three feet wide, *The Timucuan Chiefdoms*, 1:113).

39. Fray Baltasar López, "Cartas de Fray Baltasar López, Francisco Pareja y Pedro Ruiz
sobre el estado de las conversiones de indios de la Florida," in John Hann, *Troika: Three Letters
about Missions and Mission Populations from 1602* (1997), John H. Hann Collection of Colonial
Records at the University of Florida, https://ufdc.ufl.edu/hann/all, 2.

40. For the doctrinal material that Timucua adults had to learn before being baptized,
see Friar Francisco Pareja's bilingual catechism published in 1612 in Mexico. It is entitled
Cathecismo en Lengua Castellana y Timuquana, en el cual se contiene lo que se le puede enseñar a

Not unlike in Central Mexico, many baptized Indians asked to go to confession more than once a year and some of them requested communion so insistently that the friars could not deny it to them.[41] Churches became centers of congregation on Sundays and on holy days after Mass. The friars reported that the Timucua had a love of music and took "part in the chanted divine services."[42] In perhaps an overly optimistic letter to the governor of Cuba in 1602 reminiscent of the exalted outlook of Motolinía's *Historia*, veteran missionaries Fray Baltasar López and Fray Francisco Pareja wrote that there were "many pagans from the hinterlands" coming to the missions asking to be taught Christian doctrine and urging the friars to raise crosses in their villages.[43] The friars also underscored how in spite of their utter poverty, the Timucua of their coastal missions of San Pedro and San Juan del Puerto supported the confraternity or brotherhood of the True Cross which mounted two processions during Holy Week. They assisted their priests in making monuments to encase the Eucharist and armed warriors guarded the structure until it was opened up on Good Friday to reveal the host. [44] With their miserly savings, the Timucua purchased candles and banners for the processions. They even assembled to receive notice of papal decrees.[45]

John E. Worth observes that missions were established in chiefdoms by "strictly voluntary acts" from the caciques, whose consent was mainly obtained with gifts and diplomacy.[46] For in La Florida Christianity was never

---

los adultos que an de ser bautizados (Catechism in Castilian and Timucua in which is contained everything that should be taught to the adults who are to be baptized). This work is comparable to the best produced by the Franciscans in Mexico, who published approximately thirteen bilingual catechisms and doctrines in Nahuatl–Spanish during the sixteenth century. See Luis Resines, *Catecismos americanos del siglo XVI* (Salamanca: Junta de Castilla y León, 1992).

41. López, "Cartas de Fray Baltasar López," 3.

42. López, "Cartas de Fray Baltasar López," 3; Fray Alonso de Jesús and John H. Hann, "1630 Memorial of Fray Alonso de Jesús on Spanish Florida's Missions and Natives," *The Americas* 50, no. 1 (1993): 100.

43. López, "Cartas de Fray Baltasar López"; de Jesús and Hann, "1630 Memorial," 101.

44. John H. Hann, *A History of the Timucua Indians and Missions* (Gainesville: University Press of Florida, 1996), 160–61.

45. López, "Cartas de Fray Baltasar López," 4; Fray Francisco Pareja, "Cartas de Fray Baltasar López, Francisco Pareja y Pedro Ruiz sobre el estado de las conversiones de indios de la Florida," in Hann, *Troika*, 1997, *Three Letters about Missions and Mission Populations from 1602*, https://ufdc.ufl.edu/hann/all, 7.

46. Worth, *The Timucuan Chiefdoms*, 1:40.

imposed as a direct result of military defeat.[47] Alliances with caciques were officially sealed in Saint Augustine with ceremonies in which expensive European gifts were exchanged for obedience to the Spanish governor as representative of the crown.[48] These globalizing gifts were silk shirts, hats, socks from Brussels, cotton shirts from Ruan, doublets from Holland, ribbons and buttons, axes and hoes, and many other items.[49] Understandably, the goods from faraway lands enhanced the political prestige and status of a cacique among his people and in neighboring villages. On most occasions, but not all, the caciques were also baptized when they pledged obedience. No less than the governor and his wife would serve as godparents. The new Crown subjects returned to their villages sometimes in full Spanish attire, with Spanish names and the noble title of "don," displaying their capacity to engage and ally themselves with modernity and the new political power in the land. In exchange, the caciques promised to allow missionaries in their territory and even to persuade their subjects to baptize. Caciques would also provide organized labor to build a church and monastery in large villages where friars would reside.[50] In 1595, Governor Domingo Martínez de Avendaño performed the obedience ritual that Cortés had inaugurated in Tenochtitlan seventy years before to empower the religious. Avendaño accompanied five newly arrived friars and a novice to the missions in the Guale region where they would be stationed. In his flamboyant official

---

47. John H. Hann and Bonnie G. McEwan, *The Apalachee Indians and Mission San Luis* (Gainesville: University Press of Florida, 1998), 31–32.

48. On the Indian fund or "situado" for gift-giving, see Worth, *The Timucuan Chiefdoms*, 1:36–40; and Jerald Milanich, *Laboring in the Fields of the Lord*, 106–9. For a more skeptical view of the Spanish diplomatic strategy, see Amy Bushnell, *Situado, and Sabana: Spain's Support System for the Presidio and Mission Provinces of La Florida*, Anthropological Papers of the Museum of Natural History, 74 (Athens: University of Georgia Press, 1994), 108–10.

49. Francis and Kole, *Murder and Martyrdom in Spanish Florida*, 37.

50. Worth, *The Timucuan Chiefdoms*, 1:40–43. The friars also introduced new agricultural technologies in the villages for the production of corn. The thousands of charred cobs found in the fire pits of recently excavated missions exceeded by many times the number found in all of Florida and Georgia before contact, according to Milanich, *Laboring in the Fields of the Lord*, 146–47. The friars' intention in multiplying the production of corn was not only to improve the quality of life for the Florida Indians. They also sought to supply St. Augustine, and even to export the remaining surplus to Cuba. In addition, the friars brought new animals to the missions, especially chickens and pigs, as well as new fruits and plants such as peaches, watermelons, figs, hazelnuts, and garbanzo beans (Milanich, *Laboring in the Fields of the Lord*, 145).

garb, the governor knelt in front of each friar and kissed his hand. [51] As in Mexico-Tenochtitlan, the Indians from La Florida missions surely picked up immediately that the ceremony was meant to let them know that the friars were fully supported by the Spanish *mico*.[52] On their part, the caciques understood that if they wanted to keep having access to the Spanish luxury goods and foodstuffs that consolidated their authority among the people in the new state of affairs of the land, the chiefs had to guarantee the safety of the friars in their territories.

THE GUALE UPRISING OF 1597

However, missionizing in sixteenth-century La Florida was a precarious, hypersensitive affair that would suffer unexpected setbacks. Written ca. 1619 by the Franciscan Francisco de Oré, *The Account of the Martyrs in the Provinces of La Florida* is one of the most important narratives written about missionary activity in sixteenth-century La Florida. The title focuses on the slaughter of the Jesuits in the Chesapeake Bay rebellion of 1570 mentioned above but especially on the murder of the Franciscans in the second Guale uprising now of 1597. As the title closes up on martyrdom to the exclusion of everything else, Oré foregrounds the deadly consequences of failed intercultural communication as evidence of the ever-present risk of the ultimate sacrifice in the missionary path.

Although the friars as a rule always attempted to preserve indigenous cultural and political practices compatible or indifferent to Christianity,[53] the introduction of Catholicism inevitably entailed a restructuring of indigenous life with new regimes of emotions and beliefs, new agricultural technologies, animals, alien disciplines of the body, and monogamous

---

51. Maynard Geiger, O.F.M. *The Franciscan Conquest of Florida (1573–1618)* (Washington, DC: The Catholic University of America, 1937), 65.

52. There is no record of Governor Avendaño having been called a mico or "principal chief." However, there is documental evidence that Pedro Menéndez de Avilés was referred to by the Guale as *mico Santa María*. Francis and Kole point out that it is significant that Menéndez's title as mico was associated not with territory (namely, St. Augustine or La Florida), but with a supernatural figure or deity, the Virgin Mary. They hypothesize that this may mean that the power of the mico for the Guale rested more on his access to supernatural power than on territorial control (Francis and Kole, *Murder and Martyrdom in Spanish Florida*, 29). If so, by kneeling in front of the Franciscans and kissing their hand, the Guale may have well interpreted that Avendaño, the Spanish principal chief or mico, was performing a direct transfer of supernatural powers to the religious.

53. Milanich, *Laboring in the Fields of the Lord*, 130.

family formations. According to Oré's account, the rebellion started when the resident friar in the village of Tolomato, Father Pedro de la Corpa, warned the Christian heir to the high chiefdom of Guale, don Juan, that "he could not take a second wife. He was rebuked and told to live as a Christian and not as a heathen."[54] Even Oré's paraphrase of Corpa's reprimand seems harsh. One of the seven young Guale Indians that the Spaniards captured after crushing the rebellion declared in 1598 that the cacique "don Juan from Tolomato had ordered the murder because Fray Corpa had punished him for following his native laws and customs."[55] Other youngsters declared that the reasons the friars were killed was because they were "wicked," "belligerent," and "cunning" in keeping the men away from their custom of taking more than one woman as wife.[56] It can be conjectured by the statements that although baptized, the high cacique don Francisco and his son don Juan had not accepted the Christian prohibition of polygamy. When confronted by their refusal, Fray Corpa transgressed Guale protocol and politics. His stern, public reprimand to the heir to the major cacicazgo of the region was perceived as an offense and challenge to mico authority that demanded ritual retribution.[57] For according to Oré, Fray Corpa was not killed on the spot. Rather, a few days later, don Juan and some Guale warriors under his command came back under the cover of night smeared in red paint and with feathers in their head, which meant war.[58] They then clubbed Fray Corpa to death and decapitated him. He had lived among the Guale people for two years and knew their language. Namely, Fray Corpa was not an inexperienced neophyte preacher. We

---

54. Luis Jerónimo Oré, *Account of the Martyrs in the Provinces of La Florida*, 118.

55. Francis and Kole, *Murder and Martyrdom in Spanish Florida*, 108, is a study on the documents generated by the Guale uprising of 1597. On the youngsters' testimony, see especially 101–14

56. Francis and Kole, *Murder and Martyrdom in Spanish Florida*, 103.

57. Maynard Geiger states that Fray Corpa had berated don Juan first privately, then publicly. Moreover, apparently along with Fray Blas Rodríguez, he had attempted to impede don Juan from his hereditary rights as mico of the region (Geiger, *The Franciscan Conquest of Florida*, 88–89). Therefore, the rebellion was not only because of the prohibitions of Christianity against polygamy, but also because of Franciscan interventionism in the politics of the region. Perhaps this is why don Juan felt that all friars in his sphere of influence were challengers of his authority, and therefore had to be eliminated. Worth also thinks that Father Corpa crossed a red line in his interference with chiefly succession on account of the don Juan's polygamy (*The Timucuan Chieftans of Spanish Florida*, 1:114–15).

58. de Oré, *Account of the Martyrs in the Provinces of La Florida*, 118.

will never know if he could have acted with more cultural sensitivity while retaining his missionary integrity and pastoral authority in front of don Juan's people. Be this as it may, the fact is that Fray Corpa miscalculated his power because there is no indication in the records that he was expecting his death.

Don Juan's retribution did not stop with Father Corpa's murder. The slight to Guale authority had been deep. He sent orders to caciques in the region to kill any resident friars in their villages. The Franciscans in the Guale island mission were next.[59] Although the friendly cacique of this mission warned the lay brother Antonio de Badajoz of their impending death, he could not believe that they were in danger and refused to escape. Don Juan's warriors arrived to check that their mico's order had been obeyed. Because the friendly cacique still refused to comply, don Juan's warriors themselves executed the lay brother and Father Friar Miguel de Auñón. Nonetheless, they were able to say mass and to have four hours of deep prayer before their death. Oré adds the possibly fictitious detail that the non-Christian Indian who struck Fray Miguel hung himself a few days later and that such an act of despair "impressed the villagers mightily."[60]

The following victim was Father Blas Rodríguez, who had lived among the Indians of the Guale town of Topiqui for more than ten years. When attacked he asked his executors to allow him to say Mass. This they did and gave him four additional hours to pray and prepare for death. When time was up Father Blas tearfully tried to reason with the Indians he had baptized. He certainly did not want to die and felt deeply hurt that his charges would not stand up for him. He gained forty-eight more hours with his tears and then was executed by a blow that split his skull in two. The fourth friar, Francisco de Avila, escaped death but the Indians subjected him to a humiliating and cruel captivity for ten months until the Spanish governor rescued him. The last friar to be martyred was Fray Francisco de Veráscola. He had gone to St. Augustine to pick up some items for his cell and for his indigenous charges in the mission of Asao in present day Saint-Simon Island, Georgia. Traveling by boat, as soon as

59. This is St. Catherine's Island in Georgia.

60. de Oré, *Account of the Martyrs in the Provinces of La Florida*, 119.

he landed he was killed and then cut up with axes.[61] It is clear that in all the deaths consigned by Oré in his account, none of the friars expected their fate and some even attempted to dissuade their executioners. Fray Corpa also bore responsibility if only because of his likely mismanagement of the admittedly thorny issue of polygamy. Nonetheless, all five friars were represented by Oré as martyrs to his readers if only because they had died in the line of a globalizing apostolic duty that was full of risks, hardships, and the uncertainties of sensitive cultural difference. In the case of Ávila, although he did not die, he endured harsh slavery and constant threats of death.

FRANCISCAN BLOOD BEARS FRUIT

If the first two decades of Franciscan missionization did not yield an impressive harvest of indigenous souls in La Florida, the sacrificial blood shed by the Friars Minor martyrs in its vast, alien lands would bear plentiful fruit in the next century. New friars would be back by 1605 to the southern missions of Guale[62] with an unbending intent to resume their pastoral care of 1,200 Christian Indians and to continue their work with the Timucua in the region of present-day southern Georgia and northern Florida. According to a letter to the king by friars Francisco Pareja and Alonso de Peñaranda in 1607, there were more than 6,000 Christian Indians in Timucua mainland and coastal territories.[63] By 1633, the Franciscans established the first missions in the fertile Apalachee territory to the west of present-day Tallahassee.[64]

By the time Oré wrote his account, the missions in La Florida had become the Franciscan Province of Santa Elena and had taken off to the so-called decades of their golden age. Indeed, the Friars Minor in La Florida performed philological feats comparable to those of their brothers in Mexico a century earlier, although the indigenous convert population never approached half a million even at the height of their missionary effort. Fray Francisco Pareja had produced by 1614 an art or grammar of

---

61. de Oré, *Account of the Martyrs in the Provinces of La Florida*, 129.

62. Milanich, *Laboring in the Fields of the Lord*, 114–15.

63. Quoted in Hahn, *A History of the Timucua Indians and Missions*, 168.

64. John H. Hahn and Bonnie G. McEwan, *The Apalachee Indians and Mission San Luis* (Gainesville: University Press of Florida, 1998), 24.

the Timucua language, three bilingual catechisms, and a bilingual confessional, which ranks among the most extensive and accomplished in the genre compared to those written in Nahuatl.[65] In 1635, Fray Gregorio de Movilla published his translation into Timucua of Cardinal Roberto de Bellarmine's *Doctrina Christiana* of 1597.[66] Commissioned by Pope Clement VIII, Bellarmine composed this text for teaching a standardized Christian doctrine in the Catholic world. The *Doctrina* was translated in all European languages spoken at the time as well as in Arabic, Chinese, Quechua, and Tagalog, among many others. With Movilla's translation, the Timucua language—spoken in the tiny barrier island of San Juan del Puerto in the southern corner of present-day Georgia—rose to stand next to the major languages of the world.

CONCLUSION

The Friars Minor labored hard and steady in Central Mexico and in La Florida during the sixteenth and early seventeenth centuries to globalize the peoples of the New World through the universality of the word of Christ. With the force of their faith and the material accomplishments of their missionary activity, they were major players and forgers of the early modern era at an intercontinental scale. Some could certainly argue that along with the salvific word of Christ came devastation, servitude, and death to millions of Nahuas during the sixteenth century. In the case of La Florida, besides epidemics, the Guale, Timucua, and Appalachee Indians of the prosperous but vulnerable Florida missions of the seventeenth century would eventually be crushed by the hands of Indian enemies allied with and armed by the English colonists. Critics may point out that the friars were accomplices of the destruction—even if unwitting—because

---

65. For a bibliography of Pareja's five Spanish-Timucua works, see Fernando Rodríguez de la Torre, "Francisco Pareja," in *Diccionario bibliográfico de la Real Academia de la Historia*, http://dbe.rah.es/biografias/63916/francisco-pareja and Luis Resines, *Catecismos americanos del siglo XVI*, 178–85.

66. Fray Gregorio Movilla, *Explicacion de la doctrina que compuso el Cardenal Belarmino por mandado del Señor Papa Clemente 8. Traducida en lengua Floridana: por el Padre Fr. Gregorio de Movilla (Explanation of the Doctrine that Cardinal Bellarmine Composed by Order of the Pope Clement 8, Translated in Floridan Language by the Father Fray Gregorio de Movilla)*. A second work by Movilla was also published in Mexico in 1635. It is a short manual in Latin, Spanish, and Timucua for administering the sacraments to the Indians and Spaniards. According to the title of the work, the part in Timucua was a translation not from Spanish, but from Nahuatl.

by brokering Nahua, Timucua, Guale, and Appalachee cultures in the service of Christianity, they facilitated colonization and its intended and unintended consequences of demographic catastrophe and relentless exploitation.

Indeed, the tragic and unexpected turn of events brought about by the early modern binding of the world in which the figure of Christ played such a central, connective role, was disconcerting. It made unreadable the providential outlook that had framed the overwhelming success of the Franciscans in Central Mexico during the sixteenth century and their high hopes in La Florida during the first decades of the seventeenth. Yet, perhaps without the imagination of the Word and the strenuous efforts to spread it, the shock of contact and onslaught of modernity would have been even more painful and morally devastating for the indigenous populations. For there would be no turning back after the apple of connectivity was bitten in 1492. Thus, the sacrificial work of the friars, the virtue of their astounding philological output, the fortitude of their inexhaustible energy, and of the blood of their martyrs not only bound the world but also expiated—at least in some measure—the ever-present limits of fallen human agency. For if only, the truth of the materiality of the friars' very best apostolic labor evidences the scope of their beliefs and of their most deeply felt convictions, beyond whose horizons at the time, it was not possible to see what can be known today.

BIBLIOGRAPHY

Baudot, George. "Amerindian Images and Utopian Project: Motolinía and Millenarian Discourse." In *Amerindian Images and the Legacy of Columbus*, edited by Rene Jara and Nicholas Spadaccini, 375–95. Minnesota: University of Minnesota Press, 1992.

———. *La pugna franciscana por México*. México, DF: Alianza Editorial Mexicana, 1990.

———. *Utopia and History in Mexico: The First Chronicles of Mexican Civilization. 1520–1569*. Translated by Bernard R. Ortiz de Montellano and Thelma Ortiz de Montellano. Niwot: University of Colorado Press, 1995.

Berdan, Frances. "Trauma and Transition in Sixteenth-century Central Mexico." *Proceedings of the British Academy* 81 (1993): 163–95.

Brickhouse, Anna. *The Unsettlement of America: Translation, Interpretation and the Story of Don Juan Velasco, 1560-1945*. New York: Oxford University Press, 2015.

Burkhart, Louise. *Holy Wednesday: A Nahua Drama from Early Colonial Mexico*. Philadelphia: University of Pennsylvania Press, 1996.

Bushnell, Amy. *Situado and Sabana: Spain's Support System for the Presidio and Mission Provinces of La Florida*. Anthropological Papers of the American Museum of Natural History, 74. Athens: University of Georgia Press, 1994.

Carrasco, Davíd. *Quetzalcoatl and the Irony of Empire: Myths and Prophecies in the Aztec Tradition*. Boulder: University Press of Colorado, 2000.

————, and Scott Sessions. *The Daily Life of the Aztecs: People of the Sun and Earth*. Westport, CT: Greenwood Press, 1998.

Coe, Michael D., and Rex Koontx. *Mexico: From the Olmecs to the Aztecs*. New York: Thames and Hudson, 2008.

Díaz Balsera, Viviana. *The Pyramid under the Cross: Franciscan Discourses of Evangelization in Sixteenth Century Mexico*. Tucson: University of Arizona Press, 2005.

————, and Rachel E. May, eds. *La Florida: Five Hundred Years of Hispanic Presence*. Gainesville: University Press of Florida, 2014.

Duverger, Christian. *La conversión de los indios de Nueva España: Con el texto de los Coloquios de los Doce de Bernardino de Sahagún (1564)*. Translated by Maria Dolores de la Peña. México: Fondo de Cultura Económica, 1993.

Francis, J. Michael, and Kathleen M. Kole. 2011. *Murder and Martyrdom in Spanish Florida: Don Juan and the Guale Uprising of 1597*. Anthropological Papers 95. New York: American Museum of Natural History, 2011.

Geiger, Rev. Maynard, O.F.M. *The Franciscan Conquest of Florida (1573-1618)*. Washington, DC: The Catholic University of America, 1937.

Gibson, Charles. *The Aztecs under Spanish Rule: A History of the Indians of the Valley of Mexico, 1519-1810*. Stanford, CA: Stanford University Press, 1964.

Graziano, Frank. *The Millenial New World*. Oxford: Oxford University Press, 1999.

Hann, John H. "1630 Memorial of Fray Alonso de Jesús on Spanish Florida's Missions and Natives." *The Americas* 50, no. 1 (1993): 85–105.

————, and Bonnie G. McEwan. *The Apalachee Indians and Mission San
Luis*. Gainesville: University Press of Florida, 1998.

————. *A History of the Timucua Indians and Missions*. Gainesville: University Press of Florida, 1996.

————. *Troika: Three Letters about Missions and Mission Populations from
1602*. John H. Hann Collection of Colonial Records at the University of Florida, 1997. https://ufdc.ufl.edu/hann/all.

Hermann, Placid, O.F.M. "Introduction and Notes to *St. Francis of Assisi*."
In *Writings and Early Biographies: English Omnibus of the Sources
for the Life of St. Francis*. Edited by Marion A. Habig. London: The
Society for Promoting Christian Knowledge, 1979.

Hoffman, Paul. "Until the Land Was Understood: Spaniards Confront La
Florida, 1500–1600." In *La Florida: Five Hundred Years of Hispanic
Presence*. Edited by Viviana Díaz Balsera and Rachel E. May, 69–82,
Gainesville: University of Florida Press, 2014.

Kobayashi. José María. *La educación como conquista (empresa franciscana
en México)*. México: El Colegio de México, 1974.

Lafaye, Jacques. *Quetzalcoatl and Guadalupe: The Formation of Mexican
National Consciousness, 1531–1813*. Translated by Benjamin Keen.
Chicago: University of Chicago Press, 1987.

Lockhart, James. *The Nahuas after the Conquest: A Social and Cultural History of the Indians of Central Mexico: Sixteenth through Seventeenth
Centuries*. Stanford, CA: Stanford University Press, 1992.

López, Fray Baltasar. "Cartas de Fray Baltasar López, Francisco Pareja
y Pedro Ruiz sobre el estado de las conversiones de indios de la
Florida." In John H. Hann, *Troika: Three Letters about Missions
and Mission Populations from 1602*, 1997, 2–6. https://ufdc.ufl.edu/
hann/all.

Mendieta, Gerónimo. *Historia eclesiástica Indiana*. México, DF: Porrúa,
1870, 1993.

Milanich, Jerald T. *Laboring in the Fields of the Lord: Spanish Missions and
Southeastern Indians*. Washington, DC: Smithsonian Institution
Press, 1999.

Motolinia, Fray Toribio de Benavente. *History of the Indians of New Spain.* Translated by Francis Borgia Steck. Washington DC: Academy of American Franciscan History, 1951.

Movilla, Fray Gregorio. *Explicacion de la doctrina que compuso el Cardenal Belarmino por mandado del Señor Papa Clemente 8. Traducida en lengua Floridana: por el Padre Fr. Gregorio de Movilla.* Mexico: Imprenta de Juan Ruiz, 1635.

———. *Forma breue de administrar los sacramentos a los Indios, y Españoles que viuen entre ellos lo q[ue] estaua en le[n]gua Mexicana traducido en lengua Floridana.* Mexico: Imprenta de Juan Ruiz, 1635.

Nicholson, Henry B. *Topiltzin Quetzalcoatl: The Once and Future Lord of the Toltecs.* Boulder: University Press of Colorado, 2001.

Oré, Luis Jerónimo de. *Account of the Martyrs in the Provinces of La Florida.* Edited and translated by Raquel Chang-Rodríguez and Nancy Vogeley. Albuquerque: University of New Mexico Press, 2017.

Pardo, Osvaldo F. *The Origins of Mexican Catholicism: Nahua Rituals and Christian Sacraments in Sixteenth-Century Mexico.* Ann Arbor: The University of Michigan Press, 2004.

Pareja, Francisco. *Three Letters about Missions and Mission Populations from 1602.* In John H. Hann, *Troika: Three Letters about Missions and Mission Populations from 1602,* 1997. https://ufdc.ufl.edu/hann/all.

———. *Cathecismo en Lengua Castellana y Timuquana, en el cual se contiene lo que se le puede enseñar a los adultos que an de ser bautizados. Compuesto por el P.F. Pareja, Religioso de la Orden del Seraphico P.S. Francisco, Guardián del Convento de la Purissima Concepcion de N. Señora de S. Agustín, y Padre de la Custodia de sancta Elena de la Florida.* México: Viuda de Pedro Balli, 1612.

Phelan, John L. *The Millenial Kingdom of the Franciscans in the New World.* Berkeley: University of California Press, 1970.

Pollnitz, Aysha. "Old Words and the New World: Liberal Education and the Franciscans in New Spain, 1536-1601." *Royal Historical Society (London, England). Transactions of the Royal Historical Society* 27 (2017): 123–52.

Reeves, Marjorie. *Joachim of Fiore and the Prophetic Future.* New York: Harper and Row, 1977.

Resines, Luis. *Catecismos americanos del siglo XVI.* 2 vols. Salamanca: Junta de Castilla y León, 1992.

Ricard, Robert. *La conquista espiritual de México.* Translated by Ángel Garibay K. México: Fondo de Cultura Económica, 1986.

Rodríguez de la Torre, Fernando. "Francisco Pareja." In *Real Academia de la Historia, Diccionario Biográfico Electrónico.* http://dbe.rah.es/biografias/63916/francisco-pareja.

Sahagún, Bernardino de. *Coloquio de los Doce.* In Christian Duverger, *La conversión de los indios de la Nueva España con el texto de los Coloquios de los Doce de Bernardino de Sahagún (1564),* 53–87. México: Fondo de Cultura Económica, 1993.

———. *Historia de las cosas de la Nueva España.* 2 vols. Edited by Josefina García Quintana y Alfredo López Austin. México: Consejo Nacional para la Cultura y las Artes, Alianza Editorial Mexicana, 1989.

Sanders, William T. "The Population of the Central Mexico Symbiotic Region, the Basin of Mexico and the Teotihuacan Valley in the Sixteenth Century." In *The Native Population of the Americas in 1492,* edited by William M. Denevan, 85–150. Madison: University of Wisconsin Press, 1992.

Steck, Francis Borgia. *El primer colegio de América. Santiago de Tlatelolco.* Centro de Estudios Franciscanos, 1944.

Tavárez, David. "Nahua Intellectuals, Franciscan Scholars, and the "Devotio Moderna" in Colonial Mexico. *The Americas* 70, no. 2 (2013): 203–35.

Worth, John E. *The Timucuan Chiefdoms of Spanish Florida.* 2 vols. Gainesville: University of Florida Press, 1998.

16

—

THE INSTITUTIONAL INNER LOGIC OF SIXTEENTH-CENTURY DISCALCED FRANCISCAN MISSIONS

Rady Roldán-Figueroa

The long sixteenth century marked the beginning of the first global age of Catholicism. Catholic missionaries spread around the globe and were active in all continents, laying the foundations of peripheral Roman Catholicism. The adaptation of existing institutional structures as well as the creation of new ones was of critical importance for the global spread of Catholicism during this period. Changes in existing religious orders constituted a significant aspect of the kind of institutional change that occurred in response to the new context. This chapter will examine the missionary trajectory of the Discalced Franciscans, an eremitic branch of Franciscanism that originated in Spain. Their quick institutional and organizational development as well as their geographical reach was quite remarkable.

The spread of Catholic missionaries around the globe in the early modern period was made possible by institutional structures that provided a matrix of coordinated missionary activity. In other words, Catholic missionaries were *organized* for mission. Organizational structures facilitated the recruitment of religious personnel, their formation and training, and the allocation of material resources. The vast majority of Catholic missionaries during the early modern period were regular clergy, or members of religious orders that were organized under a religious rule. The immediate organizational structures of these religious orders were set up in their respective rules. The complexity that religious orders acquired in the early modern period requires a new institutional approach in order to assess not only their religious impact, but also their capacity to respond and shape political and economic developments. Moreover, it also requires that religious orders be viewed as locations for the production of goods and practices of enduring cultural value that transcended their organizational confines.

The Discalced Franciscans were no exception and their important missionary role in the sixteenth century is coming under greater focus. In his book, *Franciscan Spirituality and Mission in New Spain, 1524-1599*, Steven E. Turley deals with some important aspects of the movement's early institutional history.[1] He carefully examines the impact of Franciscan Observant eremitic spirituality upon missionary practice in New Spain for the period spanning from 1524 to 1599. He gives close attention to the Franciscan eremitic movement that emerged in the region of Extremadura in the late fifteenth century and that eventually led to the formation of the province of San Gabriel.[2] He also traces the trajectory of missionaries associated with the movement during the initial stages of colonization of New Spain. He initially posited that the rigors of missionary work among the indigenous people of New Spain would debilitate the eremitic spirituality of the Franciscan friars. As Turley states, "Effective mission work—both in the initial evangelization stage and the later pastoral stage—was ultimately incompatible with eremitic spirituality."[3] Throughout the book he argues that, in fact, missionaries lost their eremitic fervor over time.[4] Turley then compares the spiritual fervor of the first waves of Franciscan missionaries to New Spain with that of the first cohort of Discalced Franciscans that arrived there in 1577.[5]

The Discalced Franciscans not only quickly gained the favor of ecclesiastical authorities in New Spain, but also changed the attitude of Philip II (r. 1556-1598) towards their movement.[6] Since the inception of his reign

---

1. Steven E. Turley, *Franciscan Spirituality and Mission in New Spain, 1524-1599: Conflict Beneath the Sycamore Tree (Luke 19:1-10)* (London and New York: Routledge, 2014).

2. Turley, *Franciscan Spirituality*, 22-23.

3. Turley, *Franciscan Spirituality*, 160.

4. Turley, *Franciscan Spirituality*, 160.

5. Turley, *Franciscan Spirituality*, 163-81.

6. Turley, *Franciscan Spirituality*, 154-58 and 175-78.

in 1556, Philip II intended to implement among the Franciscans the reform program initiated by Cardinal Francisco Jiménez de Cisneros (1436–1517) under Isabella I (r. 1474–1504) and Ferdinand II (r. 1479–1516). The aim of this reform program was to fully dissolve the Conventual Franciscans, which for a time comprised the Discalced Franciscans, among the Observants, uniting in this way both families of Franciscanism under the Observant branch.[7]

How did the Discalced Franciscans avoid dissolution? Turley surmised that there were two reasons why the Discalced Franciscans escaped total demise under Philip II. First, the Discalced Franciscans successfully defended their reforms in Rome, and not only avoided dissolution, but also instead gained a significant degree of autonomy in 1578.[8] Second, the Discalced Franciscans embraced the idea of taking on the Christianization of the Philippines. Indeed, Turley argued that it was their willingness to go as missionaries to the Philippines that helped change Phillip II's religious policy towards the eremitic group.[9]

An ancillary explanation that Turley does not entertain, however, is that under the charismatic leadership of Pedro de Alcántara (1499–1562), the discalced movement experienced a marked level of institutional development. Such changes, in turn, laid the foundation for discalced involvement in missionary work. In fact, Turley misread the figure of Fray Francisco de los Angeles Quiñones (1482–1540) by not recognizing his role as the promoter of recollect houses as an Observant institutional alternative to the more austere discalced eremitism.[10] Standing firmly within the Observant family, Quiñones did not represent the fulfilment of discalced aspirations; Pedro de Alcántara did.[11] His extreme austerity and rigorist approach to

---

7. José García Oro, *Cisneros y la reforma del clero español en tiempo de los Reyes Católicos* (Madrid: Consejo Superior de Investigaciones Científicas, 1971), 173; Juan de Santa María, *Chronica de la Provincia de san Joseph de los descalços de la Orden de los Menores de nuestro Seraphico Padre s. Francisco; y de las provincias, y custodias descalças, que della han salido, y son sus hijas* (Madrid: Imprenta Real, 1615), 58.

8. Turley, *Franciscan Spirituality*, 177.

9. Turley, *Franciscan Spirituality*, 177.

10. Turley, *Franciscan Spirituality*, 24–28.

11. "La mayoría de edad de la Recolección empezó, sin embargo, a partir del año 1523, por el empuje que le dio el Rdmo. P. Francisco Quiñones, Ministro General de toda la Orden, no obstante ser él hijo de la provincia de los Ángeles." Ángel Uribe, "Espiritualidad de la descalcez franciscana," *Archivo Ibero-Americano* 22, nos. 85–86 (1962): 133–61 (136); Fidel de Lejarza,

apostolic poverty earned Alcántara ample recognition among Spanish and Portuguese elites as well as among the leading Catholic reformers in Spain. He either directly founded new houses or participated in the reform of existing ones, leaving an imprint of his spiritual discipline in the charters of some of the movement's most important monasteries and provinces, in particular the Discalced Province of San José.

The corresponding institutional build-up in the middle decades of the sixteenth century allowed the Discalced Franciscans to navigate more efficiently the political landscape of the Spanish Empire, as well as the intricacies of ecclesiastical diplomacy in Rome. This institutional build up was especially important after Alcántara's death as the Observants amplified their efforts to suppress the discalced movement. Moreover, their growing institutional development gave them the organizational capacity to take on missionary work not only in the Philippines, but also in Japan and New Spain.

PEDRO DE ALCÁNTARA AND THE
DISCALCED FRANCISCANS

Also known as the Alcantarines, the discalced movement intended to reform Franciscanism by the adoption of a rigorous form of eremitism.[12] Historians of late-medieval Iberian Franciscanism—including Fidel de Lejarza, José García Oro, and Hipólito Amez Prieto—concur in identifying Fray Pedro de Villacreces (d. 1422), Fray Luis de la Puebla (1453–1495), and Juan de Guadalupe (1450–1505) as forerunners of the Discalced Franciscans.[13]

"Orígenes de la Descalcez Franciscana," *Archivo Ibero-Americano* 22, nos. 85–86 (1962): 15–131 (75); J. García Oro, "Los frailes del Santo Evangelio. El eremitismo franciscano en Extremadura," *Edad de Oro* 8 (1989): 77–96 (94–96); Rafael Sanz Valdivieso, ed., *Vida y escritos de san Pedro de Alcántara*, Místicos franciscanos españoles 1 (Madrid: Biblioteca de Autores Cristianos, 1996), 193.

12. Hipólito Barriguín Fernández, ed., *Registro y libro de memoria de la santa provincia de los padres descalzos de San Francisco, 1594–1835*, vol. 1, *Liceo franciscano* (second series) 65, nos. 202–4 (2015): 9.

13. Lejarza, "Orígenes," (1962); García Oro, "Los frailes del Santo Evangelio" (1989); Hipólito Amez Prieto, "Los Descalzos de San Francisco en Extremadura, desde Fray Juan de Guadalupe hasta fray Pedro de Alcántara," in *San Pedro de Alcántara. Hombre universal: Congreso de Guadalupe, 1997*, ed. Francisco Sebastián García Rodríguez (Guadalupe, Cáceres: Ediciones Guadalupe, 1998), 113–222; José García Oro, "San Pedro de Alcántara," in *Real Academia de la Historia, Diccionario Biográfico electrónico*, http://dbe.rah.es/biografias/8229/san-pedro-de-alcantara.

Fray Juan de la Puebla, a former Hieronymite monk-turned Franciscan, was the founder of the custody of Nuestra Señora de los Ángeles.[14] Fray Juan de Guadalupe was in turn directly inspired by De la Puebla's strict observance. He cooperated with De la Puebla between 1491 and 1495.[15] He established a series of hermit houses in the region of Extremadura and parts of Portugal. In 1501, these foundations were gathered in the newly established Custody of the Holy Gospel, or Santo Evangelio.[16] With time, the Custody of Santo Evangelio became known as Custody of San Gabriel and was elevated to the rank of province in 1519; this was confirmed by Pope Leo X in 1520.[17] In this way the province of San Gabriel became the first province of the discalced movement in Spain. Fray Juan Pascual (d. 1553) continued the work of Juan de la Puebla and Juan de Guadalupe. He founded new houses in the region of Galicia between 1541 and 1551.

The origins of the movement were marked by conflict, as the leadership of the Observant branch of Spanish Franciscanism was consistently opposed to their reform efforts. Tension between Discalced and Observant Franciscans colored the historiography of the movement. For instance, in the early decades of the seventeenth century, the chronicler of the Province of San José, Fray Juan de Santa María, still narrated with bitterness the "persecution" that the Observants made his discalced brethren endure half a century earlier. "The devil found in them," stated the resentful Juan de Santa María about the Observants, "occasion to convince them of this purpose, disguised under the shadow of better government and greater perfection."[18] While his narrative accentuated differences between Observants and Discalced Franciscans, he also emphasized parallels between the

---

14. On Fray Juan de la Puebla see Lejarza, "Orígenes," 16–33; on the founding of the custody of Nuestra Señora de los Ángeles see Lejarza, "Orígenes," 24; see discussion of Puebla's spiritual practices in Turley, *Franciscan Spirituality*, 16–17; Barriguín Fernández, ed., *Registro y libro*, 10; Ángela Atienza López, *Tiempos de conventos: una historia social de las fundaciones en la España moderna* (Madrid: Marcial Pons, Ediciones de Historia; La Rioja: Universidad de La Rioja, 2008), 90–91.

15. On Fray Juan de Guadalupe see Lejarza, "Orígenes," 34–95.

16. Lejarza, "Orígenes," 63; Atienza López, *Tiempos de conventos*, 91.

17. Sanz Valdivieso, *Vida y escritos*, lxx; García Oro, "Los frailes del Santo Evangelio," 79 and 82, note 20; Turley, *Franciscan Spirituality*, 20–23.

18. Juan de Santa María, *Chronica de la provincia de san Ioseph de los Descalços de la Orden de los Menores de nuestro seraphico padre s. Francisco; y de las provincias, y custodias descalças, que della han salido, y son sus hijas, parte primera* (Madrid: Imprenta Real, 1615), 302.

Discalced and Capuchins. He considered Franciscans to be divided into three "forms of life," so "different that they each seem a different religion." These "ways of life" were the Observants, Conventuals, and "Capuchins and Discalced."[19]

Moreover, historiographical controversy over the movement's origins persisted long after tensions between Discalced and Observant Franciscans had subsided. The eighteenth-century Discalced chronicler, Marcos de Alcalá, sustained that Pedro de Alcántara was the "chief, only, and singular founder of the strictest discalced reform" of the Franciscans.[20] He argued that Pedro de Alcántara was the sole founder of the Discalced Franciscans, and that the discalced reform did not go back to Guadalupe. Alcalá first advanced this claim in 1736, in his *Chronica de la santa provincia de San Joseph*.[21] Fray Juan de San Antonio, chronicler of the discalced Province of San Pablo, responded to Alcalá's assertion in 1737. He argued that the "foundational primacy" ("primacía fundamental") of the discalced movement belonged to Fray Juan de Guadalupe.[22]

The debate was neither spurious nor trivial; a conclusion that could be drawn from the fact that both authors belonged to the discalced branch. However, who should be regarded as the founder of the discalced movement ought to be treated as a legitimate historical question, even if one that cannot be fully explored in this chapter. After all, there was a significant gap between Guadalupe's death in 1505 and the time when Alcántara became the official leader of the movement as Commissary General of the Reformed Conventuals in 1559. Moreover, the discalced movement experienced significant growth after the elevation in 1561 of the Custody of San José to the rank of province under Alcántara's leadership. Lastly, but more importantly, Alcántara responded with a remarkable degree of success to

---

19. Juan de Santa María, *Chronica*, 22.

20. Marcos de Alcalá, "Prologo al lector," in *S. Pedro de Alcántara defendido contra los opositores de sus glorias* (Madrid: Imprenta y librería de Manuel Fernández [ca. 1739]), no pagination.

21. Marcos de Alcalá, *Chronica de la santa provincia de San Joseph: Vida portentosa del penitente admirable, y contemplativo altissimo san Pedro de Alcántara, fundador de toda la descalcez seraphica, redemptor de la observancia mas estrecha de la regla de nuestro gran padre san Francisco* (Madrid: Imprenta de Manuel Fernández, 1736).

22. Juan de San Antonio, *Primacía fundamental del v. padre fray Juan de Guadalupe, vindicada por el R. P. fray Juan de San Antonio (Salmantino)* (Madrid: Imprenta de la Causa de la V. M. de Agreda, 1737).

Observant opposition. Indeed, by the time of his death in 1562, Alcántara had overseen a significant level of institutional buildup that gave organizational consistency to the movement and cemented a stronger sense of identity among the discalced friars. The provincial statutes that he crafted for the Province of San Gabriel in 1540 and for the Province of San José in 1561 (year of the "short text"), provided the movement with internal coherence around a complex of spiritual practices that were inspired by a radical ideal of apostolic poverty. Together, these elements allowed the Discalced Franciscans to avoid dissolution after Alcántara's death. In this sense, Pedro de Alcántara laid the foundations of the sixteenth and seventeenth century history of the movement.

Baptized as Juan de Sanabria, he later adopted the name of Pedro de Alcántara after the town of his birth in the region of Caceres.[23] He studied in Salamanca from 1511 to 1515. He became a Franciscan in 1516, after completing his novitiate at the Convent of Santa María de los Majaretes, at the time part of the Custody of Santo Evangelio.[24] He was ordained to the priesthood in 1524, and practiced a form of extreme eremitism and rigorous observance of apostolic poverty.[25] In 1537, he went to Portugal at the behest of King John III (r. 1521–1557), where his reform program gained support among segments of the nobility.[26] He returned to Portugal in 1542, after serving as provincial of San Gabriel since 1538.[27] The occasion for his second visit to Portugal came about when João de Lencastre, first Duke of Aveiro (d. 1571), asked the Minister General, Fray Vicente Lunel (1480–1549; Minister General 1535–1541), to accept his offer of land for the establishment of a hermitage.[28] In Portugal he cofounded with Fray Martín de Santa María

---

23. I am following Sanz Valdivieso, "Cronología de san Pedro de Alcántara y de otros acontecimientos franciscanos," in Vida y escritos, lxix–lxxvii; Arcángel Barrado Manzano, Vida de san Pedro de Alcántara, in Vida y escritos de san Pedro de Alcántara, ed. Rafael Sanz Valdivieso (Madrid: Biblioteca de Autores Cristianos, 1996), 9.

24. Barrado Manzano, Vida de san Pedro, 23.

25. Barrado Manzano, Vida de san Pedro, 27.

26. Sanz Valdivieso, "Cronología," lxxii; Arcángel Barrado Manzano, "San Pedro de Alcántara en las provincias de san Gabriel, la Arrábida y san José," Archivo Ibero-Americano 22, nos. 85–86 (1962): 423–561 (487); Barrado Manzano, Vida de san Pedro, 39.

27. Barrado Manzano, "San Pedro de Alcántara," 476; Sanz Valdivieso, "Cronología," lxxii–lxxiii; Barrado Manzano, Vida de san Pedro, 45–54.

28. Barrado Manzano, "San Pedro de Alcántara," 473–75.

the Custody of the Arrábida; the statutes that he wrote for the Province of San Gabriel served as a model for the new custody.[29]

Alcántara's growing network of relations proved to be beneficial in the 1540s as he continued to gain notoriety for his asceticism and as he sought to consolidate the discalced reform program. He cultivated an epistolary relationship with members of the Portuguese court. In 1540, both King John III and the queen, Catherine of Austria (r. 1557–1562), wrote letters assuring him of their patronage.[30] He remained involved in the affairs of the Custody—and later Province—of Arrábida years after he returned to Spain. In fact, in the late 1540s he made common cause with Infante Luís of Portugal, Duke of Beja (1506–1555), in the defense of his discalced brethren against Observant efforts to change their spiritual regiment. Alcántara had established a close relationship with Francisco de Borja (1510–1572), at the time Viceroy of Cataluña and future third Superior General of the Society of Jesus, as early as 1541.[31] Drawing on this relationship, Alcántara enlisted Borja's support and influence with the pope in this matter.[32] In addition to his correspondence with Infante Luís of Portugal, Alcántara also exchanged letters with other members of the Portuguese court including Francisco de Portugal, third Count of Vimioso (d. 1582), Isabel of Braganza, Duchess of Guimarães (d. 1576), and María of Portugal, Duchess of Viseu (1521–1577).[33]

---

29. Barrado Manzano, "San Pedro de Alcántara," 476–77.

30. John III of Portugal, "Carta del Rey de Portugal Don Juan II a Fr. Pedro de Alcántara," Lisbon, October 29, 1540, in Barrado Manzano, "San Pedro de Alcántara," 551; Catherine of Austria, Queen of Portugal, "Carta de la Reina de Portugal Doña Catalina a Fr. Pedro de Alcántara," Lisbon, October 29, 1540, in Barrado Manzano, "San Pedro de Alcántara," 552.

31. Sanz Valdivieso, "Cronología," lxxii; Barrado Manzano, Vida de san Pedro, 43.

32. Barrado Manzano, "San Pedro de Alcántara," 481; Francisco de Borja, "Sancto Petro de Alcantara," February 13, 1549, in Sanctus Franciscus Borgia Quartus Gandiae Dux et Societatis Jesu Praepositus Generalis Tertius, vol. 3 (Madrid: Typis Gabrielis Lopez del Horno, 1908), 35-36

33. In order of appearance, "Carta del Infante de Portugal Don Luis a san Pedro de Alcántara," Almerín, 28 November 1551, in Barrado Manzano, "San Pedro de Alcántara," 557; "Carta del Conde de Vimioso a san Pedro de Alcántara," Santarén, September 20, 1551, in Barrado Manzano, "San Pedro de Alcántara," 553-54; "Carta del Conde de Vimioso a san Pedro de Alcántara," 28 November 1551, in Barrado Manzano, "San Pedro de Alcántara," 558; "Carta de la Infanta de Portugal Dña: Isabel a san Pedro de Alcántara," Almerín, 1551 [?], in Barrado Manzano, "San Pedro de Alcántara," 555-56; "Carta de la Infanta de Portugal Doña Isabel a san Pedro de Alcántara," in Barrado Manzano, "San Pedro de Alcántara," 556; "Carta de la Infanta Doña María a san Pedro de Alcántara," September 21, 1552 (?), in Barrado Manzano, "San Pedro de Alcántara," 558-59; "Carta de la Infanta Doña María a san Pedro de Alcántara," Lisbon, February 2, 1553, in Barrado Manzano, "San Pedro de Alcántara," 559. In addition, see

In the midst of his many accomplishments, Alcántara remained a hermit at heart. In several occasions throughout the decade of the 1550s, he withdrew from public life in order to live as a hermit.[34] His reputation for holiness continued to grow. Indeed, the Emperor Charles V (r. 1519–1558) called him to his retreat at the Monastery of Yuste as he neared the end of his life.[35] In 1559, Alcántara became General Commissary of the Reformed Conventuals in Spain.[36] The previous year he founded the custody of San José, which was elevated to a province in 1561.[37] The province of San José became the center of the Discalced Franciscan movement as it spread around the globe.

THE ORGANIZATIONAL INNER LOGIC OF DISCALCED FRANCISCAN MISSIONS

The Franciscan ideal of apostolic poverty governed the organizational inner logic of Alcantarine missionary work. The central aspiration of the Discalced Franciscans was to restore the Order to the primitive rule of St. Francis as a condition for the perfect emulation of their patron saint. In this regard, Alcántara's charismatic figure served to kindle the apostolic passion of his Franciscan confreres. Alcántara modeled himself after St. Francis. His austerity and harsh discipline were expressions of his vehement desire to reach apostolic perfection. He set in this way a pattern of extreme austerity that became emblematic of the ideals of masculine holiness of the Catholic Reformation in Spain.

Juan de Santa María, Alcántara's biographer, noted that for Alcántara, a friar's poverty "ought to be poor and laborious."[38] He would not allow

---

his own letters to Isabel of Braganza, Duchess of Guimarães, and María of Portugal, Duchess of Viseu, in Sanz Valdivieso, *Vida y escritos*, 374–78.

34. Barrado Manzano, *Vida de san Pedro*, 65–73.

35. Sanz Valdivieso, "Cronología," lxxv; Barrado Manzano, *Vida de san Pedro*, 76.

36. Barrado Manzano has revised the traditional dating of Alcántara's appointment as General Commissary of the Reformed Conventuals in Spain. While previously it was believed to have occurred in 1558, Barrado Manzano has convincingly argued that it occurred in 1559. Barrado Manzano, *Vida de san Pedro*, 92–94.

37. M. de Castro, "Alcántara, Pedro de," in *Diccionario de historia eclesiástica de España*, ed. Quintín Aldea Vaquero et al., vol. 1 (Madrid: Instituto Enrique Flores, Consejo Superior de Investigaciones Científicas, 1972), 34; Atienza López, *Tiempos de conventos*, 91.

38. Juan de Santa María, *Chronica*, 95; Alcántara was not a prolific writer, but a summary of his spirituality can be found in his *Tratado de la oración*; see Pedro de Alcántara, *Tratado de*

friars to have in their cells anything that could be a distraction, not even "relics or images, contrary to the opinion of others."[39] Santa María remarked that while "pious painting moves the affections and awakens devotion," it is nevertheless contrary to discalced discipline. Sacred paintings, Santa María sustained, also awaken "curiosity, which is very contrary to the purity of this religion."[40] Part of Alcántara's rigid discipline was absolute abstention from consuming meat and drinking wine.[41]

Alcántara's charismatic influence radiated beyond Franciscanism. He gave his support to Teresa de Jesús (1515–1582) as she advanced the discalced principles of extreme poverty among the Carmelites. Teresa de Jesús described some of his rigorous practices, which included self-inflicted depravation of sleep and food. He would sleep for one and a half hours in a chair, "resting his head against a piece of wood hanging from the wall."[42] Sometimes he would go eight days without eating and more commonly he would eat every third day.[43] According to Teresa de Jesús, Alcántara had a "great love for poverty" because he assiduously kept it for many years. Consequently, he knew very well the "wealth" that was found in poverty. "He helped me greatly," she wrote, "and commanded me not to give up on my intentions."[44] In fact, in a letter of April 14, 1562, he encouraged her to proceed to establish new convents without endowments ("rentas").[45] Following his advice, she decided to do away with rents and to embrace institutional poverty.

The great struggle of the Discalced Franciscans in the early part of the sixteenth century was to give enduring institutional form to their reform program in face of the great opposition of the Observants and the Spanish monarchy. Thus, the foundation of new hermitages, their gathering in new custodies, and the establishment of new provinces represented

la oración y meditación, ed. Raquel E. López Ruano (Madrid: Biblioteca de Autores Cristianos, 2012).

39. Juan de Santa María, *Chronica*, 95.

40. Juan de Santa María, *Chronica*, 96.

41. Juan de Santa María, *Chronica*, 96.

42. Teresa de Jesús, *Libro de la vida*, in *Obras completas: edición manual*, ed. Efrén de la Madre de Dios and Otger Steggink (Madrid: Biblioteca de Autores Cristianos, 2006), 147 [27,17].

43. Teresa de Jesús, *Libro de la vida*, 147 [27,17].

44. Teresa de Jesús, *Libro de la vida*, 191 [35,5].

45. Juan de Santa María, *Chronica*, 98–99; Sanz Valdivieso, *Vida y escritos*, 379–81.

decisive landmarks signaling their progress. In turn, provincial statutes gave expression to their guiding aspirations. Juan de Guadalupe drafted the first rules of the Custody of Santo Evangelio in 1501. Pedro de Alcántara, on the other hand, drew up the provincial statutes of San Gabriel of 1540, as well as the 1561 and 1562 versions of the statutes of the Province of San José.[46] Alcántara himself used the statutes of the Province of San José to institutionalized his views on apostolic poverty. The statutes of the Province of San José differed from those of the Province of San Gabriel (1540) in important ways. In fact, the 1562 version of the statutes of the Province of San José had a greater resemblance to those of the Custody of Santo Evangelio of 1501.

The statutes of the Custody of Santo Evangelio summarized the discalced reform program in seven articles. A leading principle of the statutes was the assertion of apostolic poverty by means of visible claustral austerity. Indeed, the opening article stipulated that future houses and oratories in the custody be "small buildings" made of "boorish materials" ("materiales toscos"). According to the rule, discalced friars should construct their sacred spaces just like "the poor of the world" ("los pobres del siglo") build their own homes.[47] Through their claustral austerity, they fashioned a primitive discalced "architecture" that did away with the mundane vanity associated with worldly wealth. In this way, their "holy poverty and humility" would shine forth from their houses and oratories.[48]

The discalced rule of the Custody of Santo Evangelio prescribed a liturgical esthetic of simplicity. In the second article, the discalced rule instructed that vessels neither of gold nor silver be accepted for the service of the altar. Only a small silver box, or pyx, could be used to keep the consecrated host. In addition, the altar could be provided with a small vessel

---

46. Barrado Manzano published the statutes of Santo Evangelio (1501), San Gabriel (1540), and San José (1562). He described the latter as published in 1561. However, Sanz Valdivieso published the 1561 and 1562 versions of the statutes of San José, clearly showing that the version that Barrado Manzano published in 1962 was in fact that of 1562 and not of 1561. Certainly, Barrado Manzano acknowledged in 1962 that the statutes he published could have been adopted in 1562. Barrado Manzano, "San Pedro de Alcántara," 531–39; Sanz Valdivieso, *Vida y escritos*, 391–407.

47. "Ordenaciones Provinciales del Santo Evangelio," Article 1, Barrado Manzano, "San Pedro de Alcántara," 532.

48. "Ordenaciones Provinciales del Santo Evangelio," Article 1, Barrado Manzano, "San Pedro de Alcántara," 532.

for the oil of extreme unction and two or three small unadorned calices of silver. The article proscribed the use of silk, requiring instead the use of wool or common cloth without embroidery.[49]

Discalced Franciscans intended to do away with the corrupting influence of material wealth. Thus, the third article prohibited that pecuniary alms be accepted, not even for the more urgent needs that may arise. Instead, only alms in kind, such as bread, fish, and oil could be accepted. Alms in kind could not be stored or hoarded, with the exception of oil of which there should be a sufficient amount to last one or two months.[50] Friars were instructed not to accept remuneration for masses, and to preach their sermons without taking into consideration any "temporal interests."[51]

Discalced dietary restrictions were rigorous and they constituted an important component of their regular discipline. Fish and meat were for the exclusive consumption of the elderly and sick. Everyone else was instructed to be satisfied by consuming "herbs and dried pork" ("yervas y tocino") in days in which the eating of meat was allowed, while on days of fasting and abstinence they could eat "legumes, fruits, and sardines." Drinking of wine was prohibited and only permitted in rare situations in which it was necessary for health reasons, and only after properly approved by the superior of the custody. Lastly, there would be a communal fast every Wednesday and Saturday throughout the year in addition to Fridays and Lent, which were a common observance.[52]

Discalced aesthetics of apostolic poverty were not peripheral or incidental. Dress was another prominent concern for the Discalced Franciscans, and probably the most visible way of expressing their renunciation of the world and embrace of abject poverty. The friars of the Custody of Santo Evangelio were instructed to use "patched," "humble sackcloth" ("sayal grosero") as per the instructions of St. Francis. Moreover, with the exception

---

49. "Ordenaciones Provinciales del Santo Evangelio," Article 2, Barrado Manzano, "San Pedro de Alcántara," 533.

50. "Ordenaciones Provinciales del Santo Evangelio," Article 3, Barrado Manzano, "San Pedro de Alcántara," 534.

51. "Ordenaciones Provinciales del Santo Evangelio," Article 5, Barrado Manzano, "San Pedro de Alcántara," 536.

52. "Ordenaciones Provinciales del Santo Evangelio," Article 4, Barrado Manzano, "San Pedro de Alcántara," 535.

of the sick, all friars should be discalced or barefoot ("pies por tierra"). Those who needed an exception could use open sandals, without heels.[53]

Only in the last article did the statutes of the Custody of Santo Evangelio deal with the divine office. The divine office should be observed night and day. All should be standing, not sitting, with reverence and devotion. If the divine office was song, it should be in plain and low tone. There should be two and a half hours of mental, silent prayer for the entire community every day. Self-flagellation ("disciplina") was to take place every day of advent and lent, with the exception of Sundays. The practice should also be observed on Mondays, Wednesdays, and Fridays during the year, including vigils and vespers of the leading holy days.[54]

The statutes of the Province of San Gabriel (1540) diverged significantly from those of the Custody of Santo Evangelio, especially when the continuity between these two ecclesial entities is taken into consideration. In eleven articles, the new constitutions showed an increased concern with the proper observance of the divine office. In contrast to the status of the Custody of Santo Evangelio, those of the newly created province opened up with the first article dedicated to the suitable implementation of the divine office. For instance, singing the divine office was proscribed.[55] The second article required that the Office of Our Lady be done every day after the daily office, and that the Office of the Dead be said daily after giving grace. In addition to other prescribed structured prayers, it instructed that the Sermon on the Mount be read at the table every Saturday.[56] Moreover, it bade a mass for the Virgin with commemoration of the angels and for St. Francis.[57] The new statutes gave greater structure to the practice of the "discipline" by clearly identifying the accompanying prayers.[58] Time

---

53. "Ordenaciones Provinciales del Santo Evangelio," Article 6, Barrado Manzano, "San Pedro de Alcántara," 536.

54. "Ordenaciones Provinciales del Santo Evangelio," Article 7, in Barrado Manzano, "San Pedro de Alcántara; Uribe, "Espiritualidad," 159–60.

55. "Ordenaciones Provinciales de San Gabriel," Article 1, Barrado Manzano, "San Pedro de Alcántara," 532.

56. "Ordenaciones Provinciales de San Gabriel," Article 2, Barrado Manzano, "San Pedro de Alcántara," 533.

57. "Ordenaciones Provinciales de San Gabriel," Article 3, Barrado Manzano, "San Pedro de Alcántara," 534; Barrado Manzano, Vida de san Pedro, 42.

58. "Ordenaciones Provinciales de San Gabriel," Article 4, Barrado Manzano, "San Pedro de Alcántara," 535; Uribe, "Espiritualidad," 159–60.

was again allotted for mental prayer, but a new provision was made for designated times of silence.[59]

Certainly, the new rubrics represented an early stage in Alcántara's formation as an ascetic reformer. Those provisions related to apostolic poverty, which were the majority in the statutes of the Custody of Santo Evangelio, were now relegated to the closing articles. Moreover, the number of these provisions was significantly reduced from six to three. Provisions related to the austerity of diet and dress remained. However, all provisions related to cloistral austerity and architectural simplicity were gone. Similarly, provisions related to liturgical modesty were eliminated and there was no mention of the former rejection of pecuniary alms.

Scholars of Discalced Franciscanism have remained oblivious to the just cited changes in the statutes of the Province of San Gabriel. However, these changes were indicative of the institutional trajectory of the province. Moreover, they help us understand the importance of the Province of San José in the history of the discalced movement. In the 1561 and 1562 versions of the statutes of the Province of San José, Alcántara took the opportunity to redefine the direction of the movement. He was now in the position to identify the movement's marks of distinctiveness as well as institutional priorities.

The statutes of the Province of San José combined at least three layers of ideational materials in the final autograph version of 1562. First, the statutes incorporated some provisions related to the divine office, preserving in this way the characteristic emphasis of the Province of San Gabriel.[60] Second, the new statutes returned to the priorities, and even language, that Fray Juan de Guadalupe codified in the statutes of the Custody of Santo Evangelio. For instance, the statutes once more specified that friars were required to wear "humble sackcloth" ("sayal").[61] The prohibition of vessels of gold and silver as well as the banning of the use of silk for ornaments of the sacristy was restored; although this time vessels with a "golden interior"

---

59. "Ordenaciones Provinciales de San Gabriel," Article 5, Barrado Manzano, "San Pedro de Alcántara," 536; "Ordenaciones Provinciales de San Gabriel," Article 6, Barrado Manzano, "San Pedro de Alcántara," 536.

60. See for instance Articles 3–5, Sanz Valdivieso, *Vida y escritos*, 402.

61. Article 10, Sanz Valdivieso, *Vida y escritos*, 403.

were allowed.[62] Even the claustral austerity that was so paramount to the Custody of San Gabriel was recovered.

The new statutes of the Province of San José also incorporated a third layer of ideational material. In fact, several provisions reflected and captured Alcántara's own imprint on the destinies of the discalced movement. The constitutions required that no friar could claim any kind of ecclesiastical exemptions.[63] His chief emphasis was the recovery of apostolic poverty. For that purpose, the new statutes returned to the rejection of "pecuniary alms" ("limosna pecuniaria"), or any other kind of alms, in exchange of masses.[64] Furthermore, an innovation of the statutes was the explicit elimination of the office of syndic. The constitutions indicated that none of the houses of the province should have a syndic, or "any other designated person who receives pecuniary alms."[65]

He also concluded that claustral austerity was not sufficient. For sure, the new statutes not only recovered, but also intensify the theme of claustral austerity. The constitutions now barred the use of "hewed stones" ("cantería labradas") and required the use of rustic timber ("no labrada a cepillo").[66] The physical dimensions of structures such as houses, oratories, and churches were enunciated in very specific detail in order to ensure that they were built in "conformity with holy poverty."[67] Monastic complexes were envisioned to include small and independent hermitages.[68]

However, Alcántara reminded his confreres of their Franciscan vocation. Citing St. Francis's *Testament*, he summoned them to "always be guests" in their houses and temples, "as pilgrims and strangers."[69] In order to accomplish this, Alcántara went on to institutionalize a form of claustral renunciation, which was an expression of Franciscan itinerancy. He instructed that "no house, from here on, be accepted without a patron." In the 1561 version, the stipulation went on to state that the patron could

---

62. Article 14, Sanz Valdivieso, *Vida y escritos*, 404.
63. Articles 1 and 2, Sanz Valdivieso, *Vida y escritos*, 401–2.
64. Article 15, Sanz Valdivieso, *Vida y escritos*, 405.
65. Ibid.
66. Article 18, Sanz Valdivieso, *Vida y escritos*, 405.
67. Article 18, Sanz Valdivieso, *Vida y escritos*, 405–6.
68. Article 19, Sanz Valdivieso, *Vida y escritos*, 406–7.
69. Article 18, Sanz Valdivieso, *Vida y escritos*, 405.

not "relinquish" the patronage in favor of the pope, but that instead the patron would continue to own the property with the authority to "throw out the friars."[70] The 1562 version did not include this provision. However, it included a ceremony—also stipulated in 1561—by which the friars every year would return the "keys" to the patron, symbolizing their condition of "guests," "pilgrims," and "strangers." Furthermore, every year friars were expected to bring the keys to the patron giving thanks because the patron has "allowed them to reside for a year in the house, begging by the love of God, if it is pleasing, to allow them to reside there for another year."[71]

THE MISSIONARY REACH OF THE DISCALCED FRANCISCANS

In 1563, shortly after Alcántara's death, Pope Pius IV (r. 1559-1565) removed the Discalced Franciscans from the tutelage of the Conventuals in order to place them under the authority of the General of the Observants.[72] By 1579, the Discalced Franciscans had gained complete autonomy within the Observant family.[73] The institutional development of the Alcantarines reached a climatic point in the seventeenth century. In 1622, Pope Gregory XV created the office of the General Vicar of the Discalced who was to respond directly to the pope. Pope Urban VIII (r. 1623-1644), however, annulled the office in 1624.[74]

One of the most distinguished aspects of the history of the Discalced Franciscans was their missionary reach. The movement spread very quickly, acquiring transnational dimensions by the end of the seventeenth century. In fact, in 1682 the *novohispano* chronicler, Baltasar de Medina, listed a total of sixteen provinces. Among those he catalogued were the provinces of San Gabriel in Extremadura, San José in Castilla la Nueva, San Juan Bautista in Valencia, San Pablo in Castilla la Vieja, San Diego in

70. Article 9 (1561), Sanz Valdivieso, *Vida y escritos*, 399-400.

71. Article 20, Sanz Valdivieso, *Vida y escritos*, 407.

72. Sanz Valdivieso, "Cronología," lxxiv.

73. Barriguín Fernández, *Registro y libro*, 12; García Oro, "San Pedro de Alcántara."

74. Baltasar de Medina, *Chronica de la santa provincial de san Diego de Mexico, de religiosos descalços de N.S.P.S. Francisco en la Nueva-España: Vidas de ilustres, y venerables varones, que la han edificado con excelentes virtudes* (Mexico: Juan de Ribera, impressor, y mercader de libros, 1682), 7r-7v.

Andalucía, San Antonio in Portugal, San Gregorio in the Philippines, San Diego in New Spain, and San Antonio in Brazil.[75]

Founded in 1586, the province of San Gregorio was the first overseas province of the discalced movement. Fray Antonio de San Gregorio, a lay Franciscan brother who was a missionary in Peru, traveled in 1575 from Lima to Madrid to request Philip II to send missionaries to the Islands of Solomon.[76] On his way, he stopped in the newly established Monastery of San Bernardino of the Discalced Franciscans. Founded in 1570, the monastery was meant to represent the Discalced Franciscans in Madrid.[77] Indeed, the monastery's patron was Philip II's accountant, Francisco de Garnica. The king instead authorized Fray Gregorio to organize a mission to the Philippines.[78] Manila had just been conquered under the leadership of Miguel López de Legazpi (1502–1572). Fray Gregorio organized the mission, and in 1576 set sail with twenty other missionaries to the Philippines by way of Veracruz and Acapulco. A decade later, in 1586, Pope Sixtus V (r. 1585–1590) promoted the custody of San Gregorio Magno to the rank of province and authorized the new province to erect convents and churches throughout the East, including China.[79] In this way the Province of San Gregorio became the center of discalced missionary activity in the Philippines, Southeast Asia, and even New Spain.

Particularly significant was the administrative relationship that was developed between the province of San Gregorio in the Philippines and the Discalced Franciscans of New Spain. The Franciscan presence in modern-day Mexico dates to 1524, with the arrival of a missionary group of twelve under the leadership of Fray Martín de Valencia. The first Franciscans in New Spain became known to posterity as the "Twelve Apostles." The first Franciscans were Observants and their success soon

---

75. Medina, *Chronica*, 7.

76. Juan de Santa María, *Chronica*, 383–84; Marccelo de Ribadeneira, *Historia de las islas del Archipiélago Filipino y reinos de la Gran China, Tartaria, Cochinchina, Malaca, Siam, Cambodge y Japón* (Madrid: La Editorial Católica, 1947), 35–37.

77. Paloma Vázquez Valdivia and Carmen Soriano Triguero, "El Convento de San Bernardino de Madrid de franciscanos descalzos," *Archivo Ibero-Americano* 61, nos. 238–239 (2001): 251–72.

78. Ribadeneira, *Historia*, 35–37.

79. Ribadeneira, *Historia*, 92–96.

lead to the creation of the province of Santo Evangelio of New Spain. The Discalced Franciscans, however, arrived later in the sixteenth century.

In fact, in 1580 Discalced Franciscans on their way to Manila from Spain founded their first discalced convent in New Spain. The custody of San Diego de Mexico was part of the province of San Gregorio for nearly two decades, until, on September 16, 1599, Pope Urban VIII created the new province of San Diego de Mexico, with Fray Gabriel Baptista as provincial.[80] By 1682 the province of San Diego had a total of fourteen convents, namely the Ermita de San Cosme, México (1576–1591), and the convents of San Diego, México (1591), Santa María de los Ángeles, Huitzilopochco (Churubusco, 1591), Santa Bárbara, Puebla (1591), San Ildefonso, Oaxaca (1592), San Bernardino, Taxco (1595), San Francisco, Pachuca (1596), San Antonio de Padua, Zultepec (1599), Nuestra Señora de Guía, Acapulco (1607), San Antonio de Padua, Querétaro (1613), Santa María Magdalena, San Martín Texmelucan (1615), San José, Cuautla (1640), San Pedro Alcántara, Guanajuato (1663), and Nuestra Señora de la Concepción, Aguascalientes (1667).

The global reach of the Discalced Franciscans led Baltasar de Medina to compare their missionary advance to that of the Jesuits. He took issue with the claims of Julio Nigrono.[81] The latter was of the opinion that the Discalced Franciscans had not extended beyond Spain.[82] To the charge, Medina retorted that by the year in which Nigrono first published his work—that is, 1614—the Discalced Franciscans had already transcended Spain and traversed the globe. "Not only was it already consolidated in Spain," Medina pronounced, "but it had spread throughout Europe, with the provinces of Extremadura, Valencia, both [Old and New] Castile, Andalucía, and Portugal."[83] Moreover, via Portugal's mercantile empire, it also reached East India, embracing Asia in a circle with the provinces of the Madre de Dios in Malaca, and San Gregorio in the Philippines. He also rushed to add the missionary work of the Discalced Franciscans in Africa, and the establishment of the new provinces of Brazil, Marañón, and even

---

80. Medina, *Chronica*, 41v.

81. Medina, *Chronica*, 8v.

82. Although Medina cited the 1614 edition, the comment can be found in the 1617 edition as well, Julio Nigrono, *Regulae communed Societatis Iesu, commentariis asceticis illustratae* (Cologne: Joannem Kinchiunn, 1617), 509.

83. Medina, *Chronica*, 9r.

the province of San Diego de Mexico. Medina concluded: "Accordingly, before Father Nigrono had written his book, the Discalced had already surrounded the four parts of the world."[84]

CONCLUSION

There are many contextual factors that cannot be addressed with an institutional analysis exclusively focused on the "inner logic" of the Discalced Franciscans. The relationship between Discalced Franciscans and Capuchins, for instance, calls for closer examination, especially during the formative period under Alcántara. The role that Discalced Franciscans played after Alcántara's death in spreading the values of apostolic poverty is another area that calls for closer scrutiny. The institutionalization of claustral renunciation occurred as Alcántara was advising Teresa de Jesús to do away with rents and, thus, it represents the Discalced Franciscan equivalent.[85] Lastly, Alcántara's institutional affirmation of Franciscan itineracy cannot explain by itself the missionary mobility of the Discalced Franciscans. Franciscan missionary mobility was rooted in Franciscan itinerancy; that is, itinerancy was a common thread running through all Franciscan families, harking back to St. Francis. However, his institutional reforms were meant to secure itinerancy, freeing Discalced Franciscans from claustral attachments. In their historical context, in the face of Observant opposition and a centralized reform program driven by the monarchy, the institutional responses of the Discalced Franciscans under Alcántara's leadership can explain their transition from an eremitic group to a missionary branch of the Franciscan family.

BIBLIOGRAPHY

Alcalá, Marcos de. *Chronica de la santa provincia de San Joseph: Vida por-tentosa del penitente admirable, y contemplativo altissimo san Pedro de Alcántara, fundador de toda la descalcez seraphica, redemptor de la observancia mas estrecha de la regla de nuestro gran padre san Francisco.* Madrid: Imprenta de Manuel Fernández, 1736.

---

84. Ibid.

85. For the significance of the renunciation of rents for Discalced Carmelite reform see, Jodi Bilinkoff, *The Avila of Saint Teresa: Religious Reform in a Sixteenth-Century City*, 2nd ed. (Ithaca, NY: Cornell University Press, 2015).

———. *S. Pedro de Alcántara defendido contra los opositores de sus glorias.* Madrid: Imprenta y librería de Manuel Fernández, ca. 1739.

Alcántara, Pedro de. *Tratado de la oración y meditación.* Edited by Raquel E. López Ruano. Madrid: Biblioteca de Autores Cristianos, 2012.

Amez Prieto, Hipólito. "Los Descalzos de San Francisco en Extremadura, desde Fray Juan de Guadalupe hasta fray Pedro de Alcántara." In *San Pedro de Alcántara. Hombre universal: Congreso de Guadalupe, 1997,* edited by Francisco Sebastián García Rodríguez, 113–222. Guadalupe, Cáceres: Ediciones Guadalupe, 1998.

Atienza López, Ángela. *Tiempos de conventos: una historia social de las fundaciones en la España moderna.* Madrid: Marcial Pons, Ediciones de Historia; La Rioja: Universidad de La Rioja, 2008.

Barrado Manzano, Arcángel. "San Pedro de Alcántara en las provincias de san Gabriel, la Arrábida y san José." *Archivo Ibero-Americano* 22, no. 85–86 (1962): 423–561.

———. *Vida de san Pedro de Alcántara.* In *Vida y escritos de san Pedro de Alcántara,* edited by Rafael Sanz Valdivieso. Madrid: Biblioteca de Autores Cristianos, 1996.

Barriguín Fernández, Hipólito, ed. *Registro y libro de memoria de la santa provincia de los padres descalzos de San Francisco, 1594–1835.* Vol. 1, *Liceo franciscano* (second series) 65, nos. 202–4 (2015).

Bilinkoff, Jodi. *The Avila of Saint Teresa: Religious Reform in a Sixteenth-Century City.* 2nd ed. Ithaca, NY: Cornell University Press, 2015.

Borja, Francisco de. *Sanctus Franciscus Borgia Quartus Gandiae Dux et Societatis Jesu Praepositus Generalis Tertius.* Vol. 3. Madrid: Typis Gabrielis Lopez del Horno, 1908.

Castro, M. De. "Alcántara, Pedro de." In *Diccionario de historia eclesiástica de España,* edited by Quintín Aldea Vaquero et al. Vol. 1. Madrid: Instituto Enrique Flores, Consejo Superior de Investigaciones Científicas, 1972.

García Oro, José. *Cisneros y la reforma del clero español en tiempo de los Reyes Católicos.* Madrid: Consejo Superior de Investigaciones Científicas, 1971.

———. "Los frailes del Santo Evangelio: El eremitismo franciscano en Extremadura." *Edad de Oro* 8 (1989): 77–96.

———. "San Pedro de Alcántara." In *Real Academia de la Historia, Diccionario Biográfico electrónico*. http://dbe.rah.es/biografias/8229/san-pedro-de-alcantara.

Jesús, Teresa de. *Libro de la vida*. In *Obras completas: edición manual*. Edited by Efrén de la Madre de Dios and Otger Steggink. Madrid: Biblioteca de Autores Cristianos, 2006.

Lejarza, Fidel de. "Orígenes de la Descalcez Franciscana." *Archivo Ibero-Americano* 22, nos. 85–86 (1962): 15–131.

Medina, Baltasar de. *Chronica de la santa provincial de san Diego de Mexico, de religiosos descalços de N.S.P.S. Francisco en la Nueva-España: Vidas de ilustres, y venerables varones, que la han edificado con excelentes virtudes*. Mexico: Juan de Ribera, impressor, y mercader de libros, 1682.

Nigrono, Julio. *Regulae communes Societatis Iesu, commentariis asceticis illustratae*. Cologne: Joannem Kinchiunn, 1617.

Ribadeneira, Marccelo de. *Historia de las islas del Archipiélago Filipino y reinos de la Gran China, Tartaria, Cochinchina, Malaca, Siam, Cambodge y Japón*. Madrid: La Editorial Católica, 1947.

San Antonio, Juan de. *Primacía fundamental del v. padre fray Juan de Guadalupe, vindicada por el R. P. fray Juan de San Antonio (Salmantino)*. Madrid: Imprenta de la Causa de la V. M. de Agreda, 1737.

Santa María, Juan de. *Chronica de la Provincia de san Joseph de los descalços de la Orden de los Menores de nuestro Seraphico Padre s. Francisco; y de las provincias, y custodias descalças, que della han salido, y son sus hijas*. Madrid: Imprenta Real, 1615.

Sanz Valdivieso, Rafael, ed. *Vida y escritos de san Pedro de Alcántara*. Místicos franciscanos españoles 1. Madrid: Biblioteca de Autores Cristianos, 1996.

Turley, Steven E. *Franciscan Spirituality and Mission in New Spain, 1524–1599: Conflict Beneath the Sycamore Tree (Luke 19:1–10)*. London and New York: Routledge, 2014.

Uribe, Ángel. "Espiritualidad de la descalcez franciscana." *Archivo Ibero-Americano* 22, nos. 85–86 (1962): 133–61.

Vázquez Valdivia, Paloma and Carmen Soriano Triguero. "El Convento de San Bernardino de Madrid de franciscanos descalzos." *Archivo Ibero-Americano* 61, no. 238–39 (2001): 251–72.

SUBJECT INDEX

—

Anabaptist(s), x, 2–3, 5, 11, 34, 62, 68, 130, 132, 188–222

Bethlehem Chapel, 39, 42–44

Bibliander, Theodor, ix, 15, 18, 168–187

Bohemia, 37–40, 42–43, 57–59

Brazil, ix, xi, xvi, 2, 27–28, 32, 118–119, 134, 138–141, 143, 145–155, 157, 159–161, 163, 165, 167, 188, 234, 332, 363, 365

Bucer, Martin, 2, 9, 12, 15, 20, 25–26, 32, 105–107, 176

Buddhist(s), Buddhism, 238–239, 246, 248, 250, 252–255, 258–261

Calvin, John, ix, xv, 1–2, 7, 9, 13–16, 18–20, 27–36, 57, 62, 91–92, 98, 106, 108–109, 111–112, 114–137, 142–143, 146, 150–154, 159–160, 162–166, 209–210

Carmelite(s), 68, 72, 152, 285, 287, 289–290, 295–297, 302, 356, 365

China, Chinese, x, 2, 114, 143, 225, 235–263, 271, 341, 363, 367

Christendom, 17, 62, 67, 75–76, 88, 178, 190, 192, 195, 201, 203–204, 206, 210, 212, 251, 276

Columbus, Christopher, 305–307, 311, 321, 323, 342

Confucius, Confucian, Confucianism, x, 2, 237–240, 243–244, 246, 248, 253–263

De las Casas, Bartolomé, x–xi, xv, 304–321

Denmark, 60, 62–69, 71–72, 75, 79–88, 201

Dominican(s), 3, 68, 75, 77, 234, 262, 269, 306, 309–312, 316–317, 319, 327, 329

Farel, Guillaume, xv, 92, 94, 96–97, 99–103, 105, 107–113, 121–122, 132, 141, 144

Finland, 60, 62, 76–79, 81–84, 90

Florida, x, xi, 322–323, 332–338, 340–346

France, French, ix, 2, 9, 16, 18–20, 27, 33, 37–38, 42, 46, 47, 59, 67, 91–97, 99–107, 109–113, 117–119, 121–124, 130, 138–151, 153, 155–167, 169, 174, 186, 201, 210, 226, 234, 265, 284, 288, 333

Francis of Assisi, 139, 310, 355, 358–359, 365

Franciscan(s), x, xv, xvii, 3, 67–68, 75, 96, 99, 105, 112, 148, 226–227, 234, 262, 295, 309–310, 322–335, 337–340, 342–353, 355–359, 361–365, 367

Geneva, x, xvi, 10, 18–19, 27–28, 33, 74, 87, 92, 109–111, 114–125, 127–138, 141–144, 146, 149, 151–152, 154, 160–161, 166, 169, 182–184, 210

Germany, German, 8, 20, 61, 62–66, 68–69, 71–72, 74–79, 83–85, 91–93, 95–96, 99–101, 106–107, 112, 115, 124, 130, 141–142, 151, 190, 196, 201, 209, 212, 218–219, 234–235, 286, 310

Hus, Jan, xv, 37–59

Ignatius of Loyola, 1, 225–226, 231–232, 238, 242–243, 249, 263, 295, 299, 308

Japan, 234–236, 238, 245, 247, 255, 263, 271, 332

Jesuit(s), Society of Jesus, x, xv–xvi, 1–3, 140, 209, 225, 227–283, 287, 295–296, 298–300, 308–309, 332–333, 337, 354, 364

Jews, 12, 24–25, 115, 119, 130–131, 178–180, 212, 288

Kongo (Congo), x, xvi, 2, 264–284

Luther, Martin, xv, 1–2, 7–9, 11, 14–18, 20–25, 34–35, 40, 57, 61–67, 69–70, 72–78, 80–84, 86–94, 96–98, 103, 106, 108, 111–112, 168, 176–178, 185, 209, 211, 216, 218, 289

Mexico, Mexican(s), x, 304–305, 309, 322–335, 337, 340–346, 362–365, 367

Portugal, Portuguese, 2, 8, 138–140, 149–150, 153, 158–159, 219, 235–236, 245, 251, 253, 262, 265–272, 275–285, 304, 308, 350–351, 353–355, 363–364

Muslims, Islam, 18, 130, 170, 172–176, 178–179, 181–186, 204, 206, 210, 324

Paris, 92–99, 103, 105–111, 138, 141, 144–145, 148, 152, 157, 161, 227, 266, 271, 314

Ricci, Matteo, x, xv, 225, 234–235, 237–249, 251–263

Scandinavia, ix, xv–xvi, 2, 18, 60–63, 65–89, 168

Spain, Spanish, xv, 2, 8, 94, 102, 107, 130, 139–140, 153, 219, 226–227, 234, 236, 251, 285, 288, 290, 298, 304–311, 313–315, 318, 324–339, 341, 343–348, 350–351, 354–356, 363–364, 367

Sweden, 60, 62–63, 72–77, 79–83, 86–87, 168, 201

Turks, 11–12, 15, 24–25, 115, 146, 172–178, 182, 184, 186, 204, 312

Valignano, Alessandro, 225, 235–238, 241, 244–245, 247, 249, 251, 253–254, 256

Ward, Mary, x, xv, 285–287, 289, 294, 296–298, 302–303

Warneck, Gustav, 8–9, 11–17, 20, 22, 25, 27–28, 35, 61, 115, 117, 137, 168, 176, 186

Wittenberg, ix, xvi, 19, 21, 23, 34, 60–86, 88, 93–96, 99

Teresa of Avila, x, 1, 285, 287–297, 299, 301–303, 366

Zwingli, Huldrych, 91, 96, 100–101, 169–170, 175, 209, 212–213